RELIGIOUS TRANSFORMATIONS
IN NEW COMMUNITIES OF INTERPRETATION
IN EUROPE (1350–1570)

NEW COMMUNITIES OF INTERPRETATION

CONTEXTS, STRATEGIES, AND PROCESSES OF RELIGIOUS TRANSFORMATION IN LATE MEDIEVAL AND EARLY MODERN EUROPE

VOLUME 3

Religious Transformations in New Communities of Interpretation in Europe (1350–1570)

Bridging the Historiographical Divides

Edited by
ÉLISE BOILLET and IAN JOHNSON

BREPOLS

D/2022/0095/209
ISBN 978-2-503-60177-9
eISBN 978-2-503-60178-6
DOI 10.1484/M.NCI-EB.5.130893

Printed in the EU on acid-free paper.

Table of Contents

Contributors

Erminia Ardissino (erminia.ardissino@unito.it; PhD, Yale University; Dottorato di Ricerca, Università Cattolica del Sacro Cuore, Milan) is Associate Professor at the University of Turin. Her research deals with Italian literature from Dante to the Baroque Age, with particular attention on its relationship with the history of ideas and religious experience. She has published several books and articles in the main journals in the field of philology and literary studies. Among her most relevant publications are *Tasso, Plotino, Ficino: In margine a un postillato* (Rome: Edizioni di Storia e Letteratura, 2003); *Tempo storico e tempo liturgico nella 'Commedia' di Dante* (Vatican City: LEV, 2009); *Galileo: La scrittura dell'esperienza: Saggio sulle lettere* (Pisa: ETS, 2010); *L'umana 'Commedia' di Dante* (Ravenna: Longo, 2016), and *Le donne e la Bibbia nell'Italia della prima età moderna: Riscritture e comunità ermeneutiche* (Turnhout: Brepols, 2020). She has also edited critical editions of ancient texts such as Giovanni di Bonsignori's *Ovidio Metamorphoseos Vulgare,* Giambattista Marino's *Dicerie sacre,* and Lucrezia Tornabuoni's *Poemetti biblici.*

Élise Boillet (elise.boillet@univ-tours.fr) is a CNRS researcher at the Centre d'études supérieures de la Renaissance of the University of Tours, France. She is the author of a monograph on Aretino's biblical works, *L'Arétin et la Bible* (Geneva: Droz, 2007) and published the critical edition of these texts for the Edizione Nazionale delle Opere (Rome: Salerno, 2017). She is also the author of several papers on Renaissance Italian literature on the Psalms. She has co-edited several collections of essays on European and Italian biblical literature and culture. An important bibliographical tool in this field, *Repertorio di letteratura biblica a stampa in italiano (ca 1462–1650)* (Turnhout: Brepols), co-edited with Erminia Ardissino, is forthcoming [2023]. She has recently directed a research project on religious practices and European urban space during the modern era (EUDIREM, https://eudirem.hypotheses.org/), which has resulted in several collections of essays on this topic.

Daniela Solfaroli Camillocci (daniela.solfaroli@unige.ch) is Professor of Cultural and Religious History, and currently Director of the Institute of Reformation History at the University of Geneva. Her field of research covers anticlericalism, religious dissent, confessional identities, women, and gender roles in the Reformed communities of the French-speaking regions in the sixteenth and seventeenth centuries. Among her latest publications are *La construction internationale de la Réforme et l'espace romand à l'époque de Martin*

Luther, ed. with Nicolas Fornerod, Karine Crousaz and Christian Grosse (Paris: Garnier, 2021); *Pierre Viret et la diffusion de la Réforme*, ed. with Karine Crousaz (Lausanne: Antipodes, 2014), and the article 'Le chapelet entre dénonciations et défenses: La critique du rosaire dans la littérature religieuse et la culture visuelle réformées du XVIe siècle', in *Connecteurs divins: Objets de dévotion en représentation dans l'Europe moderne (XVIe-XVIIe siècle)*, ed. with Frédéric Cousinié and Jan Blanc (Paris: Éditions 1 : 1, 2020).

Marleen Cré (marleen.cre@usaintlouis.be) is Maître de Langues Principale in English and Professor of Civilisation of the English-Speaking Countries at the Université Saint-Louis in Brussels and is an associated researcher at the Ruusbroec Institute, University of Antwerp. Her research focuses on late medieval mystical and devotional texts in their manuscript contexts, on devotional compilations and on authors Julian of Norwich, Walter Hilton, and Marguerite Porete. She has published *Vernacular Mysticism in the Charterhouse: A Study of London, British Library, MS Additional 37790* (Turnhout: Brepols, 2006) and with Diana Denissen and Denis Renevey co-edited the collection *Late Medieval Devotional Compilations in England* (Turnhout: Brepols, 2020).

Ottó Gecser (gecsero@tatk.elte.hu) is Associate Professor in the Faculty of Social Sciences at Eötvös Loránd University in Budapest. He holds an MA and a PhD in Medieval Studies from the Central European University, as well as an MA in Sociology from Eötvös Loránd University. His research has focused on preaching and the cult of saints between the thirteenth and fifteenth centuries, as well as on religious and medical interpretations of the plague in the later Middle Ages. His publications include "Fuir ou bien faire une procession? Peste, religion et peur de la contamination à Pérouse au XVe siècle", in *Textes et pratiques religieuses dans l'espace urbain de l'Europe moderne*, ed. by Élise Boillet and Gaël Rideau (Paris: Honoré Champion, 2020), pp. 51–72 and *The Feast and the Pulpit: Preachers, Sermons and the Cult of St Elizabeth of Hungary, 1235–c. 1500* (Spoleto: CISAM, 2012).

Ian Johnson (irj@st-andrews.ac.uk) is Professor of Medieval Literature and Head of the School of English at the University of St Andrews. He was Co-Director of the Queen's Belfast-St Andrews AHRC-funded project *Geographies of Orthodoxy: Mapping English Pseudo-Bonaventuran Lives of Christ, 1350–1550* (2007–2011). With Alastair Minnis he edited *The Cambridge History of Literary Criticism: Volume II. The Middle Ages* (2005). He is founding General Editor of *The Mediaeval Journal* (Brepols) and was for many years General Editor of *Forum for Modern Language Studies* (Oxford University Press). His latest books are *The Middle English Life of Christ: Academic Discourse, Translation and Vernacular Theology* (Turnhout: Brepols, 2013); *The Pseudo-Bonaventuran Lives of Christ: Exploring the Middle English Tradition*, edited with Allan Westphall (Turnhout: Brepols, 2013); *The Impact of Latin Culture on Medieval and Early Modern Scottish Writing*, edited with Alessandra

Petrina (Kalamazoo: Medieval Institute Publications, 2018); *Geoffrey Chaucer in Context* (Cambridge: Cambridge University Press, 2019), and *Religious Practices and Everyday Life in the Long Fifteenth Century (1350–1570): Interpreting Changes and Changes of Interpretation* (Turnhout: Brepols, 2022), edited with Ana Maria S. A. Rodrigues. He was a Working Group Coordinator and Management Committee member of the COST Action *New Communities of Interpretation: Contexts, Strategies and Processes of Religious Transformation in Late Medieval and Early Modern Europe* (2013–2017).

Waldemar Kowalski (waldemar.kowalski@ujk.edu.pl) is Professor of Early Modern History at Jan Kochanowski University in Kielce, Poland. He is interested in popular religiosity *c.* 1500–1650 in its medieval and Tridentine contexts and also in early modern emigration from Scotland. His major publications include *The Great Immigration: Scots in Cracow and Little Poland, circa 1500–1660* (Leiden: Brill, 2015); '"Verily, This Is the Sheepfold of that Good Shepherd": The Idea of the "True" Church in Sixteenth-Century Polish Catechisms', *Odrodzenie i Reformacja w Polsce [Renaissance and Reformation in Poland]*, SI 01 (2016), 5–47; 'Man and God: The First Three Commandments in the Polish Catholic Catechisms of the 1560s–1570s', in *The Ten Commandments in Medieval and Early Modern Culture*, ed. by Youri Desplenter, Jürgen Pieters, and Walter Melion (Leiden: Brill, 2017); 'The Reformation and Krakow Society, *c.* 1517–1637: Social Structures and Ethnicities', in *Krakau – Nürnberg – Prag: Stadt und Reformation*, ed. by Michael Diefenbacher, Olga Fejtová, and Zdzisław Noga (Prague: Červený Kostelec, 2019).

Marco Mostert (m.mostert@uu.nl) is Professor of Medieval History at Utrecht University. He is interested in the social history of communication in the Middle Ages. His publications from 1996 onwards can be found at https://www.uu.nl/medewerkers/MMostert/Publicaties. He is Editor of *Utrecht Studies in Medieval Literacy* (https://medievalliteracy.wp.hum.uu.nl/home-2/utrecht-studies-in-medieval-literacy/).

Melina Rokai (melinarokai85@hotmail.com) is currently a Senior Research Associate at the Department of History, Faculty of Philosophy, University of Belgrade. She was a member and a Management Committee Substitute member of the COST Action 1301 *New Communities of Interpretation: Contexts, Strategies and Processes of Religious Transformation in Late Medieval and Early Modern Europe*. Her interests encompass cultural history, women's history, and the history of concepts and ideas in late medieval and modern Europe. Her latest publication is 'Continuity and Discontinuity in Everyday Religious Life in Southern Hungary before 1526 in the Light of Supplications to the Holy See', in *Religious Practices and Everyday Life in the Long Fifteenth Century (1350–1570): Interpreting Changes and Changes of Interpretation*, ed. by Ian Johnson and Ana Maria S. A. Rodrigues (Brepols, forthcoming 2022). With a PhD from the University of Belgrade and an MSt from the University of Oxford, she is the author of two monographs.

Daniela Rywiková (daniela.rywikova@osu.cz) is Associate Professor of Art History at the University of Ostrava, where she focuses her research and teaching on Central European and Czech Late Medieval Art History and Christian Iconography, and the relationship between the visual culture of the high and late Middle Ages and devotion and religious practice. At the University of Ostrava, she teaches courses in Czech medieval art, European Gothic art, iconography, and the historiography of art. She has published a number of books and scholarly articles dedicated to, for example, Eucharistic devotion and medieval art, visualization of the Seven Deadly Sins, visual culture in Bohemia after the Fourth Lateran Council, and Death as personified in late medieval painting.

Wojciech Świeboda (woj.swieboda@uj.edu.pl) has a PhD from Jagiellonian University, Cracow. He is a Polish historian, medievalist, and researcher at the Manuscript Department of the Jagiellonian Library, Cracow. He is co-author of two printed catalogues: *Catalogus diplomatum pergameneorum quae in collectione Bibliothecae Jagellonicae Cracoviae asservantur* (Cracow: Towarzystwo Naukowe Societas Vistulana, 2014) and *Catalogus codicum manuscriptorum medii aevi Latinorum qui in Bibliotheca Jegellonica Cracoviae asservantur*, XI (Cracow: Biblioteka Jagiellońska, Księgarnia Akademicka, 2016). He focuses on the relations between Catholic Church and non-Christian world and the Inquisition in medieval Europe. He has published *Innowiercy w opiniach prawnych uczonych polskich w XV w. Poganie, żydzi, muzułmanie* (Cracow: Towarzystwo Naukowe Societas Vistulana, 2013) and *Universitas contra haeresim: Działalność antyheretycka Stanisława ze Skarbimierza jako przedstawiciela Uniwersytetu Krakowskiego* (Cracow: Towarzystwo Naukowe Societas Vistulana, 2021).

Václav Žůrek (zurek@flu.cas.cz) received his PhD in 2014 from Charles University, Prague and École des hautes études en sciences sociales, Paris. He is Research Fellow in the Centre for Medieval Studies at the Institute of Philosophy of the Czech Academy of Sciences. He is author of *Karel IV: Portrét středověkého vládce* (Prague: NLN, 2018) and, with Pavlína Cermanová, Jaroslav Svátek, and Vojtěch Bažant, is co-author of *Přenos vědění: Osudy čtyř bestsellerů v pozdně středověkých českých zemích* (Prague: Filosofia, 2021). He is co-editor, with Julia Burkhardt, Martin Bauch, and Tomáš Gaudek, of *Heilige, Helden, Wüteriche: Herrschaftsstile der Luxemburger (1308–1437)* (Cologne: Böhlau, 2017) and, with Pavlína Cermanová, co-edited *Books of Knowledge and their Reception: Circulation of Widespread Texts in Late Medieval Europe* (Turnhout: Brepols, 2021). He works on late medieval Central Europe, political thought, and medieval historiographies.

IAN JOHNSON

Introduction

Investigating and Reconsidering Medieval and Early Modern Divides and Connections

This volume brings together medievalist and early modernist specialists, whose research fields are traditionally divided by the jubilee year of 1500, in order to concentrate on the role of the laity (and to a lesser extent those in holy orders) in the religious transformations that occurred during the 'long fifteenth century' from the flourishing of the *Devotio Moderna* to the era of the Reformation and the Counter-Reformation.

Recent historiography has described the Christian Church of the fifteenth century as a world of 'multiple options', in which the laity was engaged with the clergy in a process of communication and negotiation leading to the emergence of hybrid forms of religious life. The religious manifestations of such 'new communities of interpretation' appear in an array of biblical and religious texts which widely circulated in manuscripts before benefiting from the new print media. In addition to the reconsideration of vitally important developments in textual culture, recent historiography has provided new perspectives on such turning points as the posting of the ninety-five theses by Luther in 1517 and the institution of the Roman Inquisition by Pope Paul III in 1542, thereby invigorating the investigation of the rich, creative, long-lasting, and at times violent, damaging, and prejudicial religious debates in which laypeople and clergy in both the Protestant and the Catholic worlds participated to varying degrees.

These essays have their origins in an international colloquium, 'Religious Transformation in Late Medieval and Early Modern Europe: Bridging the Chronological, Linguistic, Confessional and Cultural Divides (1350–1570)', hosted by the Centre d'études supérieures de la Renaissance at the University of Tours in October 2015 as part of the ongoing programme of activities under the umbrella of the European Union-funded COST Action IS1301, *New Communities of Interpretation: Contexts, Strategies and Processes of Religious Transformation in Late Medieval and Early Modern Europe*, which ran from

Ian Johnson • (irj@st-andrews.ac.uk) is Professor of Medieval Literature and Head of the School of English at the University of St Andrews.

Religious Transformations in New Communities of Interpretation in Europe (1350–1570): Bridging the Historiographical Divides, ed. by Élise Boillet and Ian Johnson, New Communities of Interpretation, 3 (Turnhout: Brepols, 2022), pp. 11–20.

DOI 10.1484/M.NCI-EB.5.131211

September 2013 to September 2017. This COST Action involved over 300 researchers from twenty-four countries. Its remit was to re-examine, and open up dialogues about, the traditional religious, cultural, social, linguistic, and geographical rifts and connections of late medieval and early modern Europe, as well as the common national narratives that have influenced and distorted (and continue to influence and distort) the construction and maintenance of historical identities and beliefs.

The essays in this volume therefore develop the philosophy and approach of the COST Action by modifying and adding to existing scholarship (or the lack of it) on religious change in the 'long fifteenth century'. The Action's 'Memorandum of Understanding' spells out the context for this:

> In spite of the pivotal importance of the analysis of the long fifteenth century as a turning point in European history, the period is relatively understudied in its complexity, multiplicity and fluidity, i.e. as a period in which the simultaneous presence of tradition and innovation and old and new media and modes of communication, offered multiple and divergent options for the formation of religious and cultural identities.[1]

Following on from the sentiments and goals of the 'Memorandum', the studies in this collection, as with all activities of the Action, aim to cast a spectrum of new yet profoundly historical light on themes of seminal relevance to present-day European society — doing so by analysing patterns of inclusion and exclusion, and examining shifts in hierarchic and non-hierarchic relations articulated through religious practices, texts, and other phenomena featuring in the lives of groups and individuals.[2] The academic team assembled for this particular collective output of *New Communities of Interpretation* (with editors from France and the United Kingdom and contributors with institutional affiliations in Belgium, the Czech Republic, France, Hungary, Italy, the Netherlands, Poland, Serbia, and Switzerland) is internationally European as well as interdisciplinary and multidisciplinary in its methodology.

The authors of the contributions to this book have developed studies on the multiplicity, complexity, and fluidity of religious transformations promoted by laypeople (and to a lesser extent the clergy) during the so-called 'long fifteenth century'. In so doing, many of them explore two main directions: the religious textual traditions which ran from the late Middle Ages to the early modern era, and the uses of religious texts in various historical, social, and cultural contexts. This collection accordingly participates in the re-nuancing of traditional historiography on the subject of religious change. Value and evidential force are added to this nuance by the range and variety of comparable/contrastable and mutually informing subject matters — from

---

1 'Memorandum of Understanding', p. 5.

2 See 'Memorandum of Understanding', p. 2.

recusant English-speaking nuns in the Francophone Spanish Netherlands to Bohemian Hussites in the Balkans; from pagan-friendly donnish Latin juridical theorizing to reactionary Catholic lowborn lay vernacular polemic; from a multi-confessionally hospitable Moravian wall painting to a ferociously sectarian Swiss denunciation of the Rosary's alleged Mariolatry. This collection therefore combines and juxtaposes, in fresh ways, reconsiderations of the continuity and transformation of textual traditions and text-based practices alongside such familiar and important factors as the print 'revolution', the 'Protestant paradigm', and the effects that ecclesiastical censorship and the Inquisition had on the religious life of Christian society and the religious lives of individuals within it.

Some of the essays in this book are more overt than others in addressing the themes of bridging chronological, linguistic, confessional, and cultural divides; others do so more obliquely — whether, in their different ways, commuting back and forth over a combination of particular divides, or straddling them connectively, or blurring them concealingly yet revealingly. Though the topics of individual chapters show rich variety and range, it is the hope of the editors that readers of this volume, bringing their own expertise and interests to bear on the book, will be prompted to form their own comparative insights and connections that may gather in momentum and complexity as readers move through its chapters and develop a sense of the volume as a whole.

The eleven chapters of this book have been arranged loosely into five groups. These groups are far from being mutually exclusive, as all essays have considerable, if shifting, thematic and methodological affinities with their cousins in other groups, and each offers perspectives on others. The first group, 'Lay and Clerical Cultures on Heaven and Earth: Divides, Interactions, and Negotiations', is a trio of studies focusing on how medieval and early modern people negotiated the most fundamental and life-shaping divide of all — the one between this mortal life on earth and the heavenly otherworld and its celestial inhabitants. They deal respectively with a nun's contemplation of the divinity in prayerful meditation, layfolk's transactions with saints, and the pieties of praise or prayer to be offered (or, rather, disapprovingly denied) to the Virgin Mary.

In the opening essay of the collection, Marleen Cré's 'Gertrude More's *Confessiones Amantis* and the Contemplative Identity of the Cambrai Benedictine Community', we are given a richly contextualized account of the textually articulated attitudes of a significant contemplative who crossed some key divides. The English recusant Helen (later Gertrude — after Gertrude of Helfta) More, a great-great-granddaughter of Thomas More, co-founded and became a member of a Benedictine Convent in Cambrai in the Francophone Spanish Netherlands. Her *Confessiones Amantis* is not only a work that crosses the divide between earth and heaven, but it also reaches back over a chronological gap into traditions of late medieval vernacular theology and monastic contemplation. She also crosses interpersonal divides by revoicing

Julian of Norwich and making aspects of her textual interiority her own. In the same vein, the shareable voice and experiences of her *Confessiones* are designed to be relived intersubjectively by a following community of nuns. Gertrude's text aims not only to be formative of her own spiritual self but also of the larger collective selfhood and identity of a community of nuns projecting themselves into the future. Gertrude, it would appear, bequeathed to her sisters their own programmatic spiritual identity, one in defiance, over a gender divide, of their Douai Benedictine *confrères*, who would have them behave otherwise in their devotional lives.

With the next essay, Ottó Gecser's 'Helper Saints and their Critics in the Long Fifteenth Century', we are still poised petitioning on the heaven-earth divide, only this time it is the one between layfolk and their helper saints. It was one thing in this period for a saint to be petitioned in penitential sincerity for intercession with the Almighty; it was another thing altogether to bargain with a saint as a craft specialist in order to effect rescue from an unwelcome earthly plight or, worse, to procure worldly advantage or benefit. This study examines the gaps and clashes between Catholic and Protestant views on this topic, thereby refining the larger study of the cult of saints. It also enlightens us about contemporary discussions and attitudes surrounding the specialization of the labours of saints in German-speaking territories in the sixteenth century, and on the programmes of reformists to critique, criticize, and invalidate their cults. Gecser rightly points out that although individual helper saints have enjoyed a fair deal of modern scholarly attention, the topic of helper saints in general, and the disquiet that the cult of such saints provoked, has been relatively overlooked.

We move next from disquiet and fractiousness over saints to contention over the most powerful heavenly intercessor of them all, the Virgin Mary, who is at the centre of the third essay, 'Censoring Popular Devotion in French Protestant Propaganda: The Reformer Pierre Viret, the Rosary, and the Question of the Proper Honouring of the Virgin Mary', by Daniela Solfaroli Camillocci. The Lausanne reformer Pierre Viret's extraordinary sustained textual attack on the cult of the Virgin sought both intellectually and psychologically to discredit and displace an emotionally charged tradition of devotional practice that evidently needed a major effort to dislodge — an effort he was prepared to make with passionate zealotry. For Viret, the beads of a rosary were no less than snake eggs. Clearly, he wanted to shatter any confidence or credence that any laypeople may have invested in the powers of the Virgin to protect or intercede for them. Viret even went so far as to manipulate the divides of class, sex, and gender for his own ends, condemning and stereotyping Marian devotion as essentially the practice of bawdy females of low social status and greedy monks. It is interesting, however, that later in his polemical career, Viret took a slightly more moderate tack that seemingly adjusted his downgrading of the Virgin's cult by highlighting the right kind of honouring due to the mother of Christ. Praise of Mary, then, was acceptable in a way that petitioning her was not.

Perhaps he did this because his onslaught on Mary could have been perceived as having gone too far. Perhaps, too, there may have been a process of having to accommodate an invincible pre-existing tradition of Marian devotion? Viret, it would appear, simply had to soften a border that he wanted to be bright, sectarian, and very hard.

The next two essays in the collection, constituting a group entitled 'Lay Literacy and the Press: Forms and Transformations of Religious Writing and Rewriting', are both about the adaptability and portability of texts — and in particular the forms they take. Each study complements the other; the first attends to the disposition and redisposition of the authoritative material text in the formal terms of its layout and punctuation, whereas the second addresses the diverse adaptabilities of the biblical text via the formal terms of genre. In the first, the presentation of the physical text is adapted — made legible — to meet the perceived needs of its users; in the second, the biblical text is re-articulated variously through generic adaptation and transformation. In both cases, the divide between production and reception is to be negotiated through strategies and repertoires of readability. Accordingly, Marco Mostert, in 'Changes in the Grammar of Legibility: Influences on the Development of "New Communities of Interpretation?"', explains, and illustrates through textual examples, some of the most important ways in which, through the material disposition of the letters, words, spaces, and rhetorical and linguistic structures on the physical page, legibility functioned variously in manuscript and printed texts. At a time of profound change from predominantly manuscript to predominantly print culture, the changing grammar of legibility is an important topic. Another vital divide addressed in this study (one relevant to so many other studies in this book) is that between whoever wrote the text and whoever used it, whether by reading it aloud to others, or by taking it in themselves silently, or by quietly mouthing the words on the page. Consideration too is afforded to a repertoire of, on the one hand, punctuation geared to the effective oral delivery and thereby the aural comprehensibility and affective impact of the text, and, on the other hand, punctuation designed to direct and safeguard its legibility and also to communicate desired meaning through the eye of the beholder.

The historically evident variety with which texts were remade to be read is also at the centre of the next essay, Erminia Ardissino's 'Biblical Genres through the Long Sixteenth Century: Italy as a Case Study'. Wycliffites, Hussites, Lutherans, and Calvinists had the Bible in their vernacular languages. It would, however, be a mistake to continue to think that pious mainstream medieval readers and hearers and early modern Catholic users of holy books were ill served or not served at all when it came to the Bible. This erroneous assumption, one that persists even in recent scholarly accounts, is put right by our contributor in her substantial case study of Italian print culture in the early modern period. Here, she taxonomizes and explains the various literary genres (for example, history, meditation, sermon, translation, and even the novel) that were deployed in order to disseminate the Bible and its teaching to diverse readers and places throughout Italian culture in the long sixteenth century. Particularly fascinating in this chapter is the account of how the biblical text was tactically reshaped in response to the pressures of ecclesiastical censorship. Our contributor remarks appositely on the surprising potency of literary forms in adapting the Bible: 'It may seem strange that a literary perspective can determine research in a religious field and especially research into the use of the foundational religious text, the Bible'. Here, then, is a disciplinary crossing of the methodological divide, from literary-textual studies to religious and historical studies: a divide well bridged.

The same corpus of Italian biblical literature is also the subject matter of the next essay, which commences the third group of studies, 'Vernacular Culture and Ecclesiastical Censorship', whose two chapters shed light on people and texts subjected to ecclesiastical prohibition. In 'Printed Italian Vernacular Biblical Literature: Religious Transformation from the Beginnings of the Printing Press to the Mid-Seventeenth Century', Élise Boillet provides a careful recalibration of familiar chronological frameworks and reference points for the massive catalogue of Italian biblical literature that she has prepared with Erminia Ardissino. At the same time as accommodating the 'long fifteenth century', the 'long sixteenth century', and the important year of 1570, this essay incorporates, for the purpose of consideration of its materials, the notion of 'religious transformation' that is intrinsic to the overall approach of *New Communities of Interpretation*. This it does with reference to the never-ending processes of negotiation amongst various ecclesiastical and lay forces, whose interaction provides an informative context for the nature of the Italian biblical texts that found their way into the print market and the hands of their readers.

The next essay, by Melina Rokai, homes in not on the prohibition of texts but on the prohibition of whole communities, and on where and how these people went where they went, did what they did, and taught what they taught, as indicated by its title, 'Communities of Interpretation of the Bible along the European Margins: Hussite Teachings, the Hussite Bible, and the Bogomils, from the South of Hungary to the Periphery of Eastern Europe in the Long Fifteenth Century'. Here, it is explained how a group of Hussites initially managed to thrive, remarkably enough, in a part of southern Hungary now in Serbia, but how in due course they were persecuted by the Inquisition, which drove them to flee to what is now eastern Romania, where their community survived until the early seventeenth century. The chronological and geographical spans covered by this study are unusually vast, to say the least, extending to Hussite activities persisting well after the early modern period in territories as far flung from central and south-eastern Europe as Norway, Greenland, and the Danish West Indies (now the American Virgin Islands). One of the most fascinating achievements of this study is the light it sheds on the complex mutuality of relations between Hussites and Bogomils, evidenced most eloquently in a telling comparative analysis of the similarities and differences there were in the transmission of the textual details of the Paternoster in the teachings of the Hussites of southern Hungary and the Bogomils of Bosnia. In this single example (representative of an approach that may be carried out elsewhere), we are presented with a significant new interpretation of mutual influence and a new understanding of the porosity of social, theological, and textual divides.

The next pairing of essays forming the fourth group, 'Political and Religious Cultures', sees academics in dispute about how the Church should deal with and live with the sharpest of confessional divides: those concerning heretics and infidels. The first essay in this group discusses a debate about not only whether the Eucharist should be taken in one or both kinds but also about the legitimacy of using the vernacular for theological purposes. The second essay has as its topic the dilemma, as addressed by medieval jurists, of whether it is virtuous or not to make alliances with non-Christians in pursuit of war.

In the first essay of the pair, 'Language as a Weapon: Hilarius of Litoměřice and the Use of Latin and the Vernacular Language in Religious Polemics in Fifteenth-Century Bohemia', Václav Žůrek analyses the remarkable debate of 1464, which took the form of letters exchanged between, on the orthodox Catholic side, Hilarius of Litoměřice, and on the reformist side, the Utraquist Václav Koranda the Younger. Both of these men were academics, well learned in Latin. What divided them theologically was the question of whether the wine as well as the bread should be taken at the Eucharist by laypeople. This dispute was complicated, however, by Hilarius conducting his side of the debate in Latin, whereas Koranda insisted on the vernacular. To a theological divide was thereby added a linguistic divide that was often taken to typify division between laity and clergy. This debate raises the issue of divided audiences as well; for Koranda (who, for all his education and his professional distinction as a University of Prague academic, advertised his lay status) addressed his arguments not just to his opponent but also opened them up to the burghers and gentlefolk who typically supported his party, and, most vitally, to the Utraquist King, George of Poděbrady — not forgetting any Catholic laity and whom he might additionally win over. The choice, however, of Latin and the vernacular is not always as straightforward as it would appear to be in this debate. Although in this exchange of correspondence Hilarius condemned the use of Czech for matters theological, he was happy to use it elsewhere when trying to win over layfolk to his position. Conversely, Koranda was a notable theological writer in Latin. In multi-confessional Bohemia, then, the divides of heterodoxy/orthodoxy and Latin/vernacular were able, for tactical reasons, to switch within themselves and also with each other.

For tactical reasons also, a rather more dramatic flipping was at the heart of a ferocious military and legal struggle at the beginning of the 1400s between the Poles and the Teutonic Knights. In 'The Legitimacy of Making Alliances between Christians and Infidels: Arguments of Polish Jurists in the First Half of the Fifteenth Century', Wojciech Świeboda describes the response of Polish jurists to the Teutonic Knights' allegation against the Polish-Lithuanian Commonwealth that they had committed grave mortal sin by allying themselves with non-Christians in warfare. The jurists argued, by drawing on authorities in the best academic manner of the age, that it was acceptable to ally with infidels in a just war. Moreover, whereas the Teutonic Knights afforded no rights to infidels and saw them as fit only for slaughter or subjugation, the Polish legalists took the position, coherently argued, that pagans had a right to their own territories and jurisdiction over them: neither should non-Christians be converted by force. This rather tolerant position did not enter the traditional mainstream of European intellectual culture, however. Our contributor points out that when, in the 1500s and the 1600s, European intellectuals came to discuss once more the issue of what powers the pope should be able to exercise over infidels in newly discovered territories, they did not come up with anything like the same degree of rights that the Polish jurists judged appropriate at the beginning of the fifteenth century.

Both essays in the final section deal with everyday problems and practices encountered by various players in the multi-confessional societies that endured for quite a while in Central Europe until they were extirpated by the forces of the Counter-Reformation. The group commences with two tales of 'Confessional Coexistence, Conversion, and Confusion', staying in Poland with Waldemar Kowalski's 'Peasants and "Sectarians": On the Ineffectiveness of Evangelical Persuasion in Sixteenth-Century Poland'. This chapter provides some rather intimate insights into how and why Protestantism was moderately successful in Lesser Poland. Our contributor here rightly points out that, amongst the peasants, Protestantism was not necessarily making many inroads either before the Council of Trent (1545–1563) or in the decades when Tridentine reforms renewed the vigour of Polish Catholicism. At the heart of this essay is a revealing account of two Polish neighbours in the Cracow palatinate, showing how they managed to get along across a confessional and social divide without rancour even though one was an Evangelical gentleman trying to win his peasants over to the new religion and the other was the local Catholic priest. That we know so much about this is due to the survival of the collected letters between the two neighbours, both gentlefolk who presumably knew each other of old. In this astonishing correspondence, the priest, for example, writes at one point to the squire, telling him that his peasants are coming along to him, in his priestly vocation, for spiritual support and are definitely not turning into good Evangelicals. Evidently, in this part of Europe Protestant teaching and indoctrination were not as well organized or as penetrating as they were elsewhere. Moreover, the local Catholic establishment and popular culture were robust enough to fend them off. Harking back to the different tactical uses of Latin and the vernacular detailed in Václav Žůrek's chapter, it is interesting to note in this context that, as Waldemar Kowalski assumes, 'the letters were published in Polish — to retain the expression and authenticity of speech, while the comments were formulated in Latin — for the convenience of the Papal Nuncio'. These letters have an illuminating companion text in a verse polemic, published in Polish in 1549, stoutly defending the traditional practices of the Catholic laity. In claiming to be a text by a lowborn man, this work provides telling evidence of how and why the Polish laity were reluctant to leap over the confessional divide into reformism or Protestantism, even when Evangelical persuasion was the tool and motivating force of powerful and prestigious local landowners. For all that Polish Protestantism failed to gain a lasting hold, it is nevertheless salutary to observe a substantial period of multi-confessionalism in this part of Europe — one in which it can be shown that people were able to live together cooperatively in civility and even good-willed cordiality, despite their differences.

For the purposes of Waldemar Kowalski's study, the divide across which neighbours communicated was a relatively straightforward one between the Evangelical nobility and Catholic clergy. In multi-confessional Moravia, however, there was a more complex triple divide amongst neighbouring Catholics, Utraquists, and Lutherans. The next essay shows how this divide was maintained at the same time as being breached via a subtle visual and exegetical medium of shared devotional material circumstances. In 'Religious Transformation on the Early Modern Periphery. Law and Gospel: Image, Place, and Communication in the Multi-Confessional Community of Sixteenth-Century Moravian Ostrava', Daniela Rywiková sheds instructive light upon another mixed community, this time in Ostrava, the focus of her study of an intriguingly ambiguous religious wall painting made and used in the years before the Jesuit annihilation of multi-confessionalism in this Moravian town. The painting in question, an allegory of the Old and New Testaments in the local church, seems to have been a site of religio-cultural hospitality for Lutheran, Utraquist, and Catholic alike. Our contributor suggests very credibly that the local priest may have been behind the design of an artwork accommodating 'a sort of umbrella-like Christian "supra-identity"' that would sustain both diversity and cohesion by pragmatically ignoring yet recognizing confessional divides. From such a perspective, divisions and meeting points start to look like each other. It is fitting that the book should end with a complex divide bridged so intriguingly.

Repeated themes and observable features and processes have emerged during the assembly of this collection: the exceptionality yet comparability of local circumstances; the incompleteness and ambivalence of many cultural/educational processes and directives; the proximity of hospitality and conflict; the richly innovative and sometimes fragile means used to address or accommodate multi-confessional cultures. All in all, the individual studies in this collection uncover, and engage with, familiar yet strange composites of continuity and transformation across chronological, linguistic, confessional, and cultural divides — divides that may sometimes also be seen and re-understood as junctures, joins, and meeting points.

Acknowledgement: The editors would like to express their considerable gratitude to Abe Davies for compiling the index.

Works Cited

Online Resource

'Memorandum of Understanding for the implementation of a European Concerted Research Action designated as COST Action: New Communities of Interpretation: Contexts, Strategies and Processes of Religious Transformation in Late Medieval and Early Modern Europe' (Brussels: COST Association, 2013), accessible at: https://www.cost.eu/actions/IS1301/ [click on: MoU]

MARLEEN CRÉ

Gertrude More's *Confessiones Amantis* and the Contemplative Identity of the Cambrai Benedictine Community

Helen More: A Catholic Nun in Exile

In 1623, a seventeen-year-old girl called Helen More (1606–1633) journeyed across the Channel to Cambrai, France, to co-found and become a member of the Benedictine Convent of Our Lady of Consolation. A great-great-granddaughter of Thomas More, and daughter of Cresacre More (1572–1649) and Elizabeth Gage (died *c.* 1611), Helen grew up in a recusant family. Her father Cresacre (named after his paternal grandmother) went to the Jesuit school of Eu when he was twelve, and later trained for the priesthood at the English College at Rheims and studied theology at the English College at Douai. On his brother's death, he was called back to England as his father's heir. Cresacre and Elizabeth had three children: Helen, Bridget, and Thomas. Both their daughters would become Benedictine nuns.[1] Thomas, too, wanted to become a priest, but, like his father before him, was called upon to continue the family name and marry.

In early seventeenth-century England, for Catholics to pursue a vocation meant exile to the Continent, more particularly to France and the Spanish Low Countries. The Douai, and later Cambrai, that Helen More and her seven companions travelled to at the instigation of Benet Jones, her Benedictine confessor, was at the time part of the Southern Low Countries (the Seventeen Provinces) under the governance of Isabella Clara Eugenia, daughter of

1 See Anderson, 'More, (Christopher) Cresacre' and Bolton Holloway, 'More, Helen' [*name in religion Gertrude*]' in the *Oxford Dictionary of National Biography* and *The Life*, ed. by Wekking, pp. x–xv.

Marleen Cré • (marleen.cre@usaintlouis.be) is Maître de Langes Principale in English and Professor of Civilisation of the English-Speaking Territories at the Université Saint-Louis in Brussels and is an associated researcher at the Ruusbroec Institute, University of Antwerp.

Religious Transformations in New Communities of Interpretation in Europe (1350–1570): Bridging the Historiographical Divides, ed. by Élise Boillet and Ian Johnson, New Communities of Interpretation, 3 (Turnhout: Brepols, 2022), pp. 21–42.
 DOI 10.1484/M.NCI-EB.5.131212

Philip II of Spain. This was a time during which cultural and religious life prospered.[2] Benet Jones wanted to found a new convent for Benedictine nuns, and the dowry that Cresacre More was willing to give his daughter would make this possible. Despite the absence of a clear vocation, and despite her age, Helen resolved to go. She kept this resolve throughout the difficult early years of her life as a monastic at Our Lady of Consolation: she was clothed on 31 December 1623 and took her vows on 1 January 1625.[3]

Helen, who in religion had taken the name of Gertrude, did not have a happy spiritual life. Her inability to settle truly into her life as a nun was exacerbated by the uncongeniality for her of the Ignatian method of prayer introduced to the convent by the three sisters who had joined the eight English novices from the English Benedictine Monastery of Brussels.[4] When Augustine Baker was appointed as the confessor to the sisters in 1624, initially only Catherine Gascoigne stuck to Baker's instruction, while More ridiculed his teachings, which sought to help the sisters follow their personal paths to the divine as it manifested itself in their souls — paths that could be completely different for each sister, just as their personalities, needs, and inclinations were different.[5]

Some months after More took her vows, she was persuaded by the novice-mistress once again to try going to Baker for spiritual counsel, and this time, his reading of a passage of Constantin de Barbanson's *Les Secrets Sentiers de l'Amour Divin* struck a chord. This moment would prove to be a turning point and the start of a fulfilling contemplative life in which writing played a major role.[6]

The Author Gertrude More

Indeed, like many in her family, More was not only a devoted Catholic, but also a writer. Her literary legacy — in printed form and in research — is

---

2 Isabella had been Governor of the Spanish Low Countries with her husband Albert of Austria from 1598 to 1621, when Albert died. After Albert's death, she governed on her own from 1621 to 1633, roughly the years that Helen More lived in Cambrai. See also *Histoire de Cambrai*, ed. by Trenard, pp. 125–44.

3 *The Life*, ed. by Wekking, p. x.

4 These eight novices included Catherine Gascoigne (1600–1676), who would become the Abbess of Our Lady of Consolation in 1629. One of the Brussels nuns was Frances Gawen (1576–1640), who became the first abbess of the new house. Prudentia Deacons was another. She became novice-mistress. *The Life*, ed. by Wekking, p. xi.

5 Baker's methods were controversial, and Francis Hull, the chaplain and confessor of the Cambrai Benedictine nuns, questioned his orthodoxy. Baker's works were examined in 1633 and declared orthodox. *The Life*, ed. by Wekking, p. xxii. Hull's actions were in keeping with the post-Tridentine Church's suspicion of creativity and any deviation of controlled methods in personal worship. McNamara, *Sisters in Arms*, p. 506.

6 *The Life*, ed. by Wekking, pp. 37–38. De Barbanson's *Les Secrets Sentiers* was printed in French by Jean Kinckius in Cologne in 1623.

closely intertwined with Augustine Baker's.[7] He wrote *The Life and Death of Dame Gertrude More* and edited her *Ideots Deuotions* (which he named *Confessiones Amantis*). More's devotions were prepared for a printed edition by 'F. G.', Francis Gascoigne, Catherine Gascoigne's brother, most likely from documents left by Augustine Baker, and were printed in 1657 and 1658 by Lewis de la Fosse in Paris, twenty-four years after More's death and sixteen years after Baker's. In *The Life*, which is a life of Gertrude as well as a lengthy discussion of Baker's spiritual method he taught to the Cambrai nuns, Baker often quotes More's *Confessiones*.

The text of the *Confessiones Amantis* also survives in full in one manuscript, Oxford, Bodleian Library, MS Rawlinson C. 581, and in fragments in Paris, Bibliothèque Mazarine, MS 1202;[8] York, Ampleforth Abbey, MS 127; Stafford, Colwich Abbey, MSS 22 and 23, and Stratton-on-the-Fosse, Downside Abbey, Baker MS 33. In what follows, I use the form of More's *Confessiones Amantis* as it occurs in Oxford, Bodleian Library, MS Rawlinson C. 581 as edited by J.P.H. Clark. This is a mid-seventeenth-century manuscript copy — in two English hands — of the *Confessiones*, which is preceded by three poems also by More: *Amor ordinem nescit*, *Of suffering and bearing the crosse*, and *To our blessed Laidy the Aduocate of sinners*.[9] The provenance of this manuscript is uncertain. The differences from the 1658 edition suggest that the work may have been copied regularly, and that F. G.'s edition does indeed present a version 'stiled' by 'Her only Spiritual Father and Directour, the Ven. Fa. Baker', as the title page records.[10]

The manuscript version of the *Confessiones Amantis* is used here because in its handwritten form it is a more direct witness of the intimate spiritual culture of the small Benedictine convent in Cambrai. Rather than evidencing a process of dialogue between the female monastic communities and lay urban communities in Cambrai or Catholic communities in England, both text and manuscript show a very different type of negotiation within a community that sought its place in the early modern town. Exiled from a country hostile to their religion and life choice, the Cambrai nuns sought to conserve the Catholic monastic tradition. Though the catalogue of the books owned by the Cambrai nuns *c.* 1793 shows that their spiritual reading included contemporary as well as more traditional texts,[11] this

---

7 The extent to which this is the case shows in the title of the edition of More's *Confessiones Amantis* used in this paper: *Confessiones Amantis*, ed. by Clark. The title of this edition seems to have been taken from the 1658 print rather than from Oxford, Bodleian Library, MS Rawlinson C. 581, which is the text Clark edits. The edition is also part of Analecta Cartusiana's efforts to publish editions of all of Augustine Baker's writings and related texts. All references to this edition are by Confessio number, followed by page and line numbers.

8 For an edition of this manuscript, see *'Colections'*, ed. by Holloway.

9 *Confessiones Amantis*, ed. by Clark, pp. 1–17.

10 See *Confessiones Amantis*, ed. by Clark, p. ii.

11 *Catalogue des livres*, ed. by Rhodes. As Rhodes edits the catalogue made by the French authorities after the expulsion of the nuns from their convent by the French Revolutionary authorities on 18 October 1793, I assume that the date in the title of the edition is a typographical error, and should read 1793 rather than 1739.

essay will focus on Gertrude More's *Confessiones Amantis* as a text that both records the author's personal search for her identity as a monastic and functions as a text that helps define the community's identity as enclosed and inward-looking, thus conserving the community's roots in centuries-old contemplative monasticism.

More's personal struggle with her enclosed life and her coming to terms with it through Baker's teaching can also be placed in the wider context of the Catholic response to the Reformation in the aftermath of the Council of Trent (1545–1563). When women began to adopt roles in the religious life that previously were the prerogatives of men, the Church authorities imposed claustration and strict observance on women's communities. Mary Ward, a contemporary of More's, is an interesting example of a woman who chose an unenclosed and missionary life, founding schools on the Continent, and travelling to England as a missionary. Initially, Pope Paul V supported her, but as she came to be criticized by the Jesuits, she was condemned as a heretic 'because of her refusal to accept cloistering'.[12] Though her excommunication was lifted, the damage done to her work was irreversible in her lifetime.[13] In the broader context of the post-Tridentine Church, with its restrictions placed on female religious, More's text offers an interesting example of how one individual woman made her life of claustration meaningful to both herself and others.

The text of the *Confessiones* presents itself as Gertrude More's outpourings of feeling and thought during moments of inspiration, written down to help her through times of spiritual barrenness when such inspiration was lacking:[14]

> And to hearten & encourage my soule by speakeing & writing thus to thee, was the cause that these things haue bin mentioned by mee, which I read ouer when I cannot (for some indisposition in body or minde) other wayes thinke vpon thee; and when I am ouerwhelmed in any miserie, it becometh most tolerable by haueing this such conference with thee, who neuer disdainest me; for withall glorie be giuen to thee, who art my Lord & my God, blessed for all eternitie. Amen. Alleluia.[15]

> Ffor, as thou well knowest, if I should not, when I enioy some more interior light, set down in writing some things which I may peruse att other tymes, I should be apt to forgett to praise thee, yea & euen wither away with the griefe & anguish, which ofteen by thy sweet permission ouerwelmeth my soule.[16]

12 McNamara, *Sisters in Arms*, p. 463.

13 See Lux-Sterritt, 'Mary Ward's English Institute' and McNamara, *Sisters in Arms*, pp. 462–63.

14 The *Confessiones* are silent on the question on whose initiative More started writing. In the quotations from the text, I follow Clark's edition of MS Rawlinson C. 581. I reproduce its many idiosyncratic spellings, though I have silently expanded abbreviations. When the meaning is unclear from the spelling, I add the emendation in square brackets.

15 *Confessiones Amantis*, ed. by Clark, Confessio 8, p. 56, ll. 3–9.

16 *Confessiones Amantis*, ed. by Clark, Confessio 15, p. 79, l. 21 – p. 80, l. 1.

Writing is just another form of communication with God:

> And verily, my God, to whome I speake & writt with much content to my soule.[17]

Yet More's *Confessiones* were soon regarded as suitable for reading by Gertrude's fellow sisters (and, possibly, English Catholics more widely)[18] as part of their spiritual practice, which under Augustine Baker, and, ostensibly, after his time as well, was explicitly bookish.[19] In *The Life*, Baker suggests that, even though More's writings were indeed intended as 'prayers with the hands' that she could return to when her inner life was barren and she lacked divine inspiration, they quickly became part of the convent's store of edifying texts:

> She sticking to her Praier, and being diligent and industrious, as she was, by reason of the aforesaid Propension aided or caused by the divin grace, and using at the first onlie out of necessitie such ejaculations, as she gotte out of bookes, she camme in a short time to use other meerelie of her owne framing, as suggested to her by her owne nature or spirit, or by the divin spirit, which often times she used to sette downe in writing for her helpe in times of more ariditie. And those so expressed in writing, some others in the howse coming to see them, liked so well of them, that they used to copie them out. By this meanes there was in the howse great store of those Amorous affections of her collection or framing, that were written or scattered heere and there in divers and sundrie bookes and papers. The 2nd, or 3rd parte, or both of them of the bookes called the Idiots Devotion, that are in this howse, do consist of her said doengs, the Author having onlie reduced them into some order and into certein exercises.[20]

This passage from *The Life* nuances both Wekking's assertion that 'after More's death papers were found in her room, which constitute the body of her devotional writings' and Bolton Holloway's statement that More's writings were 'discovered after her early death in 1633'.[21] Clearly, her writings were read and copied by her fellow-sisters before that time. This reminds us that, in spite of her enclosed state, More was not an isolated mystic, but was

17 *Confessiones Amantis*, ed. by Clark, Confessio 18, p. 87, ll. 7–8.

18 It seems likely that Lewis de la Fosse's 1657 and 1658 print of More's *Confessiones* was first and foremost aimed at the 'English nuns, friars, monks, and other regulars on the continent'. Further research will have to establish whether the book also made its way to England. *English Catholic Books*, ed. by Clancy, p. x. An intriguing question, also, is whether a manuscript version of More's works would ever have made its way to England to her family, or whether the *Confessiones* remained enclosed reading as its author remained enclosed.

19 'She redde over all the bookes, that were in the howse, or he could gette from abroade for her purpose, printed and Manuscript, and redde them seriously: and store of bookes there were in the howse'. *The Life*, ed. by Wekking, p. 22.

20 *The Life*, ed. by Wekking, pp. 44–45.

21 *The Life*, ed. by Wekking, p. xv and Bolton Holloway, 'More Helen' [*name in religion Gertrude*].

an author whose texts played an important role in shaping the identity of her community.

Though *The Life* might give that impression, Baker does not seem to have urged More to write as part of her spiritual life just so that his teaching method could be vindicated, and her sanctity and orthodoxy proven (*vidas por mandato*).[22] Nor, would I argue, are Gertrude's *Confessiones* spiritual autobiography only, though the text came to serve as both *vida por mandato* on Baker's behalf and as spiritual autobiography. I would contend that both in writing and reading, re-reading and copying the text, More and her fellow sisters were bridging a historical divide: in More's writings and her fellow sisters' appropriation of them (mediated by Baker or not) these Cambrai nuns were shaping an enclosed spirituality continuous with medieval traditions.

Augustine Baker describes More as a great reader,[23] yet More's voice is authorial rather than compilational — she does not rely on passages from existing texts to form a new, unified text,[24] but confidently writes her own work. Her writing is conventional: she is God's lover, full of desire for him, eagerly enjoying his presence and yearning for it in his absence. Like medieval religious writers before her, she quotes from the Bible — a text Baker reports that she had read in great detail — to illustrate a point she has been making, thus anchoring her book to the Book.[25] In this essay, the focus will be squarely on the *Confessiones* as Gertrude's text. I am fully aware that this focus at present excludes issues that need to and will be addressed elsewhere: first and foremost the relationship between all versions of More's *Confessiones Amantis*, both printed and in (fragmented) manuscript form, and the question whether Gertrude's text can be extricated from later appropriations of it, and the connections of More's work with medieval and early modern contemplative texts,[26] in particular the influence of Augustine's *Confessions* and the writings of More's namesake Gertrude of Helfta, both of which she names as inspirations in her text.[27] Equally crucial is the question of to what extent More may have been influenced by Julian of Norwich's *A Revelation of Love* and Walter Hilton's *Scale of Perfection*, texts that we know Augustine

---

22 Van Hyning, 'Expressing Selfhood', pp. 219–20.

23 See *The Life*, ed. by Wekking, p. 22.

24 This is the definition of what is called a 'compilation' as opposed to an authorial text. See Dutton, *Julian of Norwich*, p. 3 and the introduction to *Late Medieval Devotional Compilations in England*, ed. by Cré, Denissen, and Renevey, pp. 1–2.

25 *The Life*, ed. by Wekking, p. 22.

26 For two assessments of More's literary and spiritual legacy, see Norman, 'Dame Gertrude More' and Latz, 'The Mystical Poetry'.

27 As the Latin edition of *The Herald of Divine Love* was published by the Cologne Carthusians in 1536, it may have been known by Gertrude More. Seven copies of Gertrude of Helfta's text (edited between 1578 and 1687) occur in the catalogue of books owned by the Cambrai nuns around 1793. One of these copies is an English translation (in manuscript). More may have known the earlier copies. *Catalogue des livres*, ed. by Rhodes, pp. 68–69.

Baker was interested in and that were available to the Cambrai nuns,[28] and by Constantin de Barbanson's *Sentiers Secrets*, which Baker read to her, translating from the Latin (*De semitis occultis*) into English. The possible influence of Julian of Norwich's *A Revelation* on More's text will be briefly treated below.

Starting from the assumption that the text as it survives in Oxford, Bodleian Library, MS Rawlinson C. 581 was copied by scribes (fellow sisters?) close to Gertrude herself,[29] the focus will be on the themes in More's text — the themes that define her and her fellow sisters' spirituality: apology for her sinfulness and her lack of ardour at the start of her life as a nun, love of God related to knowledge of him, and religious instruction and the role of teacher that More evolves towards in the later *Confessiones*.

Gertrude More's '*Confessiones Amantis*'

Apology

Gertrude More's *Confessiones Amantis*, in Rawlinson C. 581 a collection of fifty confessions of varying length, is loosely inspired by Augustine's *Confessions* in their combination of meditative prose addressed to God and autobiographical elements, though More's collection is not as vast and detailed as Augustine's, whom More names as an inspiration at several points in her text.[30] Like Augustine's *Confessions*, they are apologetic in character, but

---

28 *The Writings of Julian of Norwich*, ed. by Watson and Jenkins, p. 16. Baker may have been instrumental in acquiring the medieval manuscript(s) that the seventeenth-century copies of *A Revelation* (in Paris, Bibliothèque Nationale, MS Fonds Anglais 40 and London, British Library, MS Sloane 2499) are based on. More may have read the Paris text. The Sloane manuscript may have been copied by Sister Clementina Carey, a Cambrai nun who later became the abbess at the Paris daughter house, years after More's death, around 1650. See *The Writings of Julian of Norwich*, ed. by Watson and Jenkins, p. 458. The *Catalogue des livres* lists printed copies of *Revelations* (the 1670 Serenus Cressy version) and Hilton's *Scale* (1653 and 1659) that postdate More. See *Catalogue des livres*, ed. by Rhodes, pp. 76 and 81. These could of course be printed copies bought to replace manuscript copies. That the Cambrai nuns owned fifteen copies of *Revelations* might point to a longer-standing popularity of the writer among the nuns. Margaret Gascoigne (d. 1637) wrote meditations on Julian's text. See *The Writings of Julian of Norwich*, ed. by Watson and Jenkins, pp. 437–46.

29 This is a working assumption that will need to be backed up by further research. It is based on the fact that Rawlinson C. 581 contains five more Confessiones than the 1658 print (Confessiones 46 to 50), and that — even though the provenance of the manuscript is unknown — it would be exactly the kind of volume to be the result of More's fellow sisters copying out her text, as Baker describes it (see *The Life*, ed. by Wekking, pp. 44–45).

30 See for instance Confessio 18, p. 88, l. 25–p. 89, l. 3: 'and also my beloued ffather & patron St Augustine, whome thou hast giuen me in a most particular manner to be an helpe to mee in doubts & ffeares, an incouragement by his bookes to hope for pardon ffor my innumerable sinnes, & as a fire in all his words to sett my soule also on fire to seeke after & aspire to thy diuine loue, & to wish only þat that may wholy possesse my soule; which grant ffor his sake, as also for thy owne, who art blessed ffor euer. Amen'.

whereas Augustine, as a public figure, may have felt a more pressing need to explain his tumultuous past, More's *Confessiones* initially present themselves, in Walter Hilton's words, 'intimate love letters between a loving soul and Jesus who is loved'.[31] They gradually also include more didactic commentaries on biblical passages read out in the offices (or read during private prayer), and — especially in the later *Confessiones,* meditations in which More expresses her own sinfulness more explicitly.

Gertrude's apologetic statements initially refer to the sorry state of her religious practice in the early years of her life in Cambrai, to her realization that her behaviour was unworthy of a nun, and to her gratitude that Augustine Baker (who is not named in the text, just as he is called 'Father Anonimus' in *The Life*) showed her the way out of the dead-end life she was living:

> Ffor till I resolued, what difficulties so-euer I endured, to make thy will my law, & thy disposition my consolation, I found noe stabilitie in any thing or exercise what-soeuer; & since that time I haue ffound certainty & quiett in all the incerteinty of contrarie occurrences.[32]

In a later Confessio, More discusses her difficulties and their solution in greater detail:

> Ffor when I sinned, he recalled me, & forsooke me not in that my miserie of offending such an infinite goodnes so shamefully, & when entering into wholy [holy] religion before I knewe the happinesse thereof, by which meanes I grew wearie of bearing his sweet yoake and light burthen, which is heauy only through our one fault, & not of itselfe, & through which default & ignorance of mine it grew so greiuous and intolerable to me, that I wished often that it mought haue bin shaken of lawfully by me, pretending that it was so incompatible with my good, that I could scarcely worke my saluation in this my state & profession, & this, my God, thou art witness of, is true; & so did it continue with me three yeares after I had in shew forsaken thee world, & the world indeed forsaken me; when, I say, after this plight entering into religion, did my Lord in these my bitter afflictions forsake mee? No, no, but he prouided such an helpe for me by meanes of a faithfull seruant of his, that quicly was my sorrow turned into ioye; yea, into such an vnspeakbable ioye, that it hath sweetned all my sorrowes that since that tyme haue befallen me. Ffor as soone as my soule was sett in a way of tending to God by abnegation, I found al my misseries presently disperse themselues and come to nothing. Yea, euen in 5 weekes my soule became so enamored with the yoake of this my deare Lord, that if I must haue made not only 4 but 4000 vowes to haue become wholie dedicated to him, I should haue imbraced his state with more ioye and content then

31 'swete lettre-sendyngys made atwix [a] louynge soule and Jesu loued'. Hilton, *The Scale,* Book II, Chapter 43, ed. by Hussey and Sargent, p. 336.

32 *Confessiones Amantis,* ed. by Clark, Confessio 18, p. 87, ll. 14–17.

> euer I did desire to obteine that whicheuer I most of all wished or desired. Yea, and as thou knowest, my God, by 6 weekes my soule, being putt into a course of prayer, I seemed to haue found a true meanes whereby I might loue without end or measure, & that without any perill or danger. Ffor who can loue thee, my God, too much?[33]

It is worth quoting this passage in full, for it gives us a very clear view of Gertrude's aims and themes. A first theme is her own spiritual history, which is shaped as a conversion story: the shameful life of misery and ignorance, which is turned around by the help of God's faithful servant (the unnamed Augustine Baker), whose methods of setting the souls in his care on the way to abnegation (the true humility of recognizing that, compared to God's all, the soul is infinitely small, yet can obtain the fullness of his love in humility) provided her with the true means to love God without end or measure, and without any danger, in a period of five to six weeks. That this is a relatively short period in which to emerge from a spiritual crisis that lasted for years, shows the soundness of Baker's spiritual method — and can thus be seen as a strong endorsement — and simultaneously proves God's endless mercy and willingness to forgive the contemplative's sins. One can see how this would have been considered edifying reading for all the Cambrai sisters, while at the same time it presents More as both completely dedicated to the spiritual life and especially blessed.

More's own predicament leads her to take strong positions on what she considers a good 'souperiour' or spiritual adviser:

> souperiours reflecting one theire owne authority rather then on what in thy behalfe they ought to exact in this or that case, & rather on what by theyre power they ought to exact in this or that case, & rather on what by their power they may commaund, then on what according to thy pleasure were best to be done, gouerne more in theire owne power then in thine; & the effect, (vnles it be very streight betweene his subiects hearts and thee), will consequently be more humaine then diuine; & then they (whilst sensible of theire one honour onely) doe abuse the power giuen by thee, & euen loose whate otherwise they would haue found; & the subiects, lookeing rather to discouer the defects of theire superiours then performe theire one obligations & offices, both faile in theire duties towards thee, to thy dishonour, who so sweetly & iustly disposest all things, so long as we doe not peruert thy order with seekeing not thee & thy honour, but our-selues & our owne honour.[34]

In this passage we see a confident early modern woman speaking her mind. She suggests that superiors who seek their own authority before God's create

33 *Confessiones Amantis*, ed. by Clark, Confessio 25, p. 104, l. 16 – p. 105, l. 20.
34 *Confessiones Amantis*, ed. by Clark, Confessio 14, p. 77, l. 11 – p. 78, l. 4.

disobedient communities who fail to give God his due and fail to find God in true contemplation, losing themselves in worldly friendships. She reports what she experienced in herself, and — possibly — observed in others, as seems to be suggested by her use of the plural:

> But being ignorant how to conuerse with thee and haue in all things relation to thee, theire yoake becomes more & more burdensome to them, and euery day, they fall into new deficulties & inconueniences, and are in danger att last to fall into open rebelion with their lawfull superiours, and some into strang ffrindshipps; a thing which is worthy to be bewailed with bloody teares, that hearts capable of thy love & wholy consecrated thereto, should soe miserably loose them-selues in poring out them-selues where & from whome noe true comfort can be found or had.[35]

A good superior can guide any contemplative to the spiritual life that suits her by making her find the way in which to 'converse' with God most suited to the individual nun, but always leading to the ardent, exclusive love for God that overcomes worldly attachments:

> But I wish that those that do this [i.e. hold the internal spiritual life in contempt] simply by being vnapt for a spirituall life, might giue them-selues to that, which by superiours should be found for them most fitt; and not be a cause that thy sweet mercy and goodnesse should haue such wrong, as that other soules that are fitt should be hindred ffrom haueing relation to thee, by which theyre soules would be turned wholy into loue, by a vehement desire and longing after thee, that one thing which is necessary.[36]

The soul can only match God's infinity, his 'all', in her boundless love for him. More even expresses this boundlessness in figures: even when she would be bound by four thousand rather than four vows (obedience, chastity, poverty, and stability of abode), she would desire God more ardently than she ever desired any worldly thing. Again, the spiritual bedrock on which all More's statements rest is the contemplative soul's realization that, in comparison to God, she is nothing, and that she can only receive the fullness of God in her soul in true humility. Because only God is fullness of being, the soul cannot find rest in the worldly things from which God is absent. In her writings, rather than marrying the practical requirements of convent life — More was the Cambrai Abbey's cellaress — with the spiritual side of it, More resolutely turns inwards, stressing the spiritual consequences of physical enclosure — a radical renunciation of the world and its creatures, in which and in whom no comfort can be found. More

35 *Confessiones Amantis*, ed. by Clark, Confessio 1, p. 21, ll. 18–26.
36 *Confessiones Amantis*, ed. by Clark, Confessio 5, p. 43, ll. 9–15.

expresses this repeatedly throughout the *Confessiones*, but most eloquently and succinctly in the following passages:[37]

> therefore misserable are wee, when wee seeke any-thing besides thee[38]

> Lett vs leaue pretending anie-thing but thee.[39]

> O lett all creatures be to me as if they were not, to the ende I may fully attend to thee in the bottome of my soule, where I will in silence hearken to thee.[40]

In a passage in Confessio 45 in which More discusses the transience of people's opinions, we might possibly see More dealing with her fellow sisters' responses to her writings, urging herself not to set too much store by their appreciation or lack of it:

> O how little true peace doth the soule enjoy, who careth for the praises of men, or feareth their dispraises, since nothing is more slippery, nothing more vnconstant, nothing more vncerteine, then men! To-day one will be thy friend and extoll thee to the skeyes, and to-morrow none shall haue thee lesse in esteeme then he. And thus it standeth with all human flesh: this is the frailty of man.[41]

Though the sentiment she expresses is commonplace — the slippery and changeable world full of inconstant people is opposed to the stability and certainty found in the love of God, who never wavers and is ever present — the later *Confessiones* have other characteristics that can be read and understood as the consequence of Gertrude's growing reputation as a spiritual writer and exemplary nun.[42] Thus, in the later *Confessiones*, More repeatedly presents herself as a sinful wretch in language absent from the earlier *Confessiones*. Fairly neutral expressions such as 'I haue bin twenty-fiue yeares in my infirmity of most loathsome sinnes'[43] make way for expressions of self-abasement in stronger language:

> If it were euer possible to be lawfull for thy creatures to exclaime against thee, & taxe thee of iniustice, it might be admitted them, in this thou hast done and doest for me, *the most sinfull and contemptible of all thy Majesties creatures*.[44]

---

37 Other passages that express the same teaching are Confessio 20, p. 95, l. 18 – p. 96, l. 4; Confessio 43, p. 132, l. 23 – p. 133, l. 2, and Confessio 45, p. 140, ll. 16–22.

38 *Confessiones Amantis*, ed. by Clark, Confessio 14, p. 79, ll. 5–6.

39 *Confessiones Amantis*, ed. by Clark, Confessio 37, p. 124, l. 22.

40 *Confessiones Amantis*, ed. by Clark, Confessio 40, p. 128, ll. 18–20.

41 *Confessiones Amantis*, ed. by Clark, Confessio 45, p. 140, ll. 16–22.

42 That she indeed had this reputation can also be seen in the deathbed accounts written by her fellow nuns included in *The Life*. See *The Life*, ed. by Wekking, pp. 312–26.

43 *Confessiones Amantis*, ed. by Clark, Confessio 14, p. 76, ll. 3–4.

44 *Confessiones Amantis*, ed. by Clark, Confessio 33, p. 116, ll. 15–18; italics mine.

> Thou only art just, thou only holy, and *I the most vile and contemptible of all creatures*. Thou who discernest most clearly how it standeth with me for *my pride, and other abominable sinnes*, wash me in thy blood and I shall yet become whiter then snowe.[45]

These passages of self-abasement are also linked to the spiritual commonplace that 'happy [are] they that are approved by thee, my God, though here they be despised, neglected and contemned by the whole world',[46] and they also play on the consciousness that, compared to God's 'strong and faithfull seruants' of the past, his little children's sufferings are but 'flies and gnatts'.[47]

Love and Knowledge

More frequently responds to her experience of God's overwhelming 'all' with boundless desire for him. God is the lover 'who is more mine then I am my owne',[48] and who draws the soul to him and showers it with his abundant mercy:

> O lett me melt wholy into loue, to record these thy most abundant mercies! Lett me be neuer werie in singing thy praise, who thus hath inuited & drawne me euer, whether I would or noe, to a perfect contempt of all created things, that I may adhere to thee aboue all guifts what-so-euer! This I doe so particularly writt downe, because my frailty is so great, that I may perhapps growe vnmidnfull of thee, notwithstanding all this that thou hast done for me.[49]

More's love of God is closely linked to the urge to write. She has to record her love, lest in her insufficiency she forgets God's greatness. Yet the urge to write equally derives from those moments in which More is sick with love for her absent lover, when writing to or of him is one of the only consolations she has. In her reference to other people who speak to her about her beloved, we once more see More as a member of her community, as she suggests conversations with her fellow sisters and her spiritual adviser and confessor:

> To speake with him is impossible, the distance of place being so great; but yet she may heare others who speake of him, which a little mittigateth her miserie, though while his absence is all irksome to her, because the delaye afflicteth her heart: but is shee yet without all comfort? Noe, for she may writt to & of him; & if none will carry it to her deare beloued, it shall remaine / by her, that he may see att his returne hou shee languished for loue, & could take comfort in nothing all creatures could offer or propose

45 *Confessiones Amantis*, ed. by Clark, Confessio 45, p. 137, l. 31 – p. 138, l. 2; italics mine.
46 *Confessiones Amantis*, ed. by Clark, Confessio 45, p. 138, ll. 12–14.
47 *Confessiones Amantis*, ed. by Clark, Confessio 24, p. 103, ll. 4–9.
48 *Confessiones Amantis*, ed. by Clark, Confessio 13, p. 69, ll. 11–12.
49 *Confessiones Amantis*, ed. by Clark, Confessio 25, p. 105, l. 21 – p. 106, l. 3.

> to her soule, & how shee possessed not what shee only desired, her life by loue being more with her beloued then where shee liued: for which cause shee heareth & yet mindeth not what is said; vnless perhapps they treat feelingly of her absent loue, & speake in his praise, shee seeth & yet cannot take comfort in what shee beholdeth; shee sleepeth, but yet her heart waketh: & in fine, whilst she canot enioye her beloued, nothing cane satisfie her vnquiett heart.[50]

For More, as for religious writers before her, her loving experience of God and her amorous desire for him also desires greater knowledge of him, and this knowledge of him comes in contemplation. This realization is expressed early on in the *Confessiones*, and is repeated throughout the text. In these passages, More also expresses the overwhelming greatness of God in hyperbolical figures, as she did earlier when speaking about the vows she would like to take for God:

> For one learneth more in prayer of thee in one houer then all the creaturs in the world could teach one in 50 yeares; for that which thou teachest is sound, solid & secure, because it tends to nothing but to loue thee & neglect itselfe; thy words bring force & strength in themselues, thy words are words of peace to the soule; thy words are not like þe words of men, which passe as sound through the ayre; but thine peirce the very bottome of oure soules.[51]

> Because once to haue seene thee is to haue learned all things.[52]

This loving knowledge of God, how it can be acquired and what it can lead to, is further nuanced. In Confessio 5, More teaches that knowledge of God and of the self can be acquired not just in private prayers, but in the saying of the Office too:

> and sometymes thou teachest a soule to vnderstand more in [the Office] of the knoweledge of thee and of them-selues, then euer could haue bin by all the teaching in the world shewed to a soule in 500 yeares.[53]

Because of God's fullness, knowledge of him is a multiplication of knowledge of the world arrived at by other means. Later in the *Confessiones*, More expresses again that knowledge of God and knowledge of the self are 'inseparable companions', quoting and expounding Augustine's *Soliloquies* 2. 1. 1:

> In this light the glorious St Augustine walked in an extraordinarie manner, when he cried out with a most amorous heart: 'Lord, lett me knowe thee, & lett me know my-selfe'.

---

50 *Confessiones Amantis*, ed. by Clark, Confessio 13, p. 71, ll. 3–16.
51 *Confessiones Amantis*, ed. by Clark, Confessio 1, p. 23, ll. 9–16.
52 *Confessiones Amantis*, ed. by Clark, Confessio 19, p. 90, l. 18.
53 *Confessiones Amantis*, ed. by Clark, Confessio 5, p. 39, ll. 27–29.

> These two knowledges are inseparable companions, and increase the one by the other. Ffor who can knowe thee, vnles he knowe himselfe? And who cane knowe himselfe, vnles he be tought by thee? Those that would knowe something of thee, and would be fauored by thee, for any end but to loue thee and to learne to dispise them-selues, shew them-selues to be in perill of a most dangerous ruine: for those that walke the true way of loue, which is the way of the Crosse, desire noe fauour, but to be able without all comfort to be faithfull to thee, my Lord God.[54]

Religious Instruction

If we take the *Confessiones* at face value, and read them as letters to God by Gertrude More that have been transmitted in the order in which she wrote them, we can see her developing into a commentator on the Scriptures and a teacher. She may first and foremost be pondering the texts she reads or encounters in the Office for herself, but if it was the case that her fellow sisters started reading her *Confessiones* as she was still writing them, she may also have been teaching them. An interesting recurrent interest in the *Confessiones*, more particularly in Confessiones 27, 36, and 39, is in Mary Magdalene. She is a person More identifies with, and she ponders Jesus' responses to her in the Gospel, seeking to draw conclusions about how he deals with a contemplative soul, and how contemplatives should respond to him. In Confessio 27, Mary Magdalene is understood to be one of the women going to Jesus's grave early in the morning on the third day, bearing spices to anoint his body (Luke 24. 1–10).[55] Here Mary Magdalene is presented as the soul yearning for God and looking for him, and satisfied by nothing or no one but him:

> Was it any comfort to Marie Magdalen, when she sought thee, to find two angelles, which presented them-selues instead of thee? Verily, I cannot thinke it was anie ioye vnto her.[56]

In Confessio 36, we follow More as she is thinking while she writes, groping for answers after she heard what could have been John 20. 11–18, the Gospel

---

54 *Confessiones Amantis*, ed. by Clark, Confessio 8, p. 52, ll. 16–26.

55 The Gospel does not explicitly name one of the women as Mary Magdalene. The women going to the tomb carrying spices are not named in Luke 24. 1, and are referred to as 'mulieres quae cum ipso venerant de Galilaea' (the women who came with him from Galilee) in Luke 23. 56. Though in Luke 24. 10, Mary Magdalene is named, it is unclear whether of the group of women mentioned, she was one of the two who went to the grave: 'erat autem Maria Magdalene et Johanna et Maria Iacobi et ceterae quae cum eis erant quae dicebant ad apostolos haec' (and it was Mary Magdalen and Joanna and Mary, mother of James and the other women that were with them, who told these things to the Apostles).

56 *Confessiones Amantis*, ed. by Clark, Confessio 27, p. 110, ll. 20–22.

for Easter Sunday in the Tridentine Rite.[57] More contrasts John 20. 17 ('noli me tangere') with Luke 7. 38 and 7. 45, where 'a woman who was in that city, a sinner' — commonly identified with Mary Magdalene in the medieval period and beyond — washes Jesus's feet with tears, kisses them, and dries them with her hair. More is struck with bewilderment that Jesus will allow Mary Magdalene, still a sinner, to kiss his feet, whereas later, when she 'had bin a long time trained vp in thy schoole of perfection, and had accompanied thee in thy Passion, and morned for thee at thy tombe, takeing noe rest till thou, her beloued, returned to her againe',[58] he no longer allows her to kiss his feet (or, as John 20. 17 has it, to touch him). Would it be possible, More ventures, that as contemplatives love God more, he loves them less? 'Noe, God forbid I should euer admitt of such a thought'.[59] She then explains that God asks Mary to lift her love for him 'to a loue more spirituall then that with which shee loued thee, when thou conuersedst with her before thy death and Passion'.[60] God becomes more severe with his advanced contemplatives so that they do not fall into the temptation of attributing their progress in the spiritual life to themselves. By giving them stronger trials, he aims to show them their frailty. Like Mary Magdalene, advanced contemplatives should consider themselves unworthy to kiss Jesus's feet, and should 'conuerse with thee in a more spirituall manner then before';[61] and like her, they should not reflect on the pain and suffering Jesus's denial causes them, 'for, as thou knowest, loue feeleth no labour, nor complaineth of anie burthen; and onlie to haue seene thee aliue againe was sufficient to haue made her forgett all former afflictions'.[62]

In Confessio 39, More meditates on Luke 7. 36–50, the reading 'in tertio Nocturno' on 22 July,[63] and more particularly on verses 7. 47 and 7. 48. Returning to Jesus's reaction to Mary Magdalene ('the sinner who was in that town'), she despairingly asks 'O my Lord and my God, if none haue much forgiuen them, but those that loue much, what will become of me'.[64] More laments that she is not like the woman who had 'the necessarie disposition for a soule to heare that comfortable word, "Thy sinnes are forgiuen thee, goe in peace"' because her soul 'is destitute of that pure loue which soe preuaileth with thy diuine Majestie'.[65] She describes herself as 'blown downe with the least blast of temptation', and unable to 'endure anie disgrace, desolation, or

57 *Confessiones Amantis*, ed. by Clark, p. 121.
58 *Confessiones Amantis*, ed. by Clark, Confessio 36, p. 121, l. 27 – p. 122, l. 1.
59 *Confessiones Amantis*, ed. by Clark, Confessio 36, p. 122, ll. 6–9.
60 *Confessiones Amantis*, ed. by Clark, Confessio 36, p. 122, ll. 9–10.
61 *Confessiones Amantis*, ed. by Clark, Confessio 36, p. 122, l. 23.
62 *Confessiones Amantis*, ed. by Clark, Confessio 36, p. 122, ll. 24–27.
63 *Confessiones Amantis*, ed. by Clark, p. 126.
64 *Confessiones Amantis*, ed. by Clark, Confessio 39, p. 126, ll. 7–8.
65 *Confessiones Amantis*, ed. by Clark, Confessio 39, p. 126, ll. 18–19.

difficultie what-soeuer, as it beseemes a true lover of his'.[66] At the end of the meditation, she identifies herself with Mary Magdalene again, and imagines herself at Jesus's feet, where she will

> sigh & weepe, both for my sinnes and for my defect in loueing thee, who art so worthy of all loue & praise and what-so-euer. There I will begge this loue, so much to be desired. There I will wish & long for it, and from thy feete I will not depart, till thou denounce to me: 'Thy sinnes are forgiuen thee', and sayest to my soule: 'Goe in peace'.[67]

We can see here how More's very personal response to readings in the Office takes shape in writing, and how the writing process helps her express the joys of contemplation (in the exclamation of Confessio 27 that the angels at the grave cannot have been a source of joy for Mary Magdalene) as well as deal with the difficulties she experienced in the life she has chosen (the realization of the insufficiency of her love and her sinfulness). We can equally imagine how, in this textual embodiment, her meditations and commentaries could have been useful for her fellow nuns, who I argue would have had access to her writings even when she was alive.

More and the Medieval English Mystical Tradition: Julian of Norwich's 'A Revelation of Divine Love'

Because More writes in an authorial rather than a compilational voice, the medieval influences on her work do not show in the explicit borrowing of passages that can be isolated and identified. Her work does, however, linger on themes that were important to the medieval mystics, and this may mean that More's response to her experience continued on from what she had read (or had heard Augustine Baker read aloud) in the medieval texts, such as Julian's *A Revelation*.

More's assertion that, 'enamored with the yoake of this my deare lord' she would 'haue made not only 4 but 4000 vowes'[68] to completely dedicate her life to God, she might well be appropriating Julian of Norwich's repeated expression of Christ's boundlessly abundant gifts to the soul:[69]

---

66 *Confessiones Amantis*, ed. by Clark, Confessio 39, p. 126, ll. 27–29.

67 *Confessiones Amantis*, ed. by Clark, Confessio 39, p. 127, ll. 3–7.

68 *Confessiones Amantis*, ed. by Clark, Confessio 25, p. 105, ll. 12 and 14.

69 A similar idea occurs in an exclamation in Confessio 2: 'O noe, but if I had tenn thousand hearts, all were too little to bestowe on thee' (26/15–16) and in Confessio 5, a passage quoted earlier: 'sometymes thou teachest a soule to vnderstand more in [the Office] of the knoweledge of thee and of them-selues, then euer could haue bin by all the teaching in the world shewed to a soule in 500 yeares'. *Confessiones Amantis*, ed. by Clark, Confessio 5, p. 39, ll. 27–29.

> For methought that alle the pain and traveyle that might be suffrede of all living men might not haue deservede the wurshipful thank that one man shalle have that wilfully haue servede god.[70]
>
>> (For it seemed to me that all the pain and travail that might be suffered by all living men might not have deserved the worshipful thanks that one man, who has willingly served God, shall have.)

Though Christ suffered only once, not only did he suffer 'more paine than alle men might suffer [...] from the first beginning into the last day',[71] he repeatedly assures Julian that, if he 'might suffer more', he 'wolde suffer more'.[72] These words lead to Julian's understanding of Christ's love for the soul which she expresses in terms of large numbers. More's four thousand vows express the soul's reciprocation of Christ's gift of his suffering in similar terms of love and dedication.

> And in these wordes — 'If I might suffer more, I wolde suffer more' — I saw sothly that as often as he might die, as often he wolde, and love sholde never let him have rest tille he had done it. And I behelde with grete diligence for to wet how often he wolde die if he might. And sothly the nomber passed my understanding and my wittes so ferre that my reson might not, nor cold not, comprehende ne take it. And when he had thus ofte died, or shuld, yet he wolde set it a nought for love.[73]
>
>> (And in these words – 'If I might suffer more, I would suffer more' – I saw truly, that as often as He might die, as He often would, love should never let Him rest till He had done it. And I beheld this with great diligence in order to know how often He would die if He were able to. And truly, the number passed my understanding and my wits so far that my reason was not able and could not comprehend or take it in. And when He had in this manner so often died or should die, yet He would set it at nought for love.)

In Confessio 1, More points out that those who cannot arrive at connecting with God in meditation and prayer 'soo miserably loose them-selues in powring out them-selues where & from whome noe true comfort can be found or had',[74] and she prays to God 'to remoue these impediments from those that are thine by soe manie titles; lett them knowe thee and of thee,

70 All references to *The Writings of Julian of Norwich*, ed. by Watson and Jenkins, by chapter and page numbers. *A Revelation*, p. 14, ll. 14–16.

71 *The Writings of Julian of Norwich*, ed. by Watson and Jenkins, *A Revelation*, p. 20, ll. 3–5.

72 *The Writings of Julian of Norwich*, ed. by Watson and Jenkins, *A Revelation*, p. 22, ll. 4–5.

73 *The Writings of Julian of Norwich*, ed. by Watson and Jenkins, *A Revelation*, p. 22, ll. 21–27.

74 *Confessiones Amantis*, ed. by Clark, Confessio 1, p. 21, ll. 21–27.

that they may loue nothing but thee'.[75] Again, her text is reminiscent of *A Revelation*, where Julian teaches that too many people look for comfort and rest where they cannot be found:

> For this is the cause why we be not all in ease of hart and soule: for we seeke heer rest in this thing that is so little, wher no reste is in, and we know not our God, that is al mighty, all wise, and all good. For he is very reste. God will be knowen, and him liketh that we rest us in him.[76]
>
> > (For this is the reason why we are not all at ease in heart and soul: for we seek here rest in this thing that is so little, in which there is no rest, and we do not know our God, Who is almighty, all wise, and all good. For He is very rest. It is God's will that He be known, and it pleases Him that we rest ourselves in Him.)

A third instance in which More seems to be appropriating Julian's voice is when she discusses the importance of the common over the singular in the context of spiritual exercises:

> Ffor this proceeding [i.e. observing one's personal path towards God] doeth not make a soule singuler in her acctions & carriage (for singularity is a vice w[ch] thou extreamly hatest), but rather makes one exceedingly loue the common obediences & externall exercises, all of them putting ones soule in mynde of her duetie towards thee in all things.[77]

The aside in parentheses may well be an echo of Julian's understanding that God prefers the general, the common, and the all to the singular:

> And when God almighti had shewed so plentuosly and so fully of his goodnesse, I desired to wit of a serteyn creature that I loved if it shulde continue in good leving, which I hoped by the grace of God was begonne. And in this singular desyer it semed that I letted myselfe, for I was not taught in this time. And then was I answered in my reson, as it were by a frendfulle mene: 'Take it generally, and beholde the curtesy of thy lorde God as he sheweth to the. For it is more worshipe to God to beholde him in alle than in any specialle thing'.[78]

Further research will have to establish whether or not More gleaned these ideas from a reading of Julian of Norwich's *A Revelation*, or whether they could have come to her through other channels, from contemporary authors such as Constantin de Barbanson, whose *Secrets Sentiers* is itself continuous with medieval mystical texts such as John Ruusbroec's *Spiritual Espousals*. It could be argued that More would have mentioned Julian as an influence directly in

75 *Confessiones Amantis*, ed. by Clark, Confessio 1, p. 21, l. 26 – p. 22, l. 1.
76 *The Writings of Julian of Norwich*, ed. by Watson and Jenkins, *A Revelation*, p. 5, ll. 21–25.
77 *Confessiones Amantis*, ed. by Clark, Confessio 5, p. 39, ll. 13–17.
78 *The Writings of Julian of Norwich*, ed. by Watson and Jenkins, *A Revelation*, p. 35, ll. 1–7.

her text, but she does not. Here, too, she might be seen to follow medieval examples, as recent authors were far less likely mentioned as sources, whereas authors of authoritative texts were.[79]

Conclusion

In the *Confessiones* More can be seen to bridge a historical divide as she adopts contemplation as the only valid and fruitful way to live her vocation, a way of life that in her text she also offers to her fellow sisters as the one that defines them as a true Benedictine community. By returning to the roots of the monastic life — the renunciation of the world to turn inwards to God — More is able to break her spiritual deadlock. In addition, when her text becomes part of her community's spiritual legacy, she is also pointing to what she believes is the way forward for the Cambrai community. Just as Gertrude More's *Confessiones* shored up her hard-won stability in spiritual exercises, and 'certainty & quiett in all the incerteinty of contrarie occurrences',[80] as taught her by Augustine Baker, this text, both in its initial manuscript transmission and later in its printed form, may also have given the Cambrai community a sense of its contemplative Benedictine identity, turning inwards to prayer and meditation so that the nuns could transcend the world, and turn to God:

> Ffor this is a rule, thou knowest, giuen to me by a faithful seruant of thy diuine Majestie, who indeed gaue most generall rules, that we might not be tied to him or anie other creature, but being leaft more free to thee, flie alsoe more freelie with the wings of diuine loue, which carieth a soule, euen in humain flesh, aboue all that is not thy verie selfe; of such force is thy grace concurring with our will, which is by nature capable off an infinite extent towards thee, when as it neither seeketh, intendeth, desireth, willeth or resteth in anything but thee.[81]

It is intriguing to see that this inward movement (not only evidenced in More's work, but also in the defence of Baker when his orthodoxy was investigated in 1633,[82] as well as in the tenaciousness with which the community held on to Augustine Baker's contemplative writings when they were ordered to give

79 Though the compiler of *The Chastising of God's Children* borrows extensively from John Ruusbroec's *Spiritual Espousals* and Alphonse of Pecha's *Epistola solitarii ad reges*, neither author is acknowledged in the compilation. *The Chastising*, ed. by Bazire and Colledge.

80 *Confessiones Amantis*, ed. by Clark, Confessio 18, p. 87, ll. 16–17.

81 *Confessiones Amantis*, ed. by Clark, Confessio 20, p. 95, l. 18 – p. 96, l. 4.

82 See Appendix D in *The Life*, ed. by Wekking, pp. 347–50, which has 'A Protestation of Father Anonimus and his Scollers: or a Declaration of his doctrine and practise in the matter of the Divine Call [...] penned by Father Anonimus; but at the instance of Dame Gertrude'.

them up in 1655),[83] coincided with an outward movement sometime after her death. We have seen that her text was copied, and was printed in 1657 and 1658, and therefore disseminated outside the boundaries of Cambrai Abbey. In addition, the community was disseminated too, when in 1651 the Cambrai's daughter house, The Monastery of Our Lady of Good Hope, was founded in Paris, with Gertrude's sister Bridget as its first prioress.[84] The inward movement is in keeping with the post-Tridentine Church's strict enforcement of female enclosure. However, the Cambrai English Benedictines' insistence on their right to shape their contemplative lives according to their personal needs and away from any kind of method imposed by the Douai Benedictine monks who were critical of the freedom Baker's teaching afforded can be seen as an anomaly. It illustrates the diversity of religious practice in the period and the strength of these relatively small convents in exile in the Spanish Netherlands.

Works Cited

Manuscripts and Archival Sources

London, British Library, MS Sloane 2499
Oxford, Bodleian Library, MS Rawlinson C. 581
Paris, Bibliothèque Mazarine, MS 1202
Paris, Bibliothèque Nationale, MS Fonds Anglais 40
Stafford, Colwich Abbey MSS 22 and 23
Stratton-on-the Fosse, Downside Abbey, Baker MS 33
York, Ampleforth Abbey, MS 127

Primary Sources

Augustine Baker, O.S.B.: The Life and Death of Dame Gertrude More, ed. by Ben Wekking, Analecta Cartusiana, 119.19 (Salzburg: FB Anglistik und Amerikanistik Universität Salzburg, 2002)

Catalogue des livres provenant des religieuses angloises de Cambray: Book List of the English Benedictine Nuns of Cambrai c. 1739, ed. by J. T. Rhodes, Analecta Cartusiana, 119.42 (Salzburg: FB Anglistik und Amerikanistik Universität Salzburg, 2013)

The Chastising of God's Children and the Treatise of Perfection of the Sons of God, ed. by Joyce Bazire and Eric Colledge (Oxford: Basil Blackwell, 1957)

83 For epistolary evidence of Abbess Catherine Gascoigne's reluctance to do as she was asked, see *English Convents in Exile*, III, ed. by Hallett, pp. 285–93.

84 Rowell, 'Baker's Continuing Influence', p. 82.

'Colections' by an English Nun in Exile: Bibliothèque Mazarine 1202, ed. by Julia Bolton Holloway, Analecta Cartusiana, 119.26 (Salzburg: FB Anglistik und Amerikanistik Universität Salzburg, 2006)
Constantin de Barbanson, *Les secrets sentiers de l'amour divin: Edités en 1623 chez Jean Kinckius libraire à Cologne* (Paris: Desclée, 1932)
English Convents in Exile, 1600–1800: Volume 3, Life Writing, ed. by Nicky Hallett (London: Pickering and Chatto, 2012)
Fr. Augustine Baker O.S.B.: Confessiones Amantis: The Spiritual Exercises of the Most Vertuous and Religious Dame Gertrude More, ed. by John Clark, Analecta Cartusiana, 119.27 (Salzburg: FB Anglistik und Amerikanistik Universität Salzburg, 2007)
Hilton, Walter, *The Scale of Perfection, Book II: A Critical Edition based on British Library MSS Harley 6573 and 6579*, ed. by Stanley Hussey and Michael Sargent, Early English Text Society, o.s., 348 (Oxford: Oxford University Press, 2017)
The Writings of Julian of Norwich: 'A Vision Showed to a Devout Woman' and 'A Revelation of Love', ed. by Nicholas Watson and Jacqueline Jenkins, Medieval Women Texts and Contexts, 5 (Turnhout: Brepols, 2006)

Secondary Studies

Anderson, Judith H., 'More, (Christopher) Cresacre (1572–1649), in *Oxford Dictionary of National Biography* (Oxford: Oxford University Press, 2004), <https://doi.org/10.1093/ref:odnb/19174> [accessed 15 September 2022]
Bolton Holloway, Julia, 'More, Helen [name in religion Gertrude] (1606–1633), in *Oxford Dictionary of National Biography* (Oxford: Oxford University Press, 2004), <https://doi.org/10.1093/ref:odnb/19178> [accessed 15 September 2022]
Dutton, Elisabeth, *Julian of Norwich: The Influence of Late Medieval Devotional Compilations* (Cambridge: Brewer, 2008)
English Catholic Books 1641–1700: A Bibliography, ed. by Thomas H. Clancy (Aldershot: Scolar Press, 1996)
Histoire de Cambrai, ed. by Louis Trenard (Lille: Presses Universitaires de Lille, 1982)
Late Medieval Devotional Compilations in England, ed. by Marleen Cré, Diana Denissen, and Denis Renevey, Medieval Church Studies, 41 (Turnhout: Brepols, 2020)
Latz, Dorothy L., 'The Mystical Poetry of Dame Gertrude More', *Mystics Quarterly*, 16.2 (1990), 66–82
Lux-Sterritt, Laurence, 'Mary Ward's English Institute and Prescribed Female Roles in the Early Modern Church', in *Gender, Catholicism and Spirituality*, ed. by Laurence Lux-Sterritt and Carmen M. Mangion (Basingstoke: Palgrave Macmillan, 2011), pp. 83–98
McNamara, Jo Ann Kay, *Sisters in Arms: Catholic Nuns through Two Millennia* (Cambridge, MA: Harvard University Press, 1996)
Norman, Marion, 'Dame Gertrude More and the English Mystical Tradition', *British Catholic History*, 13.3 (1976), 196–211

Rowell, Benedict, 'Baker's Continuing Influence on Benedictine Nuns', in *That Mysterious Man: Essays on Augustine Baker OSB (1575–1641)*, ed. by Michael Woodward, Analecta Cartusiana, 119.15 (Salzburg: FB Anglistik und Amerikanistik Universität Salzburg, 2001), pp. 82–91

Van Hyning, Victoria, 'Expressing Selfhood in the Convent: Anonymous Chronicling and Subsumed Autobiography', *British Catholic History*, 32 (2014), 219–34

OTTÓ GECSER

Helper Saints and their Critics in the Long Fifteenth Century

The title page of the second edition of Thomas More's *A Dialogue Concerning Heresies* (1531, first published in 1529) advertised it as a work 'wherein be treated divers matters: as of the veneration and worship of images and relics, praying to saints, and going on pilgrimage.[1] With many other things touching the pestilent sect of Luther and Tyndale'.[2] Even though the *Dialogue* is not about heterodox views on saints and their worshippers in the first place, the printer, William Rastell, or the author himself, apparently found this topic the most characteristic of the 'sect' in question or the most interesting for potential customers. This advertising strategy was not entirely unfair, as the interlocutors of the dialogue — the young Messenger, whose role is to present the views of the 'heretics', and the narrator who has to confute them — discuss a wide range of arguments concerning all aspects of the cult of saints in sixteen chapters (2–17) of book I and again in five additional chapters (8–12) of book II, that is, in roughly a quarter of the whole work.

1 This article is based on research carried out at the Institute for Advanced Study in Princeton with the support of the Herodotus Fund. The finishing touches were put on the text during a research stay as a Humboldt Fellow at the Seminar für Mittlere und Neuere Geschichte of the Georg-August-Universität in Göttingen. I am grateful to Dorottya Uhrin for her feedback on a previous version of the text, and to the editors of the volume for their thorough comments on it. Unless indicated otherwise, all translations and emendations of the quoted sources are mine.

2 More, *A Dialogue Concerning Heresies*, ed. by Gottschalk, p. 3. Gottschalk's edition relies on More, *A Dialogue Concerning Heresies*, ed. by Lawler, Marc'Hadour, and Marius with corresponding page numbers but provides the text with standardized spelling and modernized punctuation. For the work itself, see Duffy, '"The comen knowen multytude of crysten men"'; for the cult of saints as discussed in it, see Mitjans, 'On Veneration of Images, Praying to Saints, and Going on Pilgrimages'.

Ottó Gecser • (gecsero@tatk.elte.hu) is Associate Professor in the Faculty of Social Sciences at Eötvös Loránd University in Budapest.

Religious Transformations in New Communities of Interpretation in Europe (1350–1570): Bridging the Historiographical Divides, ed. by Élise Boillet and Ian Johnson, New Communities of Interpretation, 3 (Turnhout: Brepols, 2022), pp. 43–70.

DOI 10.1484/M.NCI-EB.5.131213

In chapter 10 of book II, upon admitting to the narrator that 'ye have in my mind very well touched the matter concerning that it is not in vain to pray to saints, nor to worship them and to have their relics in some reverence', the Messenger goes on to expound his objections to 'the manner of the worship'.[3] Firstly, he criticizes worshipping the saints as God himself; secondly, worshipping the images of saints as the saints themselves; and thirdly, 'the harm that goeth by going of pilgrimages — roiling about in idleness, with the riot, reveling, and ribaldry, gluttony, wantonness, waste, and lechery'.[4] Finally, he turns to the specializations of saints, their assignments to specific kinds of assistance, in the following way:

> 'What say we then', quoth he, 'to that I spoke not of yet in which we do them little worship, while we set every saint to his office and assign him a craft such as pleaseth us? Saint Eligius we make a horse leech and must let our horse rather run unshod and mar his hooves than to shoe him on his day — which we must, for that point, more religiously keep high and holy than Easter Day! And because one smith is too few at a forge, we set Saint Hippolytus to help him. And on Saint Stephen's Day we must let all our horses' blood with a knife because Saint Stephen was killed with stones. Saint Apollonia we make a tooth-drawer, and may speak to her of nothing but of sore teeth. Saint Zita women set to seek their keys. Saint Roch we set to see to the great sickness, because he had a sore. And with him they join Saint Sebastian because he was martyred with arrows. Some serve for the eye only. And some for a sore breast. Saint Germanus only for children. And yet will he not once look at them but if the mothers bring with them a white loaf and a pot of good ale. And yet is he wiser than Saint Wilgefortis; for she, good soul, is, as they say, served and content with oats. Whereof I cannot perceive the reason but if it be because she should provide a horse for an evil husband to ride to the devil upon. For that is the thing that she is so sought for, as they say. Insomuch that women hath therefore changed her name, and instead of "Saint Wilgefortis" call her "Saint Unencumber" — because they reckon that for a peck of oats she will not fail to unencumber them of their husbands'.[5]

It is the 'manner of the worship' concerning these specialized saints that constitutes the last objection to the cult of holy men and women not only in this chapter but in the entire work as well. The remaining two chapters of book II are reserved for the narrator's answer and further comments. The problem of specialization (which the Messenger 'spoke not of yet') has been left to the very end. Why? Was it a minor issue considered only for the sake of completeness? Or was it a major issue of the day to be treated at the end

3 More, *A Dialogue Concerning Heresies*, ed. by Gottschalk, p. 226.
4 More, *A Dialogue Concerning Heresies*, ed. by Gottschalk, p. 226.
5 More, *A Dialogue Concerning Heresies*, ed. by Gottschalk, pp. 226–27.

to make the most lasting impression on the reader? Was it an issue easy to examine due to a large body of arguments made available by others? Or was it an issue requiring much rhetorical invention to discuss?

Answering these questions (or, at least, attempting to do so) needs the rest of this article. My main goal is to reconstruct how the cult of helper saints or holy helpers — that is saints specialized in particular kinds of assistance — emerged as a problem in its own right in the course of the fifteenth century. The holy helpers in general have received little attention by scholars even if the cult of specific saints who came to be venerated as helpers or that of the famous Fourteen Holy Helpers have been studied by many experts in many publications. I have already tried to fill parts of this gap in an article focusing on the differences between holy helpers and other types of patron saints as well as on the growth and diffusion of their cults.[6] Here I will concentrate on the criticisms, tracing them back to their presumable origins, following their transformations, and placing them in a broader context as a contribution to the history of debates on the cult of saints on the eve of the Reformation.

The Identity of the Helpers

Helper saints constitute a rather elusive category as it is difficult to know when a saint is venerated *qua* helper saint. Art historians frequently run into this problem when trying to explain the representation of a particular saint. In many cases, it seems to work as an *ultima ratio*: if the saint in question cannot be shown to have been a patron of the church or other ecclesiastical institution where his or her image is located, or a former member of the religious order that commissioned it, or a generally venerated local holy man or woman, or a personal favourite or protector of a rich donor, then his or her (alleged) specialism may serve as a last resort. Unfortunately, however, the sources for such specialisms are very limited, so it is difficult to be certain if that particular specialism was known to have belonged to the saint in question in that place and time. A large part of the information we have about the assignment of specific kinds of assistance to specific saints in the Middle Ages comes from critics like More's Messenger. At least one of these critics, Erasmus, also noticed the variability of such assignments, that they 'differ with each nation, so that in France Paul has the same importance that Hiero has for us, while James and John are not equally powerful in all places'.[7]

In addition to such variability, going back in time we find less and less information about specialisms altogether. The 178 authentic chapters of the *Legenda aurea*, reconstructed by Giovanni Paolo Maggioni, tell the story of

6 See Gecser, 'Holy Helpers and the Transformation of Saintly Patronage'.

7 Erasmus, *The Handbook of the Christian Soldier*, trans. and ann. by Fantazzi, p. 64. See also the comments at footnotes 56–57 below.

153 different saints or groups of saints.[8] Out of these 153, five — Blaise, Giles, Katherine, Leonard, and Margaret — are portrayed as having a particular commitment to help. Although their capability to do so always appears as a divine gift, they differ among themselves in its reception and scope. Leonard is said to have obtained it from God ('a deo [...] impetrauit') without any specification of how or why; the martyrs — Blaise, Katherine, and Margaret — pray for it right before their death and a celestial voice announces a positive answer; Giles receives it as an extra, without asking for it, as he is praying for the remission of a horrible unnamed crime of King Charles (the Great). As to its scope, only three saints of this group had a real specialism: Blaise is said to help against ailments of the throat, Margaret in giving birth to healthy children, and Leonard against being imprisoned; Katherine's responsibilities, by contrast, are extended to help 'in exitu anime uel in quacumque necessitate' (at the end of life or in any necessity), and 'quisquis sanctum Egidium pro quocumque commisso inuocaret, si tamen ab illo desisteret eius meritis sibi remissum non dubitaret' (whoever invokes St Giles with regard to any crime, and refrains from doing it again, should not doubt in being pardoned through his merits).[9] Later on (at least) two further saints promising assistance to anyone were added to the corpus: Barbara and Dorothy. Both of them received this gift of God in the same way as the other three martyrs, and its scope remained rather general. Barbara is said to have been invested with securing the remission of sins for her faithful worshippers, while Dorothy was credited with seeing to it that they 'in omnibus salvarentur tribulationibus et praecipue a verecundia, paupertate et a falso crimine liberarentur et in fine vitae contritionem et remissionem omnium peccatorum obtinerent, mulieres vero parientes nomen ejus invocantes celerem sentiant in doloribus profectum' (be saved from all tribulations and freed, in particular, from shame, poverty, and false accusation and, at the end of [their] lives, have contrition and pardon for all [their] sins, as well as that women in labour invoking her name experience quick relief from their pains).[10]

What characterizes these seven saints is not specialization in the first place but socially unrestricted assistance. They are willing to help *anyone*, that is not only a specific group of worshippers, be it from a given city, region, ethnic group, or dynasty. Even in the case of the Fourteen Holy Helpers, the helper saints *par excellence*, it was, most probably, not the complementarity of their specialisms, not their being a well-selected team of experts that made them attractive to their earliest worshippers but their independence

---

8 James of Voragine, *Legenda Aurea*, ed. by Maggioni. I deducted the Christological and the other non-hagiological feasts, and I counted once only those saints who have more than one feast and thus more than one chapter in the book (like the Virgin Mary or St Paul).

9 James of Voragine, *Legenda Aurea*, ed. by Maggioni, I, 294 (Blaise); I, 692 (Margaret); II, 988 (Giles); II, 1188 (Leonard); II, 1356 and 1358 (Katherine).

10 James of Voragine, *Legenda aurea*, ed. by Graesse, pp. 901 (Barbara) and 911 (Dorothy).

and their collectivity.[11] They were not (known to have been) 'reserved' as the patron saints of others somewhere else and thus they were free to help anyone. Plus, they could be invoked as a group which made them look more powerful and enhanced the aura of the individual members as well. Readers of the Life of St Erasmus in the Middle High German legendary *Der Heiligen Leben*, composed in Nuremberg around 1400, were informed that 'er is der vierzehen nothelfer ainer vnd mag avch alln menschen wol zv helf kvmen jn alln irn noten an sel vnd an leib' (he is one of the fourteen helpers in need and he is willing indeed to come to the help of all people in all their needs of the soul and the body).[12] He is not yet the helper specializing in intestinal diseases; his identity comes from belonging to a group of powerful saints who are willing to help anyone with anything.[13]

They were also addressed as a whole in the oldest known written sources featuring all fourteen of them (in the selection called the *Normalreihe*), in variants of the following short prayer transmitted by Bavarian manuscripts from around the turn of the fourteenth and fifteenth centuries: 'Georgius Blasius Erasmus | Pantaleonque Vitus Christophorus | Dyonysius et Cyriacus Achatius | magnus Eustachius Egidiusque | cum Margareta cum Barbara cum Katharina | pro nobis orent et celica munera rorent' (George, Blaise, Erasmus and Pantaleon, | Vitus, Christopher, Denis and Cyriacus, | Achatius the Great, Eustace and Giles, | with Margaret, with Barbara, with Katherine, | let them pray for us and make heavenly favours pour forth).[14]

Of course, the fact (if it is one) that the Fourteen Holy Helpers were initially venerated as a group of unconditionally helpful generalists does not exclude the possibility that some of their members were individually venerated as specialists as well. As we have seen above, Blaise and Margaret were singled out as veritable specialists already by the *Legenda aurea*. In addition, if the cult of holy helpers was a phenomenon of popular religion, as it is sometimes assumed, then a large number of saints could be venerated as specialists without their specialisms appearing in written sources until the coming of the critics at the end of the Middle Ages.

There is, however, a major difference between the cult of *few* helper saints and that of *many*. On the one hand, the veneration of some saints as specialists is very old. St Blaise, for example, was regarded as particularly helpful against diseases of the throat in Eastern Christianity as early as the sixth century. The

11 For the origins of their cult, with emphases which partly differ from mine, see Guth, 'Vierzehnheiligen und die Anfänge der Nothelferverehrung' and Pötzl, 'Die Verehrung der Vierzehn Nothelfer vor 1400'.

12 *Der Heiligen Leben*, ed. by Brand, Freienhagen-Baumgardt, Meyer, and Williams-Krapp, p. 136.

13 The importance of group formation in this cult and related ones is emphasized by Schreiber, *Die Vierzehn Nothelfer in Volksfrömmigkeit und Sakralkultur*, pp. 11–15.

14 Dünninger, 'Sprachliche Zeugnisse über den Kult der Vierzehn Nothelfer', p. 345 (quoting from München, BSB, MS lat. 26926).

Byzantine doctor, Aetios of Amida, suggests that, when trying to remove a bone or another sharp object stuck in the throat, the practitioner has to say the following incantation: 'Blasios the martyr and servant of God says, "Come up, bone, or go down"'.[15] Similar practices may have stood at the beginning of other saintly specializations as well.[16]

On the other hand, for *many* saints being (also) helper saints, a sufficient number of saints must be venerated in a given place and at a given time. In the simplest model, with one specialty per saint, there must be as many saints as kinds of assistance. Counting saints venerated in a given area in a given period is quite a difficult task in itself,[17] and it becomes even more difficult if the question is that of how many saints were venerated by the *same larger community* of worshippers in a given area in a given period. Diocesan calendars would count as obvious sources but most of their feasts were observed by the canons of the cathedral or some other local clerics alone. And even the feasts of precept do not necessarily imply any involvement on behalf of most laymen and laywomen beyond not working and hearing Mass. Sources reflecting the appropriation of cults on behalf of the laity, like donations or last wills, are far more difficult to study than calendars, especially in a comparative framework. Nevertheless, as it has been pointed out by Jacques Chiffoleau for the diocese of Avignon, there was a major shift in the fourteenth and fifteenth centuries in the number of saints whose benevolence testators wanted to secure for themselves and for members of their families.[18] If this was the case elsewhere too, then, other things being equal, the conditions in the later Middle Ages were more favourable for the emergence of an extensive division of labour among saints than before.

In other words, even if we regard the cult of holy helpers as a phenomenon of popular religion and explain its invisibility or difficult visibility in written sources as a consequence of this social position, it could hardly have been a typical feature of the cult of saints right from its beginnings in late Antiquity, as this would have required the appropriation of a sufficient number of cults by the laity. The *when* of reaching such a sufficient number was probably different from region to region, but may well have been catalysed to a significant extent by the growing importance of preaching about saints. Separate volumes of sermons dedicated to this purpose became more frequent from the thirteenth century onwards, including not only collections of *sermones de sanctis* but also those of *sermones de communi sanctorum*.[19] The latter type — by offering sermons not on specific saints but on general categories of them, such as

---

15 Quoted in Zellmann-Rohrer, 'The Tradition of Greek and Latin Incantations', p. 16 (see also pp. 140–41).

16 For early incantations invoking St Zachary against bleeding in the Eastern Church, see Barb, 'St Zacharias'.

17 See Bartlett, *Why Can the Dead Do Such Great Things?*, pp. 137–50.

18 Chiffoleau, *La comptabilité de l'au-delà*, pp. 386–87.

19 Bériou, 'Les sermons latins après 1200', p. 388.

martyrs, confessors, virgins, and so on — enabled any preacher having such a sermonary to preach about, theoretically, any saint. Another sign of the growing importance of preaching about saints is the parallel emergence of *abbreviationes* or *legendae novae*, that is, collections of short *vitae* arranged in the order of the ecclesiastical calendar, primarily as background material for preachers, with the *Legenda aurea* being the most famous among them.[20]

Apart from preaching, the number of saints venerated by the same larger community could also increase as a function of the gradual replacement of relics by images as the privileged means of contact between the saints and their worshippers. From the thirteenth century onwards, the diffusion of images of saints, in various formats, in more and more geographical areas and social circles, first in Italy, contributed to the dissociation of cults from pilgrimage sites. Worshippers could dedicate themselves or pray to a saint in front of a local image instead of visiting his or her tomb and, eventually, they could even hope for a miraculous cure from their bodily contact with or proximity to an image just as they could from touching or approaching the relics.[21] Such a 'delocalization' of devotion to holy men and women, as André Vauchez put it, made the importation of new cults to any given place easier and the 'reservation' of saints as local patrons more difficult.

Nevertheless, the transition from cults of saints centred on the grave to their counterparts centred on visual representations was gradual and far from absolute. Pilgrims visiting 'glorious bodies' remained crucial for processes of canonization, and miraculous images gave rise to new pilgrimage sites. Specialization was not in the interest of the orchestrators of new cults even at the end of the Middle Ages, since any filtering of the potential worshippers diminished the chances of success. Without pilgrims there is no spread of the saint's *fama sanctitatis*, no possibility of hearing witnesses to the saint's *virtus*, and thus no *inquisitio in partibus*, and no canonization. New saints have to be generalists. This must be the main reason why canonized *sancti moderni* were slow to appear among the holy helpers in the late Middle Ages.[22] The latter tended to be old saints, in the first place, whose cults nobody wanted or could keep local and general.

Invoking the Helpers

It seems that the first theological reflections on the cult of saints *qua* specialists also go back to the thirteenth century. They appear in commentaries on the *Sentences* of Peter Lombard, more precisely the forty-fifth distinction of the fourth book. Here, in the sixth chapter, the Lombard inquired into '[q]uomodo

20 Philippart, *Les Légendiers latins et autres manuscrits hagiographiques*, pp. 45–48.

21 Vauchez, *Sainthood in the Later Middle Ages*, pp. 444–53.

22 See the end of the next section.

Sancti et glorificati et Angeli audiunt preces supplicantium et intercedunt pro eis' (how the saints and those in glory and the angels hear the prayers of their supplicants and intercede for them).[23] Originally, his problem had nothing to do with the holy helpers, but in the thirteenth century new questions were added to it. Thomas Aquinas may well have been the first to reflect on the cult of holy helpers in this context. With reference to the same passage of the *Sentences*, he asks '[u]trum debeamus sanctos orare ad interpellandum pro nobis' (if we have to pray to the saints to intercede on our behalf), and considers the following point among the potential arguments for a negative answer:

> [S]i eos ad orandum pro nobis interpellare debemus, hoc non est nisi quia scimus eorum orationem esse Deo acceptam. Sed quanto aliquis est sanctior inter sanctos, tanto ejus oratio est magis Deo accepta. Ergo semper deberemus superiores sanctos pro nobis intercessores constituere ad Deum, et nunquam minores.[24]
>
> (If we need to request them to pray for us, this can only be the case because we know that their prayers are heard by God. But the more someone is saintly among the saints, the better God hears his prayer. Therefore, we should always choose greater saints as our intercessors with God and never lesser ones.)

In his *solutio* for this objection, Aquinas points out that 'quamvis superiores sancti sint magis Deo accepti quam inferiores, utile tamen est etiam minores sanctos interdum orare; et hoc propter quinque rationes' (even if greater saints are better received by God than lesser ones, sometimes it is useful to pray to the lesser ones as well; and this is because of five reasons). One of these five is that 'quibusdam sanctis datum est in aliquibus specialibus causis praecipue patrocinari, sicut sancto Antonio ad ignem infernalem' (certain saints are given special patronage over some particular matters as St Anthony over hellfire).[25]

Anthony was another early example of saintly specialization, if not as early as Blaise mentioned above. Anthony emerged as a healer of a range of pathological conditions referred to as 'fire' (*ignis*) — typically exhibiting gangrenous symptoms including, quite probably, the effects of ergotism as well — in the course of the twelfth century, in connection to his relics in Saint-Antoine-de-Viennois.[26] Aquinas's reference to 'hellfire' is baffling at first sight, but the disease name 'fire' was frequently qualified as *sacer*, *infernalis*, or 'of St Anthony', which some authors considered semantically identical. Thus, for example, Aquinas's contemporary and fellow Dominican, Stephen of Bourbon, discussing the immense destructive potential of hellfire in the literal sense, asks that 'si ignis iste qui dicitur sacer uel sancti Anthonii, uel

---

23 Peter Lombard, *Libri IV sententiarum*, bk. IV. dist. XLV. ch. VI, vol. II, 1009.

24 Aquinas, *Commentum in quartum librum Sententiarum*, ed. by Fretté, dist. XLV. qu. III, p. 382.

25 Aquinas, *Commentum in quartum librum Sententiarum*, ed. by Fretté, dist. XLV. qu. III, p. 383.

26 Foscati, *Ignis sacer*, pp. 121–33.

inferni, hic sic deturpat membra, quanto magis ille cum iste non sit nisi signum uel umbra illius' (if the fire called sacred or of St Anthony or of hell disfigures the limbs to such an extent, how much more does that [fire] do so, as this is but a sign or shadow of that one)?[27] Thus Aquinas must have simply referred to a disease by one of its names — otherwise he would have attributed too much power to St Anthony.

We do not know how many other examples of saintly specialization Aquinas was familiar with, but his above *solutio* implies that helper saints are lesser saints: neither Apostles, nor evangelists, but belonging to more populous categories, the rank and file of the heavenly court, such as martyrs and confessors. And, indeed, even among the holy helpers mentioned by their critics at end of the Middle Ages we hardly find anyone belonging to the highest levels of the celestial hierarchy. The multiplication of saints venerated by the same larger community of worshippers in a given place and at a given time could not jeopardize the position of the most important, most generally celebrated, best-known saints, but it may well have pushed the lesser ones toward particular niches in the growing division of saintly labour. Apart from this, Aquinas's solution also implies that prayers should not be addressed to helper saints (and other lesser saints) in the first place. Not because it is doctrinally wrong, but because it is less efficient. In other words, he seems to have regarded the cult of holy helpers as an existing but largely irrelevant phenomenon.

It appears that authors other than Dominicans did not consider saintly specialization in their commentaries on distinction forty-five, but Aquinas's *confrères* tended to rely heavily on his treatment of the passage. Thus, for example, Durandus of St Pourçain made use of Aquinas's above-discussed *solutio* by quoting it almost word for word, including his reference to saintly specialization: 'quibusdam sanctis datum est in aliquibus specialibus casibus precipue patrocinari, ut sancto Anthonio ad extinguendum ignem, qui dicitur infernalis, et quibusdam aliis sanctis in aliis specialibus infirmitatibus' (certain saints are given special patronage over some particular calamities as St Anthony over extinguishing the fire called infernal, and certain other saints over other particular diseases).[28] The only novelty here is the allusion to other holy helpers but without specific examples and keeping their responsibilities limited to diseases. One of his fellow Dominicans, Peter of Palude, despite

---

27 Stephen of Bourbon, *Tractatus de diuersis materiis predicabilibus*, ed. by Berlioz and Eichenlaub, I. IV, p. 112. Before St Anthony, the fiery diseases had been associated with other saints as well — first of all St Martial of Limoges and the Virgin Mary — but these associations largely remained limited to the catchment areas of specific shrines competing for pilgrims, even if names like *ignis/malum/morbus sancti Marcialis* or *ignis/malum/morbus Beate Marie/Nostre Domine* had a broader diffusion; see Foscati, *Ignis sacer*, pp. 39–52, 61–75, 80–82.

28 Durandus of St Pourçain, *Scriptum super IV libros Sententiarum*, ed. by Jeschke, bk. IV. dist. XLV. qu. IV, p. 227.

many disagreements on other points, followed here exactly in Durandus's footsteps, quoting Aquinas and adding the same allusion to other unnamed saintly experts in specific diseases.[29]

By the fifteenth century the Aquinian citation of holy helpers as an argument for invoking lesser saints came to be imitated by authors outside the Order of Preachers and in contexts unrelated to the *Sentences* as well. '[M]elius est atque utilius oratione et devotione pro adiutorio ad Matrem Christi recurrere quam ad alios sanctos inferiores; et plus ad superiores quam ad inferiores' (it is better and more profitable to have recourse, with prayer and devotion, to the Mother of Christ than to other lesser saints; and rather to the greater than the lesser ones) — writes Bernardino of Siena in his sermon-treatise *De sanctissima oratione et de circumstantiis eius*.[30] 'Utile tamen est etiam sanctos minores orare, et maxime propter tres rationes' (it is, nevertheless, profitable to pray to the lesser saints as well, and especially for three reasons), the second being that:

> quibusdam sanctis divinitus datum est in aliquibus specialibus causis praecipue patrocinari, sicut sancto Antonio de Padua Ordinis Minorum quotidie eius patrociniis gratias et miracula impetrare; sancte Luciae multi pro conservatione corporalis luminis, et sancto Nicolao, ut evadant a maris periculis, devotione recurrunt; et sic de multis aliis sanctis.[31]
>
> (certain saints are given special patronage by God over some particular matters as St Anthony of Padua of the Friars Minor to procure favours and miracles daily through his patronages; many have recourse, with devotion, to St Lucy for the preservation of their eyesight and to St Nicholas for evading the dangers of the sea; and likewise to many other saints).

Bernardino seems to make an attempt to include Anthony of Padua here instead of Anthony the Great, but he fails to mention his specialism. On the other hand, he — just like his Dominican predecessors — places the holy helpers among the lesser saints whose help, not being as effective as that of the greater ones, is not really worthwhile to seek frequently.

---

29 '[Q]uibusdam sanctis datum est in quibusdam specialibus casibus patrocinari, ut sancto Antonio ad extinguendum ignem, qui dicitur infernalis et quibusdam aliis sanctis in quibusdam aliis infirmitatibus.' Peter of Palude, *Scriptum in quartum Sententiarum*, bk. IV. dist. XLV. qu. II, cons. III, fol. 218vb. For his disagreements with Durandus, see Dunbabin, *A Hound of God*, pp. 37–43.

30 Bernardino of Siena, *Sermones de tempore et de diversis*, II. 1, p. 82.

31 Bernardino of Siena, *Sermones de tempore et de diversis*, II. 1, pp. 82–83. This edition, the modern Quaracchi edition, reads 'aliquibus *spiritualibus* causis' instead of 'aliquibus *specialibus* causis'; I emended the text on the basis of the eighteenth-century Venice edition (Bernardino of Siena, *Sermones eximii*, ed. by de La Haye, p. 148) as *spiritualibus* makes little sense here and, if abbreviated in a manuscript, it is easily confused with *specialibus*.

Preaching in the vernacular about the same topic, *Come e che si de' domandare a Dio*, Bernardino does not even mention the helpers. Among the saints it is, first of all, the Virgin Mary he advises his compatriots to address in their prayers. God listens to her requests more than to

> tutte l'orazioni che ma' feceno o fanno o faranno tutti li apostoli, tutti li martiri e tutti li confessori e tutti i vergini e tutti i Serafini e tutti e Cherubini e Troni e Dominazioni e Podestà e Virtù e Arcangioli e Angioli e tutte l'anime giuste.
>
> > (all the prayers that were or are or will be ever said by all the apostles, all the martyrs and all the confessors and all the virgins and all the Seraphim and all the Cherubim and Thrones and Dominions and Powers and Virtues and Archangels and Angels and all the souls of the righteous).[32]

Apart from her, the Sienese should only turn to their local patron saints, Ansanus, Crescentius, Sabinus, and Victor:

> Noi aviamo anco delli altri avocati: chi n'ha uno, e chi n'ha un altro, e anco chi n'ha più d'uno. Voi sapete che noi n'aviamo quatro; cioè i martori nostri del Duomo. [...] Avendo questi martori e avocati de la città nostra, sempre li doviamo invocare.[33]
>
> > (We have other protectors too: some have one and some have another and some have more than one, too. You know that we have four, namely our martyrs of the Cathedral. [...] Having these martyrs and protectors of our city, it is them whom we have to invoke at all times.)

The Aquinian model of the helper saint as lesser saint standing low in the hierarchy of efficient intercessors remained alive until the end of the Middle Ages. The main novelty seems to have been the attempt, already seen in Bernardino of Siena, to add saintly *confrères* to the list. The Hungarian Observant Franciscan preacher, Pelbart of Timişoara/Temesvár (d. 1504), for example, in his answer to the Aquinian question — 'utrum utilius sit semper homini implorare pro patrocinio aliquem sanctum maiorem, quam minorem' (whether it is always more profitable for a human being to implore the patronage of a greater saint than that of a lesser one)? — makes his own variant of the usual point:

> [Q]uibusdam sanctis est concessum seu est datum a Deo in aliquibus specialibus causis praecipue patrocinari, sicut beato Antonio liberare ab

32 Bernardino of Siena, *Prediche volgari sul Campo di Siena*, ed. by Delcorno, XXVI. 15, vol. II, 746. The omission of referring to the helpers in the vernacular sermon was most probably not motivated by any marked disapproval of invoking them, as Bernardino was not shy to make his criticisms explicit regarding other aspects of the cult of the saints; see Bartolomei Romagnoli, 'Osservanza francescana e disciplina del culto dei santi', pp. 132–33.

33 Bernardino of Siena, *Prediche volgari sul Campo di Siena*, ed. by Delcorno, XXVI. 20, vol. II, 747.

igne infernali ipsum invocantes, item beato Nicolao defendere itinerantes, beato Brictio praecavere a confusione, beato Gratiano ad recuperandum res perditas, beato Francisco ad subveniendum in morte et in Purgatorio, et sic de aliis.[34]

> (Certain saints are granted or given special patronage by God over some particular matters, such as St Anthony to free from hellfire those who invoke him, or St Nicholas to protect travellers, St Brixius to guard against shame, St Gratian to find lost things, St Francis to help in dying and in Purgatory, and similarly concerning others.)

Interestingly enough, here — just as with Bernardino — the *confrère* helper saint has no real specialization comparable to that of Anthony the Great, Nicholas, Brixius, or Gratian. One possible interpretation of this deficiency is that Francis — or Anthony of Padua in the earlier case — had no generally acknowledged 'office' yet (to use More's term), and his inclusion in the list meant to promote his invocation in a cultic landscape where saints were increasingly considered in their specialized capacities by their worshippers.

In the second half of the fifteenth century, more concerted efforts to fashion canonized mendicant saints as holy helpers also appeared. In the canonization process of Vincent Ferrer in Brittany in 1453, several witnesses claimed to have recovered, or that their community was saved, due to the intercession of the saint. Some of these healing narratives — and others inspired by them — found their way into biographies of the saint, and from there to other vehicles of the cult. Thus, for example, the Dominican preacher Gabriele Barletta (d. after 1481) hails Vincent for having saved, still in his lifetime, an entire monastery from the plague and for having effected, *post mortem*, sixty-six plague cures. Accounting for these prodigious deeds, Barletta writes that 'datum est quibusdam sanctis patrocinari super infirmitates, ut Antonio super igne, Lucia super oculos, Sebastiano et Rocho super pestem et huic datum est' (certain saints are given special patronage over diseases as Anthony is given over [those called] fire, Lucy over [those of the] eyes, Sebastian and Roch, and this one [i.e. Vincent] over plague).[35] In contrast to St Anthony of Padua and St Francis in the above examples, Vincent has a veritable specialization here, and Barletta's reference to it is entirely detached from the context of invoking lesser saints (even if the formulation resembles the original Aquinian one).

---

34 Pelbart of Timişoara/Temesvár, *Pomerium sermonum de sanctis*, winter part, sermon LXXXII: 'In festo omnium sanctorum: Sermo primus de veneratione sanctorum', § . E.

35 Barletta, *Sermones*, pt. II (*Sermones de sanctis*), 'In festo s. Vincentii confessoris Ordinis Predicatorum', fols 21vb–23vb. For Vincent as a plague saint, see Smoller, *The Saint and the Chopped-Up Baby*, pp. 105–09 and 193–94.

Problems Arising

Going by the sources considered in the previous section, the cult of holy helpers seems to have been entirely unproblematic, even if largely irrelevant, in the later Middle Ages. By contrast, Gabriel Biel, in his *Canonis misse expositio* finished in 1488, dedicates a rather long section to saintly specialization with the intention of defending it from criticism. In lesson XXXII, where this section belongs, he discusses the *Communicantes* prayer of the canon, a hierarchical catalogue of heavenly intercessors with Mary on top followed by St Joseph, *eiusdem Virginis sponsus*, as well as a list of Apostles and martyrs, and a general reference to all (other) saints 'quorum meritis precibusque concedas, ut in omnibus protectionis tue muniamur auxilio' (through whose merits and prayers you grant us being safeguarded in everything with the help of your protection). Commenting on the prayer Biel notes that:

> in hac sanctorum invocatione non tantum sancti maiores, ut Petrus et ceteri apostoli in beatitudine et gloria deo proximiores, sed etiam inferiores et mediocres, ut Linus et ceteri martyres, ex nomine exprimuntur. Etiam certi nominandi eliguntur, ut per hoc instruamur quod licite nunc ad hunc, nunc ad illum maiorem vel minorem orationes fundere possumus, et ad speciales recurrere, devotione et fiducia speciali. Quo illorum error reprobatur, qui non ad varios sanctos pro variis sublevandis defectibus recurrendum dogmatizabant.[36]
>
>> (in this invocation of saints not only major saints are mentioned by name, like Peter and other apostles – who, in [the state of] beatitude and glory, are closer to God – but also middling and lesser ones, like Linus and other martyrs. Likewise, some are chosen to be named for our instruction so that we can legitimately direct our prayers now to this, now to that major or minor one, and have recourse to specific ones with particular devotion and trust. Through which the error of those is condemned who propound it as a dogma not to have recourse to different saints for assistance with different problems.)

It is difficult to tell who these critics were, as Biel makes no specific reference to anyone. But it seems clear from his argument in defence of the helpers that the purported error of the critics lay in attacking the very foundation of saintly specialization:

> Consideranda est varietas donorum etiam in sanctis tam in via, quam in patria discretorum. Verum enim est et in sanctis illud Virgilianum: 'non omnia possumus omnes', quoniam nec omnia, nec eadem omnibus data sunt, sed diversi diversa receperunt dona, omnia tamen ad communem

---

36 Biel, *Canonis misse expositio*, ed. by Oberman and Courtenay, XXXII, vol. 1, 340 (with slight changes in capitalization).

ecclesie utilitatem. Quod pulchro paradigmate deducit apostolus, I Cor. xii: 'Divisiones' inquit 'gratiarum sunt, unus autem Spiritus. Divisiones ministrationum sunt, unus autem dominus. Divisiones operationum sunt, idem autem deus, qui operatur omnia in omnibus, alii enim datur sermo sapientie; alii gratia curationum; alii operatio virtutum; alii prophetia; alii genera linguarum'.

> (We have to consider even in saints, both in the state of wayfaring and in the fatherland [i.e. in heaven], the variety of diverse gifts. The Virgilian maxim [Virgil, *Eclogues*, VIII, 63], 'not all things can we all do', is, indeed, true of saints as well, because neither everything, nor the same thing is given to everyone, but different ones receive different gifts, yet all for the general benefit of the Church. The apostle explained this with beautiful examples, I Corinthians xii [4–10]: 'There are', says he, 'diversities of graces, but the same Spirit. There are diversities of ministries, but the same Lord. There are diversities of operations, but the same God, who worketh all in all; to some indeed is given the word of wisdom; to another, the grace of healing; to another, the working of miracles; to another, prophecy; to another, diverse kinds of tongues'.)[37]

Given that earlier discussions of invoking the holy helpers took their specialization for granted, it must have been quite difficult to find authorities to underpin the thesis that specialization on earth continues to exist — or exists in some other form — in heaven too. The words of the apostle in their original context refer to *this world* alone, and thus they merely prove the rather obvious element of the thesis, namely that the Church Militant is functionally differentiated. The difficult part is to show that the same holds for the Church Triumphant as well.

Biel cites two theological authorities: Augustine and Gerson — Augustine from chapter 26 of *De sancta virginitate*, where he discusses the meaning of the one denarius in the parable of the vineyard in Matthew 20. 1–16: '"So what relevance", they ask, "has that denarius which is bestowed equally upon all, once the work in the vineyard is done, whether on those who worked from the first hour or on those who worked for a single hour?"' Augustine's answer is that it merely refers to the very fact of salvation, 'the reward gained by all', not to 'the varying rewards of the saints'.[38] According to the passage quoted by Biel:

> [V]ita eterna pariter erit omnibus sanctis, equalis denarius omnibus attributus est; quia vero in ipsa vita distincta fulgebunt lumina meritorum, 'multe

37 Biel, *Canonis misse expositio*, ed. by Oberman and Courtenay, XXXII, vol. I, 340–41 (with slightly different typography). Quotations from the Bible in English follow the Douay-Rheims version. The English translation of Virgil, *Eclogues*, VIII. 63 is by H. Rushton Fairclough from the 1916 Loeb edition.

38 Augustine, *De bono coniugali, De sancta uirginitate*, ed. by Walsh, p. 99.

> mansiones sunt' [John 14. 2] apud patrem ac per hoc in denario quidem non impari non vivit alius alio prolixius, in multis autem mansionibus honoratur alius alio clarius.
>
> (Eternal life will itself be alike for all the saints, and so the denarius has been allotted equally to all. But because in that [eternal] life the lights of their merits will shine differently, 'there are many dwelling-places' [John 14. 2] with the Father. Accordingly, since the value of the denarius remains the same, one does not live longer than another, but in those numerous dwelling-places one obtains brighter glory than another.)[39]

In contrast to Biel's thesis, what Augustine talks about here is hierarchical rather than functional differentiation in the Church Triumphant: some receive more in heaven, some receive less. This is the basis of the traditional distinction between greater and lesser saints. There is no mention here of different ministries or gifts in the state of glory. Such a view was not yet on the agenda in Augustine's time.

Biel's reference to Gerson is closer to his point. Gerson in his *De modo orandi*[40] discusses, among other things, three considerations for choosing a saint as the addressee of one's prayer. One is the saint's proximity to God, another is the worshipper's familiarity with the saint, while the third is the saint's specialization. In terms of the last one, the reader is advised 'aliquem sanctorum convertere pro necessitatibus aliquibus sublevandis vel pro impetranda speciali quadam gratia, qui sanctus vel sancta privilegiatum donum recipisse memoratur a Deo ut pro talibus opem ferat' (to turn for assistance in certain necessities or obtaining some special favour to any saint who, as a holy man or woman, is remembered to have received from God a special gift of bringing help in such cases).[41] Gerson then refers to the same scriptural passage as Biel ('There are diversities of graces', I Corinthians 12. 4) and notes that 'quod verum est nedum de viatoribus sed beatis' (it holds not merely for the wayfarers but for the blessed too). It is this note that Biel quotes from him.[42]

Thus Gerson, as opposed to Augustine, did talk about the continuity or renewed existence of individual ministries or gifts of saints in glory. There is no sign, however, that his motivation to do so was that of responding to

---

39 The Latin text is quoted according to Biel, *Canonis misse expositio*, ed. by Oberman and Courtenay, XXXII, vol. I, 341 (with slight typographic changes). I adapted Walsh's English translation (Augustine, *De bono coniugali, De sancta uirginitate*, ed. by Walsh, p. 101) to the minor divergences between his Latin text and that of Biel.

40 Gerson, *Œuvres*, ed. by Glorieux, no. 37, II, 169–74. Combined with *De valore orationis et attentione* (Gerson, *Œuvres*, ed. by Glorieux, no. 38, II, 175–83), it was printed as *De oratione et valore eius* first around 1470 in Cologne and several times later.

41 Gerson, *Œuvres*, ed. by Glorieux, II, 172.

42 Gerson, *Œuvres*, ed. by Glorieux, II, 172; Biel, *Canonis misse expositio*, ed. by Oberman and Courtenay, XXXII, vol. I, 341 (with minor typographic differences): '"Quod verum est" (ait Gerson, tractatu *De oratione*) "nedum in viatoribus sed etiam in beatis"'.

criticism. Originally, he sent *De modo orandi* as a letter to one of his younger brothers, Jean the Celestine, from the Council of Constance in 1416.[43] Jean the Celestine was a religious in a rather strict order, so he knew enough of prayer and the saints. The point was not to introduce him to the topic or providing a concise summary of theological views related to it, but to give personal, or even fatherly advice to a sibling twenty years younger than the author. This is probably why no specific helper saints are mentioned as examples: Gerson was sure that his brother knew what he was talking about.

In the course of the next year Gerson composed another text, the *De directione cordis*,[44] which also touched on the holy helpers. In this work, apparently unknown to Biel, he approached their cult from a different angle, that of superstitious practices instead of invocation and prayer. Superstitious practices connected to saints include the following:

> offeratur tale munus vel tale, sicut gallus pro pueris, gallina pro puellis beato Christophoro et beato Joanni Baptistae; quod ad sanctum Hubertum pro morsu canis rabidi, fiant innumerae particulares observantiae quae nullam videntur habere institutionis rationem; et ita talis ritus transit in superstitionem quae nihil aliud est quam vana religio. Dicitur autem vana, quia caret ratione vel effectu. Similiter est de hoc quod sanctus Antonius habeat plus virtutis in curando sacrum ignem quam alii sancti. Rursus quod in hac ecclesia dedicata beatae Virgini, ipsius virtus sit potentior ad faciendum miracula quam in altera; et hoc ratione talis imaginis suae vel solitae peregrinationis; et ita de similibus absque numero.[45]
>
> (one gift or another, like a rooster for boys and a hen for girls, should be offered to St Christopher and to St John the Baptist; that countless particular rites are to be performed to St Hubert against the bite of a rabid dog, which have no rational foundation whatsoever. And, hence, such ritual borders on superstition, because it is nothing else but false religion. It is called false because it is without reason or effect. It is a similar case that St Anthony has more power to cure sacred fire than other saints. Or again that in this church, dedicated to the Blessed Virgin, her power is greater to perform miracles than in another; and this is because of a certain image of hers, or because of a customary pilgrimage; and so on in countless similar cases.)

The example of St Anthony strikes the eye as standing in clear contradiction not only to the tradition of using him as the prime example of saintly specialization from Aquinas onwards but also to Gerson's advice in *De modo orandi* seen above. If a saint like Anthony has no special *virtus* to resolve specific kinds of problems, then why choose him as the addressee of one's prayer when such

---

43 McGuire, *Jean Gerson*, p. 263.

44 Gerson, *Œuvres*, ed. by Glorieux, no. 412, VIII, 97–115.

45 Gerson, *Œuvres*, ed. by Glorieux, VIII, 108. See also McGuire, *Jean Gerson*, pp. 272–73.

a problem exists? Possibly, *virtus* means here 'power to perform miracles' as opposed to a 'special privilege of intercession' with God. Gerson may have wanted to emphasize that all supernatural help comes from God. But whatever his intention was, this (seeming) contradiction shows that, as paying attention to popular superstitions became more and more important for churchmen — and Gerson was a protagonist of this process — the cult of holy helpers tended to lose its unproblematic status.[46] Gerson was, otherwise, quite lenient with this type of superstitious practice, in contrast to those which (supposedly) involved demonic intervention. For him they belonged to a category between what was required and what was forbidden by the Church, being neither the one nor the other. While preachers were obliged to discuss the practices of the two opposite categories, they needed to be very cautious when it came to those of the intermediate one 'ut nec nimis generaliter assertive et absolute approbentur [...] nec etiam reprobentur absolute et simpliciter' (that they neither be approved all too generally, emphatically, and absolutely [...] nor rejected absolutely and straightforwardly).[47]

Some forty years later, in 1455, the diocesan synod of Brixen/Bressanone presided over by Nicholas of Cusa may have acted on similar principles when it forbade that 'populo praedicentur superstitiosa, quae in legenda lombardica habentur de S. Blasio, Barbara, Catharina, Dorothea, Margaritha, etc'. (superstitious things about St Blaise, Barbara, Katherine, Dorothy, Margaret, and so on, contained in the *Legenda aurea*, [are not to] be preached to the people).[48] As we have seen above, these five saints are portrayed by James of Voragine and the supplementers of his work as being committed to socially unrestricted assistance and as having received this commitment as a divine gift right before their death. What Cusanus probably regarded as superstitious about them was not their specialization itself (which some of them did not even have in any stricter sense) but their unconditional empowerment: they do not appear as intercessors but as plenipotentiary legates able to exercise divine power at their own discretion.[49]

But Cusanus and the synod went further than banning the preaching of certain topics. According to a note appended to the constitutions, Cusanus,

---

46 On Gerson and superstition in a broader context, see Bailey, *Fearful Spirits, Reasoned Follies*, pp. 127–47 (esp. p. 140: 'no earlier figure nearly as influential as Gerson ever addressed superstitions among the common laity to the extent that he did'). See also Hobbins, 'Gerson on Lay Devotion'.

47 Gerson, *Œuvres*, ed. by Glorieux, VIII, 109.

48 *Synodi Brixinenses*, ed. by Bickell, p. 41. For Cusanus's activity in Bressanone/Brixen, see Pavlac, 'Nicolaus Cusanus as Prince-Bishop of Brixen'. On his preaching there, and his limited interest in sermons on saints except for the Virgin Mary, see Gaffuri, 'I sermoni brissinesi di Niccolò da Cusa', esp. pp. 334–35.

49 Cf. Reames, *The Legenda aurea*, p. 234 n. 15: 'they [i.e. these chapters of the *Legenda aurea*] promise in unequivocal terms that acts of devotion to the saints in question will magically guarantee one's deliverance from certain evils, among them illnesses, poverty, and damnation itself'.

having experienced great uncertainty among the priests of his diocese about which feasts of saints were to be observed and how, made a thorough inquiry into local ways and came up with a scheme of four types of feasts. The first type is observed 'ex jure scripto, secunda ex generali consuetudine cleri et populi, tertia ex particulari quadam consuetudine certorum locorum, quarta ex proprio sensu et superstitione' (by written law, the second by general custom of the clergy and the people, the third by a particular custom of certain places, the fourth by one's own consideration or superstition).[50] The strictly forbidden fourth type looks like a mixture of problematic cases, including the observance of certain feasts, occasionally through specific rituals (such as fasting), *because* of the specialized assistance associated with the saints in question, like the octave of St Valentine against animal diseases and falling sickness, the octave of Epiphany and the feast of Sts John and Paul against tempests, or St George's day against fever.[51] As in the case of the *Legenda aurea*, Cusanus's main target was not specialization itself, but engaging in a *do ut des* relationship with the saints on the premise that they had the miraculous power themselves, or trying to force them to help through illicit practices.

It is especially this latter aspect of the cult of holy helpers that he also criticizes in a sermon written for the feast of Epiphany in 1431.[52] In a section of this sermon dedicated to the false magi who follow the star of superstition instead of the star of Bethlehem, Cusanus warns the audience that 'res consecratae, si ad alium quam proprium usum applicentur' (consecrated things, if used for purposes other than their proper ones) become vehicles of superstition. By way of illustration, he lists a range of examples for the misuse of sacred objects or practices, including:

> abstinentia a capite in honorem sanctae Apolloniae vel Blasii, [cera] luminis consecrati, crux facta de lignis palmarum etc., balnea in vigilia nativitatis et carnisprivii contra febres et dentium dolorem, non comedere carnes in die natalis Domini contra febres etc. vel ad honorandum sanctum Nicolaum propter acquirendas divitias etc., petendo eleemosynam eundi ad sanctum Valentinum contra morbum caducum, ponderando puerum cum siligine vel cera, portare crucem circumquaque campum in vere contra tempestates. Item, in certis oblatis super altare, sicut lapides in die sancti Stephani et sagittae sancti Sebastiani etc.[53]
>
> (abstaining from [the consumption of the] head [of animals] in honour of St Apollonia or [St] Blaise, [wax] from a consecrated candle, a cross

50 *Synodi Brixinenses*, ed. by Bickell, pp. 44–45.

51 *Synodi Brixinenses*, ed. by Bickell, p. 45.

52 Cusanus, *Sermones I (1430–1441)*, ed. by Bodewig, Haubst, Krämer, and Pauli, no. 2, pp. 20–40.

53 Cusanus, *Sermones I (1430–1441)*, ed. by Bodewig, Haubst, Krämer, and Pauli, p. 35 (with slightly different punctuation). For the interpretation of the passage, see Franz, *Der Magister Nikolaus*, pp. 181–82.

> made from palm twigs [used on Palm Sunday], etc.; taking a bath on Christmas Eve and in Shrovetide against fevers and toothache; not eating meat on Christmas Day against fevers, etc. or honouring St Nicholas in order to acquire riches, etc.; begging for alms for visiting St Valentine against falling sickness; weighing a boy in [measures of] wheat or wax [in order to offer this to a saint for his health]; carrying a cross around the field in spring against storms. In addition [there is superstition] in certain offerings put on the altar like stones on the day of St Stephen or arrows on that of St Sebastian).

Cusanus's point is not that no one should turn to specialized helper saints when grappling with problems that fall within their expertise. What he criticizes are, first of all, para-religious rituals performed with the aim of securing saintly assistance. Moreover, even if he looks much stricter than Gerson in his verdict about such rituals, the cult of helper saints constitutes a problem for him only insofar as it overlaps with superstition or, more precisely, one specific type of superstition, the misuse of 'consecrated things'. He was not against the cult of helper saints as such; in itself it was hardly a major problem in his eyes. In 1458, in his arguably most important text on Church reform, the *Reformatio generalis*, it is merely the authenticity of relics and the material or worldly motivations behind their exhibition and worship that Cusanus highlights in connection with saints and their cults as issues to be investigated in the course of ecclesiastical visitations. Helper saints are not even mentioned.[54]

It is still unclear how and why such occasional criticism of the cult of holy helpers relating to a generally growing attention on popular superstition could become intensified so much as to elicit a reaction like that of Gabriel Biel in the 1480s. By that time, however, the stakes had evidently risen. What Biel attempted to do was not to defend certain pious practices but saintly specialization as such. At the end of lesson XXXII, in which, as we have seen, Biel discusses this problem, he turns to four errors regarding the invocation and the cult of saints. The first of these applies if a lesser saint is celebrated more solemnly and festively than a greater one without reasonable cause (*sine rationabili causa*), such as being the local patron saint; the second if a saint is praised indiscriminately and excessively for his or her virtues and abilities; the third if an ability, virtue, or miracle is attributed to a saint fictitiously, without any written text (*scriptura*) mentioning it; and, finally, the fourth if someone who is not a saint is venerated as if he were one.[55] The source of all these errors lies in disregarding the hierarchy of the blessed, which gives us a clue to how and why the cult of holy helpers may have become problematic in the course of the fifteenth century.

The helpers had been regarded as lesser saints since at least the time of Aquinas. As long as only a few saints were venerated as helper saints, their

54 Cusanus, 'A General Reform to the Church', § 22, pp. 572–75.

55 Biel, *Canonis misse expositio*, ed. by Oberman and Courtenay, XXXII, vol. I, 348–50.

cult posed no threat to the established perception of the Church Triumphant and, through this, to the moral order of the Church Militant. Churchmen who were more interested in popular superstition from the late fourteenth century onwards could point to some superstitious practices related to the helpers, but their frame of reference was superstition more generally, not the cult of saints, and in themselves their warnings constituted no serious objection to invoking saints explicitly for their alleged specialism. But the growing number of holy helpers may well have led some to draw the inference that the cultic efforts of the faithful had come to be focused on them to an extent that was now visibly disproportionate to their standing in the celestial court. As we have seen above, in 1431 Cusanus did not go further than highlighting some forms of misusing 'consecrated things' in, *inter alia*, the cult of holy helpers. Some twenty-five years later, in his regulation concerning the observation of the feasts of saints in the diocese of Brixen, he tried to enforce a clear hierarchy. The need for such regulation implies that the ranking of saints, as well as the standard evaluation of merits and achievements signified by this ranking, had been called into question.

Of course, not only holy helpers were highly valued lesser saints. There were many of them among the local patrons of churches, cities, dioceses, and so on. But of local patrons there was only one or a few at a given place, whereas there were more and more holy helpers. Since the cult of holy helpers tended to be explicitly materialistic — the main reason for turning to them was the need to resolve a problem of everyday life — their increasing number and veneration brought about a turn towards more visible materialism in the cult of saints in general.

This seems to be the point when the well-known critics of the cult of holy helpers entered the scene and unveiled the implications of such materialism. Erasmus, who was the first in the series of these critics, pointed out paganism as an immediate consequence of venerating a high number of heavenly specialists with excessive attention. 'In this way', he wrote in his *The Handbook of the Christian Soldier* published in 1503,

> we have appointed certain saints to preside over all the things we fear or desire. [...] If this sort of piety is not turned from mere consideration of material advantages or disadvantages and redirected towards Christ, then far from being Christian it is not much removed from the superstition of those who pledged a tenth part of their substance to Hercules so that they might become rich or a cock to Aesculapius in order to recover from some illness or sacrificed a bull to Neptune for a safe crossing.[56]

In contrast to these practices, he saw the righteous way of worshipping the saints in following their example instead of trying to use them to resolve

56 Erasmus, *The Handbook of the Christian Soldier*, trans. and ann. by Fantazzi, pp. 63–64.

mundane problems: 'No devotion is more acceptable and proper to the saints than striving to imitate their virtues'.[57]

Similarly, Martin Luther, in a series of sermons on the Ten Commandments delivered in the castle church of Wittenberg between the summer of 1516 and the beginning of the next year, also criticized the cult of holy helpers for turning the attention of worshippers away from the virtues and exemplary lives of these saints and making them instruments of material needs: 'non pudet nos Christianos ita in sanctos partiri negocia rerum temporalium, ac si essent nunc facti servi et mancipia artificum' (we Christians are not ashamed to divide up worldly business among the saints in such a way as if they had been made our servants and craftsmen's apprentices).[58] Moreover, apart from treating them irreverently and not as great examples of a truly Christian life, their veneration as specialists creates the false impression that they themselves instead of God are responsible for the assistance they provide, which leads us to paganism: 'Ut rursus Romanorum illud Cahos[!] deorum et quoddam pantheon denuo extruxerimus, atque hoc ipsum non pro alia causa, quam ut hic tantummodo bene habeamus' (We would go back to the chaos of Roman gods and rebuild some sort of a Pantheon, and all this for nothing else but to be well in his world).[59] These criticisms, just like those of Erasmus, would not have been possible without a considerable growth in the number of holy helpers — now capable of filling a Pantheon — and in the importance of their cult in the course of the preceding century.

Conclusion

Why, then, was the problem of specialization left to the very end in the Messenger's critique of the cult of saints in Thomas More's *A Dialogue Concerning Heresies*? As we have seen above, his main point concerning the helpers is that 'we do them little worship, while we set every saint to his office and assign him a craft such as pleaseth us'. This seems to echo Luther's criticism that through worshipping saints as specialists we treat them irreverently, we try to use them according to our material needs as 'our servants and craftsmen's apprentices'. Accordingly, the reasons for assigning this or that function

57 Erasmus, *The Handbook of the Christian Soldier*, trans. and ann. by Fantazzi, p. 71.

58 Luther, *Decem praecepta Wittenbergensi praedicata populo*, p. 415. The German original of the sermons is now lost but a Latin version was published in the summer of 1518. By the beginning of the 1520s, it was available in six Latin, five German, two Dutch, and one Czech editions. See the editor's introduction to the work on pp. 394–98. For Luther's preaching activity in Wittenberg between 1514 and 1517, see Brecht, *Martin Luther: Sein Weg zur Reformation*, pp. 150–54. I discuss his views on saints in the 1516/1517 sermons in more detail in Gecser, 'Holy Helpers and the Transformation of Saintly Patronage', pp. 179–85; for a broader context, see Haustein, 'Luthers frühe Kritik an der Heiligenverehrung'.

59 Luther, *Decem praecepta Wittenbergensi praedicata populo*, p. 415.

to them are portrayed by the Messenger as arbitrary, based on accidental details of their lives unrelated to the essence of their sanctity. He also points to superstitious practices relating to the helpers like bringing 'a white loaf and a pot of good ale' to St Germanus to make him help with one's child, to the sometimes utterly sinful purposes for which the saints are attempted to be engaged, as in the case of St Wilgerfortis, and to the disproportionately high rank accorded to their feasts, as in the case of St Eligius's day, which worshippers 'more religiously keep high and holy than Easter Day!' So far, the Messenger's criticism of saintly specialization looks like any other at the beginning of the sixteenth century, even if he does not play the paganism card, which makes his interlocutor's job all the easier. What is surprising, however, is that More does not really want to defend the helpers *qua* helpers.

Immediately after the catalogue of helpers quoted at the beginning of this essay, the Messenger goes on to add two specific examples of abuse which take up the larger part of book II, chapter 10, dedicated to his last set of objections to the cult of saints. One of these examples is about an unnamed town, where St Martin's image is carried in procession on his feast-day and, if the weather is good, locals pour rose water on it from their windows, whereas, if the weather is bad, they do the same with their chamber pots.[60] The other example is about the visit of a young English couple to a pilgrimage site in Picardy, a chapel consecrated to St Valery, which a fellow traveller recommended as a must-see:

> And to behold, they found it fonder than he had told. For, like as in other pilgrimages ye see hung up legs of wax, or arms, or such other parts, so was in that chapel all their offerings that hung about the walls none other thing but men's gear, and women's gear, made in wax. Then was there, besides these, two round rings of silver, the one much larger than the other, through which every man did put his privy members! at the altar's end. [...] Then was there yet a monk, standing at the altar, that hallowed certain threads of Venice gold. And them he delivered to the pilgrims, teaching them in what wise themselves, or their friends, should use those threads against the stone. That they should knit it about their gear and say I cannot tell you what prayers. [...] As this gentleman and his wife were kneeling in the chapel, there came a good, sad woman to him, showing him that 'one special point' used in that pilgrimage — and the 'surest against the stone' [...]. And that was, she would have the length of his gear and that should she make in a wax candle, which should 'burn up' in the chapel, and certain prayers should there be said the while. And this was against the stone the 'very sheet anchor'.[61]

This story is a model case of all possible abuses related to sanctity. In principle, the chapel is for people striving to get rid of their kidney stones. In effect,

60 More, *A Dialogue Concerning Heresies*, ed. by Gottschalk, p. 227.

61 More, *A Dialogue Concerning Heresies*, ed. by Gottschalk, II. 10, pp. 228–29.

however, it also looks like a place for curing impotence and other sex-related deficiencies. There is a monk there who shamelessly makes profit from recommending an awkward procedure which was not a type that monks were supposed to experiment with. And the site also has a 'good sad woman', possibly a widow, representing the allegedly most superstitious type of worshippers, who suggests yet another cumbersome remedy. St Valery does have a specialization, or even more than one, but this is hardly a relevant issue here.

At the beginning of the next chapter, concerning his rebuttal of the Messenger's objections to 'the manner of the worship', the interlocutor ('More') promises to focus on three points:

> One, that the people worship the saints, and their images also, with like honor as they do God himself; another, that they take the images for the things themselves — which points do sound to idolatry. The third is the superstitious fashion of worship, with desire of unlawful things.[62]

The third focal point collapses two categories kept separate by the Messenger in the previous chapter — 'the harm that goeth by going of pilgrimages' and the cult of holy helpers — into one and reduces them to the problems of superstition and illicit goals.

The interlocutor's answer to the third point proceeds by commenting on these latter two problems. As to the first one, he claims that praying to 'Saint Apollonia for the help of our teeth, is no witchcraft, considering that she had her teeth pulled out for Christ's sake. Nor there is no superstition in such other things like'. Similarly, he considers 'the devotion to run somewhat too far if the smiths will not for any necessity set on a shoe upon St Eligius's Day and yet lawful enough to pray for the help of a poor man's horse'. In general, it would be wrong 'that all worship of saints and reverence of holy relics and honor of saints' images — by which good, devout folk do much merit — we should abolish and put away because some folk do abuse it'. A similar logic applies to endeavouring to attain illicit goals through invoking the (helper) saints: 'For whatsoever they will ask of any good saint, they will ask of God also. [...] Shall we therefore find a fault with every man's prayer, because thieves pray for speed in robbery?'[63]

It seems, then, that in the answer given by 'More' to the Messenger's objections — and, to some extent, already in the way that the Messenger has presented them — the problems that came to be associated with the cult of holy helpers in the course of the fifteenth century dissipate into the broader issue of how to defend the cult of saints in general. Something similar happens in Luther's *Large Catechism* — also written, like More's *Dialogue*, in 1529 — but with the opposite intention. Offering a range of examples of how

---

62 More, *A Dialogue Concerning Heresies*, ed. by Gottschalk, II. 11, p. 230.

63 More, *A Dialogue Concerning Heresies*, ed. by Gottschalk, II. 11, pp. 232, 233, 236–37.

people may not live up to the essence of the First Commandment, 'You are to have no other gods', Luther makes the following point:

> Again, look at what we used to do in our blindness under the papacy. Anyone who had a toothache fasted and called on St Apollonia; those who worried about their house burning down appealed to St Laurence as their patron; if they were afraid of the plague, they made a vow to St Sebastian or Roch. There were countless other such abominations, and everyone selected his own saint and worshiped him and invoked his help in time of need. In this category also belong those who go so far as to make a pact with the devil so that he may give them plenty of money, help them in love affairs, protect their cattle, recover lost property, etc., as magicians and sorcerers do. All of them place their heart and trust elsewhere than in the true God, from whom they neither expect nor seek any good thing.[64]

In his sermons on the Ten Commandments of more than a decade before, just as in other criticism around 1500, the veneration of holy helpers was a symptom of excessive materialism on the part of worshippers, which dishonoured the saints, obfuscated their real achievements, and pointed toward the reestablishment of paganism. Luther in 1516/1517 criticized the cult of holy helpers but not that of the saints in general; he criticized the former in order to restore the latter to its pristine form. Luther, in the *Large Catechism*, wanted to get rid of almost everything in the cult of saints. By then he had come to see the difference between venerating saints as helpers or personal patrons, on the one hand, and making a pact with the devil, on the other, as merely one of degree — not of substance.

Therefore, in 1529/1531 More had no reason to make his Messenger come up with the problem of the helpers earlier in the *Dialogue*. He could not leave it unmentioned entirely but it was not a central issue any more. In this context, leaving it to the very end of all the objections to the cult of saints implies that it was not considered a *topos* of rhetorical invention, a tree trunk giving rise to a crown of ramifying lines of argument; it was just a twig, not even a branch. As a significant problem in its own right, it seems to have followed a trajectory of slow ascent and quick descent over the course of the long fifteenth century. After 1517 it apparently receded from the front line of religious debate but, given its importance *within* the cult of saints, it may well have lingered on in the Catholic world — making a nice topic for another article.

---

64 *The Book of Concord*, ed. by Kolb and Wengert, p. 387. For early Protestant views on the saints, see Heming, *Protestants and the Cult of the Saints*.

Works Cited

Primary Sources

Augustine, *De bono coniugali, De sancta uirginitate*, ed. and trans. by P. G. Walsh (Oxford: Clarendon Press, 2001)

Barletta, Gabriele, *Sermones quadragesimales et de sanctis* (Brescia: Giacomo Britannico, 1497)

Bernardino of Siena, *Prediche volgari sul Campo di Siena*, ed. by Carlo Delcorno, 2 vols (Milan: Rusconi, 1989)

———, *Opera omnia*, VII: *Sermones de tempore et de diversis* (Quaracchi: Collegium S. Bonaventurae, 1959)

———, *Sermones eximii de Christo domino, augustissimo Eucharistiae sacramento, deipara Virgine, de tempore, necnon de sanctis*, ed. by Jean de La Haye (Venice: Andrea Poletti, 1745)

Biel, Gabriel, *Canonis misse expositio*, ed. by Heiko A. Oberman and William J. Courtenay, 4 vols, Veröffentlichungen des Instituts für Europäische Geschichte Mainz, 31–34 (Wiesbaden: Steiner, 1965–1967)

The Book of Concord: The Confessions of the Evangelical Lutheran Church, ed. by Robert Kolb and Timothy J. Wengert (Minneapolis: Fortress, 2000)

Der Heiligen Leben, I: *Der Sommerteil*, ed. by Margit Brand, Kristina Freienhagen-Baumgardt, Ruth Meyer, and Werner Williams-Krapp, Texte und Textgeschichte, 44 (Tübingen: Niemeyer, 1996)

Durandus of St Pourçain, *Scriptum super IV libros Sententiarum: Distinctiones 43–50 libri quarti*, ed. by Thomas Jeschke (Leuven: Peeters, 2012)

Erasmus, Desiderius, *The Handbook of the Christian Soldier*, trans. and ann. by Charles Fantazzi, in *Collected Works of Erasmus*, LXVI (Toronto: University of Toronto Press, 1988), 8–127

Gerson, Jean, *Œuvres complètes*, ed. by Palémon Glorieux, 11 vols (Paris: Desclée, 1960–1973)

James of Voragine, *Legenda aurea, vulgo Historia Lombardica dicta*, ed. by Theodor Graesse, 3rd edn (Wrocław: Koebner, 1890)

———, *Legenda Aurea, con le miniature del codice Ambrosiano C 240 inf.*, ed. by Giovanni Paolo Maggioni, Edizione Nazionale dei Testi Mediolatini, 20, 2nd edn, 2 vols (Florence: SISMEL – Edizioni del Galluzzo, 2007)

Luther, Martin, *Decem praecepta Wittenbergensi praedicata populo, 1518*, in *D. Martin Luthers Werke: Kritische Gesamtausgabe*, I (Weimar: Böhlau, 1883), 398–521

More, Thomas, *The Complete Works of St Thomas More*, VI.1: *A Dialogue Concerning Heresies*, ed. by Thomas M. C. Lawler, Germain Marc'Hadour, and Richard C. Marius (New Haven: Yale University Press, 1981)

———, *A Dialogue Concerning Heresies*, ed. by Mary Gottschalk (Irving: The Center for Thomas More Studies, 2015) <https://thomasmorestudies.org/wp-content/uploads/2020/09/DialogueConcerningHeresies2015-etext.pdf> [accessed 30 August 2022]

Nicolaus Cusanus, 'A General Reform to the Church', in *Writings on Church and Reform*, ed. and trans. by Thomas M. Izbicki, The I Tatti Renaissance Library, 33 (Cambridge, MA: Harvard University Press, 2008), pp. 550–91

———, *Opera omnia*, XVI: *Sermones I (1430–1441)*, 5 tomes, ed. by Martin Bodewig, Rudolf Haubst, Werner Krämer, and Heinrich Pauli (Hamburg: Meiner, 1970–1991)

Pelbart of Timişoara/Temesvár, *Pomerium sermonum de sanctis* (Augsburg: n. pr., 1502); online edition: <http://sermones.elte.hu/pelbart/index.php?file = ph_index> [accessed 22 February 2018]

Peter Lombard, *Libri IV sententiarum*, 2 vols, 2nd edn (Quaracchi: Collegium S. Bonaventurae, 1916)

Peter of Palude, *Scriptum in quartum Sententiarum* (Venice: Boneto Locatelli, for Ottaviano Scotto, 1493)

Stephen of Bourbon, *Tractatus de diuersis materiis predicabilibus: Prologus – Prima pars. De dono timoris*, ed. by Jacques Berlioz and Jean-Luc Eichenlaub, Corpus Christianorum Continuatio Mediaevalis, 124 (Turnhout: Brepols, 2002)

Synodi Brixinenses saeculi XV, ed. by Gustav Bickell (Innsbruck: Rauch, 1880)

Thomas Aquinas, *Opera omnia*, XI *Commentum in quartum librum Sententiarum magistri Petri Lombardi (continuatio)*, ed. by Stanislas Édouard Fretté (Paris: Vivès, 1874)

Secondary Studies

Bailey, Michael D., *Fearful Spirits, Reasoned Follies: The Boundaries of Superstition in Late Medieval Europe* (Ithaca: Cornell University Press, 2013)

Barb, Alphons Augustinus, 'St Zacharias the Prophet and Martyr: A Study in Charms and Incantations', *Journal of the Warburg and Courtauld Institutes*, 11 (1948), 35–67

Bartlett, Robert, *Why Can the Dead Do Such Great Things? Saints and Worshippers from the Martyrs to the Reformation* (Princeton: Princeton University Press, 2013)

Bartolomei Romagnoli, Alessandra, 'Osservanza francescana e disciplina del culto dei santi: Modelli di perfezione e strategie di riforma nell'opera di Giovanni da Capestrano', in *Ideali di perfezione ed esperienze di riforma in san Giovanni da Capestrano*, ed. by Edith Pasztor (Capestrano: Centro Studi S. Giovanni da Capestrano, 2002), pp. 127–53

Bériou, Nicole, 'Les sermons latins après 1200', in *The Sermon*, ed. by Beverly Mayne Kienzle, Typologie des sources du moyen âge occidental, 81–83 (Turnhout: Brepols, 2000), pp. 363–447

Brecht, Martin, *Martin Luther: Sein Weg zur Reformation, 1483–1521* (Stuttgart: Calwer, 1981)

Chiffoleau, Jacques, *La comptabilité de l'au-delà: Les hommes, la mort et la religion dans la région d'Avignon à la fin du Moyen Âge (vers 1320 – vers 1480)*, Collection de l'École française de Rome, 47 (Rome: École française de Rome, 1980)

Duffy, Eamon, '"The comen knowen multytude of crysten men": *A Dialogue Concerning Heresies* and the defence of Christendom', in *The Cambridge Companion to Thomas More*, ed. by George M. Logan (Cambridge: Cambridge University Press, 2011), pp. 191–215

Dunbabin, Jean, *A Hound of God: Pierre de la Palud and the Fourteenth-Century Church* (Oxford: Clarendon Press, 1991)

Dünninger, Josef, 'Sprachliche Zeugnisse über den Kult der Vierzehn Nothelfer im 14. und 15. Jahrhundert', in *Festschrift Matthias Zender: Studien zu Volkskultur, Sprache und Landesgeschichte*, ed. by Edith Ennen and Günter Wiegelmann, 2 vols (Bonn: Röhrscheid, 1972), I, 336–46

Foscati, Alessandra, *Ignis sacer: Una storia culturale del 'fuoco sacro' dall'antichità al Settecento*, Micrologus Library, 51 (Florence: SISMEL – Edizioni del Galluzzo, 2013)

Franz, Adolph, *Der Magister Nikolaus Magni de Jawor: Ein Beitrag zur Literatur- und Gelehrtengeschichte des 14. und 15. Jahrhunderts* (Freiburg: Herder, 1898)

Gaffuri, Laura, 'I sermoni brissinesi di Niccolò da Cusa nella pastorale del XV secolo', in *Niccolò Cusano: L'uomo, i libri, l'opera; Atti del LII Convegno storico internazionale (Todi, 11–14 ottobre 2015)*, Atti del Centro Italiano di Studi sul Basso Medioevo – Accademia Tudertina, n.s. 29 (Spoleto: CISAM, 2016), pp. 325–56

Gecser, Ottó, 'Holy Helpers and the Transformation of Saintly Patronage at the End of the Middle Ages', *Annual of Medieval Studies at CEU*, 22 (2016), 174–201

Guth, Klaus, 'Vierzehnheiligen und die Anfänge der Nothelferverehrung: Anatomie einer Wallfahrtsgenese', in Klaus Guth, *Kultur als Lebensform: Aufsätze und Vorträge*, ed. by Elisabeth Roth, 3 vols (St Ottilien: EOS, 1995–2009), I, 305–24

Haustein, Jörg, 'Luthers frühe Kritik an der Heiligenverehrung und ihre Bedeutung für das ökumenische Gespräch', *Theologische Literaturzeitung*, 124 (1999), 1187–1204

Heming, Carol Piper, *Protestants and the Cult of the Saints in German-Speaking Europe, 1517–1531*, Sixteenth Century Essays and Studies, 65 (Kirksville: Truman State University Press, 2003)

Hobbins, Daniel, 'Gerson on Lay Devotion', in *A Companion to Jean Gerson*, ed. by Brian Patrick McGuire (Leiden: Brill, 2006), pp. 41–78

McGuire, Brian Patrick, *Jean Gerson and the Last Medieval Reformation* (University Park: The Pennsylvania State University Press, 2005)

Mitjans, Frank, 'On Veneration of Images, Praying to Saints, and Going on Pilgrimages in the *Dialogue Concerning Heresies*', *Thomas More Studies*, 3 (2008), 64–69 <www.thomasmorestudies.org/tmstudies/DCH_Mitjans.pdf> [accessed 22 February 2018]

Pavlac, Brian A., 'Nicolaus Cusanus as Prince-Bishop of Brixen (1450–1464)', *Historical Reflections/Réflexions Historiques*, 21 (1995), 131–53

Philippart, Guy, *Les Légendiers latins et autres manuscrits hagiographiques*, Typologie des sources du moyen âge occidental, 24–25 (Turnhout: Brepols, 1977)

Pötzl, Walter, 'Die Verehrung der Vierzehn Nothelfer vor 1400', *Jahrbuch für Volkskunde*, n.s. 23 (2000), 157–86

Reames, Sherry L. *The 'Legenda aurea': A Reexamination of Its Paradoxical History* (Madison: University of Wisconsin Press, 1985)

Schreiber, Georg, *Die Vierzehn Nothelfer in Volksfrömmigkeit und Sakralkultur: Symbolkraft und Herrschaftsbereich der Wallfahrtskapelle, vorab in Franken und Tirol*, Schlern-Schriften, 168 (Innsbruck: Wagner, 1959)

Smoller, Laura A., *The Saint and the Chopped-Up Baby: The Cult of Vincent Ferrer in Medieval and Early Modern Europe* (Ithaca: Cornell University Press, 2014)

Vauchez, André, *Sainthood in the Later Middle Ages*, trans. by Jean Birrell (Cambridge: Cambridge University Press, 1997)

Zellmann-Rohrer, Michael Wesley, 'The Tradition of Greek and Latin Incantations and Related Ritual Texts from Antiquity through the Medieval and Early Modern Periods' (unpublished doctoral dissertation, University of California, Berkeley, 2016)

DANIELA SOLFAROLI CAMILLOCCI

Censoring Popular Devotion in French Protestant Propaganda

The Reformer Pierre Viret, the Rosary, and the Question of the Proper Honouring of the Virgin Mary

Research on the impact of the Reformation on religious practices has shown that the cult of the Virgin Mary posed a crucial problem for the Protestant movement. Several reasons have been cited to explain this difficulty: the vast and popular spread of Marian piety; the day-to-day ubiquity of prayers to the Mother of the Saviour, or the emotional character of supplications to the Virgin, which was the main reason for the deep-rootedness of the devotion in communities;[1] but also, the ambivalent attitude of the reformers towards the theological status of Mary. Indeed, Diarmaid MacCulloch has shown that Luther, Zwingli, and Calvin and, following them, most Protestant theologians were in agreement in denying the mediation of the Virgin Mary for the purposes of salvation, and in emphasizing the unique redemptive role of Jesus Christ.[2] The reformers obviously wished to distance the new communities of faith from cultic practices considered dangerous or idolatrous, arguing that they lacked scriptural foundation. On the other hand, they found themselves obliged to allow for certain aspects of the doctrinal tradition on Mary that also did not find their foundation in the Scriptures, such as her perpetual virginity, in order to defend the theology of the Incarnation from radical theological positions. However, the preaching of these reformers dealt with the cult of the Virgin very differently. Luther did not preach a rejection of traditional Marian piety but instead promoted spiritual distance from these devotions as a means of individual and communal conversion. While Zwingli defended the Hail Mary as a form of praise in laud of the Mother of Jesus, he conceived the honour due to Mary as a mere subject of moral edification.

1 Rubin, *Emotion and Devotion*, pp. 79–104.

2 MacCulloch, 'Mary and Sixteenth-Century Protestants', pp. 191–217.

Daniela Solfaroli Camillocci • (daniela.solfaroli@unige.ch) is Professor of Cultural and Religious History, and is currently Director of the Institute of Reformation History at the University of Geneva.

Religious Transformations in New Communities of Interpretation in Europe (1350–1570): Bridging the Historiographical Divides, ed. by Élise Boillet and Ian Johnson, New Communities of Interpretation, 3 (Turnhout: Brepols, 2022), pp. 71–82.

DOI 10.1484/M.NCI-EB.5.131214

Because of his high concern for the pure worship of God, Calvin pointed to the danger of honouring the Virgin Mary as a person, and defended the idea of the 'election' of the Mother as purely God's instrument.[3] As a result of the theological attack on the idolatry of creatures, Marian iconoclasm was practised in Reformed movements inspired by Zwingli and Calvin; Luther, however, criticized the violence against all the images.[4]

If we approach more closely the reorientation of practices and issues of religious confrontation, the problem that seems to arise is the following: how does one recognize the Virgin Mary's special status among created beings while at the same time forbidding or rejecting the expression of this very recognition? In other words, how does one express the honour that is due to the mother of Jesus Christ in the absence of honorific words and actions? This was the main difficulty that Protestant propaganda encountered when faced with the Marian cult. The question of the affirmation of such a theological perspective in preaching, ritual, and practices has been analysed by Beth Kreitzer, Bridget Heal, and Susan Karant-Nunn for Lutheran towns in Germany.[5] Otherwise, current research on Germany and German-speaking Switzerland shows that strong popular reactions vis-à-vis the modification of common beliefs oriented the theological debate on liturgical practices and pastoral care for both Protestant and Catholic communities.[6] How did reformed theologians react towards, and interact with, popular devotion for the Virgin Mary? For my part, I would like to present this problem beginning with an analysis focused on the geographical area that corresponds to today's French-speaking Switzerland.[7]

In the years 1530 to 1550, the gradual shift of these territories to adhering to the Reformation according to the Zwinglian perspective triggered violent religious confrontations between rival groups. As shown, for instance, by the Genevan chronicles, testimonies critical of material and symbolic aggression by evangelicals highlight the trauma of the destruction of devotional objects and images of the Virgin, while testimonies from the 'new' faithful emphasize such acts as being against idolatry.[8] In the years following the transition of Neuchâtel (1530), Geneva (1535–1536), and Lausanne (1536) to the Reformation, the geopolitical situation of the rural regions surrounding these cities, where common territories were ruled jointly by the Catholic city of Fribourg and

---

3 Oberman, 'The Virgin Mary in Evangelical Perspective', pp. 225–51.

4 Rubin, *Mother of God*, pp. 366–78.

5 Kreitzer, *Reforming Mary*; Heal, *The Cult of the Virgin Mary*; Karant-Nunn, *The Reformation of Feeling*, pp. 159–87.

6 Giselbrecht, 'Reforming a Model', pp. 137–74; see also Mudrak, 'La construction matérielle du catholicisme allemand', pp. 79–103, and Silver, 'Full of Grace', pp. 289–315.

7 We discuss here the very first results of research into the question of Mary's devotion in French-speaking Protestant literature between the 1540s and 1640s.

8 Grosse and Solfaroli Camillocci, 'Réaménager le rapport au sacré', pp. 285–324; Bruening, *Calvinism's First Battleground*, pp. 117–23.

Reformed Bern, led to the existence of neighbouring villages where inhabitants who followed the 'new' faith were confronted with those who remained attached to the 'old' belief.[9] For more than twenty years, Protestant preachers had to combat the persistence of 'papist' devotions. For instance, Marian prayers and rosaries were forbidden in the Reformed territories from 1536, but both the correspondence of the reformer Guillaume Farel and institutional sources testify to resistance against the prohibition and admonitions.[10]

Publications issued in Geneva made efforts to translate theology into the common language. A significant example is found in a reading manual published in 1533 and 1537 by Olivetan, the Evangelical translator of the Bible into French. In the frontispiece of this little book, entitled *Instruction des enfants*, the *Salutation Angelique* (Angelic Greeting), i.e. the first part of the Hail Mary, appears after the Our Father, the Articles of the Faith, and the Ten Commandments.[11] However, the corresponding chapter provides neither the text of the prayer, nor the quotation of the passage in Luke's Gospel, but rather an explanation of the difference between prayer and praise:

> Sur la Salutation angelicque autrement dicte le *Ave Maria* [...] Icy noteras la difference de oraison et salutation. Car oraison est priere requeste et demande faicte envers Dieu: comme Ton royaume advienne; donne nous aujourdhuy notre pain quotidien ec. Salutation est benediction, bien vouloir et gracieux accueil: comme quand la personne salue l'autre disant: Dieu te salue et garde; Dieu te doint bon jour ou bon soir; paix à toy; beneit soys tu ec. Laquelle forme de saluer a tenu l'ange vers Marie en sainct Luc 1. Item en Daniel 10.b. Item vers Gedeon, Juges 6.d. Item Jesus Christ vers ses apostres, Jehan 20.e. Item S. Paul et S. Pierre au commencement de leurs epistres.
>
> > (On the Angelic Greeting or *Ave Maria.* [...] Here you will notice the difference between prayer and praise. Prayer is a supplication, a request, and a solemn request to God: as your kingdom come; give us this day our daily bread, etc. Praise is a benediction, an expression of benevolence and welcome: as when a person blesses another saying: God save you and keep you; God give you good day or good night; Peace with you! Bless you! etc. It is this form of praise that the angel held towards Mary in Luke 1. See also in Daniel 10.b. and to Gideon in Judges 6.d. See also Jesus Christ to his apostles, John 20.e., and St Paul or St Peter at the beginning of their letters.)[12]

---

9 Bruening, *Calvinism's First Battleground*; see also Crousaz, 'Un témoignage sur la régulation politique de la division confessionnelle', pp. 47–66.

10 *Correspondance des Réformateurs*, ed. by Herminjard, IV, 131; Bruening, *Calvinism's First Battleground*, pp. 145, 155–60.

11 [Pierre Robert, known as 'Olivétan'], *L'Instruction des enfants*.

12 *L'Instruction des enfants*, fol. G7^{v}.

It is followed by three paragraphs with biblical quotations referring to the scriptural uses of the term 'blessed'. Their headings aid the reader in understanding the true meaning of the epithet 'Blessed' applied to the Virgin Mary, as to other women in the Old Testament, but which ultimately emphasizes the participation of all believers in this status.[13] Finally, the instruction given in the manual was that the *Ave Maria* was not a prayer but a historical narrative, and that 'Blessed' was not a specific title of honour for the Virgin Mary. We cannot find here an open criticism of the biblical quotation used as a prayer, but still, the text of the Hail Mary is nowhere offered to the reader.

In Geneva, prayers to the Virgin were indeed made the object of censure, and in 1543 a French version of the Hail Mary by Clément Marot was taken out of a Genevan printing of his translation of the Psalms, even though by all appearances it corresponded perfectly with Evangelical aims. Marot's translation emphasized the Son as Redeemer; moreover, the intercessory part of the prayer, the *Sancta Maria Dei mater ora pro nobis*, was not translated.[14]

However, in these years the registers of the Geneva Consistory, the main institutional arm for the establishment of ecclesiastical discipline, show the difficulty the pastors had in redirecting everyday individual and domestic religious practices.[15] The inhabitants of Geneva may have adapted to these prohibitions in public and abandoned acts of Marian devotion and other traditional gestures of piety, but how does one evaluate individual attitudes towards, and household participation in, the new forms of prayer? The prayer to the Virgin Mary could have been a 'marker of resistance' on the part of locals who did not accept the 'new laws' in Geneva or the manner in which the pastors were now preaching the Gospel. Core clusters

---

13 'Exemples des vertueuses femmes qui pareillement on este benites en l'Escripture' (Examples of virtuous women who were similarly blessed in the Holy Scriptures). The women mentioned are Judith, Jael wife of Heber the Kenite, and Leah). 'Pour laquelle cause la Vierge Marie fut dicte bienheureuse' (Why the Virgin Mary was called Blessed'. Quotation of Luke 1). 'Comment aussi seront bienheureux ceux qui croiront à la parolle' (How blessed will be those who believe in the Word'. Quotation of Luke 11): *L'Instruction des enfants*, fols G7^{v}–G8^{v}. These quotations correspond to the theological perspective of Zwingli's Mary sermon: Giselbrecht, 'Reforming a Model', pp. 144–47.

14 'La Salutation Angelique — *Ave gratia plena dominus tecum* — Resjouy toy Vierge Marie | Pleine de grace abondamment | Le Seigneur qui toute seigneurie| Est aveq toy divinement: | Benoiste certes tu es, entre | Celles dessoubz le firmament | Car le fruit qui est en ton ventre | Est benit eternellement' (Rejoice Virgin Mary | Full of grace abundantly | The Omnipotent Lord | Is with you divinely | You are certainly blessed among | Those under the firmament | Because the fruit of your womb | Is blessed eternally): Clément Marot, *Cinquante pseaumes de Davide*, ed. by Defaux, pp. 209–10. On the 1543 Genevan censure of Marot's work, see Defaux, 'Introduction', pp. 33–36.

15 *Registers of the Consistory of Geneva in the Time of Calvin*, ed. by Lambert and Watt, editors' Introduction, pp. xvii–xxx.

of resistance were still active in the 1560s, that is, at the time of the death of Calvin.[16]

A book by the Lausanne reformer Pierre Viret (1509?–1571) shows more clearly the pastoral effort to redirect practices. Viret was the author of a prolific collection of explanatory doctrinal treatises intended as tools for the reformed ministry as well as reading for literate 'common' people.[17] During the 1530s, the young Viret was part of a group gathered by the reformer Guillaume Farel for the promotion of religious propaganda. He often preached in Geneva, and so he probably witnessed or at least consented to iconoclasm in the churches. After the city's transition to the Reformation, Viret worked in Geneva and Lausanne organizing new churches and implementing disciplinary structures for the communities.[18] He collaborated with John Calvin and participated in the first meetings of the new Geneva Consistory; as a result, he often oversaw cases of indiscipline involving Marian devotions. One of his first instructional tracts was a criticism of the cult of the Virgin that seems to have arisen largely from his pastoral concerns. Printed in 1544, reprinted the following year and in 1549, Viret's *Little Treatise on the use of the Angelic Greeting, and on the origin of the Rosary*[19] belonged to the ample output of religious works steadily published or reprinted by Genevan presses, and dedicated to the reorientation of piety and communal liturgies. However, this treatise was the only work of these years concerning Marian prayers specifically. Because of this, we can assume that it was the authoritative summary on this subject both for educated reformed people and their pastors.

In his *Little Treatise*, Viret first of all established a link between corporeal food and spiritual food. He presented Christian prayer as food for the soul. Characterizing the reciting of prayers as a means of consuming the sacred, Viret compared the Hail Mary to good food that had been poisoned by the henchmen of Satan, so that its ingestion brought misery and death instead of well-being and salvation. Viret explained that the Gospel story from which the prayer was composed had been carved up and mixed with other expressions; once turned away from its true meaning and proper use, it was ultimately applied to inappropriate ends.

The purpose of the treatise was therefore to demystify the prayer's ritual words in order to draw the simple people away from such dangerous spiritual ingestion. To do this, Viret first of all considered the form of Marian prayer,

16 Lambert, '"Cette loi ne durera guère"', pp. 5–24; Kingdon, 'L'usage quantitatif des registres', pp. 589–91; Manetsch, 'Holy Terror or Pastoral Care?', pp. 290–99. I found Heal's discussion of the Marian devotion as a 'confessional marker' very inspiring: see Heal, *The Cult of the Virgin Mary*, pp. 132–40.

17 On Viret's works and his pastoral involvement, see *Pierre Viret et la diffusion de la Réforme*, ed. by Crousaz and Solfaroli Camillocci ; Troilo, *L'œuvre de Pierre Viret*.

18 Bruening, 'Pierre Viret and Geneva', pp. 180–85.

19 Viret, *Petit traicté*. For the editorial history of this work, see Troilo, *L'œuvre de Pierre Viret*, pp. 218–26, 324, 408.

followed by rosaries as objects, and finally the act of praying the Rosary itself. We might therefore expect an exegetical exercise aimed at denying the historical, theological, and scriptural foundations of these practices. Indeed, the doctrinal explanation is certainly there, but the instruction proposed by Viret aimed most of all at breaking the confidence of the faithful in the salvific effects of Marian protection and intercession. His criticism was done less with the goal of convincing them by arguments as by modifying the registers of the emotions that inspired their piety.

After defining as inappropriate the use of a greeting as a prayer, Viret explained that the second part of the Hail Mary (*Sancta Maria gratia plena*, etc.), which was added in order to affirm the intercessory role of the Virgin, was entirely contrary to Christian doctrine. The liturgical centrality of this prayer, like the titles for the Virgin that exalted her role as *mediatrix* (Our Lady of Grace, Queen of Heaven), were thus styled not only as abuses but as blasphemy and sacrilege. Because the sole legitimate use of the Gospel was spiritual reading, the text of this prayer — explained Viret — in the end followed the same logic as that used by sorcerers and witches, who employed the verses of Scripture in their magic formulas.[20] In this way, the very recitation of the Hail Mary itself was associated with spells, that is, with prohibited acts of witchcraft.

As far as objects of the cult, and especially rosaries, were concerned, Viret's criticism was addressed both to the objects and to their usage. The luxury of the materials from which they were produced was condemned, and their success as jewellery — even requested as wedding gifts — was censured. Feminine appreciation for rosaries was judged as an act of vanity intrinsically opposed to the simplicity of the Virgin. In contrast to the pleasing appearance of the material object, Viret explained the origin of the form of the Rosary in a different way. According to him, it was modelled on snake's eggs, threaded and tied together, as if Divine Providence wished in this way to declare the diabolical origin of these sought-after objects, which had become so trivialized by daily use.[21]

---

20 'Si nous prenons seulement une pièce de celle histoire, et la voulons reciter en maniere d'oraison, c'est abuser de la parolle de Dieu et pervertir son usage, qui ne se peut faire sans blaspheme et sacrilege: non plus que quand les sorciers, devins, enchanteurs, prenent quelques parolles des sainctes Escritures pour en faire des brevetz, charmes et sorceleries. Car il faut appliquer l'Escriture à l'usage pour lequel elle nous est donnée du Sainct Esprit' (If we take into account only a part of history, and we want to recite as a prayer, we abuse God's Word and we pervert it, which cannot be done without blasphemy and sacrilege. It is like when sorcerers, magicians, and enchanters use few words from the Holy Scriptures to make talismans, enchantments, and witchcraft. It is necessary to apply the Scripture to the use for which the Word is given to us by the Holy Spirit): Viret, *Petit traité*, fols A6^{v}–A7^{r}.

21 'Les oeufz des serpens [...] sont conjoinctz et enfilés les uns avec les autres, tout ainsi que les chapeletz, tellement qu'il n'y a choses qui mieux ressemblent l'une à l'autre. Parquoy, quant plus je considère la chose, tant plus suis-je persuadé, que ces chapeletz ont été faictz en telle forme par la providence de Dieu: à fin que par icelle il nous admonestast de quel auteur ilz procedoyent; et qu'il nous montrast plus clairement que celle superstition et idolâtrie

As for the recitation of the Rosary, Viret dwelt first of all on the logic of enumeration and allocation that, in the end, addressed prayers more to the Virgin than to God. His irony was also directed to the cumulative logic of repeated recitations — as if God needed us clearly to reiterate our requests for him to remember them — but Viret also fired his barbs at the spells of magicians and at pagan usages, like those of the priests of Baal. Indeed, this tract provided historical explanations for 'popular' religious practices that were pulled from ancient sources illustrating pagan culture, which is a fairly typical feature of Viret's work.[22] This was further developed in the rewriting of the treatise, which in 1556 was revised and augmented, with a change of title and going from seventy-six pages to 175; this new version was reprinted in 1561 and 1562.[23] Apart from a few stylistic modifications, the 1544 text did not change, but the work was now divided into chapters and split into four books. This new edition might have been an attempt to increase the pro-Reformed arguments as a polemical tactic of accumulation, but it may also have due to the need to specify reformed positions on the Virgin Mary in the face of the development of confessional controversy in France. Ultimately, this new work seemed to be aimed at a more learned reader, as if Viret were expanding the teaching he had already delivered.

However, we must first of all emphasize that the additional arguments were not entirely new. Viret had also reproduced some pages taken from his treatise on the cult of the saints written in 1542, but which had been published anonymously, and which now he was re-appropriating under his own name.[24] This long section helped to reinforce Viret's theological exposition, and especially his Mariology. The emphasis was always on practice. First, Viret evoked the manner in which the liturgy of the Virgin occupied the sensory sphere and was infused into the soundscape of the faithful through the ringing of bells for the Liturgy of the Hours. Next, he criticized the cult of images, mentioning the paintings that the people could see in convent churches. The iconography of double intercession by the milk of the Mother and by the blood of the Son at the Last Judgement was presented as a mockery and a blasphemy, an affront both to the bodily dignity of Mary due to her

---

estoit du germe, de la semence et couvée des oeufs du vieux serpent: qui de tout temps a toujours tasché de corrompre et pervertir la vraye religion, et desrober l'honneur deu à Dieu, pour l'attribuer aux creatures à fin qu'il fust honnoré in icelles au lieu de Dieu' (The eggs of snakes [...] are put and strung together as the rosaries, so that nothing is more like each other. That is why the more I consider this thing, the more I am persuaded that these rosaries were made in such form by Divine Providence and for this purpose, that by the form itself we were admonished from which author they proceeded. The form showed us more clearly that this superstition and idolatry is the grain, the seed, and the brood of the eggs of the Old Serpent, who has always tried to corrupt or to pervert the true religion, and to steal the honour due to God for attributing it to creatures, so that he could be honoured through creatures, instead of God): Viret, *Petit traité*, fols D7[v]–D8[r]. See Isaiah 59. 5.

22 Pot, 'Viret aux origines des sciences religieuses', pp. 101–25.

23 Viret, *Du vray usage*.

24 [Viret], *De la Difference*, fols M2[v]–N7[v].

uncovered breast and thus to her honour, and an affront to the Redemptive Sacrifice of the adult Jesus, who is treated as an infant cleaving to the breast of his mother.[25] Devotion to the Virgin was finally presented as an essentially feminine manifestation, propagated by monks but prevalent above all among bawdy women of ill repute (*paillardes*). Actually, Marian spirituality was in large part inspired by a clerical, i.e. a masculine, view of the Incarnation, and the Marian cult was widely practised by laymen.[26] Viret certainly seemed aware of the medieval tradition, and indeed these gendered and anticlerical remarks testify notably to his polemical approach. He aimed to devalue all intellectual implications of the cult of Mary. Moreover, Marian devotion was illustrated as a form of piety not compatible with masculinity.

In this new edition, historical and theological arguments were considerably augmented. Viret offered, in his defence, the nuanced position on the cult to the Virgin of a Greek father of the Church, Epiphanius of Salamis, taken from his *Panarion*.[27] Viret's systematic comparison of pagan cults of the Goddess and the 'papist' cult of the Virgin Mary, authorized by patristic sources themselves, was accompanied by a confession of faith in the Incarnation and by Viret's acknowledgement of the canonical title 'Mother of God' due to Mary.[28] Viret closed his treatise with a warning invoking the responsibility of the faithful. Christian idolatry aroused the ridicule of infidels as well as of unbelievers. It was therefore only in renouncing excessive, ridiculous, and

---

25 'Quelle moquerie et quel blaspheme est-ce, de peindre la vierge Marie advocate des povres pecheurs, monstrant ses mammelles à Iesus Christ son fils, comme si c'estoit un petit enfant, qui fust encore au giron de sa mere? Se faut il ainsi iouer en choses si grandes? Toutefois aux couvents de ceux qui veullent estre tenuz les plus grans serviteurs de la Vierge, on voit telles peinctures, lesquelles ne conviennent pas mal avec ce qu'ils chantent en leur *Ave maris stella*. *Monstra te esse matrem*, disent-ils, c'est à dire, Monstre que tu es la mere: qui vaut autant à dire, que s'ils disoyent, Monstre que tu as quelque puissance, credit et autorité envers ton Fils' (What mockery and blasphemy is it to paint the Virgin Mary as the advocate of poor sinners, showing her breast to Jesus Christ her son, as if he was a little child still at the bosom of his mother? Should you toy with such big matters? However, to the convents of those who want to be considered the greatest servants of the Virgin, we see such paintings, which correspond to what they sing in their *Ave Maria Stella*. *Monstra te essem matrem*, they say, that it is — Show that you are the mother — as if they say — Show that you have some power, credit and authority towards your Son): Viret, *Du vray usage*, fols 134–35. See also [Viret], *De la Difference*, fol. M8^{r}.

26 Rubin, *Mother of God*, pp. 121–37; Walker Bynum, *Holy Feast and Holy Fast*, pp. 267–69.

27 Viret, *Du vray usage*, fols 86–120.

28 Viret, *Du vray usage*, fols 123–32. This title is a translation of the Greek *Theotokos* (God-bearer) which was upheld by the Councils of Ephesus, 431 and of Chalcedon, 451; however, his later usage in Marian tradition suggests some reservations and a different attitude between Greek and Latin Fathers: see Wright, 'From "God-bearer" to "Mother of God"', pp. 22–30. The question was a stressful theological matter for the first reformers too: for instance, Calvin did not use this epithet as a title of honour for Mary in the *Institutes* nor in his sermons on Marian scriptural passages in Luke's Gospel: Calvin, *Sermons sur l'harmonie évangélique*, 'neufième sermon', cols 105–10; see also MacCulloch, 'Mary and Sixteenth-Century Protestants', pp. 203–04.

impious worship of the Mother that they could defend faith in her son Jesus Christ as the Saviour.

In conclusion, the dialectic between 'old' and 'new' generated by Viret in his work on the Rosary and Mary between 1544 and 1556 was rather complex. Sometimes it was the novelty of the practices that revealed their lack of foundation; sometimes their very antiquity testified to a centuries-old process of perversion of the doctrine and to a survival of superstitions as well as of pagan idolatry. But his discourse most of all appealed to emotions opposite to those put forth by the Marian cult itself. Thus, one passes from the emotional register of protection to one of mistrust or potential spiritual danger. The uses for Marian prayer were associated with witchcraft and spells, and the pleasant appearance of religious items was negated by their association with poisonous or repulsive objects like serpent's eggs. Much more so than his demystifying anticlerical irony, this teaching strategy was intended to modify the confident view of the faithful towards the positive appearance of the devotions censured. From this perspective, dissociation from traditional usage was done less by way of a process of theological rationalization of the practice itself than by an emotional re-reading of its meaning and implications, as well as of its distant origins. The intercession of the Virgin was emptied of its symbolic potential of mediation and thereby also of its spiritual attraction. Emphasis was now placed on the widespread diffusion of the cult, and on its roots in daily life. The critical commentaries constructed a gendered and a class perspective on Marian prayers as a popular devotion both for rude monks and ignorant women. The very point of this perspective is the spiritual intimacy with Mary, i.e. the danger of the individual prayers. It was thus by a veritable 'polemical translation' of the constitutive elements of the late medieval Marian spirituality that such popular practices were ultimately presented as being likely to contaminate the whole community of the faithful.

However, the new edition of 1556, with its insistence on the ways of giving 'true honour' to the Virgin Mary, which the new title of the treatise already declares, shows at once the necessity for Protestants to specify their theological and spiritual perspective on the Mother of Jesus vis-à-vis Catholics' accusations. Even more so, it shows a certain unease arising from the difficulty of confronting a cult that the reformed communities rejected without also calling into question the status of the figure who was the object of the devotion as the Mother of God. By his editorial refashioning of the treatise, Viret seemed aware of the fact that, on the battlefield of confessional controversy in France, this rejection would potentially turn the Reformed into Turks and Jews, or into unbelievers denying certain aspects of the Incarnation considered foundational to Christianity, and to Mary's dignity.[29]

---

29 On the confessional usages, both in Catholic and Lutheran preaching, of critiques of Turks and Jews to Marian theology, see Heal, *The Cult of the Virgin Mary*, pp. 140–47, 256–61; Rubin, *Emotion and Devotion*, pp. 45–63.

Works Cited

Primary Sources

Calvin, Jean, *Sermons sur l'harmonie évangélique*, in *Ioannis Calvini opera quae supersunt omnia*, XLVI, ed. by Guilielmus Baum, Eduardus Cunitz, and Eduardus Reuss (Brunswick: Schwetschke et filium, 1891), cols 1–826

Correspondance des Réformateurs dans les pays de langue française, ed. by Antoine-Louis Herminjard, IV, *1536–1538* (Geneva: H. Georg, 1872)

Marot, Clément, *Cinquante pseaumes de Davide mis en françoys*, ed. by Gérard Defaux (Paris: Champion, 1995)

Registers of the Consistory of Geneva in the time of Calvin, ed. by Thomas A. Lambert and Isabella M. Watt, with the assistance of Jeffrey R. Watt, trans. by M. Wallace McDonald, gen. ed. Robert M. Kingdon (Grand Rapids: Eerdmans, 2000)

[Pierre Robert, known as 'Olivétan'], *L'Instruction des enfants, contenant la maniere de prononcer et escrire en françoys. Les dix commandemens. Les articles de la Foy. L'oraison de Jesus Christ. La salutation angelique. Avec la declaration d'iceux, faicte en maniere de recueil, des seulles sentences de l'escriture saincte. Item, les figures des siphres, et leurs valeurs* (Geneva: Pierre de Vingle, 1533; 2nd edition: Geneva: Jean Girard, 1537)

[Viret, Pierre], *De la Difference qui est entre les superstitions et idolatries des anciens gentilz et payens, et les erreurs et abus qui sont entre ceux qui s'appellent chrestiens: et de la vraye maniere d'honnorer Dieu, la Vierge Marie, et les Sainctz* ([Geneva]: [Jean Girard], 1542)

[Viret, Pierre], *Petit traicté de l'usage de la salutation angelique, et de l'origine des chapeletz, et l'abuz d'iceux* ([Geneva]: [Jean Girard], 1544)

Viret, Pierre, *Du vray usage de la salutation faite par l'ange à la Vierge Marie, et de la source des chapelets, et de la manière de prier par conte, et de l'abus qui y est: et du vray moyen par lequel la vierge Marie peut estre honnorée ou deshonnorée. Reveu et augmenté* ([Geneva]: Jean Girard, 1556)

Secondary Studies

Bruening, Michael W., *Calvinism's First Battleground: Conflict and Reform in the Pays de Vaud, 1528–1559* (Dordrecht: Springer, 2005)

———, 'Pierre Viret and Geneva', *Archiv für Reformationsgeschichte*, 99 (2008), 180–85

Crousaz, Karine, 'Un témoignage sur la régulation politique de la division confessionnelle: la chronique de Guillaume de Pierrefleur', in *L'expérience de la différence religieuse dans l'Europe moderne (XVIe–XVIIIe siècles)*, ed. by Bertrand Forclaz (Neuchâtel: Éditions Alphil – Presses universitaires suisses, 2013), pp. 47–66

Giselbrecht, Rebecca A., 'Reforming a Model: Zwingli, Bullinger, and the Virgin Mary in Sixteenth-Century Zurich', in *Following Zwingli: Applying the Past in Reformation Zurich*, ed. by Luca Baschera, Bruce Gordon, and Christian Moser (Burlington: Ashgate, 2014), pp. 137–74

Grosse, Christian, and Daniela Solfaroli Camillocci, 'Réaménager le rapport au sacré: les reliques dans l'iconoclasme et la polémique religieuse aux premiers temps de la Réforme genevoise', in *Les objets de la mémoire: Pour une approche comparatiste des reliques et de leur culte*, ed. by Philippe Borgeaud and Youri Volokhine (Bern: Peter Lang, 2005), pp. 285–324

Heal, Bridget, *The Cult of the Virgin Mary in Early Modern Germany: Protestant and Catholic Piety, 1500–1648* (Cambridge: Cambridge University Press, 2007)

Karant-Nunn, Susan C., *The Reformation of Feeling: Shaping the Religious Emotions in Early Modern Germany* (Oxford: Oxford University Press, 2010)

Kingdon, Robert M., 'L'usage quantitatif des registres du consistoire de Genève', *Bulletin de la Société de l'histoire du protestantisme Français*, 153.4 (2007), 585–92

Kreitzer, Beth, *Reforming Mary: Changing Images of the Virgin Mary in Lutheran Sermons of the Sixteenth Century* (Oxford: Oxford University Press, 2004)

Lambert, Thomas, '"Cette loi ne durera guère": inertie religieuse et espoirs catholiques à Genève au temps de la Réforme', *Bulletin de la Société d'histoire et d'archéologie de Genève*, 23–24 (1993/1994), 5–24

MacCulloch, Diarmaid, 'Mary and Sixteenth-Century Protestants', in *The Church and Mary: Papers Read at the 2001 Summer Meeting and the 2002 Winter Meeting of the Ecclesiastical History Society*, ed. by Robert N. Swanson (Woodbridge: Boydell, 2004), pp. 191–217

Manetsch, Scott M., 'Holy Terror or Pastoral Care? Church Discipline in Calvin's Geneva, 1542–1596', in *Calvin – Saint or Sinner?*, ed. by Herman J. Selderhuis (Tubingen: Mohr Siebeck, 2010), pp. 283–306

Mudrak, Marc, 'La construction matérielle du catholicisme allemand au début de la Réforme', *Revue d'histoire moderne et contemporaine*, 62.1 (2015), 79–103

Oberman, Heiko Augustinus, 'The Virgin Mary in Evangelical Perspective', in Heiko Augustinus Oberman, *The Impact of the Reformation: Essays* (Grand Rapids: Eerdmans, 1994), pp. 225–52

Pierre Viret et la diffusion de la Réforme: pensée, action, contextes religieux, ed. by Karine Crousaz and Daniela Solfaroli Camillocci (Lausanne: Antipodes, 2014)

Pot, Olivier, 'Viret aux origines des sciences religieuses: de la mythologie à l'ethnographie', in *Pierre Viret et la diffusion de la Réforme: pensée, action, contextes religieux*, ed. by Karine Crousaz and Daniela Solfaroli Camillocci (Lausanne: Antipodes, 2014), pp. 101–25

Rubin, Miri, *Emotion and Devotion: The Meaning of Mary in Medieval Religious Cultures*, The Natalie Zemon Davis Annual Lecture Series (Budapest: CEU Press, 2009)

———, *Mother of God: A History of the Virgin Mary* (London: Allen Lane, 2009)

Silver, Larry, 'Full of Grace: "Mariolatry" in Post-Reformation Germany', in *The Idol in the Age of Art: Objects, Devotions and the Early Modern World*, ed. by

Michael W. Cole and Rebecca Zorach (Burlington: Ashgate, 2009), pp. 289–315

Troilo, Dominique-Antonio, *L'œuvre de Pierre Viret: l'activité littéraire du réformateur mise en lumière* (Lausanne: L'Âge d'homme, 2012)

Walker Bynum, Caroline, *Holy Feast and Holy Fast: The Religious Significance of Food to Medieval Women* (Berkeley: University of California Press, 1987)

Wright, D. F., 'From "God-Bearer" to "Mother of God" in the Later Fathers', in *The Church and Mary: Papers Read at the 2001 Summer Meeting and the 2002 Winter Meeting of the Ecclesiastical History Society*, ed. by Robert N. Swanson (Woodbridge: Boydell, 2004), pp. 22–30

MARCO MOSTERT

Changes in the Grammar of Legibility

Influences on the Development of 'New Communities of Interpretation'?

There are many continuities between the culture of the written word and that of the printed word. One of those continuities has to do with reading and its practices. Unless you are a specialist of the history of reading, you may take it for granted that readers are capable of making sense of what they find before them on the page. Nevertheless, it might be interesting to consider what makes a page 'legible'. And here research mainly undertaken by scholars of palaeography and codicology, by specialists of the handwritten word, may prove useful. They have come up with the notion of the 'grammar of legibility', and have studied legibility by paying attention to the minutest details of what is visible on the handwritten page, and how these details have developed over time.

What is needed to make a written text legible? And what contributes to an increase in legibility, allowing someone to 'read' a text? 'Reading' is understood here in the basic, down-to-earth sense of being able to 'voice' the graphic signs on the page which allow one to reconstruct the 'oral' text, the sounds of the spoken words, that were transformed into visual signs in the act of writing them down. It is this 'decoding' of the graphic signs which may enable a reader to make sense of a written text. Whether he or she in fact understands the *meaning* of the words that thus become audible once more to the outer or inner ear of the reader, is another matter. For understanding a written text, other intellectual skills may be required. I can voice the words of medieval texts on astronomy, because I can make sense of the graphic signs on the page on which those words have been written, but, having but very limited knowledge of astronomy, I cannot fully understand the words I am reading.

'Legibility' in this limited sense of the word is brought about by five kinds of knowledge. First, one needs to know the language in which the written text one tries to read is written. Much can be said on this, but let us assume for

Marco Mostert • (m.mostert@uu.nl) is Professor of Medieval History at Utrecht University.

Religious Transformations in New Communities of Interpretation in Europe (1350–1570): Bridging the Historiographical Divides, ed. by Élise Boillet and Ian Johnson, New Communities of Interpretation, 3 (Turnhout: Brepols, 2022), pp. 83–95.

DOI 10.1484/M.NCI-EB.5.131215

the moment that our reader knows the language in which the text he wants to read is written.

Secondly, a reader needs to know the alphabet and script used to write the text. As a text may be written down in different alphabets or scripts, this is an important issue.[1] Not only does our reader need to be able to identify the letters, there is also the matter of the use of capitals, or the distinction between upper-case and lower-case letters.[2] When does one use capitals, and when not? And there is the use of abbreviation, the rules of which one needs to know as well. Sometimes a polysyllable such as the Latin word for 'communicable' (*communicabilis*) may be rendered by a few letters and some signs of abbreviation, rendering the word illegible to those who did not learn the conventions of the abbreviations used.[3]

Thirdly, there is punctuation, which, together with other paratextual signs, may point the reader towards the intended ways of rendering audible the written text, or of understanding its structure, thereby helping an understanding of its sometimes complex clauses and periods.[4]

Fourthly, and most importantly, there are the spaces between the words.[5] Especially if, as happened frequently in the Middle Ages, texts were written in Latin — a language that was no longer anyone's mother tongue — it was most helpful to know where one word ended and the next word began. In areas where Romance languages, the descendants of Latin, were spoken, the introduction of spaces between words occurred as late as the tenth to thirteenth centuries. Elsewhere, as for instance on the British Isles, word-spacing was

1 A useful survey attempt to distinguish 'alphabet', 'script', and 'writing system' from a sociolinguistic point of view is provided by Bunčić, 'Introduction', in: *Biscriptality*, ed. by Bunčić, Lippert, and Rabus, pp. 20–26. A 'script' is defined as 'a set of graphic signs for writing languages'. A 'writing system' is 'an implementation of one or more scripts to form a complete system for writing a particular language' (a definition borrowed from Coulmas, *Writing Systems*, s.v.). An 'alphabet' is a script in which 'the signs essentially correspond to phonemes [...] (and its elements are called *letters*)'.

2 This has to do with the changing between 'script variants'. As Bunčić, 'Introduction', p. 22, explains: '[w]ithin a script, several graphical variants can be distinguished. For example, within the Latin alphabet the difference between the letterforms <Abcde> and the letterforms <Abcde> is in some respect considered sociolinguistically meaningful (but the letterforms <Abcde> are mainly perceived as a stylistic alternative to <Abcde>'. Bunčić, 'A Heuristic Model for Typology', p. 67, calls this 'biglyphism', which uses differences between 'glyphic variants'. See also, among the case studies, Spitzmüller and Bunčić, 'German: Blackletter and Roman'. Kaislaniemi, 'Code-Switching, Script-Switching, and Typeface-Switching', pp. 168–69 n. 6, notices that *Biscriptality* is not exhaustive, as it fails to discuss 'script-shifting' as a phenomenon.

3 See Cappelli, *Dizionario*, pp. xi–lvi, at p. xlvii, among other similar examples.

4 Parkes, *Pause and Effect*, deals with 'punctuation in the West' from the earliest Latin fragments on papyrus, dating from the first century BC, to printed works published in the eighteenth century.

5 Saenger, *Space between Words*, drawing upon a whole literature of experimental psychological studies, offering comparisons between alphabetical and other scripts, is fundamental.

developed almost as soon as texts in Latin came to be read there, from as early as the sixth century.

And finally, there was layout: the way a text is laid out on the page gives information as to what kind of text a reader is dealing with.[6] Poetry looks different from biblical texts; history from scientific texts — or so these 'genres' do nowadays; from when onwards it became necessary to distinguish historical texts, say, from astronomical texts by their layout, remains to be seen.

The most important studies for the study of the 'grammar of legibility' of manuscripts, those by Malcolm Parkes and Paul Saenger, date from the 1990s.[7] Attention to the phenomenon is fairly recent. What has attention to punctuation, space between words, and layout taught us so far?

The results come under two headings. First, there is a marked shift from the oral to the written, as might have been expected, that is accompanied by a shift from the 'aural' to the 'visual': whereas beforehand one needed to rely on one's ears to make sense of the graphical signs on the page, gradually, through a series of changes in spacing, punctuation, and layout, it became possible to read a written text without having to 'voice' it, and to rely mainly or even exclusively on visual clues.

Secondly, the shift from 'aural' to 'visual' reading is accompanied by a shift from reading aloud to reading silently. Whereas in antiquity even highly literate readers would have needed to give voice to the words on the page in order to understand them, it became increasingly less necessary to do so, so that 'reading aloud' in private reading would gradually become an object of ridicule. This was enabled by the gradual elimination of ambiguity: the use of script, punctuation, and word-spacing gave indications as to how authors and scribes wanted their products to be read.[8]

Allow me to show this by an example.[9]

WHRMBKSGLLTHWRDSTHTIGTHRNDLLTHWRDSTHTI
WRTMSTSPRDTTHRWNGSNTRNGNDNVRRSTNTHRFLG
HTTLLTHCMWHRYRSDSDHRTSNDSNGTYNTHNGHTBY
NDWHRTHWTRSRMVNGSTRMDRKNDRSTRRBRGHT

6 *Mise en page et mise en texte du livre manuscrit*, ed. by Martin and Vezin remains one of the best guides.

7 To the works by the authors mentioned above ought to be added the insightful publications by Peter Gumbert, in particular his 'La page intelligible: quelques remarques' of 1989, and 'Zur "Typographie" der geschriebenen Seite' of 1992.

8 See also *Storia della lettura*, ed. by Cavallo and Chartier, to which Malcolm Parkes and Paul Saenger contributed. The volume has been published also in French and English translations.

9 Mostert, 'Latin Learning and Learning Latin', uses a similar example, discussing it in greater detail.

To avoid complications caused by the use of a foreign language (such as Latin), here you see a text in English, as it would have been written down when alphabetic writing was invented for West-Semitic languages (Fig. 1). There is no word separation, no punctuation, no distinction between upper-case and lower-case, and you will see only consonants (when you think you see a vowel, this is meant to represent either a /v/ or a /w/ sound). Such a text could be read only by someone who already knew it by heart. Here, writing is merely an aid to memory.

WHR M BKS G LL TH WRDS THT I GTHR ND LL TH WRDS
THT I WRT MST SPRD T THR WNGS NTRNG ND NVR RST
N THR FLGHT TLL TH CM WHR YR SD SD HRT S ND SNG
T Y N TH NGHT BYND WHR TH WTRS R MVNG STRM
DRKND R STRR BRGHT

Here is the same text, now with word separation (Fig. 2). You will still be unable to make sense of it, but, when you happen to know the text beforehand, it is less likely that you will make mistakes when pronouncing it. This is the way the oldest texts in Hebrew present themselves.

WHEREMYBOOKSGOALLTHEWORDSTHATIGATHERA
NDALLTHEWORDSTHATIWRITEMUSTSPREADOUTTHE
IRWINGSUNTIRINGANDNEVERRESTINTHEIRFLIGHTTI
LLTHEYCOMEWHEREYOURSADSADHEARTISANDSING
TOYOUINTHENIGHTBEYONDWHERETHEWATERSARE
MOVINGSTORMDARKENEDORSTARRYBRIGHT

Here is our text once again, with the inclusion of vowels, an invention by the ancient Greeks (Fig. 3). This makes it possible to try and read the text, when you know the language in which it is written, but you will not be able to do so without resorting to mumbling (i.e. 'voicing') it. You see that the elimination of ambiguity by the insertion of vowels is accompanied by the curious elimination of word separation.

WHEREMYBOOKSGOALLTHEWORDSTHATIGATHERANDALLTHEWO
RDSTHATIWRITEMUSTSPREADOUTTHEIRWINGSUNTIRINGANDNEV
ERRESTINTHEIRFLIGHTTILLTHEYCOMEWHEREYOURSADSADHEAR
TISANDSINGTOYOUINTHENIGHTBEYONDWHERETHEWATERSAREM
OVINGSTORMDARKENEDORSTARRYBRIGHT

Here we have the same text, but now with a few letters which are larger than the others (fig. 4). The enlarged letters may be at the beginning of words, but also in the middle. Their use is that of guiding the eye movements of the reader from left to right and back again: they afford points of reference in the sea of letters, and their presence reduces the number of eye movements needed to make sense of the text.

WheremybooksgoAllthewordsthatIgatherAndallthewordsthatIwr
ite,Mustspreadouttheirwingsuntiring,Andneverrestintheirflight,T
illtheycomewhereyoursad,sadheartis,Andsingtoyouinthenight,Be
yondwherethewatersaremoving,Stormdarkenedorstarrybright.

The insertion of punctuation does more or less the same thing (fig. 5); it is here added to the use of larger letters, and this reduces the number of eye movements required to make sense of the text even further. Now imagine that the upper-case letters, apart from their role of points of reference, also obey certain rules — those of current English usage, for instance. And imagine that lower-case letters have a different form. And why not imagine that there is word-spacing as well?

WHERE MY BOOKS GO All the words that I gather And all the words that I write, Must spread out their wings untiring, And never rest in their flight, Till they come where your sad, sad heart is, And sing to you in the night, Beyond where the waters are moving, Storm darkened or starry bright.

This is the result: all of a sudden, the text becomes fully legible, and the number of eye movements is reduced to a minimum (fig. 6). The rationale behind the script-switching, however, is not yet clear. It is, possibly, only by adapting the layout to the way we are accustomed to perceive the genre of this particular text, that we become able to appreciate it for what it is:

WHERE MY BOOKS GO

All the words that I gather
  And all the words that I write,
Must spread out their wings untiring,
  And never rest in their flight,
Till they come where your sad, sad heart is,
  And sing to you in the night,
Beyond where the waters are moving,
  Storm darkened or starry bright.

a poem, by W. B. Yeats (fig. 7).[10] Had you been first presented with this version, the one he published, you would immediately have been able to understand it as a poem, but also to read it as a poem, with the rhythms and intonation

10 Yeats, 'Where My Books Go'.

that fit 'poems' such as we understand them. Layout does much to guide our way of reading written texts.

All these changes in word separation, script, punctuation, and layout had been possible in the culture of the handwritten word. By the end of the thirteenth century, our text, or to be more precise the poem by Yeats, might have been written down 'as poetry' (or at least in a layout that would have satisfied contemporaries' ideas of what poetry ought to look like on the page). The question now needs to be posed: what did the invention of the printing press add to the 'grammar of legibility' as defined above?

To answer this question, I looked up some of the standard works on the history of (early) printing, and was deceived. Steinberg's *Five Hundred Years of Printing* did not say anything about the legibility of printed texts.[11] Nor did Elisabeth Eisenstein in her *The Printing Press as an Agent of Change*.[12] Gaskell in his *A New Introduction to Bibliography*[13] and Henri-Jean Martin in his *Histoire et pouvoirs de l'écrit*[14] said something, but not as much as they might have done. Even the recent *Textkünste: Buchrevolution um 1500*, which deals with the 'invention' of the printed page around 1500, is silent on this.[15] There is more to be found in a recently published book, a collection on *Verbal and Visual Communication in Early English Texts*.[16] That they do talk about the grammar of legibility no doubt is due in part to the fact that some of their contributors are manuscript scholars rather than scholars of early printing. So what does one find in current scholarship on the grammar of legibility in the century after Gutenberg?

There is no interest whatsoever in word separation in print, other than as a means to arrive at straight justification of the line both left and right.[17] That once word separation had meant a huge amelioration in legibility is a lesson that seems lost on scholars of early printing.

As for script, there is an interest, with regard to the formalization of systems of script, in the standardization of typefaces which led to the elimination of the scribes' personal idiosyncrasies.[18] One also finds a tendency to value bookhand over cursive, and roman over italics.[19]

---

11 Steinberg, *Five Hundred Years of Printing*.

12 Eisenstein, *The Printing Press*.

13 Gaskell, *A New Introduction to Bibliography*.

14 Martin, *Histoire et pouvoirs de l'écrit*.

15 *Textkünste: Buchrevolution um 1500*, ed. by Schneider, accompanying exhibitions at the Universitätsbibliothek Leipzig in 2016–2017 and at the Bibliothèque municipale of Lyons, also in 2016–2017. (In Lyons the exhibition went by the name *Impressions premières — la page en revolution de Gutenberg à 1530*).

16 *Verbal and Visual Communication in Early English Texts*, ed. by Peikola, Mäkilähde, Salmi, Varila, and Skaffari.

17 Gaskell, *A New Introduction to Bibliography*, pp. 45–46 and fig. 20.

18 Eisenstein, *The Printing Press*, p. 82.

19 Cf. Eisenstein, *The Printing Press*, pp. 201–07.

As for punctuation and paratextual signs, developments seem to have been restricted to the introduction of the quotation marks known as « *guillemets* »,[20] parentheses,[21] and to the (often failed) introduction of other signs, sometimes taken from late antique traditions.[22]

As for layout, attention has been given to justification, but also to the addition of page numbers, headers, and footnotes.[23] These were all medieval inventions, made mainly by Insular, Carolingian, and thirteenth-century university scribes, but their systematization in printing was indeed important. It became financially feasible to make, for instance, indices to printed books, whereas for manuscript texts, no two copies of which are ever completely identical in their layout, and therefore reference was made to the different sections of complex texts, rather than to individual pages. But these matters have to do with other levels of reading practice, with 'consultation literacy',[24] rather than with the basic ways of making sense of graphical signs on the page that we are concerned with here.

Fortunately, the study of contemporary texts on early modern reading allows us to know more about our topic. In particular 'arts of punctuation', relatively short texts that explain how one should make use of punctuation in reading, prove interesting.[25] In summary, and this had been known already from Parkes's *Pause and Effect*, punctuation was mainly used either to help the comprehension of the written text, or to help the reading aloud of texts. In the latter case candidates might be liturgical texts, where the correct pronunciation not only of the words but also of the phrases that make up the sentences was considered to be extremely important (stories were told about supernatural punishment for the incorrect, usually sloppy, reading of liturgical texts).[26] The Latin *artes punctandi* also advocate the use of punctuation for reading aloud.

---

20 Martin, *Histoire et pouvoirs de l'écrit*, p. 189.

21 Martin, *Histoire et pouvoirs de l'écrit*, p. 189, attributing this invention to Gasparino Barzizza (*c.* 1360–*c.* 1431).

22 Gaskell, *A New Introduction to Bibliography*, pp. 358–59, and p. 339, there calling 'minor changes of spelling, capitalization, and punctuation' mere 'accidentals'.

23 Parkes, *Pause and Effect*, pp. 262–75, shows the layout of a fragment of Cicero, *In Verrem*, II. II. 2, from its oldest surviving witness (first century BC or first century AD) to the edition of Cicero's works made by Olivetus (Pierre Joseph de Thoulié) in Geneva in 1758. In this example, the footnotes appear only in 1758, but annotation was known (mainly in the margins) much earlier. See *The Annotated Book in the Early Middle Ages*, ed. by Teeuwen and van Renswoude. G. C. Huisman, 'Leesgedrag / gebruikerssporen', considers layout, punctuation, paragraph signs, chapter titles and rubrics, schemes and illustrations, tables of content and indices, headings and foliation, all parts of layout, as mnemotechnic aids for readers.

24 See *Organising the Written Word*, ed. by Mostert. For changes in pedagogical practice enabled by the possibility, thanks to the printing press, of referring to pages, lines, and words, see Ong, *Ramus*, p. 314 (quoted by Eisenstein, *The Printing Press*, p. 430).

25 I rely on Duntze, 'The sound of silence', for my knowledge on *artes punctandi*.

26 See Tubach, *Index exemplorum*, nos 1630, 5181; cf. also no. 4249.

This return to voicing the text may have been inspired by practices known from classical Latin literature. In Roman antiquity the value of what we call literature lay in the reading aloud of the literary text, which had been learnt by heart. Not the fixity of the written word, but the living word of the mouth was appreciated.[27] The 'return' to Roman values in matters literary may therefore be the cause of a renewed interest in what you could do with punctuation. A first intimation of this return to *Romanitas* can be found already in the *artes dictaminis*, manuals about the writing of, for instance, letters, that were written from the eleventh century onwards.[28]

But some of the *artes punctandi* go further. Punctuation is supposed to add indications of where one has to inset a pause, and how long that pause has to be. And punctuation also indicates matters such as the sentiment with which one has to express the following words, variation in volume (using a loud or soft voice), a higher or lower tone. Some of these marks had been known earlier on as well, as for instance the two dots preceding a title, in charters of the thirteenth century, which indicated that the title and the name following it had to be pronounced in a solemn fashion (the so-called 'points of dignity' found in northern French charters).[29] But the *artes punctandi* represent a much more formalized return to reading aloud.

The *Antonii Ciceromani ad Johannem fratrem suavissimum de arte punctuandi praefatio*, for example, printed at Lyon around 1500, gives indications on how to use five punctuation signs for reading aloud. The use of the colon is described as follows:

> Pronunciationem eius debere esse gravem: et oportunum esse ibidem facere magnam pausam: vt legens in tali mora anhelitus quiete sustentari possit.[30]
>
>> (Its pronunciation has to be grave: and it is fitting to make there [where it occurs] a long pause: so that the reader by this break may have time quietly to take a breath.)

Not only the pause is indicated by a colon, but also that the next words have to be said in a grave manner! This clearly suggests that the authors of these *artes* meant texts to be read aloud.

This observation may, incidentally, have some consequences for the performance of early music.[31] Is it too far-fetched to believe that, although

---

27 Mostert, 'Latin Learning and Learning Latin', p. 30.

28 *Le dictamen dans tous ses états*, ed. by Grévin and Turcan-Verkerk.

29 An example (from 1249) can be found in *Album palaeographicum XVII provinciarum*, ed. by Dekker, Baetens, and Maarschalkerweerd-Dechamps, Plate 13, p. 18.

30 Ciceromanus, *De arte punctandi*, fol. 2^v, quoted by Duntze, 'The sound of silence', p. 85 (with indication of abbreviations, which have been solved here).

31 For the punctuation of music, see *Ponctuer l'œuvre médiévale*, ed. by Fasseur and Rochelois, and in particular Anger, 'Ponctuation et notation dite "musicale"'; Mouchet, 'Ponctuation du texte, ponctuation du chant dans le manuscrit médiéval noté', and Dulong, 'Poésies

instrumental music might have needed visual indications about tone and volume (because by its very nature instrumental music has no text with its punctuation indicating the manner in which it has to be rendered), words set to music could do without such indications — at least for as long as the instructions of the *artes punctandi* of *c.* 1500 were still generally known? For visual indications of tone, volume, etc. as needed for instrumental music, were already given by the punctuation of the words.

At about the same time the *artes punctuandi* made their appearance, the role of rhetoric in communal religious singing was thought about in musical theory. In 1511, Johannes Cochlaeus (1479–1552) believed that the *orator* could be likened to the *cantor*, the *rhetor* to the *musicus*.[32] In 1612, Johannes Lippius (1585–1612) explicitly referred to the ('grammatical') *periodus* and *comma*, comparing them to the musical *clausulae*.[33] Musical theory understood that the effect of a text, whether it was said, chanted, or sung, could benefit from the use of rhetoric, and that the performance of sung text could be helped by the use of punctuation.

A similar use of rhetoric may be assumed in preaching. Preachers had been aware of the advantages offered by rhetoric not only when they prepared their sermons, but more in particular when they pronounced them. The topic of punctuation in written sermons has not, however, benefited from any studies I am aware of.[34] The topic of punctuation in written prayers, too, seems not to have found any students as yet. The most common prayer books, the ABC-books and books of hours which provided the faithful with the same, identical texts for their private devotion from one copy to the next,[35] may nevertheless have shown some differences in their punctuation, leading to a different rhythm of the reading of some of the basic texts Christians in the Middle Ages and later had recourse to.

---

notées du XIVe siècle'. Krones, 'Einleitung: Rhetorik und Musik', and Krones, '"Denn jedes gute Tonstück ist ein Gedicht"', provide a useful background to medieval and early modern thought about the relationship between music and rhetoric, which may have inspired the use of 'musical punctuation' in texts and punctuation in music.

32 Johannes Cochlaeus, *Tetrachordum musices*, fols A iii^{v} and A iiii^{r}; referenced by Krones, '"Denn jedes gute Tonstück ist ein Gedicht"', p. 27.

33 Johannes Lippius, *Synopsis musicae novae* (Strasbourg, 1612), fol. H 2^{r-v}, quoted by Krones, '"Denn jedes gute Tonstück ist ein Gedicht"', p. 27: 'Quod autem est periodus et comma, id in poetica musica sunt clausulae, quae tanquam partes integrum corpus constituunt... Quid autem sit comma, virgula et periodus, quibus clausulae destinantur, id potius ex grammatica quam ex musica discendum est'.

34 See *L'éloquence de la chaire entre écriture et oralité*, ed. by Aubert, Heneveld, and Meli, in which some notable attempts are made to address the problem of going beyond written sermons to preaching and its impact. However, there is no attention for the graphic representation of written sermons and what this may tell one about actual preaching. Mostert, 'Medieval Sermons as Forms of Communication', is no exception.

35 Cf. Clanchy, *Looking Back from the Invention of Printing*, pp. 9, 15, 18, 25, 27, 33, 81–83, 129, 135, 137, 144, 152, 155–62, 177, and 189.

At some stage, however, the role of punctuation as an aid to declamation was forgotten. That may have happened relatively recently. In a German book on reading aloud in schools (published as recently as 1996) one reads:

> Some learnt in school an often-senseless rule: 'at all commas lift your voice and make a short pause'. Correct would have been the principle, 'punctuation marks are not always at the same time signs for declamation!' Unfortunately, often merely grammatical reasons are responsible for our punctuation.[36]

With this quotation I wish to finish, but not before having admonished you to pay more attention to the punctuation, space between words, and layout of the manuscripts *and* printed texts you study. These small signs (and absences of signs) may provide information about the ways readers in the past read their texts. Without it, we may miss much about the reception of written texts.

Works Cited

Primary Sources

Ciceromanus, Antonius, *De arte punctandi* (Lyon: Jean de Vingle (?), *c.* 1500)
Cochlaeus, Johannes, *Tetrachordum musices* (Nuremberg: J. Weyssemberger, 1511)
Lippius, Johannes, *Synopsis musicae novae* (Strasbourg: Ledertz, 1612)
Yeats, W. B., 'Where My Books Go', in *Books and Libraries: Poems*, ed. by Andrew D. Scrimgeour, Everyman's Library: Pocket Poets (New York: Alfred A. Knopf, 2021) p. 207

Secondary Studies

Album palaeographicum XVII provinciarum – Paleografisch album van Nederland, België, Luxemburg en Noord-Frankrijk – Album de paléographie des Pays-Bas, de Belgique, du Luxembourg et du Nord de la France, ed. by C. Dekker, R. Baetens, and S. Maarschalkerweerd-Dechamps (Turnhout: Brepols, 1992)
Anger, Violaine, 'Ponctuation et notation dite "musicale": Réflexion sur les frontières', in *Ponctuer l'œuvre médiéval: Des signes au sens*, ed. by Valérie Fasseur and Cécile Rochelois, Publications romanes et françaises, 267 (Geneva: Droz, 2016), pp. 75–100
The Annotated Book in the Early Middle Ages: Practices of Reading and Writing, ed. by Mariken J. Teeuwen and Irene van Renswoude, Utrecht Studies in Medieval Literacy, 38 (Turnhout: Brepols, 2017)
Biscriptality: A Sociolinguistic Typology, ed. by Daniel Bunčić, Sandra L. Lippert, and Achim Rabus (Heidelberg: Universitätsverlag Winter, 2016)

36 Wagner, *Mündliche Kommunikation in der Schule*, p. 129.

Bunčić, Daniel, 'A Heuristic Model for Typology', in *Biscriptality: A Sociolinguistic Typology*, ed. by Daniel Bunčić, Sandra L. Lippert, and Achim Rabus (Heidelberg: Universitätsverlag Winter, 2016), pp. 51–71

———, 'Introduction', in *Biscriptality: A Sociolinguistic Typology*, ed. by Daniel Bunčić, Sandra L. Lippert, and Achim Rabus (Heidelberg: Universitätsverlag Winter, 2016), pp. 15–26

Capelli, A., *Dizionario di abbreviature latine ed italiane*, Manuali Hoepli (Milan: Ulrico Hoepli, 1929)

Clanchy, Michael, *Looking Back from the Invention of Printing: Mothers and the Teaching of Reading in the Middle Ages*, Utrecht Studies in Medieval Literacy, 40 (Turnhout: Brepols, 2018)

Coulmas, Florian, *Writing Systems* (Cambridge: Cambridge University Press, 2003)

*Le dictamen dans tous ses états: Perspectives de recherche sur la théorie et la pratique de l'*ars dictaminis *(XIe-XVe siècles)*, ed. by Benoît Grévin and Anne-Marie Turcan-Verkerk, Bibliothèque d'histoire culturelle du Moyen Âge, 16 (Turnhout: Brepols, 2015)

Dulong, Gilles, 'Poésies notées du XIVe siècle: Le point par le contrepoint?', in *Ponctuer l'œuvre médiéval: Des signes au sens*, ed. by Valérie Fasseur and Cécile Rochelois, Publications romanes et françaises 267 (Geneva: Droz, 2016), pp. 201–13

Duntze, Oliver, 'The sound of silence: Eine unbekannte "Ars punctandi" als Quelle zur Geschichte des Lesens in der Frühen Neuzeit', in *Sinn und Unsinn des Lesens: Gegenstände, Darstellungen und Argumente aus Geschichte unde Gegenwart*, ed. by Sandra Rühr and Alex Kuhn (Göttingen: V & R Unipress, 2013), pp. 81–98

Eisenstein, Elizabeth L., *The Printing Press as an Agent of Change: Communications and Cultural Transformations in Early-Modern Europe*, 2 vols (Cambridge: Cambridge University Press, 1979)

L'éloquence de la chaire entre écriture et oralité (XIIIe-XVIIIe siècles), ed. by Gabriel Aubert, Amy Heneveld, and Cinthia Meli (Paris: Honoré Champion, 2018)

Gaskell, Philip, *A New Introduction to Bibliography*, reprint with corrections (Oxford: Oxford University Press, 1974)

Gumbert, J. Peter, 'La page intelligible: quelques remarques', in *Vocabulaire du livre et de l'écriture au moyen âge*, ed. by Olga Weijers, CIVICIMA: Études sur le vocabulaire intellectuel du moyen âge, 2 (Turnhout: Brepols, 1989), pp. 111–19

———, 'Zur "Typographie" der geschriebenen Seite', in *Pragmatische Schriftlichkeit im Mittelalter: Erscheinungsformen und Entwicklungsstufen (Akten des Internationalen Kolloquiums 17.-19. Mai 1989)*, ed. Hagen Keller, Klaus Grubmüller, and Nikolaus Staubach, Münstersche Mittelalterschriften, 65 (Munich: Wilhelm Fink Verlag, 1992), pp. 283–92

Huisman, Gerda C., 'Leesgedrag / gebruikerssporen', in *Bibliopolis: Geschiedenis van het gedrukte boek in Nederland* (Zwolle: Waanders, 2003), pp. 50–51

Kaislaniemi, Samuli, 'Code-Switching, Script-Switching, and Typeface-Switching in Early Modern English Manuscript Letters and Printed Tracts', in *Verbal and Visual Communication in Early English Texts*, ed. by Matti Peikola, Aleksi

Mäkilähde, Hanna Salmi, Mari-Liisa Varila, and Janne Skaffari, Utrecht Studies in Medieval Literacy, 37 (Turnhout: Brepols, 2017), pp. 165–200

Krones, Hartmut, 'Einleitung: Rhetorik und Musik', *Rhetorik: Ein Internationales Jahrbuch*, 35.1 (2016), 1–7

———, '"Denn jedes gute Tonstück ist ein Gedicht": Rhetorik und Musik im deutschen Sprachraum: Von ca. 900 bis zur Gegenwart', *Rhetorik: Ein Internationales Jahrbuch*, 35.1 (2016), 25–56

Martin, Henri-Jean, *Histoire et pouvoirs de l'écrit* (Paris: Librairie Académique Perrin, 1989)

Mise en page et mise en texte du livre manuscrit, ed. by Henri-Jean Martin and Jean Vezin (Paris: Éditions du Cercle de la Librairie-Promodis, 1990)

Mostert, Marco, 'Latin Learning and Learning Latin: Knowledge Transfer and Literacy in the European Middle Ages', in *Theory and Practice of Knowledge Transfer: Studies in School Education in the Ancient Near East and Beyond*, ed. by W. S. van Egmond and W. H. van Soldt, PIHANS: Uitgaven van het Nederlands Instituut voor het Nabije Oosten te Leiden, 121 (Leiden: Nederlands Instituut voor het Nabije Oosten, 2012), pp. 25–37

———, 'Medieval Sermons as Forms of Communication: Between Written Text and Oral Performance', in *L'éloquence de la chaire entre écriture et oralité (XIIIe-XVIIIe siècles)*, ed. by Gabriel Aubert, Amy Heneveld, and Cinthia Meli (Paris: Honoré Champion, 2018), pp. 23–35

Mouchet, Florence, 'Ponctuation du texte, ponctuation du chant dans le manuscrit médiéval noté: Les aléas d'un dialogue en construction', in *Ponctuer l'œuvre médiéval: Des signes au sens*, ed. by Valérie Fasseur and Cécile Rochelois, Publications romanes et françaises, 267 (Geneva: Droz, 2016), pp. 101–18

Ong, Walter J., *Ramus: Method and the Decay of Dialogue: From the Art of Discourse to the Art of Reason* (Cambridge, MA: Harvard University Press, 1958)

Organising the Written Word: Scripts, Manuscripts, and Texts, ed. by Marco Mostert, Utrecht Studies in Medieval Literacy, 30 (Turnhout: Brepols, forthcoming [2023])

Parkes, Malcolm Beckwith, *Pause and Effect: An Introduction to the History of Punctuation in the West* (Aldershot: Scolar Press, 1992)

Ponctuer l'œuvre médiéval: Des signes au sens, ed. by Valérie Fasseur and Cécile Rochelois, Publications romanes et françaises, 267 (Geneva: Droz, 2016)

Saenger, Paul, *Space between Words: The Origins of Silent Reading*, Figurae: Reading Medieval Culture (Stanford: Stanford University Press, 1997)

Spitzmüller, Jürgen, and D. Bunčić, 'German: Blackletter and Roman', in *Biscriptality: A Sociolinguistic Typology*, ed. by Daniel Bunčić, Sandra L. Lippert, and Achim Rabus (Heidelberg: Universitätsverlag Winter, 2016), pp. 282–300

Steinberg, Sigfrid Henry, *Five Hundred Years of Printing*, new edition, revised by John Trevitt (Newcastle, DE: Oak Knoll Press, 1996)

Storia della lettura, ed. by Guglielmo Cavallo and Roger Chartier (Rome: Laterza, 1995)

Textkünste: Buchrevolution um 1500, ed. by Ulrich Johannes Schneider (Darmstadt: Philipp von Zabern, 2016)

Tubach, Frederic C., *Index Exemplorum: A Handbook of Medieval Religious Tales*, FF Communications, 204 (Helsinki: Suomalainen tiedeakatemia, 1969)

Verbal and Visual Communication in Early English Texts, ed. by Matti Peikola, Aleksi Mäkilähde, Hanna Salmi, Mari-Liisa Varila, and Janne Skaffari, Utrecht Studies in Medieval Literacy, 37 (Turnhout: Brepols, 2017)

Wagner, Roland W., *Mündliche Kommunikation in der Schule* (Paderborn: Schöningh, 2006)

ERMINIA ARDISSINO

Biblical Genres through the Long Sixteenth Century

Italy as a Case Study

As Northrop Frye brilliantly showed in his seminal 1982 work *The Great Code: The Bible and Literature,* the European literary imagination has in large part been constructed around the sacred book, which has determined the language, narrative models, and content of almost all literature from each cultural and linguistic area of the Old World. This certainly holds true for Italy. However, for Italy, an outdated paradigm, propagated in Reformation areas and based on Luther's observation of a supposed lack of interest in his day in the Bible in Italy, has cast a shadow over the genuine interest and familiarity that Italians felt for the Sacred Scriptures in the early modern period.[1] While it is certainly true that the ranks of the Catholic Church were not oriented towards biblical translation and the dissemination of sacred writings among laypeople, nonetheless a demand for deeper knowledge of the Sacred Scriptures was born in Italy early on, from the grassroots of the Church, from congregations and many inspired reformers such as Paolo Giustiniani and Pietro Querini.[2] Indeed, the first complete Italian translation of the Bible in print came very early, in 1471, second only to the German printed translation; other full or partial translations went to print regularly in Italy in the first half of the sixteenth century.[3]

1 On this paradigmatic view, see Gow, 'Challenging the Protestant Paradigm' and 'The Contested History of a Book'. This paradigm holds sway even today: for example, it seems to shape the essay on Italy in the *New Cambridge History of the Bible,* published as recently as 2016: Campi and Delgado, 'Bibles in Italian and Spain'.

2 The Camaldulense monks wrote to Pope Leo X promoting reform of the Church. See *Lettera al Papa,* ed. by Bianchini.

3 The bibliography on this subject is now rich, but see above all Barbieri, *Le Bibbie italiane del Quattrocento e del Cinquecento; La Bibbia: Edizioni del 16. Secolo,* ed. by Lumini.

Erminia Ardissino • (erminia.ardissino@unito.it) (PhD, Yale University; Dottorato di Ricerca, Università Cattolica del Sacro Cuore, Milan) is Associate Professor at the University of Turin.

Religious Transformations in New Communities of Interpretation in Europe (1350–1570): Bridging the Historiographical Divides, ed. by Élise Boillet and Ian Johnson, New Communities of Interpretation, 3 (Turnhout: Brepols, 2022), pp. 97–113.

DOI 10.1484/M.NCI-EB.5.131216

Moreover, knowledge of the Bible at that time also came through other channels, such as preaching, mystery plays, and, above all, the many written works based on the Bible, which together represent an extremely rich mine of material, with a wide reach among believers, lay and ecclesiastical, men and women, from the beginning of the printing age onwards.[4] This huge body of publications, of which many were produced in Italy and in Italian, is still greatly understudied, neglected as it has been by scholars primarily oriented towards the established canon. As in other Christian cultures, before and after the Reformation, in Italy this material constituted the most fundamental means by which people could improve their devotion and religious knowledge, for education or for meditation, and could even be a serious form of leisure. In the first decades of the printing age, biblical works were already widely spread across Italy, and they became even more important, useful, and in demand following the first prohibition of biblical translations by the 1558 *Index*.[5]

It is potentially of great interest to study the evolution of these works from the first age of print, through the Reformation, the decades of the Council of Trent and the confused initial censorship period, up to 1596, when, with the decree of Pope Clement VIII, access to the Bible in the vernacular became impossible for Catholics, in Italy as well as in other wholly Catholic countries. It was with this purpose, to understand the presence and evolution of biblical works, that Élise Boillet and I decided to collect data on publications based on the Bible and issued in Italian in the early modern period.[6]

The aim of the catalogue we wanted to compile was to establish not the breadth of biblical influence on literary expression, but precisely which kinds and types of readings based on the Bible were available to Italians in a given historical period. One in which the Bible was a fundamentally important and much-loved book protected by ecclesiastical hierarchies, a book which was the critical reference point for any religious and ethical proposition, although it could also be considered to endanger the unity of the Christian confession, and might be seen as a threat to orthodoxy as well as a necessary tool for religious cohesion.

---

4 On devotional printing in Italy in the early modern period, see the useful work by Jacobson Schutte, *Printed Italian Vernacular Religious Books 1465–1550*; Rozzo, *Linee per una storia dell'editoria religiosa in Italia 1465–1600*; Zardin, 'Bibbia e letteratura religiosa in volgare nell'Italia del Cinque-Seicento'; *Libri, biblioteche e cultura nell'Italia del Cinque e Seicento*, ed. by Barbieri and Zardin; Rozzo and Gorian, *Il libro religioso*.

5 See Fragnito, *La Bibbia al rogo*.

6 Thanks to Élise Boillet's project on 'The Laity and the Bible: Religious Reading in Early Modern Europe', supported by the Centre d'études supérieures de la Renaissance of the University of Tours and LE STUDIUM Loire Valley Institute for Advanced Studies, I had the chance to work for more than a year with Élise Boillet, collecting data for the catalogue that is forthcoming (Ardissino and Boillet, *Repertorio di letteratura biblica in italiano a stampa (ca 1462–1650)*).

Defining Biblical Literature

In creating a catalogue of biblical works, in Italian or in any other language, the first and biggest task a scholar must face is that of defining the kinds of works to be considered. What does biblical literature mean? What kinds of works should be considered biblical; which, of the many publications based on biblical subject matter (almost all Christian texts), should be excluded? Besides translations and obvious paraphrases, more or less creative, what other works should be taken into consideration?

Dealing with biblical literature means searching in the field of palimpsests, defined by Gérard Genette as literature in the *second degré*. According to Genette, rewriting has two types of function, 1) practical, or socio-cultural, and 2) creative. The first category includes summaries, translations, prose versions of a poem or vice versa, and recodifications for theatre, film, and the visual arts. The second category covers creative texts (poetic, narrative, artistic, or performative) or even entirely new texts based on previous expositions and transpositions.[7] Italian biblical literature falls mainly into the first category of 'second degree' literature, but it does not exclude the second category, as we find poetic inventions and even novels based on and inspired by biblical stories. Nevertheless, these works are less representative because the sacred text has undeniably been reinvented, even while it is the primary source of inspiration.

In the early 1960s, a specific field of criticism concerning works inspired by the Bible emerged with the biblical scholar Géza Vermès's use of the term 'rewritten Bible', which has been adopted and frequently used by subsequent scholars.[8] Although the term is appealing and shows affinities with our topic, it was conceived in the field of study of ancient biblical literature and applied to the reworking of biblical books in order to make them more accessible to new readers in new eras. The expression 'rewritten bible' was first used for the Old Testament, and then transferred to the New Testament. Nonetheless, Vermès's category of 'rewritten Bible' cannot be considered applicable to research on Western biblical literature. With the past tense ('rewritten') it refers more to biblical additions, rather than to transformations of biblical texts. It concerns the variants of the 'first degree' of a text, to use Genette's vocabulary, more than 'second degree' literature.

Therefore, the more generic phrase 'biblical literature' seems better suited to the purpose of exploring works based on the Bible and written in subsequent periods. It seems apt, even if the expression 'biblical literature' has to be used as an umbrella term covering the various genres of all those

---

7 Genette, *Palinsesti*, pp. 464–65.

8 Vermès, *Scripture and Tradition in Judaism*, p. 95; *Rewritten Bible after Fifty Years*, ed. by Zsengellér. Earlier considerations can be found in *Rewritten Bible Reconsidered*, ed. by Laato and Ruiten (see especially the introduction, pp. 11–39).

writings which amplify, modify, reinvent, or in some other way expand or summarize one or more books of the Old or of the New Testament, making them more suitable for modern use, especially by laypeople, who represented the new readers of such works. This literature can be in Latin (the language of theology and liturgy in Catholic Europe at the time) or in a vernacular, but research aimed at elucidating the biblical reading habits of laypeople is best focused on vernacular texts.

A catalogue of such literature, coherent in its foundations but varied in its results and purposes, would be very useful in helping us to understand attitudes towards the Bible throughout the long sixteenth century, the revolutionary age for Christendom. Such research may bring to light the multifaceted functions that the sacred book played in the history of devotion, readership, and culture in any European region (in our case study, Italy). Since printing made books cheaper and more available, and the growth of literacy rendered the book market more accessible to laypeople, biblical books entered not only literary circles but also domestic settings, and reached women as well as men. And even more importantly for Italy, a catalogue of biblical literature could answer questions that Italian historiography has faced following the interest that recent scholarship has shown in ecclesiastical censorship: how did Italians approach the Bible after the prohibition of vernacular translations following the initial ban issued in 1558, and then the definitive prohibition in 1596? Furthermore, what distinctively characterized these readers of biblical literature compared with those of the previous period?

In defining the genres that could be included in a repertoire of biblical literature, previous research in similar areas is extremely useful. Edoardo Barbieri, in his study on the dissemination of biblical translations in early modern Italy, faced the same problem. In the introduction to his catalogue of early printed Bibles in Italian he proposes a useful division.[9] In this he groups printed vernacular works derived from the fifteenth-century Bible into three categories: firstly, texts that are exclusively biblical, possibly focusing on single books of the Bible, almost without commentary; secondly, texts that elaborate on the original texts with lengthy commentaries, cuts, or through transformation into poetry; thirdly, religious texts made up of biblical matter, that use their biblical sources freely to develop an autonomous discourse, such as the *Meditationes vitae Christi* or collections of sermons. Barbieri, of course, only includes the first category in his catalogue. This schema is useful for the biblical literature in general which we are considering — it is always possible to situate a biblical text in one of the three categories — but it is not of much help when searching for works which are currently unknown. Later, in another essay on the same topic, Barbieri considered more precise categories in order to define what precisely constitutes a biblical book. He lists sermons, commentaries and

---

9 Barbieri, *Le Bibbie italiane del Quattrocento e del Cinquecento*, p. xiv.

expositions, narratives of the lives of Mary and Jesus, translations of single texts, anthologies, and collections.[10] This is certainly a richer breakdown, but it needs to be refined and tested in practice.

Another useful model is proposed by Lucie Doležalová and Tamás Visi in their seminal work *Retelling the Bible*,[11] where they organize modes of recounting the Sacred Scriptures into the following groups, mainly defined according to use:

1) Translation and Interpretation
2) Preaching and Teaching
3) Biblical Characters as Models
4) Biblical Poetry
5) Children's Bibles
6) Beyond the Text

These six groups correspond to the different topics covered by the essays in their edited volume. For research focused on the early modern period it is immediately evident that three of these groups are not useful: we have no records of *Children's Bibles* in Italian at this time, the catechism being far from a children's Bible, and even elsewhere in Europe it is hard to truly apply this category before Comenius. *Works beyond the Text* are not printed matter; and, finally, *Characters as Models* is a very general name for works inspired by the Bible and intended as ethical models, as they centre on one main biblical character. Collecting books according to their purpose, function, and use may be of some help, but cannot be the only guiding principle of research into Italian biblical literature.

A useful tool for our search would seem to be literary genres, the many different forms given to texts defined by style, technique, content, length, language code, purpose, etc., or, better: the textual tradition defined according to the connections between content and form.[12] The elements that determine a literary genre appear suitable for guiding research into biblical literature, because they offer guidelines and boundaries for classifying all texts, and because these guidelines and boundaries correspond to those chosen and followed by authors, especially in the Renaissance, when literary categories were essential features of writing clearly defined by resurgent Aristotelian rhetorical tools.[13] A search by literary genre categorized a huge number of works sharing the common denominator of biblical content in Italian. Even if new literary genres could always be created, as was the case with *sacre rappresentazioni* in the medieval period, literary genres, including the genre

10 Barbieri, *Panorama delle traduzioni bibliche.*

11 *Retelling the Bible*, ed. by Doležalová and Visi.

12 Segre, *Avviamento all'analisi del testo letterario*, pp. 234–63.

13 On Aristotelian influence on Renaissance literary composition, see Green, 'The Reception of Aristotle's *Rhetoric* in the Renaissance'; Sberlati, *Il genere e la disputa.*

of religious works, function according to basic principles of Western rhetoric and logic, and therefore of Western thought and eloquence, so that it should be possible to situate all Western speech acts and texts in these categories.

Searching by literary genre has in fact been productive, and has led to a collection of more than 3500 items of biblical works in Italian, printed between the 1460s and 1650 in a great variety of forms but all connected to a common root: biblical content.[14] All of them can be considered biblical rewritings,[15] or even biblical literature, with various degrees of closeness to their source. What makes these categories even more appealing is that they even correspond to the criteria used by the censorship processes that produced, as we shall see, the Indexes.

Biblical Genres

The genres that used biblical content in the early modern period in Italy are listed here according to their proximity to their source.

Biblical translations. Even though a translation may be very close to its original, it may still be considered biblical literature because it reflects in some way the translators' perspective on their source, especially in an age when translation was generally understood as a free re-interpretation of an original (the early Renaissance is the age of translations as beautiful but unfaithful, *belle infedeli*, and of the translator as traitor, *traduttore-traditore*).[16] Biblical translations were in fact strongly marked by the confessional allegiances of their translators. Therefore, it seems necessary to consider them as rewritings rather than simple transferrals of texts into another communication system.

Lectionaries and *anthologies*. Lectionaries in Italian were quite common from the fifteenth century onwards.[17] In the second half of the sixteenth century,

14 The *terminus post quem* is determined by the subject of the research: the first record of a biblical printed text in Italian is a fragment dated *c.* 1462. The *terminus ante quem* has been subject to much debate, as the transformations of vernacular printed biblical texts are too fluid simply to assign a date. The end of the sixteenth century does not mark the end of the humanist impulse in religious thinking. The middle of the seventeenth century, with the end of Urban VIII's papacy and of Barberini's age, seemed more suitable, as the transformation in religious production appeared to undergo a radical change at this stage, probably mainly due to the successful Clementine *Index*.

15 That is, not as rewritten Bibles, but as rewritings of the Bible, as these items are written elaborations inspired by the Bible.

16 For Renaissance ideas on translation, see Folena, *Volgarizzare e tradurre*; Korotkoff, "Traduttore traditore'?'; *Traduire les Anciens en Europe du Quattrocento à la fin du 18ème siècle*, ed. by Pradelle and Lechevalier; *Le masque de l'écriture*, ed. by Le Blanc and Simonutti.

17 The second record we have for biblical literature in Italian is in fact the following: *Inchominciano lepistole et lectioni euangeli iquali si leggono in tutto lanno nelle messi cioe domenichali feriali e festiui. Sechondo luso della sancta chiesa di roma* ([Naples: Tip. Del Terentius, *c.* 1470]).

they were even more widespread, but censorship then outlawed all but one, by Remigio Nannini. If a lectionary is a collection of biblical passages to be used in liturgy, anthologies constitute a similar category, collecting as they do passages from the Bible by various criteria. They may appear under different titles, such as *tesoro* or *collectaneo,* but *vita, lamenti,* and *passione* can also refer to collections of passages from the Bible.

Summaries. All works that recount biblical stories in summary or with captioned images can be considered biblical literature. Summaries of the Bible were a fairly popular genre from the Middle Ages onwards, with titles such as *Fiore novello estratto dalla Bibbia.*[18]

Biblia figurata. The spread of illustrated editions of the Bible was a result of print publication, for xylographic prints were vastly cheaper than illuminations.[19] Later, with the perfection of printing, the *Biblia figurata* became a popular genre.

Commentaries. All explanations, interpretations, and commentaries of biblical texts can be grouped together. The length and detail of the commentaries may vary widely, but they form a coherent group. This genre includes very different titles, called commentaries: treatises, discourses, explanations, or declarations, but also more creative titles like *giardini* and *oriente.* Savonarola, who wrote commentaries on several scriptural texts, helped foster the genre's popularity.[20] It became one of the most widely practised genres, with many works in the following centuries falling into this category.

Sermons in all their many forms, such as *lezioni, ragionamenti, prediche,* and *omelie.* All Christian sermons are based on the Bible, but not all of them truly discuss biblical subject matter. For instance, a funeral sermon cannot be considered biblical literature, nor can sermons or eulogies for saints, even if they refer to many biblical passages. Only sermons explaining the readings of the Mass can be considered biblical literature, excluding any preaching on the Holy Spirit, Trinity, etc. This genre includes preaching

---

18 This is a form of summary, with the first edition: *Questo libro e chiamato Fiore nouello molto deuoto da lezere cum certe predicatione e tuto il Testamento Vechio conmenzando da la creatione del mundo in fina alla natiuita de Christo* (Venice: Alvise da Sale, 1473). Jacobson Shutte counts twenty-four editions up to and including 1550.

19 See, for example, *Fioreti della bibia historiati in lingua fiorentina* (Venice: Antonio and Renaldo fratelli da Trino, 1493); *Epistole et Evangeli vulgare et historiate composte in lingua fiorentina* (Venice: Manfredo Bonelli, 1497) (each page has an image). A later beautiful collection of biblical images is Gabriele Simeoni, *Figure de la Biblia illustrate de stanze tuscane* (Lyon: Guillaume Rouillé, 1564).

20 Early examples are Paolo Attavanti, *Commento uolgare et latino del psalmo lxxxx uictoriale et triumphale: 'Qui habitat in adiutorio Altissimi'* (Milan: Leonhard Pachel and Ulrich Schinzenzeler, 1479); Girolamo Savonarola, *La expositione del Pater noster composta in latino da fra Hieronymo da Ferrara dellordine de frati predicatori: & traducta per gli deuoti contemplatori da uno suo amico in uulgare* (Florence: Antonio Miscomini, 1494).

for Advent or Lent (*Avventuali* and *Quaresimali*), and for the Sundays of Ordinary Time.

Catechisms, when they include biblical texts, such as the *oratio dominica* or the *salutatio angelica* or the Ten Commandments. The catechism is generally a dogmatic text, often with theological content (such as the catechism for parsons, *Catechismo a' parrochi*, which offers a summary of principal theological discussions, without biblical text). Catechisms, when they are expositions of the principles of faith and not of biblical matter, should be excluded. A small number of catechisms for children in Italian were first written in Reformed Protestant countries.

Meditations on biblical subjects, especially on the lives of Jesus and Mary, or on the Passion, had formed a very popular genre since the medieval *Meditationes vitae Christi*. Nevertheless, those which elaborate on a biblical subject in an entirely new way should be excluded; for instance, the dialogue of the soul with the cross, or the considerations on the nails of the cross, on the shroud, on Saint Anne's life, etc.

Hagiography concerned with biblical saints, such as the *Legenda aurea* by Jacobus of Voragine, specifically those parts which deal with Jesus, Mary, or the Apostles. This successful book had been translated into Italian by Nicolò Malerbi, the very same translator of the first Italian printed Bible.[21] However, this genre also includes the many stories on the Magdalen, on Joseph, etc., written as *legenda*. This genre became even more common at the end of the sixteenth century, probably because it was used as a behavioural model in an age which sought new ethical inspiration.

Devotional works based on biblical texts such as the Rosary, which include meditations on the main events of the New Testament.[22]

Books of prayer, such as the Psalms in Italian. We found no vernacular psalms set to music: they are all in Latin, with the exception of those from Reformed areas. Even if the introductory texts of a collection of Psalms set to music are in Italian, the content is always in Latin, because they were considered liturgical texts. There are few *Offici* or *officiuoli* in Italian.[23] Even those issued by confraternities are generally in Latin, with only rubrics and didactic instructions in Italian; most in the vernacular were probably lost through censorship. There are many translations and anthologies of

21 Jacobus de Voragine, *Legendario de sancti uulgar storiado* ([Venice: Bartolomeo Zani, 1475]). It had a long life, being in print until the seventeenth century, when Villegas' *Leggendario* took its place, a work strongly promoted by the Roman Catholic Church.

22 Rosary devotion spread largely because of print. The most detailed work was Alberto da Castello's *Rosario della gloriosa Vergine Maria* (1521), which went through more than forty editions in the sixteenth century.

23 A first example is Filelfo's *Comenza lofficio de la gloriosa uirgine Maria traducto et composto per lo excellentissimo doctore miser Mario philelfo poeta laureato* (Venice: Bernardino de' Cori, 1488). On the topic, see Dondi, *Printed Books of Hours from 15th-Century Italy*.

biblical prayers, such as the *oratio dominica* or the *salutatio angelica*, but generally these are accompanied by commentary.

Histories. Historical books of the time, for instance the works of Philo and Josephus Flavius, typically treat the first part of the Bible as historical fact (Creation, the lives of Noah and Abraham, etc.). Universal histories, such as that by Giovanni Tarcagnota, do likewise, always following the Renaissance order of starting with Creation according to Genesis and the history of Israel.[24]

Poems. Poetical retellings of biblical stories in Italian are numerous, totalling almost 300 in our period. They are narrative poems on the model of chivalric poems,[25] recounting the life of Christ, that of the Virgin Mary, and Old Testament histories, especially the lives of heroines like Judith, Esther, and Susanna, or heroes like Tobias, Noah, and David. Collections of poems – sonnets, madrigals, and *canzoni* – are also quite common, but generally they are focused more on spiritual rather than on biblical topics. Therefore, not many *rime spirituali* can be considered in this category, as they mainly consist of Psalms translated as a form of poetic exercise (quite common in the sixteenth century), or collections of poems on a specific biblical topic, such as the *Monte Calvario* (1609) by Giovanni Botero.[26]

Plays for the stage, such as mystery plays, but also biblical comedies and tragedies. *Sacre rappresentazioni* were widely published throughout the period. By 1650 there were still not yet many melodramas and *oratori*, but there were numerous biblical tragedies on Jephthah, Judith, Esther, etc. Many of them were written and performed in Jesuit colleges.

Novels. With the emergence of the modern novel, as distinct from the traditional romance, in the first decades of the seventeenth century, another biblical genre was created: the biblical novel. Generally, they recount biblical stories intertwined with political events, such as the history of Israel narrated by Luigi Manzini in a five-volume series. However, they were sometimes devoted to reconstructing the conversion of one individual, taking the form of an internal history, such as that of Mary Magdalene retold by Anton Giulio Brignole Sale. In a few cases the narration of biblical stories bordered on libertine free thinking, considering as they did the Bible as

---

24 Very successful histories included: Tarcagnota, Giovanni, *Delle historie del mondo [...] le quali con tutta quella particolarità, che bisogna, contengono quanto dal principio del mondo fino a tempi nostri è successo, cauate da' piu degni, e piu graui auttori, che habbiano o nella lingua Greca, o nella Latina scritto* (Venice: Michele Tramezzino, 1562); Ferentilli, Agostino and Philo Alexandrinus, *Discorso uniuersale [...] Nel quale, discorrendosi per le sei età, et le quattro monarchie; si raccontano tutte l'historie, & l'origine di tutti gl'Imperij, Regni, & nationi, cominciando dal principio del mondo, sino all'anno MDLXIX [...]* (Venice: Gabriele Giolito De Ferrari, 1570); *Giosefo Flavio historico, Delle antichità & guerre giudaiche [...]* (Venice: Giacomo Vidali, 1574).

25 Sannazaro's and Vida's poems are both based on a classical Virgilian model.

26 A list of spiritual collections of poems is found in Quondam, 'Note sulla tradizione della poesia spirituale e religiosa'.

a strictly historical narration of human events, totally detached from the divine world. This is the case with Ferrante Pallavicino's novels and with the *Adamo* by Giovan Francesco Loredan.[27]

All of the material listed above can be considered as belonging to devotional literature, of which it is a kind of subgenre with the aim of teaching on biblical subject matter in an accessible and enjoyable form. However, it has its own specificity, thanks to its close relationship with the sacred book. Theological, moral, and spiritual treatises which develop arguments grounded on biblical matters are not strictly biblical, based on Scripture though they may be.

Finally, a search by literary genre can also be useful for determining the popularity and the endurance of each genre throughout the period explored. In our results there are works that were read from the end of the fifteenth century to the middle of the seventeenth century. Some works, however, disappeared swiftly, whereas others changed aspects of content and form. Finally, some genres endured throughout the period in works by various authors, demonstrating evolution in how biblical subject matter was handled.

Biblical Literature in Transformation

During the period 1462–1650, there are some elements of continuity as well as other major changes, which can be considered responses to either continuity or change in religious attitudes as reflected in printed matter. We may wonder if the changes were also due to developments in literary trends. To a certain degree print certainly mirrors the tastes of readers as well as adapting to the requirements of the literary context. For example, this is certainly the case with biblical poems, which first responded to the success of chivalric poems and *cantari*, but later absorbed innovations first found in Tasso's epic poem *Gerusalemme liberata*, which became a favourite model for imitation.

In this long span of printing history, perhaps the most striking factor is the surprising endurance of mystery plays in the form of *rappresentazioni* of biblical events. Not only does the subject matter remain identical, but some of the same texts are reprinted for more than 150 years. The same characters, such

27 The biblical novels by Luigi Manzini are: *Le turbolenze d'Israelle seguite sotto'l gouerno di duo rè Seleuco il Filopatore, ed Antioco il Nobile. Istoria, ed osseruazioni* (Bologna: Clemente Ferroni, 1632); *Le battaglie d'Israelle: istoria e osseruazioni* (Venice: Giacomo Sarzina, 1634), *Vita di Tobia. Historia, e osseruazioni* (Rome: Pietro Antonio Facciotti, 1637), *Flegra in Betuglia. Istoria, e osseruazioni* (Bologna: Domenico Barbieri, 1649); by Anton Giulio Brignole Sale: *Maria Maddalena peccatrice e convertita* (Venice: Pietro Turrini, 1640); by Ferrante Pallavicino: *La Susanna* (Venice: Giacomo Sarzina, 1636), *Il Giuseppe* (Venice: Cristoforo Tommasini, 1637), *Il Sansone* (Venice: Cristoforo Tommasini, 1638), *La Bersabee* (Venice: Bertano, 1639); by Giovan Francesco Loredan, *Adamo* (Venice: Giacomo Sarzina, 1640).

as Abraham, Susanna, Samson, and John the Baptist, dominate the stage from the late fifteenth century right through to the beginning of the seventeenth century. The texts were also reprinted in the same form, as can be seen in the Roman *rappresentazione* of Christ's passion, which first went to print in the fifteenth century and was still in print in the seventeenth century.[28] There are undeniably changes, even in the world of the theatre, but they seem mainly due to improvements in theatrical props and backdrops, and to the development of a dramatic consciousness and thus an acting profession. This process can be seen in the works and paratexts of Giambattista Andreini, who explains how difficult it is to write a tragedy on the Fall from Eden, as it means developing a few lines of Genesis into around twenty-five scenes (five scenes for each of the five acts), with very few words to be performed, and without many of the aids normally used (no set, no costumes, no props).[29]

Some of the changes are clearly identifiable, such as the emergence of a certain tearful or lachrymose sensibility, witnessed by the many poems on the tears of penitent characters such as Peter and Mary Magdalene, or on the sorrow of Christ or the Virgin Mary.[30] It is clear that these poetic inventions tend to represent penitent models in order to inspire a penitential attitude, which appears to be a main element of religiosity in the second half of the sixteenth century, at the height of the post-Tridentine Reformation.

Considering these works in depth, it is possible for us to disrupt some well-established paradigms. Historiography has often underlined the tendency towards exteriority in religious attitudes of the period, but the popular output of poetry and meditations suggests that in the age of Catholic Reformation interiority continued to be cultivated, perhaps even more so than before. However, transformations of biblical works were primarily due to the issuing of the *Index librorum prohibitorum*. The disappearance of Italian translations of the Bible, in their entirety or in part, has already been explained by scholars.[31] The last Italian translations were issued in 1566 and 1567 in Venice, in an interlude between the permission granted by the 1564 *Index*, reintroducing the fourth rule of the Council of Trent, and the confused but restrictive period which followed. These editions still used Malerbi's translation.[32] Thereafter, new or reprinted translations only came from abroad, such as those published in

---

28 Giuliano Dati, Bernardo di Antonio, and Mariano Particappa, *Incomenza la passione di Chrifto hiftoriata in rima vulgari secondo che recita e representa de parola a parola la dignissima compagnia dela Confalone di Roma lo Venerdi santo in luocho dicto Colifeo* ([Rome]: A[ndreas] F[reitag e] J[ohann] B[esicken, *c.* 1496]). The last edition dates from 1604.

29 See the introduction in Andreini, *L'Adamo sacra rappresentatione.*

30 The first edition of Tansillo's *Le lagrime di s. Pietro* is undated, while the second is probably from 1584. It is in fact at the end of the sixteenth and beginning of the seventeenth centuries that we have large numbers of poems on religious weeping.

31 See, for instance, Fragnito, *Proibito capire.*

32 *Bibbia volgare* (Venice: Andrea Muschio, 1566) and *Bibbia volgare* (Venice: Girolamo Scoto, 1566), which came out in two different editions the same year. Eventually, *Bibbia volgare* (Venice: Girolamo Scoto, 1567).

Geneva by the printer Pineroli, or Brucioli's edition of Psalms in 1588, or even Giovanni Diodati's translation in 1607.[33]

Thus, in this period, summaries became a kind of substitute for translation, and were hugely successful publications.[34] However, even as early as 1595, as Gigliola Fragnito has shown, summaries could be suspect. In the memoirs of the inquisitor for Vercelli and Ivrea, Cipriano Uberti, it is stated that 'N.S. Clemente ottavo ha ultimamente dichiarato che non solo [non] si devono permettere le bibbie volgari ma ne anco i libri de gl'Evangelii et Epistole volgari, ne meno i compendii historici della Bibbia' (Pope Clement VIII has recently declared that not only are vernacular Bibles forbidden, but also the books of the vernacular Epistles and Gospels, and even historical summaries of the Bible).[35] Therefore, no compendia or summaries from the previous period were printed. Their place was taken by focused orthodox meditations or sermons. Stories taken from the Bible were not officially prohibited, provided that they did not feature the Bible *nudo texto* (plain text).[36]

The question of the Epistles and Gospels (lectionaries) was a little more complicated, as they were necessary for understanding the liturgy, and so were widely read and sought out even after they were initially prohibited. As we have said, only the Italian *Epistole e vangeli* translated by the Dominican Florentine Remigio Nannini were allowed, and as such were reprinted at least once a year.[37] They continued to be in print until the eighteenth century.

Commentaries were generally permitted, and might even be recommended if considered suitably orthodox. For example, when all translations of Psalms had been forbidden, work by the Franciscan Francesco Panigarola was recommended instead, because his Psalms bore a commentary and the author

---

33 *Il Nuouo Testamento di Giesu Christo nostro signore* ([Geneva], Giovanni Battista Pineroli, 1576); *Sessanta Salmi di Dauid tradotti in rime volgari italiane, secondo la verità del testo hebreo, col Cantico di Simeone e i dieci Comandamenti della legge. Ogni cosa insieme col canto* ([Geneva]: Giovanni Battista Pineroli, 1560) reprinted in 1564, 1566, 1573 and 1578. Antonio Brucioli, *I Salmi tradotti dalla lingua hebrea nella italiana* (Paris: Jamet Mettayer, 1588). Diodati's translation first came out in 1607: *La Bibbia. Cioè i libri del Vecchio e del Nuovo Testamento. Nuovamente traslatati in lingua italiana, da Giovanni Diodati, di nation lucchese* ([Geneva]: [Jean de Tournes <2>], 1607).

34 For example, Dionigi, Bartolomeo, *Compendio historico del Vecchio, e del Nuouo Testamento: cauato dalla sacra Bibbia, et da altri buoni auttori [...]. Nelquale si descriuono tutte le cose notabili, che successero nel popolo hebreo, dalla creatione del mondo, sino alla vltima destruttione di Ierusalem. Et la vita di Giesu Christo, saluator del mondo, nuouamente reuisto, et ornato di belle, e vaghe figure, con la disseminatione dell'euangelo, e della sua santa fede [...]* (Venice: Valerio Bonelli. 1587); Miliani, Crisostomo, *Sommario historico raccolto dalla Sacra Bibbia, dal Flauio, da Egesippo, et da altri scrittori, e di belle, e varie figure ornato [...]. Con la vita, passione, morte, e risurrettione di Christo nostro Saluatore* (Bergamo: Comin Ventura, 1590).

35 Fragnito, *La Bibbia al rogo*, p. 184. Translations are all mine.

36 See Fragnito, *La Bibbia al rogo*, p. 207.

37 On the success of this bestseller, see Barbieri, 'L'edizione delle *Epistole e vangeli* di Remigio fiorentino', and Zardin, 'Circolazione e usi delle *Epistole e vangeli* nell'Italia post-tridentina'.

was considered a highly observant Catholic.[38] In fact, in a letter dated 1597 Agostino Valier, a member of the Congregation of the Index, announced to the inquisitors that the pope wanted: 'conforme alla Regola 4° dell'Indice, permettere gl'Evangeli, e salmi volgari, che hanno congionto meditatione, espositione, annotatione, parafrasi cattolica del Panigarola, Remigio [Nannini], e simili, permettendo il Flos sanctorum di Alfonso Villega, prohibendosi affatto il Breviario volgare' (According to the fourth rule of the index, to allow the vernacular Gospels and Psalms, which are accompanied by meditations, expositions, annotations, and Catholic paraphrases by Panigarola, Remigio [Nannini], and others, allowing the *Flos sanctorum* by Alfonso Villega, and totally forbidding the vernacular breviary).[39]

The prohibition extended to the *Bibbie figurate*, which had been popular for decades.[40] In their place new products, conforming to orthodox standards and perfected by new printing techniques, were put on the market. Nadal's Evangelical illustrations were very successful and were soon translated into Italian.[41] Biblical illustrations tended either towards realistic representation or towards more symbolic representation through the use of emblems.[42]

Even the very popular *Meditationes vitae Christi*, a book widely read in Italy and at the time attributed to Saint Bonaventure, were touched by censorship, because the book was largely based on apocryphal texts as well as the Gospels.[43] This small book circulated widely in manuscript, and was reprinted in many editions from the fifteenth century onwards; it was never explicitly prohibited and was still reprinted, if less often. However, its place was challenged by other texts which better combined explanation with biblical passages.[44]

It seems evident from the records studied by Fragnito and presented above that even the Congregation of the Index and the Sant'Offizio considered various biblical literary genres in their decisions. In fact, much attention was paid to the prohibition of biblical poems, that is, biblical stories recounted

38 Francesco Panigarola, *Dichiaratione dei salmi di David [...] Alla serenissima Infantew signora duchessa di Savoia* (Florence: Filippo Giunta <2> e Iacopo Giunta <2>, 1585).

39 Fragnito, *La Bibbia al rogo*, p. 201.

40 Fragnito, *La Bibbia al rogo*, pp. 308–09.

41 A good example is the Italian translation of Jerome Nadal, *Euangelicae historiae imagines* (Antwerp: Martinus Nutius, 1595) by Vivaldi, Agostino, *Meditationi sopra li Euangelii che tutto l'anno si leggono nella messa, & principali misterij della vita, & passione di nostro Signore. Composte dal r.p. Agostino Viualdi della Compagnia di Giesu. Respondenti alle imagini del padre Girolamo Natale della medesima Compagnia* (Rome: Luigi Zanetti, 1599).

42 Such emblem figurations are well represented by the biblical *imprese* included in Paolo Aresi's *Imprese sacre*, a multivolume work edited in Milan and Tortona between 1616 and 1635. On the topic, see *Emblemata sacra. Rhétorique et Herméneutique du discours sacré*, ed. by Dekoninck and Guiderdoni-Bruslé.

43 On the popularity of this genre, see Barbieri, 'Forme e tipologie'.

44 For the suggested substitutes, see Fragnito, *La Bibbia al rogo*, p. 202, and Fragnito, *Proibito capire*, p. 103.

in verse. They were included in the 1574 and 1583 Indexes. The Clementine *Index* was less clear than a later decree issued in 1601, stating that only poetry which declares that the 'Sacrae scripturae textum simpliciter [...] et nudam eius versionem' (The text of the Sacred Scriptures in a faithful and literary translation) was forbidden, but not those poems that 'ex Sacra Scriptura et eius partibus diversas hystorias aut materias assumant pro subiecto poematis' (that take their matter and histories from the Sacred Scripures as the subject of their poetry).[45] Therefore it is possible to find poems which embellish upon biblical stories, such as the participation of a mythical king of Fiesole in the war of the Israelites (led by Saul) against the Philistines. This poem, *Davide perseguitato e fuggitivo*, by Maddalena Salvetti Acciaioli was not forbidden, but the reader is never informed that it is a mixture of biblical history and mythology, not a true account.[46] There were strict controls on plays which reproduced biblical events, as Fragnito shows, and some writers had problems publishing their works. However, the theatre was so richly creative at this time that new genres were created in response to censorship, including biblical tragedies, *oratori*, and melodramas.[47]

In this climate, homilies probably remained the genre most free from the attacks of censorship, because preachers were subject to severe scrutiny. It would have been almost impossible to have, after this period, figures such as Bernardino Ochino or preachers who could be attacked for their (lack of) orthodoxy, even if a later collection of sermons, *Serafici splendori*, by the Capuchin Mario de' Bignoni, was prohibited.[48] The spread of collections of sermons at the end of the sixteenth and beginning of the seventeenth centuries is due to the fact that the congregation required sermons in order to understand and appreciate Holy Scriptures in the vernacular. The importance assigned to preaching in the Church's Reformation at Trent made the sermon a fashionable genre, to the point that the poet Giovan Battista Marino even wrote three sermons. He was not a preacher, merely a lay poet wishing to explore a new genre, and yet he became a model for Italian preachers for almost a century afterwards.[49]

Conclusion

It may seem strange that a literary perspective can determine research in a religious field and especially research into the use of the foundational religious text, the Bible. But the work over many years to compile a catalogue of printed biblical books in Italian from the beginning of printing up until

---

45 Fragnito, *La Bibbia al rogo*, p. 207.

46 Salvetti Acciaioli, Maddalena, *Il Davide perseguitato o vero fuggitivo* (Florence: Giovanni Antonio Cataneo, 1612).

47 On this event, see Fabrizio-Costa, 'De quelques emplois des thèmes alchimiques'.

48 Fragnito, *La Bibbia al rogo*, p. 207.

49 Giovan Battista Marino, *Dicerie sacre* (Turin: L. Pizzamiglio, 1614).

1650 has shown the suitability of such an approach. Writing, as with every form of linguistic expression, is determined by codes of communication and their rules, which are subject to prevailing usage and the models in fashion at the time. Renaissance writing was particularly highly codified, and authors depended largely on rhetorical precursors for inspiration. Even though biblical subject matter has always been incorporated into different kind of texts, with the age of print and the wide diffusion of books the early modern period created new ways of writing and transmitting sacred matter. Authors elaborated on their sources and found inspiration to convey biblical subjects in a suitable fashion, playing an important role in the religious turmoil of the sixteenth century and enjoying great influence over the social and intellectual world in which they lived.

Works Cited

Primary Sources

Andreini, Giambattista, *L'Adamo sacra rappresentatione. Alla m.ta christ.ma di Maria de Medici reina di Francia. Dedicata* (Milan: Girolamo Bordoni, 1613)

Lettera al Papa: Paolo Giustiniani e Pietro Quirini, ed. by Geminiano Bianchini (Modena: Artioli, 1995)

Secondary Studies

Ardissino, Erminia, and Élise Boillet, *Repertorio di letteratura biblica in italiano a stampa (ca 1462–1650)*, Études Renaissantes, 27 (Turnhout: Brepols, forthcoming [2023])

Barbieri, Edoardo, *Le Bibbie italiane del Quattrocento e del Cinquecento* (Milan: Editrice Bibliografica, 1991–1992)

———, 'L'edizione delle *Epistole e vangeli* di Remigio fiorentino: un *long seller* biblico', in *Gli Italiani e la Bibbia nella prima età moderna: Leggere, interpretare, riscrivere*, ed. by Erminia Ardissino and Élise Boillet, Études Renaissantes, 28 (Turnhout: Brepols, 2018), pp. 43–72

———, 'Forme e tipologie delle *Vitae Christi* negli incunaboli volgari italiani', in *L'agiografia volgare: Tradizioni di testi, motivi e linguaggi. Atti del congresso internazionale, Klagenfurt, 15–16 gennaio 2015*, ed. by Elisa De Roberto and Wilhem Raymund (Heidelberg: Universitätsverlag Winter, 2016), pp. 351–82

———, *Panorama delle traduzioni bibliche in volgare prima del Concilio di Trento* (Milan: C.R.E.L.E.B. – Università Cattolica-Edizioni CUSL, 2011)

La Bibbia: Edizioni del 16. secolo, ed. by Antonella Lumini (Florence: L. S. Olschki, 2000)

Campi, Emidio, and Marian Delgado, 'Bibles in Italian and Spain', in *The New Cambridge History of the Bible*, ed. by Euan Cameron (Cambridge: Cambridge University Press, 2016), pp. 358–83

Church, Censorship and Culture in Early Modern Italy, ed. by Gigliola Fragnito (Cambridge: Cambridge University Press, 2001)

Dondi, Cristina, *Printed Books of Hours from 15th-Century Italy: The Transmission of the Texts, the Circulation of the Books* (Firenze, Olschki, 2016)

Emblemata sacra: Rhétorique et Herméneutique du discours sacré dans la litérature en images/The Rhetoric and Hermeneutics of Illustrated Sacred Discourse, ed. by Ralph Dekoninck and Agnès Guiderdoni-Bruslé (Turnhout: Brepols, 2007)

Folena, Gianfranco, *Volgarizzare e tradurre* (Turin: Einaudi, 1991)

Fabrizio-Costa, Silvia, 'De quelques emplois des thèmes alchimiques dans l'art oratoire italien du XVIIe siècle', *Chrysopoeia*, 3 (1989), 135–62

Fragnito, Gigliola, *La Bibbia al rogo: La censura ecclesiastica e i volgarizzamenti della Scrittura (1471–1605)* (Bologna: il Mulino, 1997)

———, *Proibito capire: La Chiesa e il volgare nella prima età moderna* (Bologna: il Mulino, 2005)

Frye, Northrop, *The Great Code: The Bible and Literature* (New York: Harcourt Brace Jovanovich, 1982)

Genette, Gérard, *Palinsesti: La letteratura al secondo grado*, [1st French ed. 1982], trans. into Italian by Raffaella Novità (Turin: Einaudi, 1997)

Gow, Andrew C., 'Challenging the Protestant Paradigm: Bible Reading in Lay and Urban Contexts of the Late Middle Ages', in *Scripture and Pluralism: Reading the Bible in the Religiously Plural Worlds of the Middle Ages and Renaissance*, ed. by Thomas J. Heffernan and Thomas E. Burnan (Leiden: Brill, 2005), pp. 161–92

———, 'The Contested History of a Book: The German Bible of the Later Middle Ages and the Reformation in Legend, Ideology, and Scholarship', *The Journal of Hebrew Scriptures*, 9 (2009), 1–37

Green, Lawrence D., 'The Reception of Aristotle's *Rhetoric* in the Renaissance', in *Peripatetic Rhetoric after Aristotle*, ed. by William W. Fortenbaugh and David C. Mirhady (New Brunswick: Transactions, 1994), pp. 320–48

Jacobson Schutte, Anne, *Printed Italian Vernacular Religious Books 1465–1550: A Finding List* (Geneva: Droz, 1983)

Korotkoff, Elie, "Traduttore traditore'? Réflexions à partir d'une expérience de traduction de textes liturgiques', in *Les mouvements liturgiques: corrélations entre pratiques et recherches: Conférences Saint-Serge: 50. Semaine d'études liturgiques, Paris 23–26 juin 2003*, ed. by Carlo Braga and Alessandro Pistoia (Rome: CLV Ed. Liturgiche, 2003), pp. 173–84

Libri, biblioteche e cultura nell'Italia del Cinque e Seicento, ed. by Edoardo Barbieri and Danilo Zardin (Milan: Vita e Pensiero, 2002)

Le masque de l'écriture: Philosophie et traduction de la Renaissance aux Lumières, ed. by Charles Le Blanc and Luisa Simonutti (Geneva: Droz, 2015)

Quondam, Amedeo, 'Note sulla tradizione della poesia spirituale e religiosa', in *Paradigmi e tradizioni*, ed. by Amedeo Quondam (Rome: Bulzoni, 2005), pp. 127–282

Retelling the Bible: Literary, Historical, and Social Contexts, ed. by Lucie Doležalová and Tamás Visi (Frankfurt am Main: Peter Lang, 2011)

Rewritten Bible after Fifty Years: Texts, Terms, or Techniques? A Last Dialogue with Géza Vermès, ed. by József Zsengellér (Leiden: Brill, 2014)
Rewritten Bible Reconsidered: Proceedings of the Conference in Karkku, Finland, August 24–26, 2006, ed. by Antti Laato and Jacques van Ruiten (Winona Lake: Eisenbrauns, 2008)
Rozzo, Ugo, *Linee per una storia dell'editoria religiosa in Italia 1465–1600* (Udine: Arti grafiche friulane, 1993)
Rozzo, Ugo, and Rudj Gorian, *Il libro religioso* (Milan: Edizioni Sylvestre Bonnard, 2002)
Sberlati, Francesco, *Il genere e la disputa: La poetica tra Ariosto e Tasso* (Rome: Bulzoni, 2001)
Segre, Cesare, *Avviamento all'analisi del testo letterario* (Turin: Einaudi, 1985)
Traduire les Anciens en Europe du Quattrocento à la fin du 18ème siècle, ed. by Laurance Bernard-Pradelle and Claire Lechevalier (Paris: PUPS, 2012)
Vermès, Géza, *Scripture and Tradition in Judaism: Haggadic Studies* (Leiden: Brill, 1961)
Zardin, Danilo, 'Bibbia e letteratura religiosa in volgare nell'Italia del Cinque-Seicento', *Annali di storia moderna e contemporanea*, 4 (1998), 593–616
———, 'Circolazione e usi delle *Epistole e vangeli* nell'Italia post-tridentina', in *Gli Italiani e la Bibbia nella prima età moderna: Leggere, interpretare, riscrivere*, ed. by Erminia Ardissino and Élise Boillet, Études Renaissantes, 28 (Turnhout: Brepols, 2018), pp. 97–124

ÉLISE BOILLET

Printed Italian Vernacular Biblical Literature

Religious Transformation from the Beginnings of the Printing Press to the Mid-Seventeenth Century

The forthcoming catalogue of early modern printed Italian vernacular biblical literature edited by Erminia Ardissino and myself seeks to reconstruct an editorial production which is especially relevant for the study of Italian religious culture as both an integrated and a specific part of Western European religious culture.[1] This essay will focus on the chronological issues relating to the catalogue. Firstly, it will give an overview of the current state of knowledge with the aim of setting out the various chronological boundaries discussed by historians. Secondly, it will explain the choice of a large framework, bringing the notion of 'religious transformation' to the discussion; this has been at the core of the COST Action project 'New Communities of Interpretation' and it allows us to put in perspective the drastic changes traditionally associated with the Reformation and the Counter-Reformation. Finally, it will focus on the year 1570, since this is the *terminus ante quem* of the COST Action project, in order to qualify this date within this process of transformation.

Printed Italian Vernacular Biblical Literature and Italian Religious History

Italian religious historiography has focused, on the one hand, on the penetration of heterodox religious ideas — those drawn from the Protestant Reformers but also derived from Erasmus's and Juan de Valdés' thinking —

1 *Repertorio di letteratura biblica in italiano a stampa (ca 1462–1650)*. This long-term undertaking began within the research project 'The Laity and the Bible: Religious Reading in Early Modern Europe' supported by LE STUDIUM Loire Valley Institute for Advanced Studies and carried out at the Centre d'études supérieures de la Renaissance (CESR) of the University of Tours in 2015.

Élise Boillet • (elise.boillet@univ-tours.fr) is a CNRS researcher at the Centre d'études supérieures de la Renaissance of the University of Tours, France.

Religious Transformations in New Communities of Interpretation in Europe (1350–1570): Bridging the Historiographical Divides, ed. by Élise Boillet and Ian Johnson, New Communities of Interpretation, 3 (Turnhout: Brepols, 2022), pp. 115–131.

DOI 10.1484/M.NCI-EB.5.131217

and, on the other, on the reaction of the Roman Catholic Church against them. This reaction, based on the re-foundation of the Roman Inquisition in 1542 and the re-definition of Catholic orthodoxy during the Council of Trent held between 1545 and 1563, has been described as late, given that Lutheran ideas had been penetrating Italy since the 1520s, but also as having been very effective so quickly after its launch. Indeed, from the early 1540s, the Italian supporters of the Reformation fled their country, while people sympathetic to the new faith but opposed to any religious schism remained in Italy and represented moderate positions which were increasingly hard to sustain in a context soon dominated by intransigent Catholics. While lay reading of the Bible in the vernacular was promoted by people from various socio-cultural and religious backgrounds (from humanists to *spirituali* and heretics), the Roman Catholic Church came to ban biblical translations in the vernacular in its universal indexes of prohibited books: the 1558 Pauline Index (published in 1559) imposed a very strict ban, which was attenuated by the 1564 Tridentine Index, but finally reinstated by the 1596 Clementine Index. While Paul F. Grendler has described the Pauline Index as 'the turning-point for the freedom of enquiry in the Catholic world', Gigliola Fragnito has illustrated the complex and non-linear history of sixteenth-century ecclesiastical censorship and has discussed its profound and lasting consequences on Italian literacy and the ability of the Italians to think critically.[2]

The field of printed Italian vernacular religious literature, including biblical literature, was first mapped by Anne Jacobson Schutte, who chose a chronological framework going from the birth of the printing press to the mid-fifteenth century.[3] She intended what she called her 'finding list' as a tool to investigate the range of publications to which Italians could have had access before the dissemination of Protestant ideas.[4] She aimed to look into what Italians interested in religion were reading during the late fifteenth and the first half of the sixteenth centuries, thus allowing us to understand the reasons for the failure of the *spirituali* to influence the Catholic Reformation.[5] The chosen *terminus ante quem* made sense with regard to the fact that, according to her, by about 1550 most of the *momentum* of Italian Evangelism was gone, while before 1550 very few works expressing Counter-Reformation piety had

2 Grendler, 'Printing and Censorship', pp. 45–46. Gigliola Fragnito discusses the linguistic and cultural consequences of the Roman ban on vernacular translations of the Bible in Italy in Fragnito, *Proibito capire*, pp. 287–300.

3 Jacobson Schutte, *Printed Italian Vernacular Religious Books*. The complete title of the book qualifies it as 'A Finding List'. The *terminus post quem* is the establishment of the first Italian press at Subiaco in 1465.

4 In a paper published three years earlier, the scholar had indeed focused on the printed Italian religious literature prior to the 1520s: Jacobson Schutte, 'Printing, Piety, and the People in Italy'.

5 Jacobson Schutte, *Printed Italian Vernacular Religious Books*, pp. 1–2.

appeared.[6] Since Jacobson Schutte's enquiries, research has shown that religious dissent was still alive in the 1560s.[7] Furthermore, certain biblical publications of the last decades of the sixteenth century show that religious ideas rooted in earlier reformation movements were still circulating.[8]

In an essay dedicated to the history of religious printing in Italy, Ugo Rozzo chose a later *terminus ante quem*, namely the end of the sixteenth century.[9] Indeed, considering that 'the printed book was born as religious',[10] and that religious books remained essential in the printing industry in terms of the number of titles and print runs, he wanted specifically to explore this significant production and its influence on the evolution of the market for printed books. He divided his essay into three chapters corresponding to three phases: first, the era of *incunabula* (characterized in particular by the publication of Nicolò Malerbi's vernacular translation of the Bible and Girolamo Savonarola's works); then the period of the Reformation and the Council of Trent (marked by Antonio Brucioli's new vernacular translation of the Bible, the diffusion of heterodox works, and the Catholic reaction against this new literature); and finally the triumph of the Counter-Reformation (which saw, in particular, revised versions of Catholic catechisms, mass books, and prayer books associating Latin with the vernacular, as well as many vernacular penitential works derived from the Bible). The inventory of more than 9500 Italian religious libraries, which was carried out between 1599 and 1602, reflects the cultural project which aimed to saturate the print market with authorized works, as defined by Antonio Possevino in his *Bibliotheca selecta* published in 1593.[11] But the inventory also registers the anomalous presence of heretical literature, revealing the limitations of ecclesiastical censorship even in religious institutions supposedly under total control.[12] While making it clear that the lay readership, having been targeted by the proponents of opposing programmes of religious reform, broadened during the sixteenth century, Ugo Rozzo's historical overview invited us to look carefully at the biblical literature actually available in the print market in the second half of the century.

Since Rozzo's study, Edoardo Barbieri and Gigliola Fragnito have shed much light on the issue of Italian vernacular translations of the Bible. The catalogue published by Barbieri in 1992 proved the long and rich presence of the Italian vernacular Bible in Italy during the fifteenth and sixteenth

6 Jacobson Schutte, *Printed Italian Vernacular Religious Books*, p. 4.

7 For instance, in Modena, heresy was eradicated through the inquisitorial trials held between 1566 and 1569. See Firpo, *Riforma protestante*, pp. 68–69.

8 An illustration, also related to Modena, is given in Boillet, 'Pellegrino degli Erri', pp. 177–81 and Boillet, '*I Salmi di David* de Pellegrino degli Erri'.

9 Rozzo, *Linee per una storia dell'editoria religiosa*.

10 'Il libro a stampa nasce "religioso"', Rozzo, *Linee per una storia dell'editoria religiosa*, p. 7.

11 Rozzo, *Linee per una storia dell'editoria religiosa*, pp. 109, 111, 115–16.

12 Rozzo, *Linee per una storia dell'editoria religiosa*, pp. 113–19.

centuries.[13] Taking into account the translations of either the whole Bible or a single book within the Bible, the catalogue underlines the importance not only of the translation referring to the original sources by the layman Antonio Brucioli, but also of the translation from the Vulgate by the monk Nicolò Malerbi. While Brucioli's translation was printed for the first time in 1532 and banned in 1558, Malerbi's translation first appeared in 1471 and was re-edited several times up to 1567; it was the last complete vernacular Bible to be printed in Italy in the sixteenth century. After Malerbi's Bible in 1567, only David de' Pomi's Ecclesiastes was printed in Italy (Venice) in 1571, while translations by Brucioli, Filippo Rustici, and anonymous authors were printed in Paris, Geneva, and Nuremberg. This context determined the *terminus ante quem* chosen by Barbieri, which allows us to witness the end of the publication of vernacular Bibles in Italy.

In her seminal work published in 1997, Gigliola Fragnito reconstructed the complex history of the Roman censorship of vernacular translations of the Bible until the ban imposed by the Clementine Index in 1596 and the provisions for its implementation in the following years.[14] It was only when Benedict XIV's 1753 bull *Sollicita ac provida* was published at the beginning of the Index of 1758 that a new watershed in the history of censorship was marked. This circumstance made the implementation of the Clementine Index in the years after its promulgation the most eligible *terminus ante quem* for an enquiry into ecclesiastical censorship and vernacular translations of the Bible.

Very importantly, however, Gigliola Fragnito has shown that ecclesiastical censorship addressed not only vernacular translations of the Bible in the strictest sense, but also a whole range of vernacular books with biblical contents. Indeed, biblical material (texts and stories) could be found in many different genres, from anthologies such as the *Gospels and Epistles* to spiritual books such as meditations on the passion of Christ. The definition of 'translations' was a principal issue at the time of the implementation of the Clementine Index, with local authorities wondering to what extent they should apply such a drastic ban, and with many Italian laypeople, literate women for the most, not only declaring their incomprehension but also showing their resistance.[15] In parallel, after having identified all Italian translations of the Bible in the strictest sense, Edoardo Barbieri also paid attention to other types of texts, such as translations rearranged in an abridged version or accompanied by a commentary.[16] He then looked at this production within the larger category

13 Barbieri, *Le Bibbie italiane*. See also Barbieri, 'La fortuna della Bibbia vulgarizzata di Niccolò Malerbi'.

14 Fragnito, *La Bibbia al rogo*. By 1603 the Congregation of the Index received the lists, compiled by local inquisitors, of prohibited books in possession of laypeople and secular and regular clergy: Fragnito, *La Bibbia al rogo*, pp. 241 and 244.

15 Fragnito, *Proibito capire*, pp. 213–31 and 275–87.

16 Barbieri, 'Panorama [...]: Parte I' and 'Panorama [...]: Parte II'.

of spiritual literature, underlining the continuity of biblical knowledge among lay and ecclesiastical Italians from the fifteenth to the sixteenth century.[17]

These enquiries into what kinds of texts were produced at this time and should therefore be now considered as biblical translations, have allowed us to see better the details of the issue of access to the Bible in the vernacular in sixteenth-century Italy. Danilo Zardin has suggested that the investigation should extend beyond the end of the sixteenth century, when an attenuation of ecclesiastical control allowed a revival of biblical literature which would not have been possible if a large range of biblical texts had not continued to circulate despite the ban.[18] He proposed a connection between the editorial production of the sixteenth century to that of the seventeenth century also for another reason, that is, the literary character of many biblical texts of the time.[19] As a matter of fact, in the last two decades, literary historians have become more and more interested in the connection between literary involvement and interest in the Bible as both a religious and a literary text, given that the authors of biblical writings were well aware of Scripture's narrative and poetic qualities. Two important essay collections, one edited by Carlo Delcorno and Giovanni Baffetti, and the other by these scholars and Ginetta Auzzas, have drawn attention to literary works derived from the Bible within a broad chronological framework ranging from the thirteenth to the sixteenth centuries.[20] Afterwards, in his census of, and essay on, the vast production of Italian spiritual poetry (including biblical poetry), Amedeo Quondam has focused on the already vast enough sixteenth-century production.[21] Carlo Delcorno and Maria Luisa Doglio, however, have then connected the spiritual poetry of the sixteenth century to that of the seventeenth century.[22]

---

17 Barbieri, 'Fra tradizione e cambiamento'.

18 Zardin, 'Bibbia e letteratura religiosa in volgare'.

19 Such as the commentary on the penitential Psalms by Francesco Panigarola, in Zardin, 'Tra latino e volgare'. Edoardo Barbieri has also underlined that biblical literature has long been neglected by literary researchers because of its essentially non-literary purpose, suggesting that these books were not written by their authors nor published by their editors for literary reasons (Barbieri, 'Fra tradizione e cambiamento', p. 9). But the reason why historians of modern literature have disdained this category of texts for so long has had more to do with considering profane literature as the true illustration of an Italian modernity conditioned neither by ecclesiastical control nor by foreign domination.

20 *Sotto il cielo delle Scritture*; *Letteratura in forma di sermoni*.

21 This research was conducted using the online catalogue Edit16, which has since continued to be enriched (Quondam, 'Note sulla tradizione della poesia spirituale', p. 139). An essential example of biblical poetry is the very successful genre of penitential poetry consisting of rewritings of the penitential Psalms and 'tears' of Mary Magdalene, Peter, the Virgin Mary, and Jesus Christ (Quondam, 'Note sulla tradizione della poesia spirituale', pp. 189–96). On penitential poetry, see also *La Bibbia in poesia*, ed. by Pettinelli, Morace, Pellegrino, and Vignuzzi.

22 See *Rime sacre*, ed. by Doglio and Delcorno.

Drastic Changes vs Progressive Transformations

As this brief overview shows, among all the factors that caused change, the confessional paradigm has strongly oriented the aims of research on Italian vernacular biblical literature and thus its chronological boundaries. Early modern Italian religious identity has been seen in the development and failure of Evangelism and the Reformation in the face of a soon triumphant Counter-Reformation which forbade the faithful direct access to the Bible and promoted essential doctrinal instruction by priests and preachers. An illustration is given by the many collections of sermons printed from the second half of the sixteenth century on. But it has to be stressed that amongst such productions there was a significant number of collections of exegetical homilies which provided, after or opposite the Latin biblical verses, a vernacular explanation often expanding on a word-by-word translation, so that a reader who was not a Latin scholar could nonetheless connect the Latin text with the Italian version.[23] Furthermore, during the Counter-Reformation, besides the disappearance of biblical translations in the strictest sense and the parallel abundance of some specific genres, such as the aforementioned collections of sermons, the field of vernacular biblical literature maintained an interesting variety of texts in verse and in prose very close to translation, such as paraphrases, meditations, commentaries, and other rewritings.[24] The field of vernacular biblical literature, still under-explored, needs to be better investigated.

On the other hand, as mentioned earlier, beside the stress put on the historical divides associated with the sixteenth-century religious reformation movements, scholars have underlined the laity's interest in the Bible as a characteristic feature of the period from the late Middle Ages to the early modern era. The forthcoming catalogue of Italian vernacular biblical books printed from the beginnings of the printing press to the mid-seventeenth century allows one to see, just by looking at the titles of the publications, that answering the lay demand with books useful 'for all' was regarded as important. Indeed, while literate lay men and women claimed the right to study the Bible and share their experience and knowledge through vernacular biblical works, members of both the old and new religious orders competed not only to educate and supervise specific ecclesiastical audiences, such as nuns, parish priests, and preachers, but also to address the lay devout.[25]

For these reasons, the analysis of change in Italian vernacular biblical production would certainly benefit from the nuanced idea of 'religious

---

23 On the collections of biblical sermons, see Boillet, 'Vernacular Sermons on the Psalms'. On the evolution of the coexistence of Latin and the vernacular in sermons re-edited several times between 1524 and 1573, see Boillet, 'La fortune du *Psalterio Davitico* de Lodovico Pittorio'.

24 On the range of vernacular books on the Psalms printed in sixteenth-century Italy, see Boillet, 'Vernacular Biblical Literature'.

25 See Boillet, 'For Early Modern Printed Biblical Literature in Italian'.

transformations' at the core of the COST Action 'New Communities of Interpretation'. Indeed, it seems that its evolution cannot be reduced to the immediate and triumphant success of ecclesiastical censorship with the instantaneous destruction of an entire heritage and the quick transition from freely shared biblical knowledge to tyrannical doctrinal propaganda. Descriptions of the transformations which took place over the whole period under consideration have to take into account the results of the continuous negotiation between different lay and ecclesiastical constituencies, as illustrated by Italian printed biblical production.

The forthcoming catalogue thus intends to give a long view of Italian biblical production from before the Reformation to well after the provisions issued by the Catholic Church against it, combining the so-called 'long fifteenth century' and 'long sixteenth century' perspectives. As for the *terminus post quem*, the publications became continuous from 1470 with several titles each year. But as evidence of an older text — a Passion of Christ probably printed in northern Italy *c.* 1462–1463 — was found, this date was registered as the starting point of the research.[26] As for the *terminus ante quem*, it was essential to cover the whole sixteenth century as well as to cross into the seventeenth century. Indeed, not only the vast and various productions of the last decades of the sixteenth century, but also production subsequent to the 1596 Clementine Index still need to be explored further. For instance, it is remarkable that the biblical paraphrases by Pietro Aretino, banned from 1557, were all re-edited in Venice around 1630.[27] The year 1650 is not related to any specific historical event, but roughly corresponds to the end of a process of transformation: after Urban VIII's pontificate, which finished with the endorsing of the cultural orientations of the Counter-Reformation, the second half of the century was characterized by a decrease in the vitality of biblical production. But the fact that vernacular biblical literature did not disappear after the 1596 Index but adapted in response to it certainly contributed to the possibility of a renewal of demand at the end of the seventeenth century, leading to Pope Benedict XIV's decision to lift the ban on vernacular biblical translations in 1758.

In the history of printed Italian vernacular biblical literature reconstructed by the forthcoming catalogue, it is worth paying attention to the date selected as *terminus ante quem* by the COST Action 'New Communities of Interpretation'. This project aimed to elucidate religious transformations in Europe during

---

26 ISTC (ip00147000) also suggests: '[Southern Germany?: n. pr., about 1462] and [Parma: Damianus de Moyllis, about 1470?]. It is a fragment of twelve leaves from an octavo originally made up of seventeen leaves with full-page illustrations.

27 The *Humanity of Christ* and the *Life of the Virgin Mary* were banned from 1557 and all Aretino's works, including the religious ones, were banned repeatedly: in 1559, 1564, 1590, and 1593. The seventeenth-century re-editions were printed in Venice under the anagram Partenio Etiro, while the edition printed in Lyon by Guillaume Barbier in 1648 (*Aretino pentito, cioè Parafrasi sovra i sette Salmi della Penitenza di Davide*) included the name of the author as part of the title of the work. See Boillet, 'David, personnage et masque'.

the 'long fifteenth century', that is, between the late Middle Ages and the early modern era. It was thought important to include the period of the Council of Trent, so as to have a more comprehensive view of the transformations which eventually led to a religiously fragmented Europe. Since the Council of Trent can be interpreted not only as one of the end points of this process but also as the foundation of the Counter-Reformation, which went on until the mid-seventeenth century, this choice gave a good opportunity for specialists in the 'long fifteenth century' and the 'long sixteenth century' to connect their respective approaches better. In the specific field of printed Italian vernacular biblical literature, combining these two chronological perspectives helps to shed light on the year 1570 in the midst of a long process of transformation.

The Year 1570

The fourth rule of the 1564 Tridentine Index empowered local ecclesiastical authorities (bishops and inquisitors) to give permission to some trustworthy readers to possess and read vernacular translations of the Bible.[28] But the commission of cardinals in charge of the revision of the Index appointed in 1571 and formalized in 1572 by Pope Gregory XIII as the Congregation of the Index,[29] immediately expressed the intention of returning to the strictest provisions of the 1558 Pauline Index (published in 1559).[30] Indeed, from that moment, the three Roman bodies in charge of censorship — the Congregation of the Index, the Congregation of the Holy Office, and the Master of the Sacred Palace — began to send to local inquisitors very severe guidelines against vernacular translations of the Bible, especially those in verse.[31] In 1583, they went so far as stipulating that the fourth rule of the Tridentine Index should not be applied.[32] These Roman decisions did not cancel the universal Tridentine Index, which remained in force until the 1596 Clementine Index, but in Italy they probably contributed to a confused and variable situation which tended towards a more severe atmosphere.

As we saw earlier, no vernacular translation of the Bible was printed after 1571. But the forthcoming catalogue shows that between the Index of Paul IV (promulgated in December 1558 and printed in 1559)[33] and the Clementine

28 Fragnito, *La Bibbia al rogo*, p. 98.

29 Fragnito, *La Bibbia al rogo*, p. 115.

30 Fragnito, *La Bibbia al rogo*, pp. 119–20.

31 On censorship between 1571 and 1583, see Fragnito, *La Bibbia al rogo*, pp. 121–42.

32 In January 1583, the Congregation of the Index decided on a strict ban of the vernacular Bibles despite the rule of the Tridentine Index (Fragnito, *La Bibbia al rogo*, p. 138). In July 1583 and April 1584, the Congregation of the Inquisition gave the instruction to the inquisitor of Venice not to release any permission to possess and read vernacular Bibles (Fragnito, *La Bibbia al rogo*, pp. 135–36).

33 Fragnito, *La Bibbia al rogo*, pp. 83–85.

Index (promulgated in March 1596), there were about 1280 editions of biblical books. Before this period, more than thirty editions a year were printed in 1539, at the end of a decade marked by renewed activity in biblical production initiated by Antonio Brucioli's publications and fed by Pietro Aretino's works. Additionally, Pietro Bembo, the famous author of the *Prose della volgar lingua*, had become a cardinal in 1539, and his nomination had constituted an immediate incentive for men of letters to show their literary skills in the religious field. After the 1564 Tridentine Index mitigated the severity of the Pauline Index, the number of thirty editions (already reached once in 1562) was very often reached and exceeded from 1566 (twenty-nine that year). In the mid-1570s, that is, when the Roman authorities, despite the Tridentine Index still being in force, began to send stricter directives, a decrease to around twenty editions is visible in 1574, 1576 and 1577, production then increased again from 1578 and reached fifty editions for several years from 1585 to 1592. Only from the 1620s, did the figures decrease significantly; they remained between approximately twenty and thirty editions until 1650, and under twenty editions only in some years during the 1620s and the 1630s.

The still-abundant production of vernacular biblical texts in the last three decades of the sixteenth century may be attributed to a number of factors. Modern scholarship on editions of Italian vernacular Bibles demonstrates their well-rooted presence in Italy before sixteenth-century ecclesiastical censorship came to interfere in what had grown to be a luxurious and lucrative printing market. Study of the archives of the Holy Office and other ecclesiastical documents has revealed not only a variety of opinions at the head of the Roman Catholic Church preventing any early consensus, but also tensions amongst the three Roman bodies in charge of censorship, and between the central authorities and the local power of bishops and inquisitors. The forthcoming catalogue will help to confirm these facts from within the vast corpus of vernacular biblical literature; it will draw attention to the many and various initiatives of lay and ecclesiastical authors willing, as individuals and as representatives of specific *milieux* and institutions (movements of religious reformation, lay and ecclesiastical courts, literary academies, devout circles, lay confraternities, religious orders, and so on), to take part in the debate by putting onto the print market what they considered necessary to support the religious life of both clergy and laity.

The case of the Psalms is paradigmatic, as they became not only an essential text in the Lutheran and Calvinist liturgy, but also one of the most frequently translated, paraphrased, and commented texts in Italy in the second half of the sixteenth century.[34] The translation of the penitential Psalms, with accompanying commentary, published in Novara in 1572 by Domenico Buelli, inquisitor of the city, is of particular interest, as it concretely and explicitly

34 See Morace, 'I Salmi tra Riforma e Controriforma', p. 55.

echoes the debate on vernacular biblical translation.[35] There is evidence that some inquisitors made extensive use of the fourth rule of the Tridentine Index, willingly granting licences for the reading of vernacular Bibles.[36] That an inquisitor who had proved himself to be a particularly fierce enemy of heresy could also be the author of a vernacular biblical translation may seem astonishing at first sight.[37] However, as we will see, his position was consistent.

In the preface of his book, the Dominican declares that he chose the penitential Psalms because the Church recommends their devotional and liturgical use.[38] He assures that he based his explanation on the commentaries by the Fathers and Doctors of the Church, and gives a long list of names (Jerome, Augustine, Ambrose, Gregory, Cassiodorus, Bernard, Basil, Hugh of Saint-Cher, the *Glossa ordinaria*, Thomas Aquinas, Nicholas of Lyra, Innocent VIII, Jaime Pérez de Valencia, and 'some other doctors').[39] As for the translation preceding the explanation, he asserts that he took care that his poetic translation would be faithful not only to the meaning but also to the letter of the Latin version.[40] At this point, the author feels compelled to anticipate a strong objection: the Church 'abhors' seeing the Bible translated into the vernacular language, since common people can easily be misled.[41] His answer is as follows:

> Ond'io dico, et dirò sempre che la pura et semplice lettera dell'uno et dell'altro Testamento è molto pericolosa nelle mani d'ogni plebeo, in volgar idioma tradotta. Di che accorgendosi la santa Chiesa, non permette che le Bibie volgari possino essere indifferentemente concesse a tutti, ma solamente ad alcuni, conosciuti per ben fermi et stabili nella fede, dalla prudenza de' Vescovi et de gli Inquisitori, il che forse non farebbe s'ella

35 See Boillet, 'Tra censura e tolleranza'.

36 Fragnito, *La Bibbia al rogo*, p. 108.

37 On Domenico Buelli, see Mazzuchelli, *Gli scrittori d'Italia*, pp. 2272–73. In the mid-1570s, and again in the 1580s, he tried many alleged witches from the Val d'Ossola, using torture to obtain confessions. He is one of the protagonists of the novel *La Chimera* published by Sebastiano Vassalli in 1990.

38 Buelli, *I sette salmi penitentiali* (edn 1572), fols [π5]v–[π6]v (the first gathering is a not numbered quaternion with no signature; in this essay I designate it π according to the Italian online catalogue OPAC SBN).

39 Buelli, *I sette salmi penitentiali* (edn 1572), fol. [π6]r. In addition Athanasius is mentioned on fol. [π5]v.

40 'io mi son sempre affaticato di star fermo non pur ne i sensi, ma anco nell'istesse parole della traduttion latina' (I always took care to remain faithful not only to the meaning but also to the letter of the Latin version: all translations are mine), Buelli, *I sette salmi penitentiali* (edn 1572), fol. [π8]v.

41 'non sai tu che la Chiesa santa abborrisce il veder i testi della sacra scrittura fatti volgari, sapendo con quanto pericolo di cader in errore siano letti dal volgo, il quale [...] non è capace di potergli sanamente intendere' (Are you not aware that the Church abhors seing the Sacred Scriptures translated into vernacular language, knowing the great dangers of being misled for common people, who [...] are not able to understand them correctly), Buelli, *I sette salmi penitentiali* (edn 1572), fol. b2^{r}.

vedesse tutto il volume delle divine scritture fedelmente tradotto da qualche eccellente spirito, veramente dotto, pio et catolico, et accompagnato da un'espositione che totalmente levasse tutte quelle difficultà ch'esser sogliono il veleno ch'uccide l'anime d'alcuni semplici, ignoranti et troppo curiosi, per non dir temerarij, imperoché un'opera tale, all'anime christiane che di molte lettere dottate non sono, apportarebbe un utile et giovamento grandissimo, conciosia che, essendo ella commune a tutti i catolici, leggendo s'anderebboro continuamente più confermando nella fede, et molti heretici si convertirebboro, ritornando al gremio della lor divina et pietosa madre [...]. Hor con questa santa intentione ho io tradotti et esposti questi miei salmi, nei quali si vede chiaramente che a tempo e luogo, et secondo che l'occasione mi si porge, non manco di far (come si dice) la contramina a gli heretici. Né mai sarei stato oso di tradur il testo solo, senza accompagnarlo con qualche spirituale et fruttuosa dichiaratione.[42]

(I say and will always say that the pure and simple letter of the Old and the New Testament is very dangerous in the hands of common people when translated into the vernacular language. For this reason, the Church does not grant the permission to read it to all, but only to a few people whose firm and steady faith is valued by the prudence of bishops and inquisitors. Perhaps it would not do so if the entirety of the sacred Scriptures were faithfully translated by an excellent mind, really learned, pious, and Catholic, and accompanied by a commentary which would resolve all the difficulties which are like a poison to simple, ignorant, and too curious – not to say reckless – minds. A similar work would greatly benefit illiterate Christian souls, because, as it would be common to all Catholics, they would be able to reinforce their faith by reading it, and many heretics would convert and come back to the bosom of their divine and pious mother [...]. So, with this intention, I have translated and given a commentary of my [translation of the] Psalms, in which, when needed and when the occasion was given to me, I have not omitted to tackle heresy. And I would not have dared to give a translation without some fruitful spiritual explanation.)

In the opinion of the inquisitor of Novara, the fourth rule of the Tridentine Index was thus a valid protection against abusive readings of the Bible and a sufficient justification, not only for granting reading licences, but also for taking the lead in writing a trustworthy biblical translation. For him, the problem was not in the very fact of translating the Vulgate into the vernacular but in the quality of the vernacular translation: it had to be faithful to the Latin version and accompanied by an unequivocal explanation. It is clear that, beyond the legitimacy of translating the Bible into the vernacular, Buelli was also defending his own authority with regard to censorship and control,

42 Buelli, *I sette salmi penitentiali* (edn 1572), fol. b2^{r-v}.

as local inquisitors still had the power to decide who was allowed to read what within the territory under their jurisdiction. From this perspective, his initiative to provide a faithful translation of the seven penitential Psalms appears consistent with actively chasing heretical or superstitious beliefs.

Later, when Carlo Bascapè, who became Bishop of Novara in 1593, showed his own ambition to follow the model of Catholic reformation offered by Carlo Borromeo in Milan, Domenico Buelli entered into jurisdictional disputes with him regarding inquisitorial matters, including the implementation of the Clementine Index.[43] In February 1597, he wrote to Cardinal Agostino Valier, a member of the Congregation of the Index, to ask for clarification about the books which needed to be confiscated.[44] He considered that, unlike books containing biblical translations alone, those in which translations were accompanied by a commentary should not be banned or confiscated. This had been the position formulated in 1595 in the version of the *Observatio circa quartam regulam* proposed by Pope Clement VIII before a much stricter version, written under pressure from the Holy Office, came to be part of the Clementine Index.[45] In 1602, Buelli had his own poetic translation with commentary re-edited, concretely anticipating the decision that the Congregation of the Index took in 1605 regarding poetic translations, which were an important issue since biblical poetry had become a widespread genre. Indeed, as the Clementine Index was not explicit on this specific matter, the Congregation of the Index, after having decided on a complete ban in 1596, eventually resolved that only poetic translations not accompanied by a commentary should be banned.[46]

Talking about poetic translations, the literary dimension of early modern vernacular biblical texts, illustrated by Buelli's work, is worth underlining. The inquisitor, valuing free verse as the most appropriate for David's epic and heroic style, declared a poetic translation to be the best choice, since only the sweetness of the verse could bring the believer to the bitterness of the devotion.[47] With such a statement, he was directly intervening in current literary matters, as the 1560s saw a number of publications dedicated to poetic translations of the Psalms.[48] Buelli also endorsed the idea that only a poetic translation could fully render a biblical text which was itself originally written

43 Fragnito, *La Bibbia al rogo*, pp. 321–22.

44 Fragnito, *Proibito capire*, pp. 102 and 220.

45 Fragnito, *Proibito capire*, pp. 62–63.

46 Fragnito, *La Bibbia al rogo*, pp. 302–03.

47 Buelli, *I sette salmi penitentiali* (edn 1572), fol. [π8]v-bv.

48 The collection *Salmi penitentiali di diversi eccellenti autori*, edited by the Carmelite Francesco Turchi and printed in Venice by Gabriele Giolito de Ferrari in 1568, is emblematic. It includes verses by Antonio Minturno (1st edn 1561), Bonaventura Gonzaga (1566), Laura Battiferri (1st edn 1564), Luigi Alamanni (1st edn 1532), Pietro Orsilago (1st edn 1546), and Turchi himself (1st edn). Unlike the other authors who chose *terza rima*, *canzone*, or ode, Francesco Turchi chose free verse. See Morace, 'I Salmi tra Riforma e Controriforma', pp. 55–81.

in a poetic form.[49] It was a common opinion, particularly illustrated, for instance, by the 1545 re-edition of the translation of the Bible of the Florentine Dominican Santi Marmochino, as the book, while not mentioning the name of the author, did advertise in its title the inclusion of a most valuable poetic translation of the Psalms.[50] Also, the vernacular Life of Christ (1548) and the translation of the Book of Acts (1549) of the Florentine Capuchin Lodovico Filicaia offered biblical literature in verse in order to divert readers from vain literature and to lead them to useful works. More generally, lay and ecclesiastical Italian authors of this time often expressed the idea that vernacular biblical writings in verse and in prose should render the original beauty of the Bible, because a literary text was more efficient at catching the readers' attention and helping them memorize contents useful for their souls.

Domenico Buelli's ambition was to provide a model for a Catholic biblical translation which could be safely used by all readers. In the early 1570s, however, his proposal was not the only one. Two books on the Psalms were printed in Florence: firstly, in 1572 (with a reprint in 1573), a commentary on two Psalms (*Deus, Deus meus, Respice in me* and *Domine quis habitabit in tabernaculo tuo*) written by the Franciscan Geremia Bucchio at the request of a man of letters, Jacopo Manucci, and dedicated to the Princess of Tuscany Giovanna of Austria; and second, in 1573, a commentary on the penitential Psalms written by Bartolomeo Marescotti, dedicated to the Bishop of Faenza and authorized by the vice-inquisitor of Florence. In Venice, in the same year, three books appeared: meditations on two Psalms (*Misere mei, Deus* and *In te Domine speravi*) by the Dominican Giovanni Alcaini; sermons on the penitential Psalms by the Augustinian Gabriele Buratelli (with a reprint in 1574);[51] and a translation of, and commentary on, the Psalter by the man of letters Pellegrino degli Erri, the translation having initially been commissioned by the Bishop of Modena Egidio Foscarari and the book being dedicated to Count Fulvio Rangoni.[52] Again in Venice, in 1574, the Benedictine Germano Vecchi published a poetic paraphrase of the penitential Psalms under the title 'penitential tears' ('lagrime penitenziali'), paving the way for what became a fashionable literary genre by the end of the century. These books, among which some reveal how lay and ecclesiastical *milieux* could be closely connected, had only one, or a few, editions. While the translation with commentary by Pellegrino degli Erri was explicitly banned in 1593, Buelli issued, as we mentioned earlier, a second edition of his book in 1602. The new dedicatory letter lists the changes: the explanation has been expanded; the poetic translation has been improved; an illustration of King David praying as a penitent precedes the Psalms; the preface

49 Buelli, *I sette salmi penitentiali* (edn 1572), fol. b^r.

50 Barbieri, *Le Bibbie italiane*, I, 291–94. The first edition of Marmochino's translation was printed in 1538.

51 Boillet, 'Vernacular Sermons on the Psalms', pp. 205–06.

52 Boillet, 'Pellegrino degli Erri'; Boillet, '*I Salmi di David* de Pellegrino degli Erri'.

has been divided into two distinct texts, and a final section of spiritual verses has been added.[53] The modification of the preface is worth noticing here, as it allows us to evaluate the author's defence ('la protestation mia') in answer to criticism about the legitimacy of translating the Bible, a defence which now appears as a separate text.[54] After three decades, in the new circumstances created by the Clementine Index and its difficult implementation, Buelli's book had indeed become topical again, and was presented as such.

At this point, it is worth looking briefly at the production of vernacular books on the Psalms during the three following decades, taking note at the same time of what survived after the end of the century. After the rich production of the first half of the 1570s, that of the second half of this decade clearly receded: an old text, the sermons on the penitential Psalms by Lodovico Pittorio, extracted from his longer work on the whole Psalter first published in 1524, was printed in 1578 in the small printing centre of Fermo. In the 1580s, however, several new books appeared, mostly commentaries by ecclesiastical authors, with the remarkable exception of the commentary by a lay woman of letters, Chiara Matraini.[55] The commentaries on the *Miserere* by Canon Cesare Calderari (Naples, 1584) and on the entire Psalter by the Franciscan Francesco Panigarola (Florence, 1585) were particularly successful, with many re-editions in the following century. While Panigarola's work was explicitly tolerated by the Church, errors were found in Calderari's, which was suspended in 1594 before being revised and re-edited in 1600.[56] As indicated earlier, the 1590s were characterized by an explosion of poetic versions of the penitential Psalms ('penitential tears') by ecclesiastical and lay authors. Among them, the translation of Pietro Orsilago, a man of letters and physician who had been connected with the *spirituali* in the 1540s, was re-edited in Venice in 1595; before that, it had been edited by Anton Francesco Doni in Florence in 1546 and by Francesco Turchi in Venice in 1568 in the collection *Salmi penitentiali di diversi eccellenti autori*. So, while a range of vernacular books on the Psalms was printed during the last three decades of the sixteenth century, adapting to the local circumstances of ecclesiastical control, some works, like those by Lodovico Pittorio, Pietro Orsilago, Domenico Buelli, and Cesare Calderari, constitute various illustrations of the ways, ranging from substantial continuation to revision and expurgation, in which the divisions created by ecclesiastical censorship in different time periods and places were bridged.

---

53 Buelli, *I sette salmi penitentiali* (edn 1602), fols ✠2v–✠3r.

54 The text is untitled: 'A tutti quelli che con pia et santa mente havranno letto, o son per leggere, la presente opera: salute et pace nel Signore' (To all those who have read, or are about to read, this work with pious and holy mind: salvation and peace in the Lord), Buelli, *I sette salmi penitentiali* (edn 1602), fol. [✠9]v.

55 On this work and its doctrinal profile, see Boillet, 'I Salmi di David al femminile in Italia tra Riforma e Controriforma', pp. 39–43 and 47–56.

56 Fragnito, *Proibito capire*, p. 210. I have consulted the two Venetian re-editions by Lucio Spineda dated to 1600 and 1605, and have seen that the text was already corrected in the 1600 re-edition.

In conclusion, after the mid-sixteenth century, vernacular biblical production continued relatively unabated at a high level in Italy, despite the fact that it was one of the Catholic areas most subject to ecclesiastical censorship and control. The year 1570 stands out as being at the intersection of several interconnected lines of evolution in the history of Roman Catholic censorship, Italian vernacular literature, and the Italian market for printed books. By 1570, Catholic orthodoxy had been re-defined and its cultural project delineated. From 1570, a more severe line was progressively defined by the Roman bodies in charge of censorship and communicated to local authorities which, however, could still find room for manoeuvre in the 1564 Index. While vernacular translations of the Bible in the strictest sense were not available any longer, a variety of biblical writings, including passages of vernacular translations, were still circulating widely. Taking advantage of previous Italian literary traditions, these productions provided forms of transmission and appropriation of the Bible which were different from translations in the strictest sense but were probably quite effective for the dissemination of biblical knowledge. The proportion of ecclesiastical and lay authors began to evolve strongly in favour of the former, but the gaps left unwillingly or willingly by ecclesiastical censorship were still exploited by both categories of authors to meet Italians' demands. In the last three decades of the sixteenth century, many orthodox, unorthodox, and heterodox biblical works were printed for the first time or re-edited. The first half of the seventeenth century also maintained some continuity through both new publications and more or less revised re-editions of earlier works.

Works Cited

Primary Sources

Buelli, Domenico, *I sette salmi penitentiali tradotti et esposti per il r.p.f. Domenico Buelli, dell'ordine de Predicatori general inquisitor di Novara. All'illustriss. & reuerendiss. mons. Gio. Paolo Chiesa cardinal amplissimo* (Novara: Francesco Sesalli, 1572)

———, *I sette salmi penitentiali, tradotti, & esposti per il molto reuer. padre fra Domenico Buelli, dell'ordine de Predicatori. Dottor di sacra theologia, & general inquisitor di Novara. In questa seconda impressione augumentati, & illustrati, come nell'epistola dedicatoria si può vedere. All'iIllustriss. sig. conte Rinato Borrromeo* (Milan: heir of Pacifico Da Ponte and Giovanni Battista Piccaglia, 1602)

Secondary Studies

Ardissino, Erminia, and Élise Boillet, *Repertorio di letteratura biblica in italiano a stampa (ca 1462–1650)*, Études Renaissantes, 27 (Turnhout: Brepols, forthcoming [2023])

Barbieri, Edoardo, 'La fortuna della Bibbia vulgarizzata di Niccolò Malerbi', *Aevum*, 53.2 (1989), 419–500

———, *Le Bibbie italiane del Quattrocento e del Cinquecento*, 2 vols (Milan: Editrice Bibliografica, 1991–1992)

———, 'Fra tradizione e cambiamento: note sul libro spirituale italiano del XVI secolo', in *Libri, biblioteche e cultura nell'Italia del Cinque e Seicento*, ed. by Edoardo Barbieri and Danilo Zardin (Milan: Vita e Pensiero, 2002), pp. 3–61

———, 'Panorama delle traduzioni bibliche in volgare prima del Concilio di Trento', *Folia Theologica*, 8 (1997), 169–97, and 9 (1998), 89–110; an. repr. *Panorama delle traduzioni bibliche in volgare prima del Concilio di Trento* (Milan: C.R.E.L.E.B. – Università Cattolica-Edizioni CUSL, 2011)

Boillet, Élise, 'La fortune du *Psalterio Davitico* de Lodovico Pittorio en Italie au XVIe siècle', *Bibliofilía*, 115.3 (2013), 563–70

———, 'David, personnage et masque de l'Arétin entre XVIe et XVIIe siècle', in *Les figures de David à la Renaissance*, ed. by Élise Boillet, Sonia Cavicchioli, and Paul-Alexis Mellet (Geneva: Droz, 2015), pp. 329–62

———, 'Vernacular Biblical Literature in Sixteenth-Century Italy: Universal Reading and Specific Readers', in *Discovering the Riches of the Word: Religious Reading in Late Medieval and Early Modern Europe*, ed. by Sabrina Corbellini, Margriet Hoogvliet, and Bart Ramakers (Leiden: Brill, 2015), pp. 213–33

———, 'Pellegrino degli Erri, un umanista modenese tra eresia e azione inquisitoriale', in *Eretici, dissidenti, inquisitori: Per un dizionario storico mediterraneo*, vol. 1, ed. by Luca Al Sabbagh, Daniele Santarelli, and Domizia Weber (Rome: Aracne Editrice, 2016), pp. 177–81

———, 'Vernacular Sermons on the Psalms Printed in Sixteenth-Century Italy: An Interface between Oral and Written Cultures', in *Voices and Texts in Early Modern Italian Society*, ed. by Stefano Dall'Aglio, Brian Richardson, and Massimo Rospocher (London: Routledge, 2017), pp. 200–11

———, 'I Salmi di David al femminile in Italia tra Riforma e Controriforma: Laura Battiferri e Chiara Matraini', in *Bibbia, donne, profezia: A partire dalla Riforma*, ed. by Adriana Valerio and Letizia Tomassone (Florence: Nerbini, 2018), pp. 39–56

———, 'Tra censura e tolleranza: Le due edizioni del volgarizzamento dei salmi penitenziali di Domenico Buelli, inquisitore di Novara (1572 e 1602)', in *Gli Italiani e la Bibbia nella prima età moderna: Leggere, interpretare, riscrivere*, ed. by Erminia Ardissino and Élise Boillet, Études Renaissantes, 28 (Turnhout: Brepols, 2018), pp. 71–91

———, '*I Salmi di David* de Pellegrino degli Erri (Venise, 1573)', *Rivista di Storia e Letteratura Religiosa*, 55.1 (2019), 79–101

———, 'For Early Modern Printed Biblical Literature in Italian: Lay Authorship and Readership', in *Lay Readings of the Bible in Early Modern Europe*, ed. by Erminia Ardissino and Élise Boillet, Intersections, 68 (Leiden: Brill, 2020), pp. 170–90

Firpo, Massimo, *Riforma protestante ed eresie nell'Italia del Cinquecento* (Rome: Laterza, 1993)

Fragnito, Gigliola, *La Bibbia al rogo: La censura ecclesiastica e i volgarizzamenti della Scrittura (1471–1605)* (Bologna: il Mulino, 1997)

———, *Proibito capire: La chiesa e il volgare nella prima età moderna* (Bologna: il Mulino, 2005)

Grendler, Paul F., 'Printing and Censorship', in *The Cambridge History of Renaissance Philosophy*, ed. by Charles B. Schmitt, Quentin Skinner, and Eckhard Kessler (Cambridge: Cambridge University Press, 1988), pp. 25–53

Jacobson Schutte, Anne, 'Printing, Piety, and the People in Italy: The First Thirty Years', *Archiv für Reformationsgeschichte*, 71 (1980), 5–20

———, *Printed Italian Vernacular Religious Books, 1465–1550: A Finding List* (Geneva: Droz, 1983)

Morace, Rosanna, 'I Salmi tra Riforma e Controriforma', in *La Bibbia in poesia: Volgarizzamenti dei Salmi e poesia religiosa in età moderna*, ed. by Rosanna Alhaique Pettinelli, Rosanna Morace, Pietro Petteruti Pellegrino, and Ugo Vignuzzi (Rome: Bulzoni, 2015), pp. 55–81

La Bibbia in poesia: Volgarizzamenti dei Salmi e poesia religiosa in età moderna, ed. by Rosanna Alhaique Pettinelli, Rosanna Morace, Pietro Petteruti Pellegrino, and Ugo Vignuzzi (Rome: Bulzoni, 2015)

Letteratura in forma di sermoni: I rapporti tra predicazione e letteratura nei secoli XIII–XVI, ed. by Ginetta Auzzas, Giovanni Baffetti, and Carlo Delcorno (Florence: Olschki, 2003)

Mazzuchelli, Giammaria, *Gli scrittori d'Italia cioè notizie storiche, e critiche intorno alle vite, e agli scritti dei letterati italiani*, II, part IV (Brescia: Giambattista Bossini, 1763), pp. 2272–73

Quondam, Amedeo, 'Note sulla tradizione della poesia spirituale e religiosa (parte prima)', in *Paradigmi e tradizioni*, ed. by Amedeo Quondam, Studi (e testi) italiani, 16 (Rome: Bulzoni, 2005), pp. 127–282

Rime sacre tra Cinquecento e Seicento, ed. by Maria Luisa Doglio and Carlo Delcorno (Bologna: il Mulino, 2007)

Rozzo, Ugo, *Linee per una storia dell'editoria religiosa in Italia (1465–1600)* (Udine: Arti Grafiche Friulane, 1993)

Sotto il cielo delle Scritture. Bibbia, retorica e letteratura (sec. XIII–XVI), ed. by Carlo Delcorno and Giovanni Baffetti (Florence: Olschki, 2001)

Vassalli, Sebastiano, *La Chimera* (Turin: Einaudi, 1990)

Zardin, Danilo, 'Bibbia e letteratura religiosa in volgare nell'Italia del Cinque-Seicento', *Annali di storia moderna e contemporanea*, 4.1 (1998), 593–616

———, 'Tra latino e volgare: la dichiarazione dei salmi del Panigarola e i filtri alla materia biblica nell'editoria della Controriforma', *Sincronie*, 4.7 (2000), 125–65

MELINA ROKAI

Communities of Interpretation of the Bible along the European Margins

Hussite Teachings, the Hussite Bible, and the Bogomils, from the South of Hungary to the Periphery of Eastern Europe in the Long Fifteenth Century

In Hungary during the Middle Ages there was no theological faculty. Students wishing to study theology were forced to attend foreign universities. At the beginning of the twelfth century, they had to leave for Paris and Bologna, and after the founding of universities closer to Hungary, young people eager to learn would visit the Universities of Padua, Vienna, and Cracow. They also studied at the prestigious University of Prague. In the first decade of the fifteenth century, theological science at Charles University in Prague was taught by the famous Jan Hus, translator of the Scriptures into the Czech language. His lectures were attended by, among others, students from southern Hungary. Amongst them was Blasius, later the parish priest of Kamenica (nowadays Sremska Kamenica, which is part of the city of Novi Sad), a town on the southern bank of the Danube. Although Hus's teachings were denounced as heresy by the official Church, his students at the University of Prague accepted them and spread them to their communities. Thus, students of Blasius in Kamenica formed around Hus's teachings a community of like-minded peers, importing and disseminating modified Hussite teachings throughout their territory, and adding to the mixture of beliefs and teachings in a liminal geographic area permeated with religious diversity.

This essay studies a community of laypeople in southern Hungary in the fifteenth century — a community that created 'multiple options' involving different interpretations of religious texts alongside different modes of studying, instructing, and preaching. It will be demonstrated that the activities and textual work of this community were tightly connected to the teachings of Jan Hus. This essay is also concerned with another group of 'heretics': those who lived in the territory of Srem, in southern Hungary, where they took up

Melina Rokai • (melinarokai85@hotmail.com) is currently a Senior Research Associate at the Department of History, Faculty of Philosophy, University of Belgrade.

Religious Transformations in New Communities of Interpretation in Europe (1350–1570): Bridging the Historiographical Divides, ed. by Élise Boillet and Ian Johnson, New Communities of Interpretation, 3 (Turnhout: Brepols, 2022), pp. 133–159.

DOI 10.1484/M.NCI-EB.5.131218

the teachings of the Cathars (better known in south-eastern Europe as the Bogomils). In order to illustrate how the historical divides, both in terms of time and space, were negotiated, this paper will concern itself with the analysis of similarities and differences in the prayer 'Our Father'/ Pater Noster as taught by the Hussites of southern Hungary and the Bogomils of Bosnia. In the case of the Hussites, as we shall see, the prayer was contained in an important manuscript, the Codex of Munich. Comparative analysis of this material will show how hybrid structures of religiosity appeared and influenced each other in eastern and south-eastern Europe during the long fifteenth century and thereafter. Although a thorough comparison of the religious learning of these two groups has already been made, the particular evidence offered by exploring side by side their respective treatments of the Pater Noster has not yet been investigated. This approach therefore offers a fresh and productive insight into one telling way in which important historical divides were bridged across eastern and south-eastern Europe down the centuries. The relevance of this becomes evident when one takes into account that the text of the Pater Noster used amongst 'the heretics' differed from that used by the Inquisition in western Europe for discovering and denouncing heretics.

In order to explore how the historical divides in question were created within their particular socio-political context, this essay will trace the evolution of religious movements in the region both before and after the given period. This narrative will be accompanied by illustration of how the creation of alternative religious forms in eastern and south-eastern Europe was strangely aided by none other than the Inquisition itself, which functioned across the region as a medium for interconnecting different communities and various religious ideas with each other.

Rumours of Wycliffism in South-Eastern Europe

Eastern and south-eastern Europe were exposed not only to a number of alternative religious teachings, but also to readings of the Bible that differed from both Catholic and Orthodox orthodoxy: such alternative readings encouraged communities to create their own interpretations of them. It was not only Jan Hus's teachings that reached the far ends of southern and south-eastern Europe; it has also been established that the teachings of John Wycliffe came as far south as the east Adriatic Coast before those of his Bohemian counterpart.[1] Prior to this, Wycliffe's theological and social ideas

1 *A Huszita biblia (János evangelista könyvö), Biblia husita, Régi magyar nyelvemlékek [A Hussite Bible (The Book of John the Evangelist), The Hussite Bible]*, ed. by Király, Décsy, and Szabó, (2012), IX, 6–11; X, 16; XI, 17; XII, 18; (2013), I, 10; II, 14; III, 14; IV, 21; V, 20; VI, 20–21; VII, 11; VIII, 20–21; IX, 20–21; X, 19–21; XI, 18–19; XII, 20–21; (2014), I, 19; II, 10–11; III, 16; IV, 10–11; V, 10–11; VI, 18–19.

had been spread throughout England by the members of the lower clergy — primarily parish priests — and the so-called Lollards, who some considered at the time to be the ideological backbone of Watt Tyler's uprising of 1387.[2]

But what of the dissemination of Wycliffism further afield? John Wycliffe's heresy spread very quickly from England all the way to south-eastern Europe. It was noted that, by 1383, Wycliffe's teachings had been received in the city of Spalato on the Dalmatian coast (nowadays Split in Croatia), where a certain preacher, identified as the heretic Walter of England (Gualterius de Anglia Hereticus), preached Wycliffe's teachings and called for the local population not to pay the church tithe (*decima papalis*). The preacher was allegedly identified as Walterom de Savare de Kirkeby, from the Hundred of Tyndering, a supporter of Wycliffe's ideas, who, as recently as January of the same year, had been witnessed preaching in England against tithes.[3] He showed up in Dalmatia after the death of the Hungarian King Louis I the Great of Anjou. Louis's title of the 'true defender of the faith' was inherited, along with the throne, by his daughter Maria. Since Maria was a minor at the time, this role, alongside other monarchical matters, fell under the regency of Maria's mother and Louis's widow, Queen Elizabeth Kotromanić. Due to the complicated political situation in Hungary, where the two queens fought in alliance against political opposition to their rule, Maria and Elizabeth were not able to take full control of the situation and act against the appearance of heresy in Spalato.[4] As can be seen from the testimony recorded by the notary, Antonio de Martin de Vonico, preaching against tithes was unsuccessful in this town. As De Vonico noted, Domnius and Burcardus, the two representatives of Ugolino, Archbishop of Spalato, succeeded, without the help of the state authorities, in collecting the papal tithe by the end of September 1383. This was subsequently delivered to the sub-collectors, Toma and Benedictus, who gathered it in instead of the collector, Vivian de Sancto Severino.[5]

The Intermingling of Hussitism and Wycliffism in Eastern Europe

Looking beyond the spread of supposed Wycliffism to the south-east of the Continent, links between John Wycliffe's teachings and those of Jan Hus, specifically in their dissemination across the historical boundaries of late medieval Europe, can be detected. When the daughter of the German

---

2 Maurois, *Povijest engleske politike* [*History of English Politics*], pp. 181–86.

3 Brandt, 'Susret viklifizma sa bogomilstvom u Srijemu' ['The Meeting of Wycliffism with Bogomilism in Srem'], pp. 7–13, 177–234, 295.

4 Рокаи, Ђере, Пал and Касаш [Rokai, Đere, Pal, and Kasaš], *Историја Мађара* [*History of the Hungarians*], pp. 122–23.

5 Brandt, 'Susret viklifizma sa bogomilstvom u Srijemu' ['The Meeting of Wycliffism with Bogomilism in Srem'], pp. 7–13, 177–234, 295.

Emperor Charles IV of Luxembourg married the English Plantagenet King Richard II (1377–1399), this alliance between these dynasties helped relations between the University of Prague and English academe to become even tighter. A group of Bohemian students attended the University of Oxford, where they listened to the lectures of Wycliffe. Having returned to Bohemia, they began to spread his ideas. This meant that not only did the critique and subsequent rejection of the teachings and clergy of Catholicism spread, but so too did the increasingly liberal social movements of the time.

Away from intellectual circles, another channel for the dissemination of Wycliffe's ideas on the Continent was through the Bohemian lower nobility, who served as mercenaries in the English army during the last phase of the Hundred Years War. One such a mercenary was Jan Žiška, later leader of the Taborites, the radical Hussites, who became acquainted with English warfare at the Battle of Agincourt and with English radical theology through Wycliffe's religious ideas.

Jan Hus too had become familiar with Wycliffe's thought, particularly in the field of philosophy. This was why his opponents, the representatives of the official Church, called him and his supporters 'Wycliffites'. Hus denied any such link. The similarities and differences between the teachings of Jan Hus and John Wycliffe have recently been analysed by Zoltan Rokay.[6] In several of his tracts, Jan Hus made public his stance regarding the teachings and practices of the Catholic Church; these were presented in 'De decimis' and 'De ablatione temporalium a clericis determinatio'. In 'De eucharistia', Hus expressed his ideas about Holy Communion. Wycliffe's and Hus's teachings were declared heretical by the Council of Constance. Even so, Hus's disciples, students of the University of Prague, accepted his teachings and spread them when they returned to their communities. His ideas, meanwhile, spread not only throughout Bohemia, but across the whole of eastern and south-eastern Europe.

Among those attending Hus's lectures in Prague were students from southern Hungary. One of these was the aforementioned Blasius, later priest of Kamenica. Throughout the fifteenth century the town of Kamenica, together with Petrovaradin and Novi Sad, belonged to French monks. Thus, Kamenica became a community where a like-minded group focused upon Hus's disciple Blasius. Those identified as being in the circle of Blasius include one Toma, one Balint, and another Balint from the nearby village of Beočin. This isolated branch of Hussitism developed after Hussitism had been suppressed in its native Bohemia.[7]

As is well-known, following Hus's execution, his supporters rebelled, which led to the Fifteen Years War between the Hussites and their opponents

---

6 Rokay, 'Luxemburgi Zsigmond teológiai kompetenciája' ['Sigismund of Luxembourg's Theological Competence'], pp. 131–32.

7 Toldy, *Analecta Monumentorum Hungariae historica*, I, 162; *Chronicon observantis provinciae Bosnae Argentinae ordinis s. Francisci Seraphici*, ed. by Fermendžin, pp. 18–19.

(1419–1434). During this war, the Hussite movement divided into two factions along the lines of the moderate Utraquists (or Calixtines) and the radical Taborites. The former were named after the fact that the first point of their teaching was support for taking of the Eucharist under both kinds: 'sub utraque specie'. They also contended that church services should be conducted in the national language, and argued for the secularization of church property and the reform of the moral conduct of clergy. These four points constituted the so-called Four Articles of Prague. The social backgrounds of Utraquists varied: they came primarily from the class of Bohemian townspeople, but there was also a large number of nobles, and even some landowners and prelates. The movement's intellectual leadership was institutionally rooted and energized in the University of Prague.

The Taborites were named after the sacred mountain, the biblical Mount Tabor. They absorbed Utraquist doctrine, but added some of their own particular teachings. With the exception of the Eucharist under both kinds and baptism, they rejected all sacraments, as well as the cults of the Virgin Mary, the angels and saints, and the worship of icons and the Cross. Services conducted in the national language took place outdoors, since neither the Catholics nor the Utraquists allowed them to use their churches. After their expulsion from towns where the Utraquists were in the majority, the Taborites founded camps on mountains in Bohemia, which they gave biblical toponyms, such as Horeb and Tabor. Over time, Tabor evolved from a tented settlement into a fortified town. There, Taborites mostly came from the lower social strata of Bohemian urban society, but also included elements of the gentry, parish priests, artisans, miners, and poor villagers.

In 1433, the Utraquists made a compromise with the representatives of the General Church Council, which had again gathered under the protection of the Emperor Sigismund. The compromise with the Catholic Church, otherwise known as the Prague Compacts, accepted the use of chalice and the Czech language in the Mass, as well as the secularization of clerical property, which had already been accomplished. Furthermore, the Bishop of Prague was supposed to be elected alternately from the ranks of the Utraquists and the Catholics. Thus united, Catholic and Utraquist forces brought a devastating defeat to the Taborites at Lipany in 1434. After this, the Taborites dispersed throughout Bohemia and into neighbouring countries.

However, the Utraquists did not stay united themselves. One group, led by a nobleman named Petr Chelčický and a cleric Jan z Rokycan (John of Rokycany), separated from the main body. This group was also termed the 'Bohemian' group. In Moravia they were known as 'Moravian', and sometimes 'Bohemio-Moravian-', or simply 'Brothers' — in Czech 'Jednota českych Bratri', 'Jednota bratrská', or simply 'Jednota'. In Latin they were called 'Unitas fratrum Bohemorum', and in German 'Böhmische Brüder', or the Moravian Church. They organized themselves into a separate Church from 1460 to 1461, moving from recognizing a Catholic, in other words Utraquist, hierarchy to definitively separating, in 1467, from the Catholic Church. Since they rejected an anti-feudal and anti-state stance, they were tolerated by the Counter-Reformation. Between 1579 and 1593, they translated the Bible into the Czech language; this became known as the Bible of Kralice (in Czech: *Bible kralická*). Of relevance to the present essay is that two of the Gospels in this Bible mention praying for 'the daily bread'.

In 1570, at the Convocation in Sandomierz, in Poland, part of the Bohemian-Moravian Brotherhood melted into the Calvinists and Lutherans. Considered hardworking artisans and farmers, some landlords settled them on their estates. For example, the Saxon Count Nikolaus Ludwig von Zinzendorf (1700–1760) renewed their organized confession of the Creed on his estate in Berthelsdorf. The name the Moravian Brothers gave to this settlement was 'Herrnhut' (in English, 'the Lord's protection'). Thus, the brothers became known as the Herrnhuter Brotherhood (in German: 'Herrnhuter Brüdergemeine'). From here, they established their missions not only in surrounding countries, but also in the Danish colonies. In the years 1732–1733 they established a mission in the Danish West Indies to two small Caribbean islands, and in November 1733 they established another mission to Greenland. The two islands, sold to the USA in 1917, are nowadays known as the American Virgin Islands. The community of the Herrnhuter Brotherhood has survived until modern times, on the far side of ecumenism, amongst the Inuits of Greenland, who translated the Bible of Kralice from the Czech.[8]

Members of the Moravian Brotherhood were the first missionaries to newly acquired slaves in the Danish West Indies. They did not have the support of the local ecclesiastical and secular authorities and were constantly under attack in an attempt to stifle their effectiveness. Nevertheless, thanks to their zeal in preaching on the sugar cane plantations and at social gatherings, the Moravian Brothers succeeded in leaving a permanent mark after only two decades of activity. The Danish Evangelical (i.e. Lutheran) Church founded its own mission only in 1755, when the islands were given crown colony status.[9]

The Moravian Brotherhood or Herrnhuter Brotherhood established missions elsewhere around the world during the eighteenth century. This included Native Americans (1735), Cape Colony (then a Dutch Territory) in South Africa (1736 and 1743), Oslo (1737), Copenhagen (1739), and Bergen (1740) and Drammen (1746) in Norway. Further missions were successful in 1771 in Labrador (nowadays Canada), and in 1792 in Christensfeld in south Jylland. In the second half of the nineteenth century, in 1859, the Herrnhuter Brotherhood established a mission in Australia. This widespread missionary activity had the consequence of transforming Hussitism from a narrow national Bohemian movement into a world religion contributing to the bridging of religious divides for several centuries after it was first established.

---

8 Cröger, *Geschichte der erneuerten Brüderkirche*; Schultze, *Die Missionfelder der erneuerten Brüderkirche*.

9 Lawaetz, *Brödremenghedens mission i Dansk-Vestindien*; Westergaard, *The Danish West Indies under Company Rule (1671–1754)*, p. 34 n. 8, p. 159.

Hussites and Bogomils in the South of Hungary, and the Bridging of Confessional Differences

After the defeat at Lipany in 1434, many Taborites found shelter in Hungary, in Transylvania, and Srem. It is a matter of historical record that in the region of Srem, between the Rivers Save and Danube, a symbiosis occurred between those believed to be adhering to Hussitism and another religious group considered heretical. This group, consisting of Bosnians classified by contemporaries as followers of Cathar teaching, were commonly known as Bogomili, Patarini, or Manichei. The sect of the Bogomils was named after the mythical priest Bogumil, and represents a Christianized version of Manicheism, with its dualistic view of the world. Even Jan Hus was aware of them, referring to them in one of his Latin *postillae* as 'Patarini'.[10]

In February 1437, the symbiosis between the Hussites and the Bosnian heretics was indisputably confirmed by the testimony of three official figures — one state functionary and two religious officials. The Comes of Požega, Tamási László, stated in his attestation given to the inquisitor Jacob de Marchia in Djakovo that in the parts of Srem where Rascians (Orthodox Serbs) and Bosnians lived together with Christians (in this instance meaning Catholics), some towns and villages had many years ago been infected by the heretical sect of Bosnians and Hussites: 'In [...] partibus Syrmie [...] Rasciani et etiam Boznenses cum Christianis mixtim commorantur; quedam civitates ac ville sectis Boznensium ac Huzytarum infecte per plurimos annos extiterunt' (In [...] parts of Srem, the Serbs also live mixed together with the Bosnians; some towns and villages had been infected by the heretical sect of Bosnians and Hussites many years ago). This sect, Jacob exterminated with (we are told) the grace of God.[11]

In July 1437, a similar confirmation to the same inquisitor by a local bishop of Srem was made in the episcopal headquarters in Banoštor, 'in Monasterio Bani, in palacio solite nostre residentie' (In the monastery of Banoštor in the Episcopal headquarters, in the palace of our usual residence). The bishop of Srem stated that Bosnian Bogomils and Orthodox Serbian Rascians of Srem were converted from their Hussite depravity by the care and words of the inquisitor Jacob de Marchia. The Latin text is as follows:

> in diversis regni partibus, et specialiter in [...] partibus Sirmiensibus, ubi Boznenses ac Rasciani, Catholice fidei emuli mixtim habentur ac inter fluvios Zawam et Danubium simul commorantur, plerosque hereticos diversis heresibus, singulariter heretica pravitate maledictorum Husitarum, Sancte Romane Ecclesie infectos.[12]

10 Friedenthal, *Joanes Husz Ketzer und Rebell, Tractatus de Corpore Christi*, p. clxiii.
11 *Acta Bosnae*, ed. by Fermendžin, no. DCCLIV, p. 159.
12 *Acta Bosnae*, ed. by Fermendžin, no. DCCLXIV, p. 163.

> (In divers parts of the kingdom, and particularly in [...] parts of Srem, where Bosnians and Rascians live intermingled, striving against the Catholic faith, living together as they also do between the Sava and the Danube rivers, many heretics of diverse heresies, singularly infected with the wicked heretical depravity of the cursed Hussites against the Holy Roman Church.)

Another confirmation with similar, if not identical, wording was issued by the Bishop of Djakovo in December 1437.[13]

Whilst historians have demonstrated that, despite different interpretations of the Bible, there was a symbiotic relationship between these different southern Hungarian communities, the question of their influence on each other remains the single most important unresolved issue in studies of their interconnections.[14] Some historians and theologians have attempted to find common features in the alternatives to orthodoxy taken by forms of religious teachings deployed by the Bosnian Bogomils (also identified as Cathars or Patarini) and the Hussites of Hungary. Tellingly, significant similarities between their teachings were identified at the time by the inquisitor in these regions, Cardinal Juan de Torquemada, in his list of the fallacies of the Moldavian Hussites issued in 1461. Torquemada recognized in these heresies a common subscription to rejection of the oath, the Cross, and other Christian symbols. Furthermore, he declared that the sixteenth article on the fallacies of the teachings of the Moldavian Hussites, according to which Jesus Christ had not suffered and died in reality, 'was of Manichean origin' (fuit primo Manicheorum' […] 'and of many other heretics' (et multorum aliorum hereticorum).[15]

---

13 *Acta Bosnae*, ed. by Fermendžin, no. DCCLXII, p. 162.

14 Asbóth, 'A bosnyák bogumilek az Árpádok és Anjouk korában' ['Bosnian Bogomils in the Age of Árpád and Anjou Dynasties'], p. 1; Asbóth, *Bosnien und die Herzegowina*, pp. 73–75; Asbóth, *An Official Tour through Bosnia and Herzegovina*; Kardos, *A huszita biblia keletkezése* [*The Creation of the Hussite Bible*], p. 82; Kardos, 'A huszita mozgalmak és Hunyadi Mátyás szerepe a magyar nemzeti egyház kialakításában' ['The Role of the Hussite Movement and Matthias Hunyadi in the Creation of the Hungarian National Church'], pp. 121–77; Kardos, 'Problematika ládání o husítství v Uhrach' ['The Problem of Research of the Hussitism in Uhrach'], p. 449; Székely, 'A huszitizmus és a magyar nép' ['Hussitism and the Hungarian People'], pp. 331–67, 556–90; Székely, 'Husítství a mad'arsky lid' ['Hussitism and the Hungarian People'], pp. 111–61; Kulcsár, *Eretnekmozgalmak a XI-XIV. században* [*Les mouvementes hérétiques aux XIe-XIVe siècles, Јеретическије движенија в XI-XIV веках*], pp. 58–60, 63, 113–38, 178, 184, 277–79, 326; Примов [Primov], 'Бъгарското богомилство и европејската реформација' ['Bulgarian Bogomilism and the European Reformation'], pp. 41–51.

15 Prohaska, 'Husitstvi a bogomilstv' ['Hussitism and Bogomilism'], pp. 10–11; Prohaska, 'Husiti i bogomili' ['The Hussites and the Bogomils'], p. 441; Šidak, 'Heretički pokret i odjek husitizma na slavenskom Jugu' ['Heretical Movement and the Echo of Hussitism in the Slavic South'], pp. 282, 286–93; Brandt, 'Susret viklifizma sa bogomilstvom u Srijemu' ['Meeting of Wycliffism with Bogomilism in Srem'], pp. 33–64; Lambert, *Medieval Heresy: Popular Movement from Bogomil to Hus*; Kolpacoff Deane, *A History of Medieval Heresy and Inquisition.*

A Comparison of Hussite and Bogomil (Cathar) Teaching as Testimony of the Successful Bridging of Historical Divides in Eastern Europe

Although extensive comparison of the learning of the sects in question has already been made, one neglected aspect merits attention. As a means of catechizing larger groups of people, Hussites in southern Hungary used the Bible, which they had translated, at least partially, into Hungarian. This is referred to in the historiography as the 'Hussite Bible'. The most important part of this translation consists of that of the four Gospels, preserved in the so-called Codex of Munich. This manuscript has been edited by Gabor Döbrentei,[16] Gyula Décsy, Gyula Farkas,[17] and Nyiri Antal.[18] The Munich Codex, in its entirety or in its parts, was ascribed to the Hussites by its very first editor, Gabor Döbrentei.[19] Other editors who attribute it to the Hussites in south of Hungary were Joseph Jireček,[20] Cirill Horváth,[21] János Melich,[22] and István Tóth Bagi.[23] However, according to Pál Tóth-Szabó[24] and István Kniezsa, the translators of this codex cannot be identified with these people.[25] Some have accredited the Franciscan order with the translation of the codex. This, however, is very unlikely, given that the Franciscans earmarked this translation of the Bible as heretical.[26] As for opinions of other scholars on the matter, Tímár Kálmán has attempted to assign the translation of the Codex to the Premonstratensians,[27] whilst Szabó Flóris has come back to

16 *A Müncheni kódex* [*Codex of Munich*], ed. by Döbrentei; *A Müncheni kódex* [*Codex of Munich*], ed. by Volf.

17 *Der Münchener Kodex*, ed. by Décsy and Farkas.

18 *A Müncheni Kódex 1466-ból* [*Codex of Munich from 1466*], ed. by Nyiri.

19 *A Müncheni kódex* [*Codex of Munich*], ed. by Döbrentei.

20 Jireček, 'Über die culturellen Beziehungen', pp. 101–13.

21 Horváth, 'Huszita emlékeink' ['Our Hussite Monuments'], pp. 3–4.

22 Melich, 'A Bécsi és a Müncheni kódex írói' ['Writers of the Codex of Vienna and Codex of Munich'], pp. 358–59.

23 Tóth Bagi, 'Ötszáz évvel ezelőtt a Szerémségi Kamenicán készítették az első magyar bibliafordítást, Huszita mozgalmak a bácsi érsekség területén' ['Five Hundred Years Ago the First Hungarian Translation of the Bible was made in Kamenica in Srem'].

24 Tóth-Szabó, *A cseh-huszita mozgalmak története Magyarországon* [*A History of the Czech Hussite Movement and Rule in Hungary*], p. 162.

25 Kniezsa, *Helyesírásunk története a könyvnyomtatás koráig* [*History of our Spelling until the Age of Book Printing*], p. 178.

26 Also Rajšli, 'A huszita biblia nyelvi valósághátteréről' ['Concerning the Real Linguistic Background of the Hussite Bible'], pp. 179–89.

27 Tímár, *Prémontrei kódexek: Huszita vagy prémontrei biblia?* [*Premonstratensian Codices: the Hussite or Premonstratensian Bible?*], pp. 39–40; Tímár, *Legrégibb bibliafordításunk eredete* [*The Origin of our Oldest Translation of the Bible*], pp. 25–29; Gyetvai, *Egyházi szervezés, főleg az egykori déli magyar területeken és a bácskai Tisza mentén* [*The Ecclesiastical Organization mostly in the Former Hungarian South and near Bács Tisza*], pp. 72–75.

the theory of its Franciscan origin.[28] Most recently, in 2015, Klara Korompai advocated a Hussite origin.[29]

The author of the Franciscan chronicles considered heretical the term 'Holy Breath', which was used in the Gospel of Luke of the Munich Codex instead of the term 'Holy Spirit', the norm in Orthodox texts.[30] The Bulgarian expert Borislav Primov, however, demonstrated that this was more a case of there being a linguistic variant. The translator translated the Latin phrase 'spiritus' as 'breath', but translated the term 'anima' as 'spirit'.[31] I would add here a detail that in the Gospel of Matthew of the 'Hussite Bible' the term used is 'the spirit', which was translated into Hungarian as 'lélek'.[32] Given these observations, I would argue that the term 'breath' used in the 'Hussite Bible' is not sufficient to prove it heretical, but instead testifies to an outdated linguistic form.

Establishing which religious books were used by the Cathars or Bosnian Bogomilsis even more difficult. It is known that at least a Gospel was necessary for the Consolamentum, since it was placed on the head of the adherent; this would necessarily be the Gospel of John. According to the Serbian historian Sima Ćirković, Bogomils usually followed the Orthodox text of Holy Scripture, but with heterodox glosses made in Old Slavonic language.[33] It is not helpful that records of the Cathars were destroyed both by the Catholic and Orthodox authorities. This problem was not new: as long ago as the twelfth century Grand Prince Stefan Nemanja (1168–1196) had ordered the burning of the Bogomils' books in Serbia.

Irrespective of the extent of differences between the religious teachings of Jan Hus's followers and the Bogomils, there was one clear similarity. As is well-known, the prayer Pater Noster or 'Our Father' played a very important part in the liturgy of both Bogomils and Hussites. The expression 'quotidianum' is often used nowadays in the Roman Catholic version of Pater Noster, although in only four Vulgate manuscripts[34] is the term to be found, whilst in all other Vulgate manuscripts 'supersubstantialem' is used instead.

---

28 Szabó, 'Huszita –e a Huszita Biblia? Bírálat és útkeresés' ['Is the Hussite Bible Hussite? The Critique and the Search for the Path'], pp. 118–26.

29 Korompay, 'Egy nyitott kérdés, több tudományterület metszéspontjában: az ún. Huszita biblia' ['One Open Question in the Meeting-point of Several Scholarly Fields: the so-called Hussite Bible'].

30 *Chronicon observantis provinciae Bosnae Argentinae ordinis s. Francisci Seraphici*, ed. by Fermendžin, p. 18.

31 Примов [Primov], 'Бѧгарското богомилство и европејската реформација' ['Bulgarian Bogomilism and the European Reformation'].

32 *Máté evangeliuma, Kapitulum VI, 11. Lukács evangéliuma, Kapitulum XI, 3, Müncheni kódex, /1466/, A négy evangélium szövege és szótára [The Gospel of Matthew Kapitulum VI, 11. The Gospel of Luke, Kapitulum XI, 3, Codex of Munich /1466/, Text and Dictionary of Four Gospels]*, ed. by Décsy and Szabó.

33 Ćirković, 'Bosanska crkva u bosanskoj državi' ['The Bosnian Church in the Bosnian State'], p. 199.

34 *Novum testamentum graece et latine, Editio septima, Imprimatur Traglia A., archiepiscopus Caesariensis, vicesgerens*, ed. by Merk, p. 25*, 42*–43*.

In the Pater Noster, God is entreated to give 'panem nostrum quotidianum', which translates as 'our daily bread'. The exception is in the edition of the Latin text of the Gospel of Matthew, published as Vulgate by the German Jesuit Augustinus Merk in 1951, and dedicated to Pope Pius XII with the imprimatur of Archbishop A. Traglie. This uses the form 'supersubstantialem'.[35]

Unlike the version used until recently by the Catholic Church, the Bogomils and Hussites prayed to God to give (them) what is in Latin known as 'panem nostrum supersubstantialem'. Although Jan Hus stated during his trial that the term 'substantia' did not have an adequate equivalent in the Czech language, the term was translated as 'hleb naš nadsušni' in Old Slavonic. Also, the Cathars, whose teaching was viewed as broadly similar to the Bogomils', prayed in Latin for 'panem nostrum supersubstantialem', the literal translation of the Greek expression 'τὸν Ἐπιούσιον', instead of 'panem nostrum quotidianum'. The term 'substantia' (or 'substantialis/substantialiter') had been present amongst the Church fathers. St Jerome used it in his translation of the Bible. It was also mentioned by St Ambrose and St Augustine. A significant point in the development of doctrine is the difference in expressing the belief (or 'credo' in Latin) formulated in the diverging ideas of Lanfranc of Canterbury and Berengar of Tours from 1078 onwards.[36]

The Cathars inserted into the 'Our Father' a sentence that reads 'because yours is the Kingdom, the virtue and the glory in centuries. Amen'. This doxology was later adopted by the Protestants, only to be taken up in a slightly altered form by the Catholics after the reform of the liturgy in the nineteenth century. Thus, the Catholics pray in the Croatian language 'Jer tvoje je kraljevstvo, slava i MOĆ u vijeke' (because yours is the Kingdom, the glory and the POWER in centuries). In the case of Jan Hus's teachings on the Eucharist, praying for 'supersubstantialem' rather than 'quotidianum' has been noted by the eminent theologian Zoltán Rokay.[37]

The similarity between the Old Slavic and Latin traditions in dualistic teaching has been pointed out by two of the leading experts on this doctrine in Europe: Franjo Rački and Jaroslav Šidak.[38] Šidak's conclusion is confirmed

---

35 *Novum testamentum graece et latine, Editio septima, Imprimatur Traglia A., archiepiscopus Caesariensis, vicesgerens*, ed. by Merk, p. 16. I thank for this data Doctor of Theology Zoltán Rokay.

36 *Boldog Lanfrancus Canterbury érsek könyve az Úr testéről és véréről Tours-i Berengár ellen – Toursi Berengár három válasza Lanfrancusnak* [*The Book of Blessed Lanfranc the Archishop of Canterbury against Berengar of Tours concerning the Body and Blood of the Lord*], trans. by Rokay, pp. 15, 21, 23, 225.

37 Rokay, 'Luxemburgi Zsigmond teológiai kompetenciája' ['Sigismund of Luxembourg's Theological Competence'], p. 131.

38 Rački, *Bogomili i patareni* [*The Bogomils and the Pataria*], pp. 529, 570–71; Šidak, 'Kopitarevo evanđelje u sklopu pitanja "Bosanske crkve"' ['Kopitar's Gospel on the Question of "the Bosnian Church"'], pp. 122–23; Šidak, '"Bosanski rukopisi" u Gosudarstvenoj publičnoj biblioteci u Lenjingradu' ['"The Bosnian Manuscripts" in the State Public Historical Library of Russia in Leningrad'], p. 156.

by the fact that 'nadsuštni' (which can be translated in English as 'supreme' or 'beyond the essential') is the shortened form of 'nadsuštastveni'. With the aim of easing pronunciation, further shortening occurred. Thus, the expression 'daily bread' is used in prayers nowadays by both Slavic Orthodox and Uniates.[39] It is interesting to note at this point that a contemporary translation of the Gospel into Serbo-Croatian reads: 'Hljeb naš potrebni daj nam svaki dan'.[40] This translates into English as 'give us our essential bread every day'. The only exception made in the Greek Orthodox terminology (in the Serbian language) involves the so-called Miroslav's Gospel. In the Gospel of Matthew in this version, the phrase used is 'хлеб неш наставшаго дне'. This translates into English as 'the bread of the nascent day', where the expression 'of the nascent day' is closer to the term 'daily'.[41] It is written 'нбш' (pronounced #/nbsh/) in Jaroslav Šidak's text, instead of 'наставшаго', probably by omission, since 'нбш' does not have a lexical meaning.[42] It therefore would seem that the terms 'nasuštni'and 'daily' are not a reliable criterion for distinguishing between 'orthodox' and 'heretical' texts of the Gospel, as Aleksandar Soloviev proposed.[43] Putting aside for the moment the consideration of the dogmatic differences between the Catholic and Orthodox Church on the one hand, and the Hussites and Cathars on the other, it should be pointed out that it was this difference in the prayer that the Inquisition in western Europe employed in finding and denouncing heretics, in this case the Cathars. This was effected primarily by forcing them to recite the entirety of the 'Our Father'.[44] Intriguingly, Emmanuel Le Roy Ladurie does not mention this difference when he speaks of the 'Our Father' prayer.[45]

It is also important to observe that, according to the Gospel of Matthew in the Munich Codex, Hungarian Hussites prayed for 'bread that is beyond our physical bread' (in Hungarian: 'my tests kenyerönk felett való kenyeret adjál minekönk'). In contrast, the Gospel of Luke in the same Bible contains the prayer for 'our daily bread', or 'Mü mendennapi kenyerönket adjad münekünk

---

39 *Свето писмо, Нови завјет господа нашег Исуса Христа* [*Holy Scripture, The New Testament of our Lord Jesus Christ*], 19, p. 157; *Нови завјет, псалтир, молитвеник* [*The New Testament, Psalter, Book of Prayers*], pp. 16, 139.

40 *Uporedno evanđelje (Sinopsis)* [*Comparative Gospel (Synopsis)*], ed. by Srnec, pp. 32, 89.

41 *Мирослављево јеванђеље* [*The Gospel of Miroslav*], ed. by Rodić and Jovanović, pp. 158, 198.

42 Šidak, 'Kopitarevo evanđelje u sklopu pitanja "Bosanske crkve"' ['Kopitar's Gospel on the Question of "the Bosnian Church"'], p. 122 n. 40. Gams, who considers that the Pater Noster is 'by its simplicity and strength a unique literary masterpiece' (translated by myself from Serbian), did not comment on this difference in his work: Gams, *Biblija u svetlu društvenih borbi* [*The Bible in the Light of Social Turmoil*], p. 89.

43 Solovjev, *Vjersko učenje bosanske crkve* [*The Religious Learning of the Bosnian Church*], p. 40.

44 Testas and Testas, *Inkvizicija* [*Inquisition*].

45 Le Roy Ladurie, *Montaju, oksitansko selo od 1294 do 1324* [*Montaillou, village occitan de 1294 à 1324*], pp. 352–54.

ma'.[46] Much later, Hungarian Calvinists, whose forerunners the Hussites are sometimes considered to be, likewise retained the 'Roman Catholic' form of prayer for daily bread.[47] Finally, in their version of the 'Our Father', the French Calvinists, or Huguenots, prayed for 'Paine de notre aujourd'hui' (bread of our today).[48]

Inquisitional Activity: An Unusual Proof of, and Catalyst for, the Merging of Religious Divides

For its part, the Catholic Church had prevented the lay population from using Holy Scripture directly. On the eve of the struggle against those deemed heretics, mainly the Cathars, in 1198, Pope Innocent III forbade secular people not only from interpreting the Bible, but also reading it. This ban was made even stricter at the Second Council of Tarragona in 1234, which forbade the lay public from even possessing a Bible.[49]

In line with this, in the fifteenth century Pope Eugene IV (1431–1447) sent an inquisitor to suppress both the Bogomil and the Hussite heresies in Hungary. The inquisitor in this case was none other than Jacob de Marchia. His real name was Domenico Gangala, and he was originally from the small town of Monteprandone in Marchia Anconitana in Italy: hence his official working name. De Marchia had a reputation as a fierce and somewhat notorious fighter against any kind of heresy, especially the so-called 'Bosnian heresy'. According to the testimony of the Canon of Tours, Gilles Charlier (known in Latin as Aegidius Carlerius), Jacob openly talked of the Bosnian king, whom he had met at the Hungarian court, as being no Christian since he was not baptized.[50]

The Inquisition in Transylvania

Between 1436 and 1437, Jacob de Marchia expanded the geographical scope of his work to southern Hungary and Transylvania, where he was sent by Emperor

46 *Máté evangeliuma, Kapitulum VI, 11. Lukács evangéliuma, Kapitulum XI, 3, Müncheni kódex, /1466/, A négy evangélium szövege és szótára* [*The Gospel of Matthew Kapitulum VI, 11. The Gospel of Luke, Kapitulum XI, 3, Codex of Munich /1466/, Text and Dictionary of Four Gospels*], ed. by Décsy and Szabó, p. 28.

47 *Biblia*, ed. by Károli, no page numbering.

48 Calvin, *Bible protestante, Confession de foi de Genève XVIe siècle*, ed. by Marot, Nous, and Olivétan. For this information I am grateful to Deacon Saša Pajković, manager of the Library of the Faculty of Orthodox Theology in Belgrade, and to Tatjana Sajlovič, librarian in the same institution.

49 Gams, *Biblija u svetlu društvenih borbi* [*The Bible in the Light of Social Turmoil*], p. 134.

50 Rokai, 'Poslednje godine balkanske politike kralja Žigmunda (1435–1437)' ['The Final Years of Sigismund of Luxembourg's Balkan Policy (1435–1437)'], pp. 95–96; Živković, *Tvrtko II*, pp. 176, 181, 184–87.

Sigismund, who had just won a victory over the Hussites in Bohemia. Earlier historiography had attributed his success to 'fiery sermons [...] held in the national language'.[51] On the basis of an authentic contemporary document, however, it has been conclusively demonstrated that Jacob did not have any knowledge of Hungarian.[52]

His success owed far more to the brutal force applied during his missionary campaign than to knowledge of the vernacular. Jacob passed verdicts even on heretics already dead, exhuming them and then burning their remains, as, for example, he did with the deceased pastor of Begečka.[53] This, however, was neither a novel nor a surprising method, as it had been previously used in the south of France in the thirteenth and fourteenth centuries. There, Dominican inquisitors had dealt in the same way with the remains of deceased and buried Cathars, so that their remains would not defile consecrated ground. Such robust methods of persuasion guaranteed that the work of Jacob de Marchia was a 'success', as evidenced by mass 'conversions'. His triumph can be deduced from the written congratulations he received from both secular and ecclesiastical authorities. Although it is unknown exactly what these 'conversions' consisted of, they were no doubt superficial.

Apart from those agreeing under pressure to abandon their 'heresy', there were cases of 'heretics' who opposed the Inquisitor. Of these, the great uprising of peasants in Transylvania (Erdely) that broke out in June in 1437 needs first and foremost to be mentioned. It occurred as an outcome of Jacob's campaign, but its immediate cause was a Transylvanian bishop's response to a financial crisis — which was to require the peasants in his diocese to pay the church tithe in the old manner. The secular authorities intervened, led by the Duke of Transylvania, who, realizing that he could not overpower the peasants, initially agreed to improve the serfs' conditions. This included the annulment of the ninth and a decrease in the church tithe, as well as the founding of a peasant

51 See Pór and Schönherr, *Az Anjou ház és örökösei* [*The House of Anjou and Heirs*], as cited in Szilágyi Sándor, *A magyar nemzet története. III* [*The History of the Hungarian Nation III*], p. 599; Tóth-Szabó, *A cseh huszita mozgalmak és uralom története Magyarországon* [*A History of the Czech Hussite Movement and Rule in Hungary*], p. 157; Burka, 'Marchiai Szt. Jakab' ['St Jacob de Marchia'], pp. 280–91, 339–52.

52 *Aegidii Carlerii Liber de legationibus, Quinta legatio (1435) Monumenta Conciliorum generalium saeculi decimi quinti, Concilium Basiliens, I*, p. 148; Rokai, 'Poslednje godine balkanske politike kralja Žigmunda (1435–1437)' ['The Final Years of Sigismund of Luxembourg's Balkan Politics (1435–1437)'], pp. 94–95; Rokay, 'Beszélt-e magyarul Marchiai Jakab?' ['Did Jacob de Marchia speak Hungarian?'], pp. 99–101.

53 *Aegidii Carlerii Liber de legationibus, Quinta legatio (1435) Monumenta Conciliorum generalium saeculi decimi quinti, Concilium Basiliens, I*, p. 148; *Acta Bosnae*, ed. by Fermendžin, nos DCCLII, DCCLIV, DCCLXII, DCCLXIII, DCCLXIV, DCCLXVI, DCCLXVII, DCCLXVIII, DCCXCI, DCCCXXVI, DCCCV, MXLII, pp. 158–77, 184, 202, 245–48; Rokai, 'Poslednje godine balkanske politike kralja Žigmunda (1435–1437)' ['The Final Years of Sigismund of Luxembourg's Balkan Politics (1435–1437)'], pp. 94–95; Rokay, 'Beszélt-e magyarul Marchiai Jakab?' ['Did Jacob de Marchia speak Hungarian?'], pp. 99–101.

assembly that would oversee compliance with the agreement. By agreeing, however, the feudal lords only wanted to gain extra time. Representatives of the Hungarian nobility made a pact against the rebellious peasants, forcing them to agree to a less favourable arrangement, whose implementation was delayed until King Sigismund of Luxembourg had ratified it. This ratification, however, never happened, as Sigismund died on 9 December 1437. The army of feudal lords attacked. A number of the rebels managed to escape and migrated to neighbouring Moldavia. These emigrants would in later years constitute the nucleus of the Hungarian colony.[54]

At the same time, Jacob de Marchia encountered opposition to his brutal actions in the form of the Hussites of Kamenica, a settlement near modern Novi Sad (in Hungarian: Újvidék) in northern Serbia. To a lesser extent, he was also opposed by other inhabitants of Novi Sad and the surrounding region. In Kamenica there was the case of a tailor named Balint, who attacked the local Judge John with a sword. The judge had been under orders from de Marchia to execute a sentence on the tailor and three others, all of whom were considered heretics. On this occasion, a conflict occurred between the Inquisitor's entourage and the villagers, resulting in the freeing of a member of the community who had been destined for execution. There is evidence that this actually occurred: the event was confirmed to Jacob de Marchia by seventeen persons out of twenty-one questioned, all of whom came from nearby places.

In 1439 the community in Kamenica fell under the threat of the Inquisition. This led to a mass migration to the town of Tatros, known in Romanian as Târgu Trotuş, on the border of Moldavia and Bukovina and near the River Prut, nowadays in eastern Romania. Here, their community and their way of teaching the Bible survived into the seventeenth century. The community joined a group of co-believers who had emigrated after the peasant uprising in Transylvania had been quelled. Reportedly, they founded a town in Moldavia named Hus (although the origin of the town has been disputed by some modern historians, including Nicolae Iorga). This was not the end of their persecution: in 1440 Pope Eugenius IV sent Fabianus de Bacia as De Marchia's successor. With this aim in mind, in 1461 the inquisitor Juan de Torquemada created a list of thirty-eight errors in the beliefs of the Moldavian Hussites.[55] This community in Moldavia was strengthened numerically when in the

54 Gombos, *Az 1437. évi parasztlázadás története* [*The History of the 1437 Peasant Uprising*].

55 *Acta Bosnae*, ed. by Fermendžin, nos DCCLII, DCCLIV, DCCLXII, DCCLXIII, DCCLXIV, DCCLXVI, DCCLXVII, DCCLXVIII, DCCLXXXIV, DCCLXXXVI, DCCLXXXVIII, DCCXCI, DCCCXXVI, DCCCV, MXLII, pp. 158–77, 184, 202, 245–48; *Chronicon observantis provinciae Bosnae Argentinae ordinis s. Francisci Seraphici*, ed. by Fermendžin, pp. 18–20: Грујић [Grujić], 'Један папски инквизитор 15. века у Војводини' ['A Papal Inquisitor in Vojvodina in the 15th Century'], p. 430; Rokai, 'Poslednje godine balkanske politike kralja Žigmunda (1435–1437)' ['The Final Years of Sigismund of Luxembourg's Balkan Policy (1435–1437)'], pp. 95–96.

mid-1560s a group of co-religionists arrived from nearby areas of Hungary and Transylvania, seeking refuge from King Matthias Corvinus's persecution (1458–1490) of the Bohemian Hussites in his country.

Bohemian Hussites came to Hungary as mercenaries for various reasons, including as a result of fighting against the Turks, and because of dynastic struggles between Wladislaw III Jagiello and Elizabeth, who was the daughter of the Emperor Sigismund, the widow of Albert of Habsburg, and the mother of Ladislaus V. Two of these mercenaries, Jan Giškra and Jan Vitovec, for more than a quarter of the century held the North of Hungary, nowadays Slovakia, in their power. One of the measures of the Hussite persecution was the third paragraph of the second article of the Law of 29 May 1462, by which Corvinus condemned the Hussites to 'the loss of head and property'.[56] Three years later, King Matthias Corvinus took the last stronghold of the Bohemian Hussites, the fortress of Kostolany in Slovakia, and executed their leader, Jan Švehla.

At the invitation of Pope Paul II (1464–1471), King Matthias waged war in 1466 against the Hussite ruler of Moravia and Bohemia, George Poděbrady (1458–1471), his former father-in-law. War broke out because Poděbrady did not keep to the agreement with the Catholic Church, the so-called Compacts of Prague.[57] It may not have been by chance that in that very year George Nemeti's son Emmerich Henze finished copying the Codex of Munich in Tatros, Moldavia. This text contains on a hundred folio pages a Hungarian calendar and the four Gospels, translated into Hungarian probably sometime after 1416. According to modern linguistic analysis, it contains a number of archaic forms characteristic of the period.[58]

Having moved to the periphery of the Roman Catholic Western world, Hungarian Hussite immigrants enjoyed the protection of Corvinus's opponent and rival, the Orthodox Moldavian Prince Stephen the Great (Stefan cel Mare, 1457–1504). This was obviously not because of his religious tolerance, as László Király stated, but as a result of his support for the internal opponents of King Matthias, Stefan had been in conflict with Matthias for a number of years, and he even led a war against him.[59] In this way, the teachings of Jan Hus, so often cast as a predecessor of the Reformation of the sixteenth century, migrated from Bohemia at the centre of Europe to the south-eastern edges of the Continent, thanks in no small part to the translation of the Bible into Hungarian.

The descendants of the Hussites of southern Hungary and Transylvania were in Moldova in the sixteenth century, where, according to the testimony

---

56 *Decreta regni Hungariae*, ed. by Dőry, Bónis, Érszegi, and Teke, p. 126.

57 Rokai, Đere, Pal, and Kasaš, *Istorija Mađara* [*History of the Hungarians*], pp. 153, 162.

58 *A Huszita biblia (János evangelista könyvö), Biblia husita, Régi magyar nyelvemlékek* [*A Hussite Bible (The Book of John the Evangelist)*], ed. by Király, Décsy, and Szabó (2012), IX, p. 6.

59 Стефановић, 'Краљ Матија према Влашкој и Босни' ['King Matthias towards Wallachia and Bosnia'], pp. 1–3, 11–14; Macurek, 'Husiství v rumunskich zemích' ['Hussitism in Romanian Lands'], p. 28 n. 2, 85.

of Franciscan missionaries, they performed the liturgy in Hungarian. Their community and religious practice on the periphery of European society was preserved until the eighteenth century, when Franciscan missionaries converted them to Catholicism. Some of them, however, embraced Protestantism. Their ability to survive in faraway places has a certain similarity with another branch of the followers of the Czech reformers, the Herrnhuter and the Moravian brotherhood, whose community to this day endures on another periphery of ecumenism amongst the Inuits in Greenland.

The Inquisition in Bosnia

In 1459, at the same time as the Hussites of southern Hungary were being persecuted, Stefan Tomaš, the penultimate King of Bosnia (1443–1461), was expelling Bogomils from his realm and ordering the forced Catholicization of the highest ranks of their hierarchy. Torquemada, considered the expert on various forms of heresy, on the order of Pope Pius II (1458–1464) produced a formal rejection of Bogumil 'fallacies' in fifty points. Although both of Torquemada's lists of Hussite and the Bogomil heretical errors have been separately subjected to thorough analysis, no comparative study of them has been made thus far.

The consequence of Tomaš's actions was that three *krstjana*, as the highest ranks of Bogomils called themselves, were sent to Rome in chains. That the bringing back of the Bogomils to the 'true Catholic faith' was surely, to an extent, successful can be seen from the report that three men, Đorđe Kučinić, Stojsav Tvrtković, and Radmilo Venčinić, solemnly rejected the listed fallacies on 9 May 1461 and were baptized according to the Catholic rite, and were sent back to Bosnia. However, one of them escaped to the lands of the Herceg Stefan Vukčić-Kosača, having probably renounced his forced conversion. Unlike the King of Bosnia, Herceg Stefan Vukčić Kosača, according to whose title the area was later named Herzegovina, did not persecute the Bogomils.[60]

One group of Bogomils, bringing with them their holy books, including the New Testament written on parchment, found sanctuary in north-western Bulgaria, which was already under the rule of the Ottoman Empire. All the books used in their sermons were written in Bosnian dialect and Cyrillic script (Bosnian Cyrillic). Thus, it is not surprising that as late as the seventeenth century, their elder, Pop (priest) Rastko of the village of Davučevo, was still giving the sermon with 'leggere in Serviano' as late as 1646.[61] Thus, the

60 *Acta Bosnae*, ed. by Fermendžin, no. MXXIV, p. 243; Ćirković, 'Bosanska', p. 320.

61 Solovjev, *Vjersko učenje bosanske crkve* [*The Religious Teaching of the Bosnian Church*], p. 42 ft. 80; Šidak, 'Kopitarevo evanđelje u sklopu pitanja "Bosanske crkve"' ['Kopitar's Gospel on the Question of "the Bosnian Church"'], p. 122 ft. 40; Ćirković, 'Глосе Срећковићевог јеванђеља' ['The Gloss of Srećković's Gospel'], pp. 207–21.

Serbian language and Cyrillic script became the official language and alphabet in north-western Bulgaria. Over the centuries, Bosnian religious emigrants merged with the indigenous Bulgarian Bogomils and Paulicians, who had been living in the area for hundreds of years.

The Bogomils had a long history in Bulgaria. Arriving from the Middle East, they appeared first in Bulgaria in the tenth century. Since their teaching was partly aimed against the secular authorities, the Byzantine Church persecuted them, so they moved westward to the medieval Serbian state, where Veliki Župan (the Grand Prince) Stefan Nemanja (1168–1196) sentenced their leader to death by burning, and expelled them from his lands. The Bogomils founded their strongest and most lasting communities in Bosnia, where they survived until the Ottoman conquests, as discussed above. These communities succeeded in remaining in Bosnia over the centuries, despite the fact that in 1203 Ban Kulin swore an oath on Bilino Polje (Bilino Field, near the town of Zenica) that he would either Christianize them or expel them.

Although they too were persecuted by the Byzantine authorities over the centuries, the Paulicians survived. Over the centuries a symbiosis relationship developed between the Paulicians and the Bogomils. Paulicians, melting into the Bogomils, outlived the Byzantine Empire, and survived the conquest of the Ottomans, who did not trouble them because of their religious affiliation. Thus, Paulicians survived in Bulgaria for the entire duration of the Ottoman Empire.[62] However, they were not left completely in peace, since Catholic missionaries, mainly Franciscans, continued trying to convert them.

Having been converted to Catholicism, Paulicians from the cis-Danubian parts of Bulgaria and Vidin Bulgaria escaped, from the seventeenth century until well into the eighteenth century, from regions held by the Ottoman Empire into Habsburg territory. They partially colonized the area of Banat with centres in the town of Vinga, in Tamis County, and in Besenovo Veche, in Torontál County.[63] One descendant of the leaders of the colonization was none other than Eusebius Fermendžin (1845–1897), the most significant collector of the sources pertaining to medieval Bosnia and Bulgaria, to whose collections this essay is heavily indebted. Bulgarian settlers soon moved from Vinga to the towns of Bresće, Deta, and Dentain, Romania, and to Ivanovo and Skorenovac in Vojvodina, Serbia.[64]

Bulgarians, converted to Catholicism, also settled in Bačka (Bachka), as a consequence of the military actions of the border regiment of Subotica against the Turks in Oltenia and north-western Bulgaria. The regiment was followed by the Franciscans.[65] Their retreat was accompanied by a part of population,

62 Vanegeim, 'Chapter 25: Paulicians and Bogomils', no page numbering.

63 Szentkláray, 'Temes vármegye története' ['History of Temes County'], p. 126; Matasović, 'Ogledi paulikijanskske historiografije' ['Experiments of Pavlikian Historiography'], p. 81.

64 Szentkláray, 'Torontál vármegye története' ['History of Torontál County'], pp. 37, 80, 166; Matasović, 'Ogledi paulikijanskske historiografije'['Experiments of Pavlikian Historiography'], p. 81.

65 Tormásy, *A szabadkai római kath* [*History of the Main Parish of Subotica*], pp. 29, 101, 175.

which settled in Subotica. There they were regarded as part of the southern Slav population as late as the end of the eighteenth century.

At approximately the same time as the last Hungarian Hussites disappeared, Bosnian Franciscans converted to Roman Catholicism the last Bogomils and Paulicians in north-western Bulgaria, who had until then kept their faith. At some point in the first half of the seventeenth century, their 'heretical' books were transferred to the Chiprovtzi headquarters of Petar Bogdan Bakšić, Roman Catholic Bishop of Sofia. In the opinion of Aleksandar Soloviev, these books were destroyed in a fire that happened in Chiprovtzi in 1688. One cannot exclude, however, the possibility that the occasional book avoided this fate, if it has been hidden in an unknown place.[66] This may have been the case with the so-called Srećković Gospel, of which historiography knows nothing more, except for the existence of two pages that were placed in the Museum of Antiquities in Tver (Kalinin). Sima Ćirkovic incorrectly identifies Tver as Kaliningrad (Königsberg), whilst Tver is Kalinin, where Panta Srecković made the discovery.[67] Srecković was a commissioner of the Serbian government in areas liberated in the war against Turkey in 1877/1878. Before the Turkish conquest these provinces had belonged to Bulgaria, and Bulgaria, which was being freed herself, naturally aspired to them. Srećković never mentioned the provenance of the Gospel that was named after him. It may have been for political reasons that the Bulgarian authorities would not make claims to it.[68]

After the conquest of Chiprovtzi and the surrounding area by the Turks in 1690, its heretical 'Bogomil' residents who had converted to Catholicism were forced to emigrate to Oltenia and Transylvania (Erdely). And so, the descendants of both groups of persecuted believers found refuge in the territory of today's Romania–Hungarian Hussites in Moldova, and Bosnian Bogomils in Wallachia and Transylvania.

The Bulgarian scholar Boris Primov believes the mythical priest Bogumil to be a direct predecessor of the Reformation of the sixteenth century. He claims this by explaining that the ideas of priest Bogumil were transferred to many nations over time, and that in Hungary were spread out by Jan Hus's followers. Furthermore, he clarifies his position by stating that the link between Bogomilism and the Reformation was well established, since the Hussites were the last representatives of Bogumil's ideas in the west and because the very leaders of the Reformation accepted Hussitism as predecessor of the Reformation.[69] Sima Ćirkovic, on the other hand, does not consider the Bosnian heretics to be precursors of the Reformation. It

66 Solovjev, *Vjersko učenje bosanske crkve* [*The Religious Teaching of the Bosnian Church*], p. 44.

67 Ćirković, 'Глосе Срећковићевог јеванђеља' ['The Gloss of Srećković's Gospel'], p. 207 n. 2.

68 Veselinović, Ćirković, and Mihaljčić, 'Срећковић Пантелија (Панта)' ['Srećković Pantelija (Panta)'], pp. 644–45.

69 Primov, 'Българското богомилство' ['Bulgarian Bogomilism'], pp. 51, 50, 34; Stojanov, *Skrivena tradicija u Evropi i tajna istorija srednjovekovne hrišćanske jeresi* [*Hidden Tradition in Europe and the Secret History of Medieval Christian Heresy*].

cannot be denied that Orthodox Serbs, from the twelfth century (when the ruler Stefan Nemanja expelled the Bogomils from the medieval Serbian state (Raška)) until the early Reformation period (as Ćirković notes), encountered heterodox teachings regarded as equally heretical by the Orthodox and Roman Catholic hierarchies alike.[70] It is also a fact that the ideas of Church reformers from the fourteenth to the sixteenth century influenced socio-religious changes — from the Peasants' Revolt of 1381 in England to the Hussite Wars of 1419–1434, the great peasant revolt in Transylvania in 1437, and the German Peasants' War of 1525.

Conclusions

The essay has endeavoured to provide a wide-ranging account of diverse but interconnected communities and phenomena that existed primarily in the territories of southern Hungary during the long fifteenth century. As we have seen, analysis of the character of the interrelations amongst such communities across time and space has extended the scope of discussion of this topic along both axes. Aiming to demonstrate the complexity of such relations, this study has not only expanded the time frame of the historical discussion well into the eighteenth century, but has also enlarged its geographical reach by including places as distant from the communities' central and south-eastern European origins as Greenland and the Caribbean Islands.

To sum up, in outline, the key events which defined this study, one of the first that drew our attention was that, in the fifteenth century, south-eastern Europe witnessed not only the appearance of Hussitism but also (in the previous century) Wycliffism. The division in the 1400s of the Hussite movement into moderate Utraquists and radical Taborites had an impact far beyond the perimeter of Bohemia and its immediate surroundings. The teachings of the former, having survived amongst its break-away fraction of Moravian Brothers, was resurrected later in the eighteenth century, extending in influence as far as Greenland and the Danish West Indies. The Taborites, on the other hand, found shelter in Hungary, in Transylvania, and particularly in Srem, where a symbiosis between the adherents of Hussite and Bogomil teaching took place and, in its own way, flourished.

During the fifteenth century, the activities of the Inquisition in the south of Hungary, Transylvania, and Bosnia can be viewed as unusual proof of, and a key vehicle for, the crossing and merging of religious divides in these areas. Inquisitorial activity caused the Hungarian Hussites to migrate from Srem and seek protection in the territory of a Moldavian Orthodox Prince, where they were joined by co-religionists from Transylvania after the Great Peasant

70 Ćirković, 'Bosanska crkva u bosanskoj državi' ['The Bosnian Church in the Bosnian State'], p. 238 n. 158; Ćirković, 'Срби и рани протестантизам' ['The Serbs and Early Protestantism'], pp. 7–25.

Uprising. The teachings of Jan Hus were thus transferred from Bohemia to the south-eastern edges of the Continent, thanks also in no small part to the translation of the Bible into Hungarian. The community descended from the Hussites of southern Hungary and Transylvania was preserved, together with its religious practices, until the eighteenth century, when Franciscan missionaries converted them to Catholicism. The Inquisition in Bosnia drove a group of Bogomils to find sanctuary in north-western Bulgaria, which was already under the rule of the Ottoman Empire; in subsequent centuries this group was converted to Roman Catholicism.

The examples collected in this study co-situate and tie together many and varied experiences of different communities of interpretating Holy Scripture originating in central and eastern Europe, whose teaching was not confined to this region. The comparison of Hussite and Bogomil (Cathar) teaching has provided a particularly telling example of the successful bridging of historical divides in eastern Europe. This is shown in our analysis of similarities and differences in the transmission of the 'Our Father', as taught by the Hussites of southern Hungary and the Cathars of Bosnia, and as contained within the Codex of Munich. In this case, it is visible, in compelling textual terms that redefine a long-held divide, how the term 'breath', as used in the 'Hussite Bible', simply is not sufficient to prove its heretical character, but merely testifies to an outdated linguistic form. In that the terms 'nasuštni' and 'daily' are no reliable criteria for distinguishing between 'orthodox' and 'heretical' texts of the Gospel (as some scholars have proposed), this essay suggests, by this single methodologically representative example, a significant new interpretation of mutual influence and a new understanding of the porosity of historical divides — a porosity that is evidenced richly not just in confinement to this one single instance but also by a more widespread porosity which may be extrapolated in terms of many other examples mentioned in the course of this study, thereby providing a bigger and more nuanced picture of change, diversity, connectivity, and continuity in the religious field over the Europe of the long fifteenth century and beyond, both in time and space.

Works Cited

Primary Sources

Aegidii Carlerii Liber de legationibus, Quinta legatio (1435) Monumenta Conciliorum generalium saeculi decimi quinti, Concilium Basiliens, I (Vienna: Typ. Aulae of Status, 1857)

Acta Bosnae potissimum ecclesiastica cum insertis editorum documentorum regestis, ab anno 925 usque ad annum 1752, ed. by Eusebius Fermendžin, in *Monumenta spectantia ad historiam Slavorum Meridionalium, XXIII* (Zagreb: Academia Scientarium et Artium Slavorum Meridionalium, 1892)

A Huszita biblia (János evangelista könyvö), Biblia husita, Régi magyar nyelvemlékek [*A Hussite Bible (The Book of John the Evangelist), The Hussite Bible*], ed. by László Király, Gyula Décsy, Ádám Szabó T. in *Moldvai magyarság* [*Moldavian Hungarians*], I, II, III, VI, V, VI, VII, VIII, IX, X, XI, XII (Hargita Megye Tanácsa: Consiliul Judetean Harghita, 2012, 2013, 2014)

A Müncheni Kódex 1466-ból [*Codex of Munich from 1466*], ed. by Antal Nyiri (Budapest: Codices Hungarici, 1971)

A Müncheni kódex [*Codex of Munich*], ed. by Gábor Döbrentei, Régi magyar nyelvemlékek, 3 (Buda: n. pub, 1842)

A Müncheni kódex [*Codex of Munich*], ed. by György Volf, Nyelvemléktár, 1. kötet (Budapest: n. pub, 1874)

Biblia, ed. by Gáspár Károli <www.bibleu-szeged.hu> [accessed 15 January 2017]

Boldog Lanfrancus Canterbury érsek könyve az Úr testéről és véréről Tours-i Berengár ellen – Toursi Berengár három válasza Lanfrancusnak [*The Book of Blessed Lanfranc the Archishop of Canterbury against Berengar of Tours concerning the Body and Blood of the Lord – Three Replies by Berengar of Tours to Lanfranc*], ed. and translated from Latin by Zoltán Rokay, Textus receptus: I (Óbecse: Lux Color Printing- Szulik József Alapítvány, 2009)

Chronicon observantis provinciae Bosnae Argentinae ordinis s. Francisci Seraphici, ed. by Eusebius Fermendžin, *Starine JAZU*, 22 (Zagreb: Jugoslovenska akademija znanosti i umjetnosti, 1890)

Decreta regni Hungariae (Gesetze und Verordnungen Ungarns), II, 1458–1490, ed. by Franciscus Dőry, Georgius Bónis, Geisa Érszegi, and Susanna Teke, Publicationes Archivi nationalis hungarici, Publikationen des Ungarischen Staatsarchivs, Fontes (Quellenpublikationen), 19 (Budapest: Archivi nationalis hungarici, 1989)

Der Münchener Kodex, ed. by Gyula Décsy and Julius Farkas (Wiesbaden: Harrassowitz, 1958, 1966)

Jean Calvin, *Bible protestante, Confession de foi de Genève XVIe siècle*, ed. by Clément Marot, Pierre Nous, and Pierre Robert Olivétan <https://oratoiredulouvre.fr/prier/notre-pere/confession-de-foi-de-geneve-xvie-siecle-jean-calvin> [accessed 24 June 2019]

Máté evangeliuma, Kapitulum VI, 11. Lukács evangéliuma, Kapitulum XI, 3, Müncheni kódex, /1466/, A négy evangélium szövege és szótára [*The Gospel of Matthew Kapitulum VI, 11. The Gospel of Luke, Kapitulum XI, 3, Codex of Munich /1466/, Text and Dictionary of Four Gospels*], ed. by Gyula Décsy and Ádám Szabó (Budapest: Európa könyvkiadó, 1985)

Мирослављево јеванђеље [*The Gospel of Miroslav*], ed. by Никола Родић, Гордана Јовановић, in Зборник за историју, језик и књижевност српског народа, I одељење, XXXIII (Београд: САНУ, Институт за српскохрватски језик, 1986) [ed. by Nikola Rodić and Gordana Jovanović (Belgrade: SANU, Institute for Serbo-Croatian Language, 1986)]

Нови завјет, псалтир, молитвеник [*The New Testaments, Psalter, Prayer Book*] (Belgrade: Publishing Foundation of Belgrade-Karlovac Serbian Church, 2014)]

Novum testamentum graece et latine, Editio septima, Imprimatur Traglia A., archiepiscopus Caesariensis, vicesgerens, ed. by Augustinus Merk (Rome: Sumptibus Pontificii instituti biblici, 1951)
Novum testamentum graece et latine, Editio septima, Imprimatur Traglia A., archiepiscopus Caesariensis, vicesgerens, ed. by Augustinus Merk (Rome: Sumptibus Pontificii instituti biblici, 1992)
Свето писмо, Нови завјет господа нашег Исуса Христа [*Holy Scripture, The New Testament of our Lord Jesus Christ*] (Belgrade: The Holy Archiepiscopal Synod of the Serbian Orthodox Church, date unestablished/unavailable)
Uporedno evanđelje (Sinopsis) [*Comparative Gospel (Synopsis)*], ed. by Želimir Srnec (Novi Sad: Dobra vest, 1985)

Secondary Studies

Asbóth, János (Asbóth, John/Johann von), 'A bosnyák bogumilek az Árpádok és Anjouk korában' ['Bosnian Bogomils in the Age of Árpád and Anjou Dynasties'], *Budapesti szemle,* 41. 97 (1885), 25–52
———, *Bosnien und die Herzegowina* (Vienna: Reisebilder und Studien, 1888)
———, *An Official Tour through Bosnia and Herzegovina* (London: Swan Sonnenschein, 1890)
Borst, Arno, *Die Katharer,* Schriften der Monumenta Germaniae Historica, 12 (Stuttgart: MGH, 1953)
Brandt, Miroslav, 'Susret viklifizma sa bogomilstvom u Srijemu' ['The Meeting of Wycliffism with Bogomilism in Srem'], *Starohrvatska prosvjeta,* Nova serija, 3.5 (1956), 33–64
Burka, Kelemen, 'Marchiai Szt. Jakab' ['St Jacob de Marchia'], *Katholikus szemle,* 38 (1924), 280–91, 339–52
Cröger, E. W., *Geschichte der erneuerten Brüderkirche,* vols I and II (Gnadau: Verlag der Buchhandlung der evangelischen Brüder-Unität, 1852–1854)
Ćirković, Sima, 'Глосе Срећковићевог јеванђеља и учење Босанске цркве' ['The Gloss of Srećković's Gospel and the Teaching of the Bosnian Church'], in *Богомилство то на Балканотвосветлина тананајновите истражувања* (Скопје: Македонска Академија на науките и уметностите, 1983) [*Bogomilism in the Balkans in the Light of the Newest Research*] (Skopje: Macedonian Academy of Sciences and Arts, 1983)], pp. 207–22
———, 'Bosanska crkva u bosanskoj državi' ['The Bosnian Church in the Bosnian State'], in *Prilozi za istoriju Bosne i Hercegovine,* I, *Društvo i privreda srednjovjekovne bosanske države* [*Contributions to the History of Bosnia and Herzegovina: I, Society and Economy of the Medieval Bosnian State*], ed. by Enver Redžić, Posebna izdanja Akademije nauka i umetnosti Bosne i Hercegovine, Knjiga, LXXIX, Odeljenje društvenih nauka, Knjiga 17 (Sarajevo: Akademije nauka i umetnosti Bosne i Hercegovine, 1987), pp. 191–254
———, 'Срби и рани протестантизам' ['The Serbs and Early Protestantism'], *Зборник Матице српске за историју [Matica Srpska Journal of History]* (1987), 7–25

Friedenthal, Richard, *Joanes Husz Ketzer und Rebell, Tractatus de Corpore Christi* (Munich: R. Piper, 1972)

Gams, Andrija, *Biblija u svetlu društvenih borbi* [*The Bible in the Light of Social Turmoil*] (Belgrade: Servis saveza pravnika Jugoslavije, 1970)

Gombos, Albin, *Az 1437. évi parasztlázadás története* [*The History of the 1437 Peasant Uprising*] (Kolozsvár: Gibbon, 1898)

Grujić, Radoslav, 'Један папски инквизитор 15. Века у Војводини' ['A Papal Inquisitor in Vojvodina in the 15th Century'], *Гласник Историјског друштва у Новом Саду* [*Bulletin of the Historical Society of Novi Sad*], 4 (1931), 437–40

Gyetvai, Péter, *Egyházi szervezés, főleg az egykori déli magyar területeken és a bácskai Tisza mentén* [*The Ecclesiastical Organization, mostly in the Former Hungarian South and near Bács Tisza*] (Munich: Görres Gesellschaft, 1987)

Horváth, Cirill, 'Huszita emlékeink' ['Our Hussite Monuments'], *Irodalomtörténeti közlemények* (1896), 3–4

Jireček, Joseph, 'Über die culturellen Beziehungen der Ungarn und Böhmen im XIV. und XV. Jahrhunderte und über die ungarischen Hussiten', *Sitzungsberichte der Königlichen böhmischen Gesellschaft der Wissenschaften, Philosophisch-historisch-philologische Klasse* (Vienna: der Königlichen böhmischen Gesellschaft der Wissenschaften, 1885), 101–13

Kardos, Tibor, 'A huszita mozgalmak és Hunyadi Mátyás szerepe a magyar nemzeti egyház kialakításában' ['The Role of the Hussite Movement and Matthias Hunyadi in the Creation of the Hungarian National Church'], *Századok*, 84 (1950), 121–77

———, *A huszita biblia keletkezése* [*The Creation of the Hussite Bible*], A Magyar Nyelvtudományi Társaság kiadványai, 82 (Budapest: A Magyar Nyelvtudományi Társaság, 1953)

———, 'Problematika bádání o husítství v Uhrach' ['The Problem of Research on Hussitism in Uhrach'], *Slavie*, 24 (1955), 444–55

Kniezsa, István, *Helyesírásunk története a könyvnyomtatás koráig* [*History of our Spelling until the Age of Book Printing*] (Budapest: MTA, 1952)

Kolpacoff Deane, Jennifer, *A History of Medieval Heresy and Inquisition* (Lanham: Rowman & Littlefield, 2011)

Korompay, Klára, 'Egy nyitott kérdés, több tudományterület metszéspontjában: az ún. Huszita biblia' ['One Open Question at the Meeting-point of Several Scholarly Fields: The So-Called Hussite Bible']. This is the text of an unpublished paper given at the Conference on Bohemio-Hungarian Cultural Ties at the Times of Jan Hus, Budapest, 10 November 2015

Kulcsár, Zsuzsanna, *Eretnekmozgalmak a XI–XIV. században* [*Les mouvements hérétiques aux XIe–XIVe siècles, Јеретическије движенија в XI–XIV веках*], A Budapesti Egyetemi könyvtár kiadványai (Bibliothèque de l'Université L. Eötvös, Библиотека Университета им. Л. Етвеша), 22 (Budapest: Tankönyvkiadó, 1964)

Lambert, Malcolm, *Medieval Heresy: Popular Movements from Bogomil to Hus* (London: Edward Arnold, 1977)

Lawaetz, H., *Brødremenighedens mission i Dansk-Vestindien 1769–1848: bidrag til en charakteristik af Brødrekirken og dens gerning og af den farvede races stilling til Christendommen* (Copenhagen: Otto B. Wroblewski, 1902)

Le Roy Ladurie, Emanuel, *Montaju, oksitansko selo od 1294. do 1324* [*Montaillou, village occitan de 1294 à 1324*] (Sremski Karlovci-Novi Sad: Izdavačka knjižarnica Zorana Stojanovića, 1991)

Maurois, André, *Povijest engleske politike* [*History of English Politics*] (Zagreb: Ante Velzek, 1940)

Macurek, Josef, 'Husiství v rumunskich zemych' ['Hussitism in Romanian Lands'], *Časopis Matice Moravske*, 51 (1927), 1–98

Matasović, Josip, 'Ogledi paulikijanskske historiografije' ['Experiments of Pavlikian Historiography'], *Glasnik Zemaljskog muzeja u Bosni i Hercegovini*, 32.1–6 (1920), 57–81

Melich, János, 'A Bécsi és a Müncheni kódex írói' ['Writers of the Codex of Vienna and Codex of Munich'], *Magyar Nyelvőr*, 27 (1898), 358–59

Pór, Antal, and Gyula Schönherr, *Az Anjou ház és örökösei (1301–1439)* [*The House of Anjou and Heirs*] (Budapest: Athenaeum Irodalmi és Nyomdai R.-T., 1895)

Primov, Borislav, 'Бʌгарското богомиʌство и европејската реформација' ['Bulgarian Bogomilism and the European Reformation'], *Исторически преглед* [*Historical Review*], 25.1 (1969), 29–51

Prohaska, Dragutin, 'Husitstvi a bogomilstvo' ['Hussitism and Bogomilism'], *Časopis pro moderni filologii a literatury*, 5 (1915), 10–11

———, 'Husiti i bogomili' ['Hussitism and Bogomilism'], *Jugoslavenska njiva*, 28.3 (1919), 437–43

Rački Franjo, *Bogomili i patareni* [*The Bogomils and the Pataria*], II izdanje u spomen stogodišnjice od rođenja Franje Račkog. Za štampu spremio Jov(an). Radonić [2nd edition in memory of one hundred years since the birth of Franjo Rački. Prepared for the press by Jov(an). Radonić] (Београд: Српска краљевска академија (Belgrade: Royal Serbian Academy, 1931)

Rajšli, Ilona, 'A huszita biblia nyelvi valósághátteréről' ['About the Real Linguistic Background of the Hussite Bible'], in *A honfoglalástól Mohácsig, Jugoszláviai magyar művelődéstörténeti tárasaság* [*From the Taking-up of the Fatherland until the Battle of Mohács*], ed. by István Bosnyák (Novi Sad: JMMT, 2002), pp. 179–89

Rokai, Petar, Zoltan Đere, Tibor Pal, and Aleksandar Kasaš, *Историја Мађара* [*History of the Hungarians*] (Belgrade: Clio, 2002)

Rokai, Petar, 'Poslednje godine balkanske politike kralja Žigmunda (1435–1437)' ['The Final Years of Sigismund of Luxembourg's Balkan Policy (1435–1437)'], *Godišnjak Filozofskog fakulteta u Novom Sadu*, 12.1 (1969), 89–108

Rokay, Péter, 'Beszélt-e magyarul Marchiai Jakab?' ['Did Jacob de Marchia speak Hungarian?'], *Hungarlógiai közlemények*, 26–27.8 (1976), 99–101

Rokay, Zoltán, 'Luxemburgi Zsigmond teológiai kompetenciája', ['Sigismund of Luxembourg's Theological Competence'], *Teológia*, 29.3–4 (2005), 121–35

Schultze, Augustus, *Die Missionsfelder der erneuerten Brüderkirche* (Bonn: A. Schultze, 1890)

Solovjev, Aleksandar, *Vjersko učenje bosanske crkve* [*The Religious Teaching of the Bosnian Church*] (Zagreb: JAZiU, 1949)

Стефановић, Велимир, *Краљ Матија према Влашкој и Босни* [*King Matthias towards Wallachia and Bosnia*], Прештампано из Летописа Матице српске [Reprinted from Letopis of Matica Srpska], 331 (Novi Sad: Izdanje knjižare Slavije, 1932)

Stojanov, Jurij, *Skrivena tradicija u Evropi i tajna istorija srednjovekovne hrišćanske jeresi* [*Hidden Tradition in Europe and the Secret History of Medieval Christian Heresy*] (Čačak: Gradac, 2003)

Szabó, Flóris, 'Huszita –e a Huszita Biblia? Bírálat és útkeresés' ['Is the Hussite Bible Hussite? The Critique and the Search for the Path'], *Irodalomtörténeti közlemények*, 93.1–2 (1989), 118–26

Székely, György, 'A huszitizmus és a magyar nép' ['Hussitism and the Hungarian People'], *Századok*, 90 (1956), 331–67, 556–90

———, 'Husítství a mad'arsky lid' ['Hussitism and the Hungarian People'], in *Mezinarodní ohlas husitství* [*International Hussitism*], ed. by Josef Macek (Prague: Nakladatelství Československé akademie věd, 1958), pp. 111–61

Szentkláray, Jenő, 'Temes vármegye története' ['History of Temes County'], in *Temes vármegye monográfija, Magyarország vármegyéi és városai* [*Monograph on Temes County: Counties and Towns of Hungary*], ed. by Ferencz Wirter (Budapest: Magyar Monográfia Társaság, [n. d.])

———, 'Torontál vármegye története' ['History of Torontál County'], in *Torontál vármegye monográfija, Magyarország vármegyéi és városai* [*Monograph on Temes County. Counties and Towns of Hungary*], ed. by Ferencz Wirter (Budapest: Magyar Monográfia Társaság, [n.d.])

Szilágyi, Sándor, *A agyar nemzet története.III* [*The History of the Hungarian Nation III*] (Budapest: Athenaeum részvénytársulat betüivel, 1895)

Šidak, Jaroslav, 'Kopitarevo evanđelje u sklopu pitanja "Bosanske crkve"' ['Kopitar's Gospel on the Question of "the Bosnian Church"'], in *Studije o 'Crkvi bosanskoj' I bogumilstvu* [*Studies on'the Bosnian Church' and Bogomilim*], ed. by Jaroslav Šidak (Zagreb: Sveučilišna naklada Liber, 1975), pp. 111–25

———, '"Bosanski rukopisi" u Gosudarstvenoj publičnoj biblioteci u Lenjingradu' ['"The Bosnian Manuscripts" in the State Public Historical Library of Russia in Leningrad'], in *Studije o 'Crkvi bosanskoj' i bogumilstvu* [*Studies on 'the Bosnian Church' and on Bogomilism*], ed. by Jaroslav Šidak (Zagreb: Sveučilišna naklada Liber, 1975), pp. 151–60

———, 'Heretički pokret i odjek husitizma na slavenskom Jugu' ['Heretical Movement and the Echo of Hussitism in the Slavic South'], in *Studije o 'Crkvi bosanskoj' i bogumilstvu* [*Studies on 'the Bosnian Church' and on Bogomilism*], ed. by Jaroslv Šidak (Zagreb: Sveučilišna naklada Liber, 1975), pp. 275–93

Testas, Guy, and Jean Testas, *Inkvizicija [Inquisition]* (Zagreb: Kršćanska sadašnjost, 1982)

Tímár, Kálmán, *Legrégibb bibliafordításunk eredete* [*The Origin of our Oldest Translation of the Bible*] (Kalocsa: Árpád rt. könyvny, 1931)

———, *Prémontrei kódexek: Huszita vagy prémontrei biblia?* [*Premonstratensian Codices: A Hussite or Premonstratensian Bible?*] (Budapest: Arpád Kiad, 1924)

Toldy, Ferenc, *Analecta Monumentorum Hungariae historica*, 1 (Pest: MTA, 1860)

Tormásy, Gábor, *A szabadkai római kath. Főplébánia története* [*History of the Main Parish of Subotica*] (Szabadka: Pertits Simon könyvnyomdája, 1883)

Tóth-Szabó, Pál, *A cseh huszita mozgalmak és uralom története Magyarországon* [*A History of the Czech Hussite Movement and Rule in Hungary*] (Budapest: Hornyánszky, 1917)

Tóth Bagi, István, 'Ötszáz évvel ezelőtt a Szerémségi Kamenicán készítették az első magyar bibliafordítást, Huszita mozgalmak a bácsi érsekség területén' ['Five Hundred Years Ago the First Hungarian Translation of the Bible was made in Kamenica in Srem: The Hussite Movements in the Territory of the Archdiocese of Bacs'] A newspaper article cut without the name of the newspaper or the pagination (1938)

Vanegeim, Raoul, 'Chapter 25: Paulicians and Bogomils', *Resistance to Christianity* <http://www.notbored.org/resistance-25.html> [accessed 17 January 2015]

Veselinović, Andrija, Sima Ćirković, and Mihaljčić Rade, 'Срећковић Пантелија (Панта)' ['Srećković Pantelija (Panta)'], in *Енциклопедија српске историографије* [*Encylopedia of Serbian Historiography*] (Belgrade: Knowledge, 1997)

Westergaard, Waldemar, *The Danish West Indies under Company Rule (1671–1754), with a Supplementary Chapter (1755–1917)* (New York: Macmillan, 1917)

Živković, Pavo, *Tvrtko II: Bosna u prvoj polovini XV stoljeća* [*Tvrtko II: Bosnia in the first half of the XV Century*] (Sarajevo: Institut za istoriju u Sarajevu, 1981)

VÁCLAV ŽŮREK

Language as a Weapon

Hilarius of Litoměřice and the Use of Latin and the Vernacular Language in Religious Polemics in Fifteenth-Century Bohemia

I

In 1436, the Emperor Sigismund proclaimed the Compacts of Basel in Jihlava. The proclamation was attended by envoys of the Council of Basel.[1] The Compacts were meant to regulate religious life in the Bohemian lands — the coexistence of Utraquists and Catholics — and to ensure that the achievements of the Bohemian Reformation would be respected by the Catholic Church. This proclamation and Sigismund's ascension to the throne marked the end of the armed-combat stage of the conflict referred to as the Hussite Revolution, in which the Utraquist reform movement was able to assert itself in the Kingdom of Bohemia. This decree, confirmed by the Council of Basel, meant that the Kingdom of Bohemia was now officially a country of two faiths. The coexistence of Bohemian Catholics and Utraquists, however, continued to suffer from problems: the military and power struggles between the two sides did not come to an end, and neither did the rivalry between both camps in questions of theology, with arguments taking the form of public and literary polemics.[2]

Utraquism had originally been a learned heresy of the educated: it was formulated by the masters of Prague University and condemned by the majority of the Catholic Church. Although it came to be formally tolerated in 1436, there were constant disputes with the Catholic party. The reform

---

1 This study was supported by grant no. 19–28415X 'From Performativity to Institutionalization: Handling Conflict in the Late Middle Ages (Strategies, Agents, Communication)' from the Czech Science Foundation (GA ČR).

2 For this set of documents negotiated between the Hussites and the Council of Basel and promulgated in 1436, see Šmahel, *Die Basler Kompaktaten*.

Václav Žůrek • (zurek@flu.cas.cz) received his PhD in 2014 from Charles University, Prague and École des hautes études en sciences sociales, Paris.

Religious Transformations in New Communities of Interpretation in Europe (1350–1570): Bridging the Historiographical Divides, ed. by Élise Boillet and Ian Johnson, New Communities of Interpretation, 3 (Turnhout: Brepols, 2022), pp. 161–188.

DOI 10.1484/M.NCI-EB.5.131219

movement, therefore, was a religious group that constantly sought to define itself: differentiation from, and polemics with, the Catholics were the basic elements of Bohemian Utraquist identity. University-educated theologians took the lead in spelling out the ideological agenda of the reform movement and were also at the helm of the movement's efforts. Following the death of Jan Hus, the principal role was assumed by Jakoubek of Stříbro (Jacobellus of Mies) and later Jan Rokycana, who was elected Archbishop of Prague in 1435, but was never recognized as such by the Catholic Church. Rokycana would, however, remain the main representative of the Hussite Church in Bohemia until his death in 1471.[3]

The daily coexistence of inhabitants of both confessions was linked to the current political situation in the kingdom. Following the proclamation of the Compacts, the situation calmed down, but political disputes and armed conflicts broke out again after the inauguration in 1458 of George of Poděbrady, who as a nobleman was elected king. A king of 'two peoples', George manoeuvred between the two sides to preserve his position in a situation of permanent political tension at both domestic and foreign levels. During his reign, confessional controversies between both sides were re-ignited, with Pope Pius II stoking the fire by revoking the Compacts in 1462 and increasing the pressure on King George to convert to Catholicism.

The confessional disputes between Catholics and Utraquists in fifteenth-century Bohemia included a debate about whether it was appropriate to use the vernacular, that is, the Czech language, in religious polemics, or whether Latin, the language traditionally used in this context, should be adhered to. Initially, the ideas of the reform movement formulated in the treatises and sermons written by university masters were disseminated in both Latin and vernacular writings. The question of the vernacularization of theological discourse was a major theme within the Hussite reform movement: this was related to the activities of the very first leading figure of the movement — Jan Hus. He began to write his theological works in Czech at the time of his forced exile from Prague after 1412.[4] Jakoubek of Stříbro, his follower and the main figure in the movement after his death, continued this practice and wrote two texts in Czech on the fundamental topic of the whole reform — laypeople's communion under both kinds.[5] Jakoubek, who himself initiated the restoration of this liturgical practice in Bohemia, felt the need to defend it in writing and did so in both Latin and Czech. In his Czech writings, he primarily responded to the prohibition of communion under both kinds by the Council of Constance in 1415. The dispute over communion under both kinds resonated very strongly in Czech society and Jakoubek, aiming at a more effective promotion of his

---

3 Heymann, 'John Rokycana'.

4 Rychterová, 'Theology goes to the Vernaculars'.

5 *Dvě staročeská utrakvistická díla Jakoubka ze Stříbra* [*Two Old Czech Utraquist Works of Jakoubek of Stříbro*], ed. by Krmíčková and Čejka.

position within the communion-from-the-cup (or chalice) debate, targeted his vernacular writings primarily at lay burghers and the aristocracy. The theological works written in Czech were used by their readers as a readily available source of argument in disputes with the Catholics.

In his detailed analysis of treatises and polemic writings, Dušan Coufal has shown that lay communion under both kinds very soon became a political topic, albeit on a textual level. It was chiefly discussed by Hussite and Catholic theologians who, in the period from the Council of Constance to the Council of Basel, kept on writing treatises debunking the opinions of the other side.[6]

An important medium for the dissemination of reform ideas was formed by sermons delivered in Czech. For example, the energetic preacher Jan Rokycana, who headed the Utraquist Church for forty years, was also the author of a very popular and widely read collection of sermons. Among other things he was a polemicist, ready to defend Utraquist beliefs and principles at all times, just as he had done at the Council in Basel, where he had helped to negotiate the Compacts securing respect for both faiths in the Kingdom of Bohemia.

Czech would also be used as the language of doctrinal polemics within the Utraquist community, especially in the vernacular treatises written between 1426 and 1430 by Jan of Příbram, who argued against the radical interpretations espoused by the Bohemian adherents of the teachings of John Wycliffe. The singing of Czech songs was also assumed to play a role in spreading the basic ideas of Utraquism.[7]

The dissemination of reform ideas in the vernacular language (both in written texts and orally, for instance through sermons) was thus instrumental in Utraquism attracting new supporters, as well as for its ideological impact. Its representatives were interested in reaching out to new audiences.[8] In this respect, they targeted laymen and, in a new development, also lay women, especially from the bourgeoisie. A substantial part of Hussite supporters was to be found among burghers and lower-ranking nobles, and the reformist teachings also tended to carry the greatest sway in this group. This is why Utraquist authors placed great emphasis on the religious education of laypersons. The improving of education in religious matters and the increasing influence of reformed ideas on this group enabled new reformist discourse to gain ground more rapidly among the wider public, which had important political implications, in forming increasingly large number of Utraquist supporters.

All of the above-mentioned Hussite writers also defended their positions through writings drafted in Latin and addressed to their Catholic opponents and authorities. They therefore did not question the importance of Latin in scholarly discourse. After all, one of their goals was to persuade the international

---

6 Coufal, *Polemika o kalich* [*Polemics Concerning the Chalice*].

7 Perett, 'Vernacular Songs as "Oral Pamphlets"'.

8 Rychterová, 'Theology goes to the Vernaculars'; Rychterová, 'Preaching, the Vernacular, and the Laity'.

community — most notably the participants at the Councils of Constance and Basel — of their truth: that there was support for Hussite teachings in the Scriptures and for their liturgical practice in the customs observed in the early Church.

As shown by Pavlína Rychterová, theological discourse in Czech had established itself as equivalent to Latin, but individual Hussite authors resorted to using Czech along with Latin, and thus did not write exclusively in the vernacular language. Although the use of the vernacular was an element of group identity for adherents to the Bohemian Reformation, Czech cannot be considered as dominant in the literature produced by Bohemian Utraquists.[9]

The choice of Czech as the language of theological treatises was also an important factor in identity formation, becoming, in its own right, a significant subject of the polemics between the Utraquists and the Catholics in the context of the dispute over the use of Czech in the liturgy.[10]

II

A controversy that took place during the reign of George of Poděbrady (1458–1471)[11] between leading figures of the two camps, Hilarius of Litoměřice, the Administrator of the Prague Archbishopric, and Václav Koranda the Younger, an Utraquist university master, offers a remarkable testimony to the conscious choice of language in the discussion of religious affairs.

Hilarius of Litoměřice was the most important proponent of Catholicism at King George's court. For a better understanding of Hilarius's works and the positions he took, it is worth providing a brief biography. He was probably born in 1412 in Litoměřice. He grew up as an Utraquist and studied at Prague University (obtaining the degrees of Bachelor of Arts in 1447 and Master of Arts in 1451). Then, as a promising student of the leading Utraquist theologian and churchman Jan Rokycana, Hilarius was sent to Italy to complete his university education and to be ordained as a priest. He seems to have spent three years (1452 to 1455) there, studying canon law in Padua and Bologna and obtaining the title of *Doctor Decretorum*. During his stay in Italy, he was influenced by Catholicism and converted to it on his return. In 1458, Hilarius became a canon within the Chapter of All Saints at Prague Castle. His career developed rather rapidly: within two years he became Dean of the Chapter of All Saints and a canon within the Metropolitan Chapter at Saint Vitus at Prague Castle, one of the most important Catholic institutions in the Kingdom of Bohemia. As

---

9 Rychterová, 'Preaching, the Vernacular, and the Laity'.

10 As shown by Rychterová with regard to the example of specific Hussite questions, see Rychterová, 'Preaching, the Vernacular, and the Laity' and also Svejkovský, 'The Conception of the "Vernacular"'.

11 Odložilík, *The Hussite King*; Heymann, *George of Bohemia, King of Heretics*; Urbánek, *Věk poděbradský IV* [*The Age of Poděbrady IV*].

a convert, he was an expert in all aspects of Utraquism, including its liturgy and theology, and he used this knowledge in disputes with his opponents. Perhaps because of this quality, and certainly thanks to his tough attitude towards the Utraquist Church in Bohemia, he was appointed administrator of the Prague Archdiocese by Pope Pius II in 1462.

In the terms of political philosophy, Hilarius was an unequivocal advocate of papal primacy in the west. Following the Great (Western) Schism and a period when it had to struggle with conciliarism over primacy within the Church, the papacy was rebuilding its power and, in Pius II (Enea Silvio Piccolomini; 1458 to 1462), it had a new, self-confident pope. Pope Pius II, drawing on his very good knowledge of the situation in confessionally divided Bohemia, entrusted Hilarius with the running of the Catholic administration there and granted him powers equivalent to those of an archbishop. It seems very likely that the pope intentionally chose Hilarius, a convert from Utraquism, to signal to King George and his court that a converted Utraquist could still become a proper Catholic and gain the pope's confidence and even be entrusted with an office.

In that same year, Pope Pius II renounced the Compacts of Basel. An administrator loyal to the pope, Hilarius tried to convince King George to cease supporting this document and the coexistence of two confessions in his kingdom, and to convert to Catholicism. George of Poděbrady, however, reaffirmed his pro-Compacts position, and Pope Paul II resorted to labelling him a heretical king in 1466 and declaring all his subjects to be free to reject his rule. In this context, Hilarius had to adopt a tougher stance. He switched the focus of his efforts at persuasion from the king to the king's powerful subjects, trying to win over Czech nobles to renounce their loyalty to George of Poděbrady. As a consequence, he could no longer feel safe in Prague and so, along with the entire administration of the Prague archdiocese, he moved to Pilsen, a traditional Catholic stronghold. His stay in Pilsen was marked by frequent diplomatic journeys (to Nuremberg, Wrocław, Rome, and Graz) aimed at forging alliances against King George. In the midst of such political activity, Hilarius died in České Budějovice (Budweis) at the end of 1468.[12]

In all the years during which he held ecclesiastical administrative office, Hilarius was also a prolific writer, commenting especially on current topics and participating in many polemics with Utraquists.[13] Some of these disputes took place in person, publicly at the royal court or at the university, and would afterwards continue in writing. Others only took place in written form, but

---

12 For Hilarius's biography, see Kalina, 'Hilarius Litoměřický' ['Hilarius of Litoměřice']; *Plzeň v husitské revoluci* [*Pilsen in the Hussite Revolution*], ed. by Hejnic and Polívka, pp. 6–15; Kadlec, 'Hilarius Litoměřický v čele duchovenstva podjednou' ['Hilarius of Litoměřice as the Head of the Catholic Clergy']; Šmahel, *Humanismus v době poděbradské* [*Humanism in the Era of George of Poděbrady*], pp. 54–55.

13 For a complete survey of his writings, see *Plzeň v husitské revoluci* [*Pilsen in the Hussite Revolution*], ed. by Hejnic and Polívka, pp. 16–27.

it can still be assumed that even then those texts would have been read by important protagonists on both sides.

The bilingual Latin-Czech controversy with Václav Koranda the Younger, which is the subject of this study, took place in 1464. As hinted above, it is a valuable testimony to the contemporary perception of the vernacular language and its relation to Latin in a theological context. Václav Koranda the Younger (*c.* 1423 to 1519), the opponent of Hilarius,[14] was an important Utraquist intellectual. He held a Master of Arts degree (1458) from Prague University, later becoming its dean and rector. Following Jan Rokycana's death in 1471, he was elected Administrator of the Utraquist Consistory.[15] During the reign of George of Poděbrady, Koranda became a leading polemicist and spokesman of the Utraquist party, participating in many polemics with the Catholics. An author of many works, he was involved in the formulation of the Utraquist theological position and defended it vigorously. Some of Koranda's personal manuscript miscellany, containing his own works as well as the texts of his opponents, has been preserved.

Theologically, Koranda followed the views espoused by Jan Hus, Jakoubek of Stříbro, and, most importantly, his teacher Jan Rokycana. He considered the issues of defending the chalice, communion for children, and the singing of Czech hymns during Mass to be fundamental when discussing specific questions in disputes with the Catholics. His surviving works clearly show that he held as the foundation of his religious doctrine the view that the Truth of God (*lex dei*) is identical to the Gospel, and that the Gospel is superior to the Old Testament, with Jesus Christ and his deeds being the key element in any interpretation. The basic duty of a Christian, according to Koranda, was to respect Christ and his Truth, and to hold on to this Truth — as revealed in the Gospel — until death. The Church, therefore, was not in a position to change Christ's ordinances, and the customs of the early Church were of more value than later practices. This argument served to support both the possibility of salvation through, and the necessity of, communion under both kinds. Regarding the validity of the Compacts, Koranda insisted that they had been recognized by the doctors of theology present at the Council of Basel as well as by Emperor Sigismund and Pope Eugene IV (which was not true), arguing that their validity must be respected (this is the position

---

14 Some of the formulations used by Koranda seem to suggest that, apart from Hilarius, a fellow Catholic university master, the forceful polemicist Václav Křižanovský was also involved in the dispute on the Catholic side. See Urbánek, *Věk poděbradský IV* [*The Age of Poděbrady IV*], p. 729. See also Kalina, 'Václav Křižanovský', pp. 333–59 and Doležalová, '*Usquoque tu, Domine, obdormis gravi sopore?*'.

15 For more details on Koranda, see Krofta, 'Václav Koranda mladší z Nové Plzně' ['Václav Koranda the Younger of New Pilsen'], and Marek, 'Polemické spisy Václava Korandy mladšího' ['Václav Koranda the Younger and his Polemical Treatises']. Marek, *Václav Koranda mladší* [*Václav Koranda the Younger*] offers the most recent summary of Koranda's polemics, based on knowledge of a larger quantity of writings.

that he formulated in Rome before Pope Pius II in 1462 and that he later repeatedly emphasized in religious controversies). A typical feature of his position was the assumption of the superiority of the Truth of the Gospel to later theological interpretations.

A very active polemicist, Koranda was involved in a number of literary disputes between 1460 and 1480. These polemics were not merely private exchanges of views, but would usually take place publicly, with Koranda sometimes going as far as resorting to the publication of some of his texts.[16]

His fundamental religious writings (*Traktát o velebné a božské svátosti oltářní* [Treatise on the divine and glorious sacrament of the altar], *O rozdávánie velebené svátosti dítkám* [Providing divine sacraments to children], and *O zpievaní a čtení českém traktát* [Treatise on singing and reading aloud in Czech]) were printed in 1493 in Czech in a single incunable. Publication in Czech was an integral part of Koranda's media strategy, aimed at broadening the community of readers of these works and summarizing the set of basic principles of Utraquist theology in the vernacular.[17]

III

The subject of the dispute between the two men was the key issue dividing Utraquists and Catholics: communion under both kinds. However, in this case, the subject was not discussed openly in the polemic; instead, both scholars formally discussed birds and their division into those who drink and those who do not. This is not the only remarkable aspect of the dispute; what is also interesting is the linguistic form of the dispute, in which Hilarius used Latin and Koranda used Czech.

The entire dispute has been reconstructed by Rudolf Urbánek in his major work on the reign of George of Poděbrady.[18] He arranged five individual letters, to which he was able to find and identify relating to the controversy into a logical sequence, as the dispute has not survived in any manuscript in its entirety.

According to Urbánek, the dispute included the following letters in the following order:

1) The opening question (Koranda, in Czech) – available in Hilarius's response;
2) 'Argute augur, queris' (Hilarius, entitled *Tractatus de avibus* [*Treatise on birds*], in Latin);

16 Marek, 'Polemické spisy Václava Korandy mladšího' ['Václav Koranda the Younger and his Polemical Treatises']. Cf. also Marek, 'Major Figures of Later Hussitism', pp. 161–63.

17 Marek, 'Václav Koranda ml. a mediální strategie obrany utrakvismu' ['Václav Koranda the Younger and his Strategy for Defending Utraquism through Public Communication'].

18 Urbánek, *Věk Poděbradský IV* [*The Age of Poděbrady IV*], pp. 729–38.

3) 'Nenie ptáčníkuov' [There are no fowlers] (Koranda, in Czech);
4) *De avibus responsum doctoris ad replicam Korande, telonearii WiklephiteI* [*The rejoinder of a doctor to the response by the Wycliffite preceptor Koranda*] (Hilarius, in Latin);
5) 'Již vstupuje v tu šermici' [I am now entering the skirmish] (Koranda, in Czech).

The texts have survived in a total of four manuscripts dating to the fifteenth century. These manuscripts are chiefly found in collections of texts compiled by Hilarius and Koranda themselves, and they were probably even written in their own hands. In his manuscript, Hilarius wrote down all his contributions to the exchange, although, according to Urbánek, he recorded the last two in reverse order.[19] The dialogue format of the letters, whose opening sections contain references to the respective opponent's previous assertions, led Urbánek to assume that their authors must have been responding to each other's letters, essentially taking turns. This is why he changed the order, contrary to that of Hilarius's manuscript, and placed Koranda's second rejoinder at the end of the exchange, considering it to be the last letter in the polemical exchange.[20] His arguments seem convincing: Koranda's last letter includes a number of direct reactions to the objections raised in Hilarius's second Latin letter. The rest of Hilarius's manuscript contains other polemical texts authored by Hilarius himself, including those aimed against the Utraquist leader Jan Rokycana, as well as letters relating to his office of Catholic Church Administrator in Bohemia.[21] His opponent Koranda only copied two of the texts in his manuscript, Hilarius's first reply and his own rejoinder to that reply.[22] This manuscript, composed by Koranda as late as the 1490s, is referred to as *Manualník Vácslava Korandy* [Václav Koranda's Personal Miscellany] by historians and contains many texts related to Koranda's activities as Administrator of the Utraquist Church between 1471 and 1489. Koranda's polemical writings concerning religion, which are often accompanied in the manuscript by the replies and reactions of Catholic masters, form an important part of this volume. The manuscript is a compilation of several previously written texts, and it is therefore possible that the versions contained therein of other authors' texts — including the texts pertaining to the dispute discussed in this paper, authored by Hilarius — are authentic.[23]

---

19 Prague, Archiv Pražského hradu, Knihovna Metropolitní kapituly [Prague Castle Archives, Metropolitan Chapter Library, hereinafter Kap.], MS N.58: the manuscript was produced during Hilarius's lifetime, that is, before 1468.

20 Urbánek, *Věk Poděbradský IV* [*The Age of Poděbrady IV*], p. 730.

21 Kap., MS N 58: see the description in Podlaha, *Soupis rukopisů II* [*Catalogue of Manuscripts, II*], pp. 448–50.

22 *Manualník M. Vácslava Korandy* [*Václav Koranda's Personal Miscellany*], ed. by Truhlář.

23 *Manualník M. Vácslava Korandy* [*Václav Koranda's Personal Miscellany*], ed. by Truhlář, Introduction, p. viii.

Compiling manuscripts from one's own texts and replies, as well as from other texts, was a common trend for fifteenth-century authors.[24] It is in such manuscripts that many polemical texts originating in fifteenth-century Bohemia have survived. The fact that both Hilarius's and Koranda's texts relating to their dispute have been preserved in their respective personal *miscellanea* manuscript collections suggests that this controversy was indeed one that took place through an exchange of personal letters. However, as will be shown below, these letters also had the aim of reaching out to other readers. They were clearly read by other people, as illustrated above all by the fact that copies of three of them have been preserved in the manuscript of Kříž of Telcz (Crux de Telcz, d. 1504), a bibliophile and collector, dating roughly to the same period.[25] An Augustinian Friar, Kříž collected texts and made copies of them in his anthologies, and he recorded — in a linguistically more elaborate form — the second, third, and fourth letters exchanged in the dispute between Hilarius and Koranda.[26] Hilarius's first Latin reply can also be found in another surviving manuscript containing his texts, which is not directly linked to him. It is obvious that copies of all these texts were made fairly soon after the controversy, which has been convincingly dated to 1464 by Urbánek based on facts mentioned in the texts.

A characteristic feature of a personal dispute between two intellectuals is the survival of the relevant texts in copies made by the protagonists themselves. It is not clear to what extent these texts were known to wider audiences at the time of their writing, but there are some minor references suggesting that both Hilarius and Koranda consulted on their contributions with their close collaborators. Copies included in Kříž's manuscript also indicate that knowledge of the texts was not exclusive to their two authors, but extended to people around them.

Critical editions of only the individual texts pertaining to the controversy are available: there is no critical edition encompassing all of them. Two full texts and the introductory question contained in Koranda's *personal miscellany* have been published in an edition of the texts contained in this manuscript.[27] Hilarius's second response has been published separately by

---

24 See, for example, Doležalová, 'Late Medieval Personal Miscellanies'.

25 See Doležalová, 'Personal Multiple-Text Manuscripts in late Middle Ages'.

26 Praha, Národní knihovna České republiky [Prague, National Library of the Czech Republic, hereinafter NK], MS XI C 8, dated between 1463 and 1477. Jindřich Marek has called attention to the fact that Kříž was residing at Prague Castle at the time of the dispute, and thus had the opportunity to become aware of the texts as they were being written. That would make his renditions of the texts more authentic, as it would seem likely that Koranda only made the copies contained in his manuscript much later and edited them to produce a model polemical text. This is, however, far from certain, as the manuscript of his *personal miscellany* does contain a correction in the word *augur* (discussed below), which is clearly a response to the reproof contained in Hilarius's reply. Cf. Doležalová, *Passionate Copying*.

27 The renditions of both surviving manuscripts are contaminated by influences from Kříž's manuscript, which the editor was also drawing on when producing the critical edition.

the historian Tomáš Kalina, based only on the manuscript of Oldřich Kříž.[28] The concluding text of the dispute by Václav Koranda is preserved only in manuscript, in a single copy.[29]

Let us now examine the individual letters and the contents of the entire dispute. The main subject of the exchange of views is communion under both kinds — a main subject of controversy between the Utraquists and the Catholics. However, the subject as such is skilfully hidden behind the metaphor of birds. Here Koranda uses an item of received knowledge shared by university-educated men of the Middle Ages, namely that birds of prey and owls and other night birds do not drink.[30] This received wisdom was included in the natural philosophy curriculum taught at medieval universities, which was essentially based on Aristotle's works on nature and the commentaries on them, of which the most popular was that of Albert the Great.[31]

Koranda's opening line in the dispute is a metaphorical, but still very transparent, question. It survives only in the Latin text of Hilarius's response, where it is included in its original Czech wording:

> Mistře! Pověz mi, kteří jsú ptáci lepší, ti-li, ježto jedie a pijí, čili ti, kteří jedie toliko a nepijí! A druhé, proč ti, kteří jedie toliko a nepijí, nevražie na ty, kteří jedie a pijí?
>
> > (Master! Tell me what kind of birds do you think are better – those that eat and drink, or those that only eat and do not drink? And, secondly, why do those [birds] that only eat and do not drink hate those that eat and drink?)[32]

Hilarius responded to this Czech question by writing his *Tractatus de avibus*, a Latin treatise on birds, which opens with 'Argute augur, queris...' (You, diviner, shrewdly ask ...).[33]

Hilarius did not hesitate to write his *Treatise on Birds*, which clearly shows that he understood Koranda's hint at the principal divisive element between the Catholics and the Utraquists: communion under both kinds. He argues that it is obvious that birds that do not drink, birds of prey, are symbolic of the Catholics who do not receive Christ's blood at Mass. The other group is that of the Utraquists who drink (that is: receive both Christ's body and blood) and are therefore naturally subject to the Catholics. Using classical authorities,

---

28 Kalina's edition is based on NK, MS XI C 8, fols 274r–279v.

29 Prague, Kap., MS N 58, fols 85r–92r.

30 I would like to thank Mr Baudouin Van den Abeele (Université Catholique de Louvain-la-Neuve) for his help and advice regarding this topic of how animals were perceived in the Middle Ages.

31 Cf. Albert the Great, *Questions concerning Aristotle's 'On Animals'*, pp. 41–42.

32 Hilarius included Koranda's Czech question in his Latin response; see *Manualník M. Vácslava Korandy* [*Václav Koranda's Personal Miscellany*], ed. by Truhlář, p. 187.

33 *Manualník M. Vácslava Korandy* [*Václav Koranda's Personal Miscellany*], ed. by Truhlář, pp. 187–93.

he reminds Koranda that it is the birds of prey that do not drink and only take in solid food (especially meat) and no liquids, arguing that birds of prey are superior to other birds in three respects. Firstly, because they need less nourishment to live. Secondly, because birds of prey indeed dominate other birds in the wild. Here, Hilarius mentions the eagle, considered the king and hence also the most noble of birds.[34] Finally, Hilarius also says that birds of prey are used by humans for hunting, which also makes them superior to other birds. The hatred between both groups of birds is only discussed indirectly by Hilarius, who explains that the mutual relationship is determined by the fact that birds of prey are stronger and, therefore, are bound naturally to rule over the birds that drink.

Koranda responded to Hilarius in his Czech letter *Nenie ptáčníkuov* (There are no fowlers).[35] In his reply, Koranda continues to play the game of discussing birds and adheres to their symbolic meaning, taking sides firmly with the birds that drink (Utraquists receiving under both kinds) and arguing that they are superior to those that do not.

The opening of Koranda's reply was provoked by his misunderstanding of the Latin word *augur* (diviner) as *auceps* (fowler). Prompted by a further response from Hilarius, Koranda later realized that he had misunderstood the meaning of the word *augur*, as evidenced by his rewriting '*auceps*' as '*augur*' in the copy of Hilarius's letter in his *personal miscellany* to hide his confusion.[36]

In his reply drafted in Czech, Koranda rejects the simple logic of comparing status and the power to dominate, and instead accuses the ruling birds of prey of tyranny and cruelty, arguing that their rule is not based on law and amounts to oppression. Koranda invokes unspecified wise men who in their books label such birds (that is, birds of prey) as violent, since these birds prey upon and devour other birds. These birds are described as tyrants, a clear charge of oppression against the Catholics.[37]

Furthermore, Koranda recalls that the state of affairs in which birds do not drink is not natural. In his view, birds that do not drink have abandoned their natural state, in which they ate and drank, for a novel state of violence and irregularity, which will not last for long. Here, Koranda uses the opportunity to remind Hilarius of the basic Hussite argument that the practice of communion under both kinds was practised in the early Church and is therefore natural.

Koranda refutes and rejects one by one Hilarius's individual propositions, listing a number of animals and their role in nature. To be able

34 *Manualník M. Václava Korandy* [*Václav Koranda's Personal Miscellany*], ed. by Truhlář, p. 188.

35 *Manualník M. Václava Korandy* [*Václav Koranda's Personal Miscellany*], ed. by Truhlář, pp. 193–202.

36 See Prague, NK, MS XVII F 2, fol. 164^{r}.

37 *Manualník M. Václava Korandy* [*Václav Koranda's Personal Miscellany*], ed. by Truhlář, p. 194.

to do this, he must clearly have had a fairly good knowledge of natural philosophy. He also rejects Hilarius's argument that since birds of prey are more expensive (in human terms) and fly higher, they are generally of more value and greater significance in nature. He also rebuts Hilarius's opinion that birds of prey are more important than other birds, since the eagle is a symbol of Saint John. Koranda counters this proposition by highlighting the fact that the Holy Ghost is symbolized by a dove, a bird that both eats and drinks.[38]

Despite invoking unknown 'wise men', Koranda — tellingly — refers to the privileged position of the Scriptures: 'O tom jest jistota netoliko z kněh mudrckých, ale z zákona božieho' (This is demonstrated beyond doubt not only by books written by wise men, but also by the Law of God).[39]

Although most of Koranda's text is devoted to birds and other animals, this symbolism is consciously used to discuss communion under both kinds. He also critically notes Hilarius's choice of answering in Latin, as well as the mistakes in his argumentation.

Hilarius, probably feeling personally offended by Koranda's Czech letter, responded with a longish Latin treatise: *De avibus responsum doctoris ad replicam Korande, telonearii Wiklephite* [*The rejoinder of a doctor to the response by the Wycliffite preceptor Koranda, relating to the topic of birds*], which opens with the phrase '*Non possum non mirari*' (I cannot but wonder).[40] In this text, apart from continuing to provide arguments along the same lines in order to defend the Catholic position, he mocks Koranda's deficient Latin knowledge, drawing on the latter's confusion between *augur* and *auceps*.

In this letter, Hilarius is very aggressive: addressing his opponent directly many times and putting a range of assertions in his mouth that he then disproves. In addition to criticizing Koranda's defective knowledge of Latin, he also reproaches him more generally for insufficient knowledge of natural philosophy and theology. For the first time in the exchange, Hilarius explicitly identifies his opponent, addressing him informally as 'Václav'. Hilarius's letter is full of rhetorical questions and appeals that highlight the theological consequences of naturalistic arguments. In general, Hilarius comes up with nothing but the usual Catholic arguments against receiving from the chalice. In the conclusion of his letter, Hilarius asks Koranda not to bother him with birds anymore, but to feel free to direct to him any other questions on his mind, which he would then be happy to answer.

The last letter of the dispute is Koranda's Czech letter *Již vstupuje v tu šermici* (I am now entering the skirmish), which includes a Latin introduction and

---

38 *Manualník M. Václava Korandy* [*Václav Koranda's Personal Miscellany*], ed. by Truhlář, p. 195.

39 *Manualník M. Václava Korandy* [*Václav Koranda's Personal Miscellany*], ed. by Truhlář, p. 199.

40 *De avibus responsum*, ed. by Kalina, pp. 8–21.

is accompanied by a Latin note preserved in the same manuscript. Hilarius included the letter in his manuscript.[41] This text has not been published to date.[42]

In the Latin introduction, Koranda first discusses the dispute as such, returning to Hilarius's reproof concerning his confusion as to the meaning of *augur*. In particular, Koranda recalls that he addressed his minor questions (*questiuncule*) to Hilarius's companion, Václav Křižanovský, a Catholic convert and university master dismissed from Prague University (for the translation see below).[43] Since Hilarius chose to join in the discussion uninvited, he is not entitled to select the language of the dispute. This right belongs to Koranda and he chose his 'mother tongue'. Koranda considers the address form *augur* to be a deliberate insinuation about him being a condemnable diviner, explaining that this is what led him to interpret the word *augur* as *ptáčník* (fowler). The short Latin introduction is then followed by a long text written in Czech.

Koranda's Czech text is chiefly devoted to scolding Hilarius. He feels offended by Hilarius calling him a diviner and a bird magician and reproaches him for a lack of humility, which is not befitting of a priest. Instead of appealing to Koranda for moderation, Hilarius should, in Koranda's view, get his own act in order, as he himself abandoned the Truth and converted to Catholicism driven only by personal gain. Koranda uses the opportunity to criticize the situation at Prague Castle (by which he means the Metropolitan Chapter at St Vitus), which he considers to be dire: with games being played, parties being thrown, and harlots running around. Koranda claims he could himself point out the sinners around Hilarius.[44]

In addition to the bird allegory, Koranda also discusses the authority of the Church, mentioning the fallibility of popes and a figure, popular among Utraquists, the female Agnes, who disguised herself as a man and became Pope Joan, in order to emphasize the imperfect authority of the Catholic Church of his time. This is why, Koranda explains, the Utraquists look to the early Church for guidance. He pays considerable attention to criticism of the Church and the Catholic prelates, who, in his view, are striving for wealth and power.[45]

This letter concluded the dispute. Hilarius probably did not write a reply. There is, at any rate, no other text in his personal collection of manuscripts. He also seems to have made it clear in his last letter that he had stated his last word in the controversy and would not discuss the subject any more.

Undoubtedly, the most interesting aspect of the dispute is its language. The controversy was debated in two languages, a fact that both participants

---

41 Praha, Kap., MS N 58, fol. 84^{r}.

42 Praha, Kap., MS N 58, fols 85^{r}–92^{r}.

43 Kalina, 'Václav Křižanovský'.

44 Praha, Kap., MS N 58, fols 87^{v}–88^{r}.

45 Praha, Kap., MS N 58, fol. 91^{v}. Cf. Marek, 'Polemické spisy Václava Korandy mladšího' ['Václav Koranda the Younger and his Polemical Treatises'], p. 8.

commented on and even used in their efforts to humiliate and ridicule each other to win the argument. The languages chosen by the authors and the debate concerning their choices are also closely related to this.

From the very first moment of the controversy, Hilarius comments on the fact, that Koranda has formulated the question in their mother tongue: 'Ita queris in lingua materna' (You ask me in our mother tongue). Hilarius, however, chose to reply in Latin, and Koranda rebukes him for that choice in his rejoinder:

> Pak že k mým otázkám krátkým a českým odpověď dáváš dobře obšírnú a latinskú, latinskými barvami, s nimiž já se neobierám, položenú, neviem, zdali proto, abych tiem méně srozuměl. Svatý Pavel volil pět slov raději pověděti k rozumu nežli k nerozumu deset tisícuov.[46]
>
> (To my short questions asked in Czech you then give a fairly long answer in Latin, embellished by ornamentations of the Latin language that are of no interest to me; I do not know if you do this in order to make it more difficult for me to understand. Saint Paul preferred [speaking] five words intelligibly to [speaking] ten thousand words unintelligibly.)

Hilarius did not pass over this critique in silence, and instead clearly explained and justified why he chose Latin to express his opinion in writing, in his response to Koranda's objection.

> Non possum non mirari, ut, qui responsa mea corrigere, et arguere cum stomacho conaris, ipse te in capite responsi tuo gladio cedas, cum mea scripta, quibus te augurem appellavi, aucupem materna lingwa interpreteris inculte.[47]
>
> (I cannot but wonder that you attempt to correct and argue heatedly with my response, and yet at the beginning of your response you kill yourself with your own sword when you translate improperly my letter in which I called you a wizard, [rendering that term] as fowler in [our] mother tongue.)

Right at the beginning of his response, Hilarius mocks Koranda's inferior knowledge of Latin, using a swordfight metaphor to describe the controversy and pointing out to Koranda that he has dropped his chief weapon in the dispute due to a lack of linguistic acumen.

Hilarius ridicules Koranda's misunderstanding of the word *augur*, but he still thinks Koranda should stick to Latin in the discussion. He argues that Latin is the only fitting language for learned dialogue and debate. After all, as Hilarius notes, Koranda himself also studied at Latin and not Slavic schools

46 *Manualník M. Václava Korandy* [*Václav Koranda's Personal Miscellany*], ed. by Truhlář, p. 194.

47 *De avibus responsum*, ed. by Kalina, p. 8.

(this is clearly an allusion to Koranda's career at Prague University as a master, dean, and rector), and should therefore pay respect to the language and, as an educated man, write in Latin.

> Causaris michi, Venceslae, quod latine tibi responsum dederim [...] sed scito, latina lingua scripsi et scribo plurima, non quod non intelligas sicut ille, qui falso tibi augurem pro aucupe interpretatus est, sed ut noveris fontem scienciarum latina proditum et parum sapienciae aput barbaras oras absque latina. Neque glorior, quod latine tibi responderim, sed quod barbarus sim, aliquid latine linguae quamquam vix apud elementa cognosco, imitatus condicionem tuam, cum te sciam eciam scolas latinas non sclawas frequentasse. Neque non gaudeo, quod Bohemus sum, sed veneror litteras et sapienciam apud nostros karacteres, nisi forte in alto translatam, non legi.[48]
>
> > (You blame me, Václav, for giving you my reply in Latin. But know that I wrote and that I am writing many things in Latin not in order for you not to understand – like when you erroneously translated diviner (*augur*) as fowler (*auceps*) for yourself – but in order for you to know that the source of the sciences has been transmitted [to us] through Latin and that there is hardly any wisdom among barbarians without Latin. I replied to you in Latin not to boast, but – being a barbarian and having some, if only basic, knowledge of the Latin language just like you – because I know that you have also studied at Latin, and not Slavic, schools. I am also not unhappy about being Czech, but I hold literature in high esteem, and I have not seen wisdom in our writings, except, maybe, where they have been translated into the higher language.)[49]

Hilarius also argues that Koranda's text must have been originally drafted in Latin and only later translated into Czech.[50]

> Nam, etsi ausim, epistola hec tua vulgaris aut ex latino venit, aut in eo concepta et hanc vulgarem enixa est. Sed sunt tibi viri litteras scientes; non mutabo meam condicionem teque hortor, ut, si quid scribere velis, latine scribas.[51]
>
> > (Because even – if I may [venture to guess] – your vernacular letter either had its origin in Latin or it was conceived in Latin and came out

48 *De avibus responsum*, ed. by Kalina, p. 8.

49 I would like to thank Mr Jan Odstrčilík for discussing the meaning of the Latin passages with me.

50 On this, see also Kalina's note on the presence of many Latinisms in his edition of Koranda's text, *De avibus responsum*, ed. by Kalina, p. 9.

51 *De avibus responsum*, ed. by Kalina, pp. 8–9.

> as vernacular. But you have educated men. I will not alter my position and I urge you, if you wish to write anything, to write it in Latin.)

Hilarius thus criticizes his opponent for being a hypocrite. In Hilarius's view, Koranda only styles himself as an author writing in Czech because of his lay audience. In reality, though, the texts that he sent to Hilarius had originally been written in Latin and were only afterwards translated into Czech. Hilarius is unwilling to change his mind about language, recommending that Koranda send further letters, if any, to him in Latin immediately. Surely, writes Hilarius to Koranda, there are men around you to help you with this. Hilarius repeats the same request at the end of his letter.

> Non me plus in hiis avibus pulses, sed si aliquid aliud, quid urget, in caritate scribe! Scribe autem latine; rescribam autem, si deligis.[52]
>
> > (Do not bother me with these birds any more, but if you have any other pressing matter, write to me with love. Write to me in Latin, if you will, then I will write back to you.)

Obviously, Hilarius attempts to use his choice of language and Koranda's mistakes to gain the upper hand in the dispute and to demonstrate his intellectual superiority. This is why he stresses that no other language but Latin should be used in discussions between learned men on topics concerning religion. This strategy reflects the broader context of the entire dispute. Ever since the beginnings of the reform movement, both language and education had been important topics. In disputes, the Utraquists found themselves criticized by their Catholic opponents for the alleged lack of education of their theologians and representatives which, according to the Catholics, made them unqualified to reprimand and correct the authorities of the Church (representatives of the Councils and of the regional establishment). In his writings, Hilarius also employs the argument about the other party lacking education, highlighting the issue of the choice of the proper language in this context. In his writings, he argues that Latin is the only possible language for religious disputes and, apart from demonstrating his knowledge of Latin, calls attention to the mistakes made by his opponent and questions his choice of Czech.

Koranda's response to the linguistic objections can be found in several parts of his last letter. His principal discussion of the topic of choice of language in polemical letters is included in the Latin introduction to his last letter.

> Questiuncule mee parvule due sunt per me destinate magistro Krzyžanowsky, qui laycorum doctor et predicator existit. Vos tamen nescio quo ductus spiritu ipsas in solucionem recepistis et me vobiscum in duellum sumpsistis et provocastis. Qua ex causa iure habeo eleccionem in hoc duello eligere

52 *De avibus responsum*, ed. by Kalina, p. 21.

> mihi modum duellandi ydiomate, videlicet materno vel latino. Eligo igitur maternum et elegi ex causa pretacta et alia, quia licet, ut scribitis, frequentaverim scolas non sclawas, sed latinas, tamen quia tempus bene XLIIorum annorum transiit, ut ipsas postposui, et quitquid fuit in me latinitatis, per campos, curias et sulcos disseminavi.[53]
>
> (My two minor questions were directed to Master Křižanovský, doctor and preacher of laymen. However – and I do not know what spirit led you to do that – you decided to answer them and you challenged me and provoked me into the duel. For this reason, I have the right to choose myself the form of fighting as regards language – [our] mother tongue or Latin. I have chosen [our] mother tongue and I have chosen it for the reason already mentioned and also because – although, as you yourself write, I did not go to Slavic but Latin schools – some forty-two years have passed since I left them behind, and whatever Latinity there was in me, I scattered it over the ground in fields, courts, and furrows.)

Koranda accepts Hilarius's wordplay and also uses the duel metaphor to discuss the dispute. He reminds Hilarius that he, Koranda (as the challenger), had the choice of weapons and that he chose Czech. He nevertheless still begins his letter in Latin, probably to demonstrate his command of the language to Hilarius (and to readers).[54] In the Latin introduction, he picks up on Hilarius's remark that he, as a graduate of Latin schools, should read and be able to write in Latin, retorting — with a rather poor excuse — that many years have passed since his studies. At the same time, however, Koranda justifies the use of the vernacular as motivated by the effort to avoid ambiguities and improper synonyms ('equivocciones et synonymaciones'). This is clearly just a pose, since Koranda had a good command of Latin: otherwise, he would not have been asked by Jan Rokycana to act as the speaker of the Utraquists before the pope in Rome in 1462; moreover, he was an active master at Prague University and a prolific Latin writer.[55]

Koranda elaborates on the metaphor of the dispute as a duel. In the Latin beginning of his last letter, he writes: 'Doctor, you call me to duel with you'.[56] According to Rudolf Urbánek, Koranda really felt like a duellist, especially

53 Praha, Kap., MS N 58, fol. 85^{r}: I am quoting the transcription of Marek, 'Polemické spisy Václava Korandy mladšího' ['Václav Koranda the Younger and his Polemical Treatises'] here, who reads "XVIorum annorum" (sixteen years). Urbánek, *Věk poděbradský IV* [*The Age of Poděbrady IV*], p. 732 is correct in his preferred reading 'XLIIorum annorum' (forty-two years).

54 Praha, Kap., MS N 58, fols 85^{r}–85^{v}.

55 Krofta, 'Václav Koranda mladší z Nové Plzně' ['Václav Koranda the Younger of New Pilsen']; Marek, 'Polemické spisy Václava Korandy mladšího' ['Václav Koranda the Younger and his Polemical Treatises'].

56 Praha, Kap., MS N 58, fol. 85^{r}: 'Domine doctor, duellare me vobiscum compellitis'.

regarding the choice of weapons — in this case language.[57] He adds some more weapon metaphors elsewhere. The beginning of the Czech text of his last letter opens with: 'I am now entering the skirmish with you, Doctor, [armed] with natural language'.[58]

Language is a sword, which in Hilarius's letter first kills its wielder, Koranda, who is not skilled at using a sword,[59] but then — in Koranda's response — it is Hilarius who is described as not apt at using his sword, since he is sharpening it against himself.[60]

As both Hilarius and Koranda essentially defended the standard views of their respective parties in the dispute, the question of language choice needs to be seen not just in the context of this dispute, but also with respect to the status of the vernacular language during the Bohemian Reformation, in which it played a significant role. Since the times of Jan Hus, the Utraquists had cultivated the tradition of vernacular writings and translations of religious and theological materials, while the Catholic party criticized this as early as at the Council of Constance and generally held that theological debates should be reserved for educated scholars and therefore be conducted in Latin.[61]

In the light of this, it is not easy to judge the dispute, as both authors did not adhere to the views presented in it, as is evident from their overall, and especially later, literary activities. Neither of them solely used the respective language he defended in the debate. The defence of Czech or Latin was therefore clearly, first and foremost, a stance: Hilarius wishes to be regarded as a scholar and a supporter of traditional genuine Latin education; Koranda, on the other hand, styles himself as a proponent of mediating theological knowledge to laypersons, among whom he counts himself. This is also apparent from an argument in his second letter, in which he speaks on behalf of laymen: 'We laymen, we hold on to what we have felt with our hands' (that is, to what we have practical knowledge of).[62]

Koranda's styling himself as a layman in the dispute is, of course, evident and repeatedly emphasized, but it needs to be noted that he was most likely a layman. Despite taking on the role of Administrator of the Utraquist Church after 1471, he was most probably not an ordained priest at that time,[63] and he was certainly not one in 1464, when the dispute with Hilarius took place. This

57 Urbánek, *Věk poděbradský IV* [*The Age of Poděbrady IV*], p. 730.

58 Praha, Kap., MS N 58, fol. 85v: 'Již vstupuje v tu šermici s vámi doktore jazykem přirozeným'.

59 Praha, Kap., MS N 58, fol. 85v: '[…] že na počátku mé odpovědi svým se sám mečem morduji […]' ([…] that I am killing myself with my own sword in the beginning of my response […]).

60 Praha, Kap., MS N 58, fol. 85v: 'sám proti sobě meč ostříš' (you are sharpening the sword against yourself).

61 For the rise of vernacular literary production in Hussite Bohemia, see Perett, *Preachers, Partisans, and Rebellious Religion*.

62 Praha, Kap., MS N 58, fol. 86r: 'My laykové, což rukama omakámy, toho se držiemy'.

63 Marek, 'Polemické spisy Václava Korandy mladšího' ['Václav Koranda the Younger and his Polemical Treatises'], p. 143.

is also supported by what Koranda writes in both of his letters (*ego tamquam laycus* which literally translates as 'I, as a layman'). He consciously contrasts his position of layman to the position of Hilarius, an ordained Catholic priest. He also alludes to this difference when he apologizes for his late response, saying that, unlike Hilarius, he has much work to attend to and was not able to answer sooner.[64]

Koranda's thinking about the lay reader is also of crucial importance, since this is what Koranda's defence of the choice of Czech over Latin is based on: he argues that he chose to write in Czech in order for the 'laymen to be able to become aware of, comprehend, and more easily accept, confirm, and approve [the content]'.[65]

This argument also shows that the dispute was not a mere exchange of views for Koranda, who clearly expected others to read the letters and wished to reach out to this audience. He seems to have assumed that his readers would include Hilarius's fellow Catholics, since he says in one of his letters that he intends to explain the question of communion not just to Hilarius, but also to his (that is the Catholic) people.[66] Koranda says that he would like to educate (the Catholics, most likely) 'through similes and stories', in order for them to get to know Christ's Truth.[67]

Koranda evidently had a wider audience in mind. This is confirmed by the fact that he included any potential reader as the addressee of his letter, using the phrase 'Kto čte, rozuměj' (Whoever reads this, should understand).[68]

For Koranda, his choice of language is therefore justified by the target audience, which goes beyond the narrowly defined group of Catholic and Utraquist theologians who must have followed the dispute. There are more places in his letters where Koranda addresses readers other than only Hilarius.

Although Koranda writes to Hilarius that he has not yet shown his letter to anybody, he mentions elsewhere that he, at the very least, consulted men with an understanding of the matter. The contemporary copies of the letters by Kříž of Telč tell us that the dispute did not remain unknown and that knowledge of it spread, at the very least, around the chapter and the king's court. After all, there were controversies between both camps and public disputes throughout

---

64 Praha, Kap., MS N 58, fol. 84^r: 'Ego tamquam laycus multo pluribus quam vos occupatus et ignarus protraxi longius vestro tempore, non imputetis, cum et vos morulam feceratis in responso.'

65 Praha, Kap., MS N 58, fol. 85^r: 'byl lid laický poučen a tak porozuměl a lepší přijal, potvrdil a schválil'. Another of Koranda's remarks signals that Koranda does see the vernacular language as suitable for laymen: namely his remark to the effect that he chose his native tongue in connection with addressing Křižanovský, who is a 'laycorum doctor', although it is not quite clear what he meant by this label, since Křižanovský, as a university master, had probably also been ordained as a priest in Italy.

66 As indicated by his use of 'non tantum vos, sed et vestros'. He uses plural forms of address elsewhere as well. Urbánek, *Věk poděbradský IV* [*The Age of Poděbrady IV*], p. 731.

67 Praha, Kap., MS N 58, fol. 85^v.

68 *Manualník M. Václava Korandy* [*Václav Koranda's Personal Miscellany*], ed. by Truhlář, p. 194.

the reign of George of Poděbrady. The nature of Koranda's line of argument clearly shows that he was targeting a wider audience.

This is also evidenced by the somewhat inflammatory language used by the two protagonists. They both stress that disputes should be conducted with love and in good faith (*in caritate, in bona voluntate*).[69] Koranda points out that an exchange of views should be conducted:

> in ea bona voluntate, ut condiximus, et si quid fuerit veritatis, eciam si displiceret, ut vir prudens suscipietis
>
> (in good faith, as we promised, and if something turns out to be true, a wise man will accept it, even if it displeases him).

However, such assurances did not prevent the two scholars from attacking each other. Both university-educated men show off their erudition and knowledge. It is clear from the outset that both strive to win the debate, not just with arguments but, if need be, also by other means: insults, mockery, and denigrating the quality of the opponent's education. This results in fallacious reasoning on both sides: indeed, the second (separate) layer of the dispute concerning the language in which it should be conducted is a fallacy in its own right, as both of them use the topic of choice of language to attack and condemn one another.

Koranda, for instance, repeatedly mentions that Catholic prelates are only interested in money and material gain. He criticizes Hilarius for his conversion (apostasy) from Utraquism and uses a very common anti-Catholic argument: the moral aberrations and improper conduct of the members of the Metropolitan Chapter at Prague Castle.[70] He also does not fail to blame Hilarius for misquoting the Scriptures,[71] or to hint at his lack of knowledge by telling him 'nebuď tak léno v knihy nahlédnúti' (don't be so lazy to look into the books).[72] At the end of his reply, Koranda reproaches Hilarius for not having provided an adequate answer to his questions and for using arguments violating the logic of reasoning as taught at university and learned by Koranda in his student years.[73]

Hilarius's reaction to these reproaches is fierce.[74] At the same time, he attempts to demonstrate his superiority by addressing his opponent informally

69 Cf. Urbánek, *Věk poděbradský IV* [*The Age of Poděbrady IV*], p. 731.

70 For Koranda's criticism of the situation at Prague Castle, see Praha, Kap., MS N 58, fol. 91^{v}: 'kuběnáře, smilníky, svatokupce [...] sám ve svém súdu máš' (there are whoremongers, lechers and simoniacs [...] at your [ecclesiastical] court).

71 *Manualník M. Václava Korandy* [*Václav Koranda's Personal Miscellany*], ed. by Truhlář, p. 194.

72 *Manualník M. Václava Korandy* [*Václav Koranda's Personal Miscellany*], ed. by Truhlář, p. 197.

73 *Manualník M. Václava Korandy* [*Václav Koranda's Personal Miscellany*], ed. by Truhlář, p. 202.

74 *De avibus responsum*, ed. by Kalina, p. 8: 'Discurris per singula mea, ut neque aliquid artis vel sciencie neque officii mei saltem vereare. Studere a me desideras, qui me errasse in scholasticis astruis; vide ne, si me tua estimacione indoctum iudices, te superferas, et cum a me doceri cupias qui me male sapuisse scribis'.

as 'Václav' time and again.[75] Koranda, by contrast, at times mentions that he is concerned about the well-being of the Kingdom of Bohemia and its reputation, which — in his opinion — is being damaged by the Catholics opposing the Utraquists, who only adhere to the Compacts proclaimed by a general council and approved by the emperor and Pope Eugene IV. Koranda criticizes the apostasy of Hilarius and others who, following their conversion, look down on the Utraquists to the detriment of the reputation of the entire kingdom as well as the Czech language (ku pohanění všemu království i jazyku českému). He adds that many Catholic lords, too, were glad that the Compacts were proclaimed:

> mnozí páni lajkové byli krve božie nepřijímajíce i jsú ještie, že sú se radovali, že jest jazyk český v tom pohanění pro krev Kristovu nezuostal.[76]
>
> (Many lay lords who did and do not receive under both species have been happy that the Czech language was not affected by reputational damage resulting from [receiving] Christ's blood.)

This is one of the means that Koranda uses to persuade the reader that he and his party care about the reputation of the kingdom more than the Catholic prelates do. Interestingly, he uses this argument against Hilarius, who — in much the same vein — asked King George to convert back to Catholicism in order to preserve the reputation of the kingdom, and thus free its population of the heretical label.[77]

In order, however, to be able to provide a more meaningful evaluation of the argument between the two scholars concerning the language appropriate for discussing religious themes and to put the 1464 controversy into its historical context, it is helpful to examine more closely how the two protagonists express their views on these issues in other texts.

IV

In order to contextualize the entire controversy better, it needs to be stressed that it was not solely aimed at strengthening the confessional identities or outlining the positions of both of its protagonists. The controversy dates back to 1464. It therefore seems that the opinions formulated therein were intended to influence the king and his aristocratic courtiers. Hilarius had been invited, by a deputation of (Utraquist) university masters, to debate the communion under both kinds in autumn 1463 — at a time when the king was not present in the capital. However, he refused to debate the issue, since he had no interest in discussing it in the absence of the king. This probably

---

75 *De avibus responsum*, ed. by Kalina, p. 8 and elsewhere.

76 Praha, Kap., MS N 58, fol. 86ᵛ.

77 Žůrek, 'Konvertiten raten dem Ketzerkönig'.

prompted Koranda to challenge Hilarius at least to express his views in an exchange of letters, with Koranda making every effort to win the ensuing learned metaphor-filled dispute.

In this instance, Hilarius was probably not keen to influence the king, who had no command of Latin, but aimed at reaching out to the learned Utraquists, especially from among the clergy. This was most likely not in order to convert them, but rather to demonstrate his educational superiority over Koranda, in particular, and also that of the Catholics over the Utraquists, in general. Had he also been targeting the king, he would have probably chosen to use the Czech language, as he had done on other occasions.

The language choices made by both protagonists in their other writings are characteristic of the particular level of vernacularization of religious and political discourse in Hussite Bohemia. While Koranda defended the need to debate issues of faith in Czech in order for the debate to be comprehensible to the lay public, in the controversy discussed in this essay he himself wrote a number of Latin polemical letters.[78] However, his position still demonstrates the long-term systematic efforts made by the Utraquists to include lay audiences in religious disputes.

Hilarius presented himself publicly as an advocate of the use of Latin, which was demonstrated by several of his texts. These include the letter he wrote in reply to the request by two Premonstratensian canons, in which he indignantly comments on the choice of language, reminding the addressees that Latin is the proper language for communication among clerics: 'Dear clergymen, contrary to custom, I am writing to you in Czech, as you did to me, for I have — thank God — some knowledge of writing, but I have not seen you [use] Latin, although you should have used it in your writing.'[79]

However, despite declaring Latin to be the only language suitable for a learned discussion of religious matters in the controversy discussed in this chapter, even Hilarius did not adhere to this principle at all times. Shortly after his dispute with Koranda, he wrote his fundamental treatise on communion under both kinds (*Tractatus catholicus triumphalis contra perfidiam aliquorum Bohemorum*, 1465), which was an academic version of the position he espoused in the public debate with Jan Rokycana.[80] However, that was not his last word on the subject. In the following year, Hilarius rewrote his treatise in Czech. To

78 Marek, 'Polemické spisy Václava Korandy mladšího' ['Václav Koranda the Younger and his Polemical Treatises'].

79 Letter to Premonstratensians, Brother Albert of Křivice and Brother Mathias of Úterý: Fratri Alberto in Křiwic et fratri Mathiae in Úterý, Praemonstratensibus (1 September 1467), *Archiv český VI* [*Czech Archive*, VII], ed. by Palacký, p. 121: 'Kněží milí! Proti obyčeji píši wám česky, jako wy mně; protož bohdá písma něco umiem, jako ste w mých listech wídali, ale wašie latiny ještě sem newiděl, jako byste psáti měli.'

80 *Tractatus catholicus triumphalis contra perfidiam aliquorum Bohemorum*, published as an incunable in Strasbourg in 1485.

be more precise, he partly translated and partly reworked his existing text, in order to adjust it to a different audience,[81] leaving out the scholarly passages and replacing them by *memorabilia* from the history of Bohemia. Although Hilarius repeatedly refused to use the vernacular language in theological debate, in this instance he sought a debate with Utraquist authors and to reach out to the royal court and noblemen as important players in the arena of religious politics in Bohemia.

Similarly, when Hilarius intended to discuss politics, he would choose the vernacular, which was more appropriate for the milieu and target audience. This is already evident in his letter of 1462 to King George. Although Hilarius wrote the letter in Latin, it was almost instantly translated into Czech.[82] When Pope Paul II pressed matters and declared the 'Hussite' King George a heretic, Hilarius's support for the king disappeared and never again returned.

Hilarius threw himself into the political struggle. From then on, the main aim of his activities would be to question the legitimacy of King George. In order to protect himself and the Catholic administration in Bohemia, he began writing and sending 'political letters' in all directions, especially to Bohemian noblemen and burghers (who had thus far been loyal to King George). This is when he realized that he needed to target wider audiences (so as to increase the impact of his production), in particular the powerful group of Bohemian noblemen. They represented the most important social class in Hussite Bohemia, as the king's position was undergoing a crisis. In order to do this, he had to change his strategy, his language, and his communication mode to adjust to the realities of the country. As a result, Hilarius wrote a series of Czech letters in an attempt to convince their addressees that they should abandon King George on the grounds that he had been proclaimed a heretic by the pope, the most important authority on earth.[83] Hilarius used historical arguments, reminding his audience that their ancestors had not practised communion under both kinds. Echoing the arguments put forward by the Bohemian aristocracy, he emphasized the importance of noblemen to the country: 'Pán zemský neb král dnes bude tento, a zajtra jiný, ale rodowé

---

81 Hilarius Litoměřický, *Traktát o nejsvětějším přijímání lidu obecného pod jednou způsobou* [*A Treatise on the Holy Communion of the Common People under One Kind*], ed. by Podlaha. See also Nováková, 'K polemice Hilaria Litoměřického s Rokycanou, zvláště k "Traktátu katolickému"' ['The Polemics of Hilarius of Litoměřice against Jan Rokycana, especially concerning the "Catholic Treatise"'].

82 Hilarius Litoměřický, *List králi Jiřímu z Poděbrad* [*The Letter to King George of Poděbrady*], ed. by Podlaha; cf. Žůrek, 'Konvertiten raten dem Ketzerkönig'.

83 His enthusiasm for Czech in this particular instance went so far that he even used it in letters addressed to towns whose populations were predominantly German (such as Most and Kadaň), asking the addressees also to respond in Czech. See *Archiv český VI* [*Czech Archive, VII*], ed. by Palacký, pp. 109–10. See Šmahel, 'The Idea of the "Nation" in Hussite Bohemia', p. 184.

zuostávají' (As for the lord of the land, there is one king today and another tomorrow, but the noble houses are here to stay).[84]

The most interesting of his vernacular letters is the one addressed to John of Rosenberg, the head of a very important and, arguably, the most powerful noble house in Bohemia. This letter is markedly longer; in fact, it is more a treatise than a letter.[85] It uses many historical and theoretical arguments to show why George is not a legitimate king any more. A king (such as George of Poděbrady) considered deposed by the Catholic Church is not to be obeyed by his subjects any longer ('as though he were dead', Hilarius explicitly states), and a deposed king challenging this is simply a heretic and follower of new and unauthorized religious ideas.

* * *

The transformation of the relationship between Czech and Latin (in both written and spoken form) is an important part of the cultural change that took place in late medieval Bohemia. Looking beyond the controversy concerning which language should be used in disputes relating to religious matters, as analysed in this study, it is obvious that neither side was any longer content to use only one of the languages (Latin or the vernacular). The linguistic situation was much more complex, and the language used depended on the discourse and on the context in which the author wanted to communicate.

It is not possible to identify Latin with the Catholics, on the one side, and the vernacular with the Utraquists, on the other side. Even Hilarius of Litoměřice, the leading Catholic theologian and intellectual in Bohemia, who had a definite preference for Latin when it came to the discussion of religious topics, would switch to the vernacular when he wished to target a different audience. This can clearly be seen in the case of political debates. When Hilarius turned to the political elite of the country, that is, the nobility, he knew that his message would be much more accessible to them in the vernacular mode. On the other hand, when Václav Koranda the Younger wrote letters to Catholic masters, he used Latin, adhering to the standards of learned scholarly debate.[86]

---

84 'Letter to the noblemen of Kolovraty', *Archiv český VI* [*Czech Archive, VI*], ed. by Palacký, p. 112.

85 Hilarius Litoměřický, *Traktát k panu Janovi z Rozenberka* [*Treatise for Jan of Rožmberk*], ed. by Tobolka.

86 Marek, 'Václav Koranda ml. a mediální strategie obrany utrakvismu' ['Václav Koranda the Younger and his Strategy for Defending Utraquism through Public Communication'], pp. 145–46. See also a version of his personal miscellany, known as Brněnský Manualník. All letters included in the *Manualník* were addressed to Catholic intellectuals and, as a result, written in Latin.

John Van Engen has captured the essence of the prevailing present-day view of fifteenth-century church life in his 'multiple options' concept.[87] He has argued that the Church of the fifteenth century was able to integrate different currents and impulses and, as a result, cater to various spiritual needs. This ability of the Church is also evidenced by religious controversies in Hussite Bohemia, where members of both religious camps would still consider themselves as belonging to a single true Church. Religious controversy was a key discourse, and religion was the lens through which everything would be interpreted in dual-faith Bohemia: this applied to politics as well as to the choice of proper language for disputes between learned men. This principle was an integral part of how texts on religious issues were disseminated.[88]

The case of Hilarius of Litoměřice and his intellectual contemporaries indicates that the choice of language had a strong symbolic meaning in Hussite and post-Hussite Bohemia. Hilarius and his bilingual writings, and the controversy with Václav Koranda the Younger, show us that the phenomenon of vernacularization in medieval Bohemia was very deeply rooted within the context of the political and, in particular, religious controversy between the Catholics and Utraquists.

Works Cited

Manuscripts and Archival Sources

Praha, Archiv Pražského hradu, Knihovna Metropolitní kapituly [Prague, Prague Castle Archive, Metropolitan Chapter Library], MS N.58

———, MS N.59

Praha, Národní knihovna [Prague, National Library], MS XVII.F.2

Primary Sources

Albert the Great, *Questions concerning Aristotle's 'On Animals'*, trans. by Irven M. Resnick and Kenneth F. Kitchell, Jr (Washington, DC: Catholic University of America Press, 2008)

Archiv český VI [*Czech Archive*, VI], ed. by František Palacký (Prague: Fridrich Tempský, 1872)

Dvě staročeská utrakvistická díla Jakoubka ze Stříbra [*Two Old Czech Utraquist Works of Jakoubek of Stříbro*], ed. by Helena Krmíčková and Mirek Čejka (Brno: Masarykova univerzita, 2009)

Hilarius of Litoměřice, *De avibus responsum doctoris ad replicam Korande, telonearii Wiklephite*, ed. by Tomáš Kalina, in *Ročenka/Program C.k. vyššího státního gymnasia v Přerově: vydán na konci školního roku 1900–1901* (1901), 8–21

87 Van Engen, 'Multiple Options'.

88 Van Dussen and Soukup, 'Introduction: Textual Controversies, Textual Communities'.

———, *List králi Jiřímu z Poděbrad* [*Letter to King George of Poděbrady*], ed. by Antonín Podlaha, in *Editiones archivii et bibliothecae s. f. metropolitani capituli Pragensis*, 23 (Prague: S.F. Metropolitanum Capitulum Pragense, 1931)

———, *Tractatus catholicus triumphalis contra perfidiam aliquorum Bohemorum* (Strasbourg: [Printer of the 1483 Jordanus de Quedlinburg (Georg Husner)], 1485)

———, *Traktát k panu Janovi z Rozenberka* [*Treatise for Jan of Rožmberk*], ed. by Zdeněk Tobolka (Prague: Česká akademie císaře Františka Josefa, 1898)

———, *Traktát o nejsvětějším přijímání lidu obecného pod jednou způsobou Stříbra* [*A Treatise on Holy Communion for the Common People under One Kind*], ed. by Antonín Podlaha (Prague: S.F. Metropolitanum Capitulum Pragense, 1905)

Manualník M. Vácslava Korandy: t.ř. Rukopis bibliothéky Klementinské [*Václav Koranda's Personal Miscellany: Manuscript of the Klementinum Library*], ed. by Josef Truhlář (Prague: Královská česká společnost nauk, 1888)

Secondary Studies

Coufal, Dušan, *Polemika o kalich mezi teologií a politikou 1414–1431: Předpoklady basilejské disputace o prvním z pražských artikulů* [*Polemics Concerning the Chalice Between Theology and Politics in 1414–1431: A Contribution to the Assumptions of the Basel Disputation on the First of the Articles of Prague*] (Prague: Kalich, 2013)

Doležalová, Lucie, 'Late Medieval Personal Miscellanies: The Case of Mattheus Beran (d. 1461), Augustinian Canon of Roudnice nad Labem', in *Collecting, Organizing and Transmitting Knowledge: Miscellanies in Late Medieval Europe*, ed. by Sabrina Corbellini, Giovanna Murano, and Giacomo Signore, Bibliologia, 49 (Turnhout: Brepols, 2018), pp. 179–96

———, '*Usquoque tu, Domine, obdormis gravi sopore?* A Newly Found Topical Song from Late Medieval Bohemia (Fragment Prague, Library of the National Museum, 1 K 618, M)', *Mittellateinisches Jahrbuch*, 53 (2018), 443–60

———, 'Personal Multiple-Text Manuscripts in Late Medieval Central Europe: The "Library" of Crux de Telč (1434–1504)', in *The Emergence of Multiple-Text Manuscripts*, ed. by Alessandro Bausi, Michael Friedrich, and Marilena Maniaci, Studies in Manuscript Cultures, 16 (Berlin: De Gruyter, 2019), pp. 145–70

———, *Passionate Copying in Late Medieval Bohemia: The Case of Crux de Telcz (1434–1504)* (Prague: Karolinum, 2020)

Heymann, Frederick G., 'John Rokycana: Church Reformer between Hus and Luther', *Church History*, 28 (1959), 240–80

———, *George of Bohemia, King of Heretics* (Princeton: Princeton University Press, 1965)

———, *Plzeň v husitské revoluci: Hilaria Litoměřického 'Historie města Plzně', její edice a historický rozbor / Quo modo Hilarii de Lithomerzicz 'Historia civitatis Plznensis' res gestas aevi Hussitici illustraverit* [*Pilsen in the Hussite Revolution: The 'History of City of Pilsen' of Hilarius of Litoměřice: Its Edition and Historical Analysis*], ed. by Josef Hejnic and Miloslav Polívka (Prague: Ústav československých a světových dějin ČSAV, 1987)

Kadlec, Jaroslav, 'Hilarius Litoměřický v čele duchovenstva podjednou' [Hilarius of Litoměřice as the Head of the Catholic Clergy], in *In memoriam Josefa Macka*, ed. by František Šmahel and Miloslav Polívka (Prague: Historický ústav, 1996), pp. 187–96

Kalina, Tomáš, 'Hilarius Litoměřický' [Hilarius of Litoměřice], *Český časopis historický*, 5 (1899), 311–21

———, 'Václav Křižanovský', *Český časopis historický*, 5 (1899), 333–59

Krofta, Kamil, 'Václav Koranda mladší z Nové Plzně a jeho názory náboženské' [Václav Koranda the Younger of New Pilsen and His Religious Opinions], in Kamil Krofta, *Listy z náboženských dějin českých* (Prague: Historický klub, 1936), pp. 240–87

Marek, Jindřich, 'Václav Koranda ml. a mediální strategie obrany utrakvismu: autorita bible' [Václav Koranda the Younger and his Strategy for Defending Utraquism through Public Communication: The Authority of the Bible], in *Amica sponsa mater: Bible v časech reformace*, ed. by Ota Halama (Prague: Kalich, 2014), pp. 143–53

———, 'Polemické spisy Václava Korandy mladšího proti papeži a představitelům katolické strany v Čechách' [Václav Koranda the Younger and his Polemical Treatises against the Pope and the Representatives of the Catholic Party in Bohemia], *Mediaevalia Historica Bohemica*, 19 (2016), 111–56

———, *Václav Koranda mladší: Utrakvistický administrátor a literát* [*Václav Koranda the Younger: Administator of the Utraquist Church and Writer*] (Prague: Nakladatelství Lidové noviny, 2018)

———, 'Major Figures of Later Hussitism (1437–1471)', in *A Companion to the Hussites*, ed. by Michael Van Dussen and Pavel Soukup (Leiden: Brill, 2020), pp. 141–84

Nováková, Julie, 'K polemice Hilaria Litoměřického s Rokycanou, zvláště k "Traktátu katolickému"' ['The Polemics of Hilarius of Litoměřice against Jan Rokycana, especially concerning the "Catholic Treatise"'], *Listy filologické*, 66 (1939), 364–72

Odložilík, Otakar, *The Hussite King: Bohemia in European Affairs 1440–1471* (New Brunswick: Rutgers University Press, 1965)

Perett, Marcela K., 'Vernacular Songs as "Oral Pamphlets": The Hussites and Their Propaganda Campaign', *Viator*, 42 (2011), 371–91

———, *Preachers, Partisans, and Rebellious Religion: Vernacular Writing and the Hussite Movement* (Philadelphia: University of Pennsylvania Press, 2018)

Podlaha, Antonín, *Soupis rukopisů knihovny metropolitní kapitoly pražské II* [*Catalogue of Manuscripts of the Metropolitan Library in Prague*, II] (Prague: Sumptibus s. f. metropolitani capituli Pragensis, 1922)

Religious Controversy in Europe, 1378–1536: Textual Transmission and Networks of Readership, ed. by Michael Van Dussen and Pavel Soukup (Turnhout: Brepols, 2013)

Rychterová, Pavlína, '*Gens, nacio, communitas – lingua, sanguis, fides*: Idea národa v českém díle Jana Husa' [The Idea of the Nation in the Czech Writings of Jan Hus], in *Heresis seminaria: pojmy a koncepty v bádání o husitství*, ed. by Pavlína Rychterová and Pavel Soukup (Prague: Centrum medievistických studií, Filosofia, 2013), pp. 75–110

———, 'Theology goes to the Vernaculars: Jan Hus, "On Simony" and the Practice of Translation in Fifteenth-Century Bohemia', in *Religious Controversy in Europe, 1378–1536: Textual Transmission and Networks of Readership*, ed. by Michael Van Dussen and Pavel Soukup (Turnhout: Brepols, 2013), pp. 231–49

———, 'Preaching, the Vernacular, and the Laity', in *A Companion to the Hussites*, ed. by Michael Van Dussen and Pavel Soukup (Leiden: Brill, 2020), pp. 297–330

Šmahel, František, *Humanismus v době poděbradské* [*Humanism in the Era of George of Poděbrady*] (Prague: Nakladatelství Československé akademie věd, 1963)

———, 'The Idea of the "Nation" in Hussite Bohemia', *Historica*, 16 (1968), 143–247; 17 (1969), 93–197

———, *Die Basler Kompaktaten mit den Hussiten (1436): Untersuchung und Edition* (Wiesbaden: Harrassowitz Verlag, 2019)

Svejkovský, František, 'The Conception of the "Vernacular" in Czech Literature and Culture of the Fifteenth Century', in *Aspects of the Slavic Language Question*, ed. by Riccardo Picchio and Harvey Goldblatt, I (New Haven: Yale Concilium on International and Area Studies, 1984), pp. 321–36

Urbánek, Rudolf, *Věk poděbradský IV: Čechy za panování Jiříka z Poděbrad: Léta 1460–1464* [*The Age of Poděbrady IV: Bohemia during the Reign of George of Poděbrady, the Years 1460–1464*], České dějiny III.4 (Prague: Nakladatelství ČSAV, 1962)

Van Dussen, Michael, and Soukup, Pavel, 'Introduction: Textual Controversies, Textual Communities', in *Religious Controversy in Europe, 1378–1536: Textual Transmission and Networks of Readership*, ed. by Michael Van Dussen and Pavel Soukup (Turnhout: Brepols, 2013), pp. 1–15

Van Engen, John, 'Multiple Options: The World of the Fifteenth-Century Church', *Church History*, 77 (2008), 257–84

Žůrek, Václav, 'Konvertiten raten dem Ketzerkönig: Zwei volkssprachliche Schriften für König Georg von Podiebrad', *Bohemia*, 58.2 (2018), 246–66

WOJCIECH ŚWIEBODA

The Legitimacy of Making Alliances between Christians and Infidels

Arguments of Polish Jurists in the First Half of the Fifteenth Century

Even though Christian missions had been conducted systematically in Europe, yet at the end of the fourteenth century paganism was still practised in Lithuania, Samogitia, and the north-eastern lands. Of these, the Lithuanians were the only people in this area capable of creating and sustaining a large, strong, and uniform independent country, the Grand Duchy of Lithuania. Although it was ruled by pagan dukes from the Gediminids dynasty, in the 1380s heathens comprised no more than one fifth of the population.[1] The majority of subjects belonged to the Orthodox Church, since several Ruthenian duchies had been incorporated into Lithuania through conquest in the first half of the fourteenth century. There were also some Catholic communities which arose as a result of missions conducted by Franciscans and Dominicans to these lands.[2] The Grand Duchy of Lithuania was surrounded by Christian countries — Poland and the State of the Teutonic Order to the west and north and Orthodox Ruthenian duchies to the east, the strongest of these being the Grand Duchy of Moscow. The Order of the Brothers of the German House of Saint Mary in Jerusalem (founded *c.* 1190 in the Holy Land) was established in Prussia in the thirteenth century to Christianize tribes living in that area such as the Prussians and Yotvingians. Meanwhile, the Teutonic Knights (the common name for the Brothers) concentrated rather on expansion and looting, neglecting the diffusion of Christianity and claiming instead that the first step to conversion of the pagans to the true faith was one of subjugation. The aggressive attitude of the Order deterred

1 Błaszczyk, *Chrzest Litwy* [*The Baptism of Lithuania*], p. 17.

2 Śliwa, 'Kościół prawosławny w państwie litewskim' ['The Orthodox Church in the Lithuanian State'], pp. 16–25.

Wojciech Świeboda • (woj.swieboda@uj.edu.pl) has a PhD from Jagiellonian University, Cracow. He is a Polish historian, medievalist, and researcher at the Manuscript Department of the Jagiellonian Library, Cracow.

Religious Transformations in New Communities of Interpretation in Europe (1350–1570): Bridging the Historiographical Divides, ed. by Élise Boillet and Ian Johnson, New Communities of Interpretation, 3 (Turnhout: Brepols, 2022), pp. 189–207.

DOI 10.1484/M.NCI-EB.5.131220

Lithuanian rulers from conversion to Catholicism.[3] The alternative was to accept baptism from the Ruthenians, but choosing the Orthodox creed did not help them to resolve their political problems. What is more, such an act would deprive the Grand Duchy of potential allies from Poland or Hungary against the Teutonic Knights.[4]

The turning point in the religious and political situation in this part of Europe was the union between the Kingdom of Poland and the Grand Duchy of Lithuania, eventually created in 1385. By virtue of the arrangement completed in Krewo, the Grand Duke of Lithuania Jagiello (d. 1434) declared that he would accept baptism, convert his subjects, and incorporate his lands into the Kingdom of Poland, while the Polish gentry offered Jagiello the crown through marriage with the young Queen Hedwig of Anjou (d. 1399), who had been elected in 1384. The Grand Duke adopted the name of Wladislas (Władysław), married Hedwig, and became the King of the Polish-Lithuanian Commonwealth in 1386.[5] Following the Grand Duke, pagan nobles officially accepted baptism in 1387. This was the symbolic demise of paganism in Lithuania; however, the process of Christianizing the populace would last at least several dozen years.[6]

As there was nobody else to be catholicized (except in Samogitia, which at this time was the only disputed area), the existence of the Teutonic Order as a state in Prussia became pointless. Merely to justify the necessity of continuing the previous politics towards Lithuania and Samogitia, the Teutonic Knights tried to prove to Europe in general that Jagiello's baptism had only been skin-deep, and that Lithuania therefore still remained heathen.[7] The conflict that arose between the Kingdom of Poland and the Grand Duchy of Lithuania on the one side and the Teutonic Order in Prussia on the other led to war in 1409. The apogee was a great battle at Grunwald (Tannenberg, 15 July 1410), where the army of the Teutonic Knights and of European knighthood, which supported them, was completely scattered. The war ended in 1411 and was concluded by a peace treaty in Toruń, by virtue of which, among other resolutions, Samogitia was returned to Lithuania.[8]

---

3 Sousa Costa, 'Canonistarum doctrina de Judaeis et Saracenis', pp. 42–49.

4 Ochmański, *Biskupstwo wileńskie w średniowieczu* [*The Bishopric of Vilna in the Middle Ages*], p. 6; Wyrozumski, 'Próba chrystianizacji Litwy w czasach Giedymina' ['Attempts at Christanizing Lithuania in the Times of Gedymin'], pp. 69–90.

5 Ivinskis, 'Litwa w dobie chrztu i unii z Polską' ['Lithuania in the Age of the Baptism and the Union with Poland'], pp. 54–60; Zahajkiewicz, 'Chrzest Litwy' ['The Baptism of Lithuania'], pp. 36–39.

6 See Błaszczyk, *Chrzest Litwy* [*The Baptism of Lithuania*], pp. 9–42; Frost, *The Oxford History of Poland-Lithuania*, I, 53–73.

7 See the manifesto of the Grand Master Henry of Plauen of 14 December 1410: *Jahrbücher Johannes Lindenblatts oder Chronik Johannes von der Pusilie*, ed. by Voigt and Schubert, pp. 395–99. See also Woś, 'Sul concetto della "guerra giusta"', pp. 599–602.

8 On the great war and the Battle of Tannenberg (Grunwald), see Ekdahl, *Die Schlacht bei Tannenberg 1410*, I; Kuczyński, *Bitwa pod Grunwaldem* [*The Battle of Grunwald*]; Biskup, *Grunwaldzka bitwa* [*The Grunwald Battle*].

This conflict also evoked polemics concerning Christian attitudes towards infidels. Both sides could take completely opposite stands, as there was no uniform or consistent statement by the Church at this time. Medieval canon law (*Corpus iuris canonici*) only contained several scattered sentences about Jews, Muslims, and pagans — which sometimes contradicted one another.[9] What is more, the Doctors of the Church and most other influential Catholic theologians and canonists who spoke about infidels did not treat this issue as the main question: all their opinions were formed as side notes.[10] The Teutonic Knights followed the vision of St Augustine (d. 430), dividing humanity into two opposing groups: *civitas Dei* and *civitas terrena*, which notoriously fight each other, and claiming that those who do not believe in God stand by Devil and, as a consequence, are permanently the enemies of Christianity.[11] Goodness can only be carried out due to direct acts of God. The Teutonic Knights' aversion to Christianizing came from the conviction that non-believers, not being in a state of divine grace, were not capable of any goodness. They maintained that to live with the burden of original sin killed both body and soul, which meant that pagans rejecting the Lord were doomed and passed a death penalty on themselves. What is more, the Brothers accepted the idea of St Augustine, transmitted through the interpretation of John Duns Scotus (d. 1308), who had opined that the highest value for humanity was love of God and neighbour, in the name of which one had to enforce respect for the Lord and the sign of the Cross. The Teutonic Knights considered that because pagans blaspheme against God, as they do not worship Him, they deserve to die.[12] Natural law was understood by the Brothers as God's harmony while, in their interpretation, disbelief destroyed the order of our world. Therefore, all Christians were obliged to do everything to rectify this, preferably by fighting non-believers.[13] The ideology of the Teutonic Order was presented in the Chronicle of Peter of Dusburg (*Chronicon terrae Prussiae*), written in the first half of the fourteenth century and continued up to 1434.[14] By contrast, Polish intellectuals followed the conception of natural law taught by St Thomas Aquinas (d. 1274). According to him, *ius naturale* existed regardless of the law of God, and its main principle was that

---

9 Muldoon, *Popes, Lawyers and Infidels*, p. 5; Świeboda, *Innowiercy w opiniach prawnych uczonych polskich* [*Infidels in the Juridical Opinions of Polish Intellectuals*], pp. 71–72.

10 Winowski, *Innowiercy w poglądach uczonych zachodniego chrześcijaństwa* [*Infidels in the Eyes of the Western Christian Intellectuals*], p. 19; Świeboda, *Innowiercy w opiniach prawnych uczonych polskich* [*Infidels in the Juridical Opinions of Polish Intellectuals*], p. 81.

11 Kwiatkowski, *Zakon niemiecki w Prusach a umysłowość średniowieczna* [*The Teutonic Order in Prussia and Medieval Mentality*], pp. 15–16.

12 Kwiatkowski, *Zakon niemiecki w Prusach a umysłowość średniowieczna* [*The Teutonic Order in Prussia and Medieval Mentality*], pp. 19–21.

13 Kwiatkowski, *Zakon niemiecki w Prusach a umysłowość średniowieczna* [*The Teutonic Order in Prussia and Medieval Mentality*], pp. 43–48; Świeboda, *Innowiercy w opiniach prawnych uczonych polskich* [*Infidels in the Juridical Opinions of Polish Intellectuals*], pp. 64–65.

14 Peter von Dusburg, *Chronicon terrae Prussiae*, ed. by Töppen, pp. 21–219.

all humans, irrespective of their religion, were equal and had the same rights to possess lands, property, and authority.[15]

The intellectual polemic between Poland and the Teutonic Order began with reference to the Great War in 1409–1411. Discussions between the two sides were the starting point for creating a general idea of methods of spreading the faith. Two more problems were also raised by the intellectuals. What was the range of the pope's and emperor's power over the infidels? And what should the Christian attitude be towards other religions? Both sides tried to accuse their opponents of violating law, using unacceptable methods, or compromising the principles of true faith.[16] In fact, it was not certain which option the Christian world would espouse, as the attitude towards infidels oscillated between an uncompromising struggle with every kind of religious otherness on the one side and a dialogue with infidels characterized by mutual respect on the other. At the beginning of the fifteenth century the first option seemed to be prevalent.[17]

One of the arguments used by the Teutonic Knights against King Wladislas Jagiello was that during the war he had allied himself against Christians with infidels, such as pagans, Muslims, and schismatics, in order to destroy the Catholic faith.[18] The great chancellor of the Kingdom of Poland, Wojciech Jastrzębiec (d. 1436), Bishop of Poznań, in his letter of 29 July 1410, two weeks after the battle of Grunwald (Tannenberg), explained that all infidels who fought in the Polish-Lithuanian army were the subjects of Vytautas (d. 1430), Grand Duke of Lithuania, so the ruler had the right to use them during the war. It was acceptable to ask the Tartars for help when the ruler needed to defend his lands. He points out that there were also pagans in the Teutonic Knights' ranks, such as unbaptized Pruthenians. Therefore any accusations against Poland and Lithuania were invalid.[19] King Wladislas Jagiello used very similar arguments in his letter of 11 November 1410, in which he pointed out that the Jasz people, Cumans, and Bosniaks, who were not Christians, served in the army of Sigismund of Luxemburg (d. 1437), the Roman king and ruler of Hungary who supported the Teutonic Knights.[20]

---

15 Kwiatkowski, *Zakon niemiecki w Prusach a umysłowość średniowieczna* [*The Teutonic Order in Prussia and Medieval Mentality*], pp. 17–18, 30; Świeboda, *Innowiercy w opiniach prawnych uczonych polskich* [*Infidels in the Juridical Opinions of Polish Intellectuals*], p. 65.

16 Świeboda, *Innowiercy w opiniach prawnych uczonych polskich* [*Infidels in the Juridical Opinions of Polish Intellectuals*], pp. 125–220.

17 Swieżawski, *Eklezjologia późnośredniowieczna na rozdrożu* [*Late Medieval Ecclesiology at the Crossroads*], pp. 24–26.

18 *Scriptores Rerum Prussicarum*, ed. by Hirsch, Töppen, and Strehlke, III, 428; *Codex epistolaris saeculi decimi quinti*, ed. by Lewicki, III, 499. In fact, at the Battle of Tannenberg there were present about one or two thousand Tartars under the command of Jalal al-Din, son of the deposed Khan of the Golden Horde, who counted on Vytautas's help in recuperating the lost throne.

19 *Scriptores Rerum Prussicarum*, ed. by Hirsch, Töppen, and Strehlke, III, 428.

20 *Codex epistolaris saeculi decimi quinti*, ed. by Lewicki, III, 499.

Similarly, some professors of canon law, for instance Stanisław of Skarbimierz, Paulus Vladimiri, and others, wrote polemical treatises in which they used both juridical and theological arguments to prove that a Catholic ruler might be supported by pagans and other infidels in a just war and that such a ruler therefore incurred no sin simply because of this fact. Interestingly, they did not use the argument which appeared in official letters but rather concentrated instead on doctrinal studies concerning the problems of infidels' rights. Looking at their complex approach to the matter, it seems that they must have realized that the case was very sensitive at that time, so the arguments that they used had to be carefully prepared, coherent, and consistent with natural and canon law, and had to serve the Polish-Lithuanian Commonwealth's interests as well.[21]

'*De bello iusto et iniusto*'

Around a presumed date of *c.* 1410 a short text was written, entitled *De bello iusto et iniusto*. It is considered to be the first Polish answer to the Teutonic Knights' accusations. Its author, Stanisław of Skarbimierz (d. 1431), was a graduate of the Faculty of Canon Law at the University of Prague and was elected the first Rector of the University of Cracow in 1400. He was also considered to be the personal confessor of Queen Hedwig and a reputable orator and preacher.[22] His work, in the form of a sermon, is a kind of juridical treatise. Its major aim was to prove that the Polish king had conducted a just war, and that because of this he was allowed to ask for help even from infidels.[23]

Stanisław of Skarbimierz, as many other jurists of that time, did not divide arguments into theological and juridical ones. Generally, the majority of juridical opinions and instances drawing on canon law invoked faith and biblical examples in support of these principles to determine legal actions in legislation.[24] The more interesting aspect is: which *auctoritates* the Polish jurist quotes? The work begins with five requirements of a just war taken from the *Summa aurea* of Raymond of Penyafort (d. 1275), which were the

---

21 Świeboda, *Innowiercy w opiniach prawnych uczonych polskich* [*Infidels in the Juridical Opinions of Polish Intellectuals*], p. 114.

22 Chmielowska, 'Stanisław de Skarbimierz – le premier recteur de l'Université de Cracovie', pp. 82–89.

23 The work *De bellis iustis* was published in print three times: Ehrlich, *Polski wykład* [*A Fifteenth Century Polish Exposition*], pp. 90–145; Stanisław ze Skarbimierza, *Sermones sapientiales*, part 1, ed. by Chmielowska, pp. 323–40; Stanisław ze Skarbimierza, *Mowy wybrane o mądrości* [*Selected Speeches on Wisdom*], ed. by Korolko, pp. 86–111. In this essay the first edition mentioned above is the one quoted.

24 Świeboda, *Innowiercy w opiniach prawnych uczonych polskich* [*Infidels in the Juridical Opinions of Polish Intellectuals*], p. 11.

following: 1) only a secular and not an ecclesiastical ruler may conduct a war; 2) a war is conducted to retake property or to defend the homeland; 3) war may be justifiable if there are no other methods of making peace apart from armed struggle; 4) respect for the ordinance of God, love, justice, and obedience must be kept; 5) a war must be conducted with the Church's authorization.[25] The assertion that the armed conflict is unacceptable if there is a possibility to bring justice by legal action is adopted from the *Apparatus ad Summam aurea Raimundi de Pennaforte* written by William of Rennes (d. *c.* 1250).[26] Stanisław of Skarbimierz notes that God sometimes punishes wicked Christians by using barbarians as a scourge, so he asks: why then are Christians not allowed to unite with infidels in a just war against vicious believers?[27] Then he argues that natural law permits us to use any means to restore peace; so, if a kingdom has not got enough forces to defend itself, asking infidels for help is justified. He also points out that, since setting up ambushes and using slingshots, war machines, and artillery to bring justice is permitted by God, in the same way pagans may be used as a weapon in a just war. The Polish jurist invokes natural law to show that both Christians and pagans have the same rights to defend themselves, and then he cites the law of nations (*ius gentium*) to prove that Catholics and infidels may cooperate with each other in order to practise justice. Nor is it even a sin to ask pagans for help to bring peace, but it is meritorious, and he concludes by referring to St Thomas Aquinas.[28]

Stanisław of Skarbimierz mentions the example of Christian soldiers who used to serve in the army of the pagan Emperor Julian the Apostate, ostensibly proving that if a leader's orders do not stand in contradiction to the ordinance of God, one should preserve obedience to them. *Per analogiam*, heathens may serve in the army of a Christian ruler. And the ruler neither is responsible for his ally's warfare nor for his subjects' intentions.[29] In this way Stanisław of Skarbimierz denies Wladislas Jagiello's responsibility for the plunder and robbery committed by his Tartar allies during the war. The treatise concludes that a Christian ruler is allowed to ask pagans for help in a just war without committing any sin, provided that he cannot find any other solutions to defeat his enemy.

Many statements about infidels included in the sermon *De bello iusto et iniusto* were taken from the works of Sinibaldo Fieschi, later Pope Innocent IV (d. 1254), the most important being that even non-believers had the right to possess their own countries, property, and authority. In his opinion, all

---

25 Erlich, *Polski wykład* [*A Fifteenth Century Polish Exposition*], pp. 94–96.

26 Erlich, *Polski wykład* [*A Fifteenth Century Polish Exposition*], pp. 15–16.

27 Erlich, *Polski wykład* [*A Fifteenth Century Polish Exposition*], p. 126.

28 Erlich, *Polski wykład* [*A Fifteenth Century Polish Exposition*], pp. 128–34. Compare with: *Summa theologica*, Prima Secundae, quaestio 65, articulo 2, in *Sancti Thomae Aquinatis Summa Theologica*, II, 349.

29 Erlich, *Polski wykład* [*A Fifteenth Century Polish Exposition*], pp. 132–34.

human beings should be protected by law; so, accordingly, non-believers are subjected to natural law which for them replaces God's law. Faith is a free act, so none should spread it by force.[30] Some theological ideas expressed in this sermon were adopted from Thomas Aquinas, for example the one stating that Christians might cooperate with pagans in fulfilling moral virtues like justice or magnanimity.[31] Foundational to the admissibility of cooperation with non-believers in a just war is natural law, which relies on common sense and which allows all human beings to defend themselves. God created the universe for all humanity irrespective of their religion, so believers as well as non-believers may take advantage of its natural resources. *Ius gentium*, which derives from natural law, regulates the relationship between all communities. The religious status of a community is therefore irrelevant when a just war is waged. Man is the most distinguished creature in the world and thus even an infidel has his dignity. The law of nations prohibits attacking heathens, and even a pope cannot give permission to plunder pagans' land or grab their possessions, as the Teutonic Knights were used to doing.[32]

As we can see, the work of Stanisław of Skarbimierz is confined to the problem of whether asking pagans for help in war is permitted. Nevertheless, the main stream of argumentation concentrates on the question of what kind of rights infidels have and why Christians must respect them. In this way, not only does he defend the Polish king from accusations of making prohibited alliances with 'enemies of the Cross', but he also turns the Teutonic Knights' accusations back on themselves.

Two weeks before the battle of Grunwald (Tannenberg), Jakub of Kurdwanów (d. 1425), Bishop of Płock, preached a sermon to Polish knights trying to argue that the war against the Teutonic Knights was just and that, because of this, the king was allowed to access Prussian lands in order to defend his subjects and territory.[33] As the precise date of the publishing of *De bello iusto et iniusto* is unknown, it is difficult to say if Stanisław of Skarbimierz's work had any influence on the sermon of Jakub of Kurdwanów — or just the opposite: if, that is, the jurist was inspired by the Polish dignitary.[34] Nevertheless, we can point out that in the views of both the problem of the just war was one of the most crucial in explaining the legitimacy of making an alliance with infidels.

---

30 Erlich, *Polski wykład [A Fifteenth Century Polish Exposition]*, p. 136; Muldoon, *Popes, Lawyers and Infidels*, pp. 8–14.

31 Erlich, *Polski wykład [A Fifteenth Century Polish Exposition]*, p. 132. Compare with: *Summa theologica*, Secunda Secundae, quaestio 58, articulo 12, in *Sancti Thomae Aquinatis Summa Theologica*, III, 342.

32 Świeboda, *Innowiercy w opiniach prawnych uczonych polskich [Infidels in the Juridical Opinions of Polish Intellectuals]*, pp. 152–53.

33 *Ioannis Dlugossii Annales*, Libri X–XI (1406–1412), ed. by Turkowska, p. 65.

34 Wyrozumski, 'L'idée de tolérance à l'Université de Cracovie', p. 139.

Paulus Vladimiri of Brudzeń

The most significant stage of the polemics between Poland and the Teutonic Order took place during the Council of Constance in a debate running from 1414 to 1418. The speaker representing the Polish legation was Paulus Vladimiri of Brudzeń (d. 1436). He graduated from the Universities of Prague, Padua, and Cracow, where he finally obtained the title of doctor of canon law. He participated in the Council of Constance as the ambassador of King Wladislas Jagiello.[35] In 1416 he wrote a work which is known as *De potestate papae et imperatoris respectu infidelium* (incipit: *Saevientibus*). He composed another treaty in tandem with it — *Conclusiones* (incipit: *Opinio Ostiensis*) — which contains conclusions of his first work and which was delivered to all the Council's nations. Both works raise the question of the authority and competence a pope and an emperor have over infidels. The main conclusion is that only the head of the Church and not a secular ruler has power over all humans, including non-believers who live outside the Christian world, but that even a pope must respect their rights, which are guaranteed by natural law and the law of nations (*ius gentium*). Although he may punish them if they do not obey the law, he is also responsible for defending non-believers from injustice and aggression.[36] Undoubtedly, the event which provided the basis for demonstrating such opinions about those who stayed outside the Church was the public appearance of the representatives of recently baptized Samogitians, whose baptism had taken place half a year earlier in February 1416. The delegates testified that they had become zealous Christians due to the patient teaching of missionaries and the pious attitude of Polish-Lithuanian rulers; they also complained about the Teutonic Knights still hounding them. They ended the speech (*Propositio Samagitharum*) with a request to Pope Martin V to stand up for them.[37] According to numerous sources the appearance of the neophytes at the Council of Constance made an outstanding impression on the delegates. One of the beneficial results of their speech was the exclusive authorization

---

35 *Paulus Vladimiri and His Doctrine*, ed. by Bełch, I, 115–50; Woś, 'Appunti per la biografia di Paulus Wladimiri', pp. 57–97. The date of his death has been corrected by Marek D. Kowalski, 'Zapomniany kalendarz-nekrolog kapituły krakowskiej' ['The Forgotten Calendar-Necrology of the Chapter of Cracow'], p. 131.

36 The trilingual edition of Paulus Vladimiri's works is quoted: Paulus Vladimiri, *Pisma wybrane Pawła Włodkowica* [*Works of Paul Wladimiri – a Selection*], ed. by Ehrlich, I, 2–112 (for the work *Saevientibus*); pp. 113–43 (for the work *Opinio Ostiensis*). Another edition with English commentary is *Paulus Vladimiri and His Doctrine*, ed. by Bełch, II, 780–844 (*Saevientibus*); pp. 846–84 (*Opinio Ostiensis*).

37 Boockmann, *Johannes Falkenberg*, pp. 206–07; Banaszak, 'Chrzest Żumdzi i jego reperkusje w Konstancji' ['The Baptism of Samogitia and its Repercussions at the Council of Constance'], pp. 65–70. For a full edition of the complaint, see *Codex epistolaris Vitoldi*, ed. by Prochaska, pp. 1018–24.

granted in the following year by the pope to Polish and Lithuanian rulers to conduct missions in Samogitia.[38]

At the beginning of his treatise Paulus Vladimiri tries to respond to the controversy as to whether a Catholic ruler is allowed to expel Muslims and Jews from his country and take their property away without reason, and whether a pope may authorize him to do it. He explains, using arguments taken from Peter of Anchorano's (d. 1416) commentary to the chapter *De regulis iuris* of *Libri Sexi Decretalium*, that in such a situation, when infidels would like to live in peace side by side with Christians, they should not be oppressed in any way. Quoting several paragraphs of the *Decretum Gratiani* and the *Decretales* of Gregory IX, he shows that neither an emperor nor a pope has the authority to deprive them of their property. Non-believers should be tolerated because this benign attitude is useful for winning over heathens to the faith.[39]

Another question is whether Christians are allowed to attack pagans and Muslims living in their own countries. Quoting the ideas of Pope Innocent IV via the works of Peter of Anchorano and Francesco Zabarella (d. 1417), Paulus Vladimiri says that all infidels have the right to possess their own power and independent lands. All kinds of things belong to God, who gave them over for man's use. At the beginning of history everything was common property, but as time passed people naturally began to expropriate all individual things, which was happening by courtesy of God (Deuteronomy 11. 24). Countries and kingdoms also arose by this process. This was the origin of the principle that nobody should take away any personal property belonging to somebody else. The universe was created both for good and bad people, and consequently countries, property, and power also belong to non-believers.[40] The doctor of canon law demonstrates that the civil law prohibits attacking peaceful people, and that canon law disallows the use of force against infidels, whereas natural law demands that one should refrain from any acts that one would not like to experience oneself, while the law of God prohibits the homicide and robbery of non-Christians. What is more, aggression universally transgresses the Decalogue's Commandment: love thy neighbour as thyself.[41] This opinion, however, opposes the position of one of the most influential canonists, Henry of Segusio (called Hostiensis; d. 1271), who had claimed that since the birth of Jesus Christ all kinds of authority, power, and property had been transferred from infidels to Christians. As a result, non-believers did not have any rights to possess their own countries or territories and everything that *de facto* belongs to them is

38 Brandmüller, *Das Konzil von Konstanz 1414–1418*, II, 160–61.

39 Paulus Vladimiri, *Pisma wybrane*, ed. by Ehrlich, I, 9–10. Compare with: *Petri de Ancharano... Super Sexto Decretalium acutissima Commentaria*, De regulis iuris, pp. 527–28.

40 See *Innocentii quarti pontifici maximi Super libros quinque Decretalium*, III. 34. 8, p. 430; *Petri de Ancharano... Super Sexto Decretalium acutissima Commentaria*, De regulis iuris, cap. 4, pp. 528–29; *Francisci cardinalis Zabarella Lectura super tertio Decretalium*, fol. 180^{v}.

41 Paulus Vladimiri, *Pisma wybrane*, ed. by Ehrlich, I, 11–14.

in iure subject to the Church.[42] The consequence of this is that all kinds of war whose purpose is to recuperate infidels' lands and properties are just. Paulus Vladimiri explicitly refuses such an interpretation; however, he makes two exceptions: the Holy Land and Spain, to which, in his opinion, Christians are entitled.[43]

Paulus Vladimiri claims that it is forbidden to force infidels to convert to Christianity, because true faith is based on free will and God's grace. Enforcing faith is an act of injustice, and one should remember that 'forced service does not please God'. Christianizing ought to be performed by personal example, not by cruelty.[44] He quotes several canons of the *Decretum Gratiani* which acknowledge this standpoint, concluding that even a non-believer is a neighbour.[45] A pope may only command infidels to accept missionaries on their lands, because, as Vladimiri explains, all rational beings were created to glorify God.[46]

In the middle part of his work Paulus Vladimiri elaborates the problem of the just war, vicariously referring to the work of his friend Stanisław of Skarbimierz. One of the aspects which he considers is whether Christians needing to defend themselves and their countries are allowed to ask infidels for help. The majority of his arguments are adopted from Giovanni d'Andrea (*Additiones Speculi iudiciales*)[47] and Oldradus de Ponte (*Consilia*).[48] They responded that in sudden necessity it is permitted to call non-believers in, unless they are aggressive and/or are waging a war against other Christian countries. But if the side which allies with non-Christians gains a military advantage in a war, or is conducting an unjust war, or the alliance is no longer necessary, such an option is not acceptable. The Polish canonist makes some analogies, for example that, just as a man in an extreme situation may use a trick, so even infidels have the right to ask Christians for help. This rule also refers to those in a state of excommunication: in both situations, believers may support them without sin. To strengthen his conclusion Paulus Vladimiri uses numerous examples from the Old Testament to show that God accepts such alliances.[49]

---

42 Winowski, *Innowiercy w poglądach uczonych zachodniego chrześcijaństwa* [*Infidels in the Eyes of the Western Christian Intellectuals*], pp. 61–66; Muldoon, *Popes, Lawyers and Infidels*, pp. 16–17.

43 Paulus Vladimiri, *Pisma wybrane*, ed. by Ehrlich, I, 20–21.

44 Paulus Vladimiri, *Pisma wybrane*, ed. by Ehrlich, I, 60–61.

45 *Decretum Gratiani*, De poenitentia, Distinctio 2, cap. 5, *Corpus iuris canonici*, ed. by Friedberg, I, cols 1191–92. This aspect was broadly elaborated by Paulus Vladimiri in another treaty of his entitled *Causa inter reges Poloniae et Cruciferos*, which begins with the words *Ad aperiendam*. See Paulus Vladimiri, *Pisma wybrane*, ed. by Ehrlich, I, 192.

46 Paulus Vladimiri, *Pisma wybrane*, ed. by Ehrlich, I, 35.

47 See Ioannes Andreae, *Additiones ad Durantis Speculum iudiciale*, IV. fol. 110^{r}.

48 *Oldradi de Ponte Laudensis Consilia*, Consilium 71, fol. 27^{r}.

49 Paulus Vladimiri, *Pisma wybrane*, ed. by Ehrlich, I, 75–77. Paulus Vladimiri claims that even magic tricks can be used in need.

The works of the Polish canonist presented to the Council of Constance in 1416 provoked a backlash from the Teutonic Knights' delegation and their supporters. As the Brothers were not educated in canon law, they had to ask intellectuals from other nations for help in entering into a polemical exchange with the Polish arguments. All defenders of the Teutonic Order, such as the Bishop of Ciudad Rodrigo Andreas de Escobar, Ardicinus of Novara, the Bamberg canonist John Urbach, the Bishop of Lodi Giacomo Balardi, Rudolph Artz, or the Dominican John Falkenberg, proceeded from the statement of Henry of Segusio that, since the birth of Jesus Christ, all infidels had lost their rights to possess power, lands, and property.[50] Giacomo Balardi writes that Catholics tolerate non-believers only if they are subjected to Christian authority. No one is allowed to make an alliance with infidels unless he is given permission directly by God.[51] In similar vein is Rudolph Artz, the alleged author of the work entitled *Utrum bella contra infideles fidelibus licitum sit movere*. Being under the influence of the conception of natural law of John Duns Scotus, Rudolph was convinced that the greatest display of love is a fight against those who do not feel love of the Lord. One order should exist in the world (this means one faith, one law, etc.), so those who refuse it are to be compelled by force. Pagans never live in peace with Christians, so the war against them is permanent and nothing justifies making alliances with them, as they serve the devil.[52] The most academic work was written by John Urbach, who maintained that no infidels living outside Christian countries have any rights to possess power, lands, and property, and that consequently all wars conducted by Christian rulers against them are just if they manage to dispose them to accept the emperor's power above themselves.[53] The most controversial polemic was a treatise written by John Falkenberg (d. 1435) called *Satira*. This Dominican friar exhorted the extermination of all pagans and their supporters, especially Poles (called dogs), who were heretics, and he claimed that a man daring to kill the Polish king Jagiello deserved salvation.[54] Except for the text of John Urbach and especially that of Falkenberg, which presented a legalistic level of argumentation but were keenly discussed nevertheless because of their

50 *Die Staatsschriften des Deutschen Ordens*, ed. by Weise, pp. 112–413; Świeboda, *Innowiercy w opiniach prawnych uczonych polskich* [*Infidels in the Juridical Opinions of Polish Intellectuals*], pp. 199–207.

51 *Acta Concilii Constantiensis*, ed. by Finke, IV, 682–84.

52 *Utrum bella contra infideles fidelibus licitum sit movere?*, ed. by Bełch, pp. 15–47; *Die Staatsschriften des Deutschen Ordens*, ed. by Weise, pp. 380–81; Boockmann, *Johannes Falkenberg*, pp. 249–51.

53 *Paulus Vladimiri*, ed. by Bełch, II, 1116–80; *Die Staatsschriften des Deutschen Ordens*, ed. by Weise, pp. 318–80.

54 Włodek, 'La Satire de Jean Falkenberg', pp. 61–95; Boockmann, *Johannes Falkenberg*, pp. 313–53.

shocking conclusions,[55] other polemics against Paulus Vladimiri were not widely known.[56]

In response to the arguments of John Urbach and especially those of John Falkenberg, Paulus Vladimiri wrote another text entitled *Quoniam error* in 1417. In this work not only does he refute his opponents' conclusions,[57] but he also tries to prove that the Teutonic Knights fell into heresy, claiming that the Teutonic Order in Prussia was established mainly to exterminate pagans and seize their lands from them.[58] In this work he also takes the opportunity to develop the issue of union with infidels. He repeats the majority of arguments expressed in his previous works, he especially recalls the five requirements of a just war and emphasizes that only non-believers who do not oppress Christians or disrupt Christian missions should be treated as potential allies. In case of the pagans who live in Prussia and Samogitia there is no proof that they repress believers or impede evangelization. Therefore, the Teutonic Knights are not allowed to declare war on them. Regardless of the truth, the first step to punish aggressive or unruly nations should be legal action. A war is the last feasible means of appealing for justice. Jesus Christ commanded the preaching of the Word of God to all nations, not bringing the sword to them.[59]

As we can see, Paulus Vladimiri's deductive approach of demonstrating that the essence of the conflict between the Polish-Lithuanian Commonwealth and the Teutonic Order in Prussia was not a question of whether Christians should be allowed to cooperate with infidels, but one of who is in fact the defender of justice. Several proofs were produced that the Teutonic Knights were permanently violating natural law, the law of nations, and the law of God by conquering peaceful peoples, whereas the only justification they claimed was that heathens did not have any rights and always did harm. Meanwhile, true Christians were obliged to help non-believers when they suffered injustice, as the *ius naturae* and *ius gentium* allowed even bad people to defend themselves. This was the reason why the Polish king made the alliance with pagans and Tartars and fought shoulder-to-shoulder with them against those who called themselves Catholics.

An essential part of Paulus Vladimiri's ideas was the Thomistic conception of man as a person possessing a dignity arising from the fact of creation in the image and likeness of God. The core statement is that the universe was created for all thinking beings, and one law was established for them — *ius*

55 Boockmann, *Johannes Falkenberg*, pp. 189–97, 239–42, 264–95.

56 Świeboda, *Innowiercy w opiniach prawnych uczonych polskich* [*Infidels in the Juridical Opinions of Polish Intellectuals*], pp. 199–205. In response to the wave of polemic by the Teutonic Order's defenders, some famous European intellectuals acted as advocates on behalf of Poland, such as Cardinal Pierre d'Ailly, Bishop of Cambrai (d. 1420). See *Die Staatsschriften des Deutschen Ordens*, ed. by Weise, pp. 265–70.

57 Paulus Vladimiri, *Pisma wybrane*, ed. by Ehrlich, II, 325–98.

58 Paulus Vladimiri, *Pisma wybrane*, ed. by Ehrlich, II, 216–315.

59 Paulus Vladimiri, *Pisma wybrane*, ed. by Ehrlich, II, 303–04, 308–15.

naturae. Natural law, according to William of Ockham, includes all human beings regardless of their religion. Every man should practise love and solidarity with one another, even non-believers. Accordingly, the law of nations enables the carrying-out of peaceful and harmonious coexistence among groups, communities, nations, and countries and the adjudication of all disputes through legal process.[60] In fact, in his works Paulus Vladimiri mostly quoted the words of *auctoritates* and seldom constructed an innovative thesis; on the other hand, he was able to collect scattered sentences, and by using theological, juridical, and historical arguments he put theoretical divagations onto practical ground.[61] This Polish doctor of canon law, like Thomas Aquinas, did not claim equal rights for all religions, which was out of the question in the Middle Ages, but he stood for religious tolerance, albeit with its medieval meaning, as one would expect.[62]

Revocatur in dubium

During the long-lasting conflict between Poland and the Teutonic Knights in Prussia, one more argument was used by the latter against King Wladislas Jagiello. The Brothers, who lost their good reputation in Europe after the Council of Constance, accused the Polish ruler of allying himself during the war with heretical Hussites from Bohemia against Christians. In fact, this accusation was not baseless, as in 1421 the Hussite delegation came to Cracow to offer the Bohemian crown to the Polish king in exchange for accepting the Four Articles of Prague. What is more, the king's nephew, Duke Sigismund, came to Prague in 1422 as a viceroy of Vytautas, Grand Duke of Lithuania, with the hope of overruling Hussite Bohemia. Although Wladislas Jagiello did not accept this offer and finally condemned the Hussite heresy, he never joined any crusades against heretics. In the eyes of the Christian world at the time the most shocking act of the Polish king was his alliance with the so-called Orphans (Sirotci), a splinter group of Hussites, with whom he made a pact in 1432 against the Teutonic Order. The presence of Bohemian warriors alongside this Christian ruler gave the Teutonic Knights an excuse for accusing Wladislas Jagiello of being the ally of heretics.[63]

---

60 Jasudowicz, *Śladami Ludwika Ehrlicha: Do Pawła Włodkowica po naukę o prawach człowieka* [*After Ludwik Ehrlich: Approaching Paulus Vladimiri for the Concept of Human Rights*], pp. 20–22, 29; Kwiatkowski, *Zakon niemiecki w Prusach a umysłowość średniowieczna* [*The Teutonic Order in Prussia and Medieval Mentality*], p. 126.

61 Reid, 'Paulus Valdimiri, the "Tractatus Opinio Hostiensis" and the Rights of Infidels', p. 422.

62 Świeboda, *Innowiercy w opiniach prawnych uczonych polskich* [*Infidels in the Juridical Opinions of Polish Intellectuals*], p. 197.

63 See Nikodem, *Polska i Litwa wobec husyckich Czech* [*Poland, Lithuania and Hussite Bohemia*], pp. 205–41; Grygiel, *Zygmunt Korybutowicz* [*Sigismund Korybut*], pp. 28–37, 53–87.

Probably during the time of negotiations with the Hussites, in 1421–1422 or 1432, an unknown Polish intellectual from the king's court wrote a juridical opinion (*Revocatur in dubium*), in which he explained, after the scholastic fashion, that a Catholic ruler was allowed to ask even heretics for help.[64] Here, he argues that natural law permits one to defend oneself, and therefore that no ruler should be condemned for making an alliance with infidels to protect his subjects. He goes on to quote the opinions of Oldradus de Ponte (d. 1335) and Giovanni d'Andrea (d. 1348) to demonstrate that, since Christians are allowed to help non-believers in a just war,[65] the opposite situation should be even more acceptable.[66] He expresses his confidence that cooperation with heretics facilitates gaining them for the Church, because contact characterized by kindness makes it easier thereafter to convince somebody of the true faith. Following Innocent IV, he repeats the opinion, used by other Polish intellectuals, that infidels as well as Christians are God's creatures and belong to the Lord's fold, and also the belief that Jesus Christ suffered and died not only for believers but also for non-believers. Because of this, there are no obstacles to socializing with infidels, provided that the authority of Church is respected and its prohibitions are not broken.[67]

The last part of the text is a polemic against arguments which criticize contacts with heretics. First of all, the author proves that for defending oneself and one's property one might unite with those who are excommunicated. Secondly, when a Christian king endures a loss, all *Christianitas* suffers, but when he allies himself with infidels, so, *per analogiam*, the majority of Christians profit from it. Thirdly, in extraordinary situations — for example, in the case of necessary defence — the prohibition against maintaining contacts with heretics no longer applies. The conclusion made by the anonymous scholar is that in extreme situations contacts with heretics are permissible without sin.[68]

Although the author of the note mainly uses arguments taken from other intellectuals, his opinion should be regarded as an original compilation, as

64 Rebeta, 'Czy notatka "Revocatur" należy do polskiej szkoły prawa' ['Does the Note "Revocatur" belong to the Polish School of the Law of International Relations'], pp. 533–39; Chmielowska, 'Notatka "Revocatur"' ['The Note "Revocatur"'], pp. 33–35. The note *Revocatur* was published in print three times: *Notatka Revocatur*, ed. by Erlich, pp. 198–203; Woś, 'Sul concetto della "guerra giusta"', pp. 624–26; Chmielowska, 'Notatka "Revocatur"' ['The Note "Revocatur"'], pp. 36–38; See also: Świeboda, *Innowiercy w opiniach prawnych uczonych polskich* [*Infidels in the Juridical Opinions of Polish Intellectuals*], pp. 156–58.

65 See Zacour, *Jews and Saracens*, p. 49.

66 Erlich, *Polski wykład* [*A Fifteenth Century Polish Exposition*], p. 200; Woś, 'Sul concetto della "guerra giusta"', p. 625; Chmielowska, 'Notatka "Revocatur"' ['The Note "Revocatur"'], p. 37.

67 Erlich, *Polski wykład* [*A Fifteenth Century Polish Exposition*], pp. 202–3; Woś, 'Sul concetto della "guerra giusta"', pp. 625–26; Chmielowska, 'Notatka "Revocatur"' ['The Note "Revocatur"'], pp. 37–38.

68 Erlich, *Polski wykład* [*A Fifteenth Century Polish Exposition*], p. 203; Woś, 'Sul concetto della "guerra giusta"', p. 626; Chmielowska, 'Notatka "Revocatur"' ['The Note "Revocatur"'], p. 38.

it undertakes the intractable and controversial problem comprehensively both from theological and juridical points of view. It is doubtful, however, that his conclusions would or could have been accepted by the Church at this time. Nevertheless, it should be appreciated that this text examines the problem in a wide context, and that all its ideas derive from a well-applied concept of peaceful coexistence with other religions.[69] There are no evident references to the writings of Stanisław of Skarbimierz or Paulus Vladimiri; however, the arguments used in the note and the *auctoritates* quoted by the author are similar to other Polish works addressing the problem of making alliances with infidels.

* * *

As we have seen, the ideas of the aforementioned Polish intellectuals concerning alliances with infidels in a just war were compatible with each other. All of these works were created not as scholastic divagations, but in the specific contexts of the conflict with the Teutonic Order; their purpose was to defend the Polish-Lithuanian Commonwealth from unjust accusations. The general conception was that infidels could not be Christianized by force and had the same rights as Christians to possess their own countries and authority. In their works these Polish jurists quoted certain paragraphs of canon law, verses of the Holy Bible, and *auctoritates* such as Pope Innocent IV, St Thomas Aquinas, Raymond of Penyafort, Peter of Anchorano, Francesco Zabarella, and others. The most precious value in their reasoning was their ability to match juridical and theological arguments deriving from canon law on the one side with distinctive beliefs on the other. This had the major result of creating a consistent and logical discourse on the relations between believers and non-believers.

The treatises of Paulus Vladimiri written during the Council of Constance played the most significant role, as they presented a comprehensive doctrine of peaceful coexistence with infidels. The fact that the majority of his arguments were adopted from *auctoritates* did not downgrade the value of his works, since Paulus Vladimiri was able to transfer the theoretical considerations onto practical ground. He also used historical facts, proving that all people had the natural and inalienable right of freedom and free will. Observing the reactions of the members of the Council of Constance, we can claim that the Polish professor's conclusions were appreciated. However, the Church did not legitimize them as official doctrine. Because of this, over the next two hundred years other intellectuals, such as Francisco de Vitoria (d. 1536) and Hugo Grotius (d. 1645), were compelled to articulate a new explanation of

---

69 Ożóg, *The Role of Poland in the Intellectual Development of Europe*, pp. 113–14; Świeboda, *Innowiercy w opiniach prawnych uczonych polskich* [*Infidels in the Juridical Opinions of Polish Intellectuals*], p. 160.

the range of the pope's power over the local inhabitants of newly discovered lands. But their opinions did not reach as far as acknowledging the rights of pagans as the Polish intellectuals had done earlier.[70]

Works Cited

Primary Sources

Acta Concilii Constantiensis, ed. by Heinrich Finke, IV (Münster: Regensbergschen Buchhandlung, 1928)

Codex epistolaris saeculi decimi quinti, ed. by Anatol Lewicki, Monumenta medii aevi historica, 14, III (Cracow: Wydawnictwa Komisyi Historycznej Akademii Umiejętności w Krakowie, 1894)

Codex epistolaris Vitoldi magni ducis Lithuaniae 1376–1430, ed. by Antoni Prochaska, Monumenta medii aevi historica, 6 (Cracow: Academiae Literarum Cracoviensis, 1882)

Corpus iuris canonici, ed. by Aemilius Friedberg, I (Leipzig: Officina Bernhardt Tauchnitz, 1879)

Innocentii quarti pontifici maximi Super libros quinque Decretalium (Francofurti ad Moenum: Sigismundus Fejerabendt, 1570)

Ioannes Andreae, *Additiones ad Durantis Speculum iudiciale* (Strasbourg: Georg Husner, 1475)

Ioannis Dlugossii Annales seu Cronicae inclyti Regni Poloniae, Libri X–XI (1406–1412), ed. by Danuta Turkowska (Warsaw: Wydawnictwo Naukowe PWN, 1997)

Jahrbücher Johannes Lindenblatts oder Chronik Johannes von der Pusilie, ed. by Johannes Voigt and Friedrich Wilhelm Schubert, Beilage III (Königsberg: Universitäts Buchhandlung, 1823)

Notatka Revocatur [*The Note Revocatur*], ed. by Ludwik Ehrlich, in Ludwik Ehrlich, *Polski wykład prawa wojny w XV wieku* [*A Fifteenth Century Polish Exposition of the Law of War*] (Warsaw: Wydawnictwo Prawnicze, 1955), pp. 198–203

Oldradi de Ponte Laudensis Consilia seu Responsia et Quaestiones aureae (Venetiis [Venice]: Franciscus Zilettus, 1570)

Paulus Vladimiri, *Pisma wybrane Pawła Włodkowica* [*Works of Paul Wladimiri – a Selection*], ed. by Ludwik Ehrlich, I–II (Warsaw: Instytut Wydawniczy PAX, 1966–1968)

Francisci cardinalis Zabarella Lectura super tertio Decretalium (Lyon: Jacobus Mareschal, 1518)

Paulus Vladimiri and His Doctrine concerning International Law and Politics, ed. by Stanislaus F. Bełch, I–II (London: Mouton & Co., 1965)

Peter von Dusburg, *Chronicon terrae Prussiae*, ed. by Max Töppen, Scriptores Rerum Prussicarum, I (Leipzig: Verlag von S. Hirzel, 1861)

---

70 See Rodriguez Bachiller, 'Paulus Wladimiri, precursor de Francisco de Vitoria', pp. 863–68.

Petri de Ancharano... Super Sexto Decretalium acutissima Commentaria (Bononiae [Bologna]: Societas Typographiae Bononiensis, 1583)

Sancti Thomae Aquinatis Summa Theologica, II: *I^{a}–II^{ae}*, III: *II^{a}–II^{ae}* (Taurini: Officina Libraria Marietti, 1928)

Scriptores Rerum Prussicarum, ed. by Theodor Hirsch, Max Töppen, and Ernst Strehlke, III (Leipzig: Verlag von S. Hirzel, 1861)

Die Staatsschriften des Deutschen Ordens in Preussen im 15. Jahrhundert, I, *Die Traktate vor dem Konstanzer Konzil (1414–1418)*, ed. by Erich Weise, Veröffentlichungen der Niedersächsuschen Archivverwaltung, 27 (Göttingen: Vandenhoeck & Ruprecht, 1970)

Stanisław ze Skarbimierza, *Mowy wybrane o mądrości* [*Selected Speeches on Wisdom*], ed. by Mirosław Korolko (Cracow: Wydawnictwo Arkana, 2001)

———, *Sermones sapientiales*, part 1, ed. by Bożena Chmielowska, Textus et studia historiam theologiae in Polonia excultae spectantia, 4 (Warsaw: Akademia Teologii Katolickiej, 1979)

Utrum bella contra infideles fidelibus licitum sit movere?, ed. by Stanisław F. Bełch, in Stanisław F. Bełch, 'Theologi Anonymi Utrum bella contra infideles fidelibus licitum sit movere?', *Mediaevalia Philosophica Polonorum*, 19 (1974), 15–63

Włodek, Zofia, 'La Satire de Jean Falkenberg: Texte inédit avec introduction', *Mediaevalia Philosophica Polonorum*, 18 (1973), 61–95

Secondary Studies

Banaszak, Marian, 'Chrzest Żumdzi i jego reperkusje w Konstancji' ['The Baptism of Samogitia and its Repercussions at the Council of Constance'], in *Chrzest Litwy: Geneza, przebieg, konsekwencje* [*The Baptism of Lithuania: Origin, Process, Consequences*], ed. by Marek T. Zahajkiewicz (Lublin: Katolicki Uniwersytet Lubelski, 1990), pp. 57–76

Biskup, Marian, *Grunwaldzka bitwa: geneza, przebieg, znaczenie, tradycje* [*The Grunwald Battle: Genesis, Process, Significance, Traditions*] (Warsaw: Interpress, 1991)

Błaszczyk, Grzegorz, *Chrzest Litwy* [*The Baptism of Lithuania*] (Poznan: Księgarnia św. Wojciecha, 2006)

Boockmann, Hartmut, *Johannes Falkenberg, der Deutsche Orden und die polnische Politik*, Veröffentlichungen des Max-Planck-Instituts für Geschichte, 45 (Göttingen: Vandehoeck & Rupprecht, 1975)

Brandmüller, Walter, *Das Konzil von Konstanz 1414–1418*, II: *Bis zum Konzilsende* (Paderborn: Ferdinand Schöningh, 1997)

Chmielowska, Bożena, 'Notatka "Revocatur" w rękopisie Biblioteki Uniwersyteckiej w Gandawie' ['The Note "Revocatur" in the Manuscript of the Library of the University of Ghent'], *Studia Mediewistyczne*, 30 (1993), 33–39

———, 'Stanisław de Skarbimierz – le premier recteur de l'Université de Cracovie après le renouveau de celle-ci', *Mediaevalia Philosophica Polonorum*, 24 (1979), 73–112

Ekdahl, Sven, *Die Schlacht bei Tannenberg 1410: Quellenkritische Untersuchungen*, I: *Einführung und Quellenlage* (Berlin: Duncker & Humblot, 1982)
Ehrlich, Ludwik, *Polski wykład prawa wojny XV wieku* [*A Fifteenth Century Polish Exposition of the Law of War*] (Warsaw: Wydawnictwo Prawnicze, 1955)
Frost, Robert, *The Oxford History of Poland-Lithuania*, I: *The Making of the Polish-Lithuanian Union, 1385–1569* (Oxford: Oxford University Press, 2015)
Grygiel, Jerzy, *Zygmunt Korybutowicz: litewski książę w husyckich Czechach (ok. 1395–wrzesień 1435)* [*Sigismund Korybut: Lithuanian Duke in Hussite Bohemia (ca. 1395–September 1435)*] (Cracow: Wydawnictwo Avalon, 2016)
Ivinskis, Zenonas, 'Litwa w dobie chrztu i unii z Polską' ['Lithuania in the Age of the Baptism and the Union with Poland'], trans. by Jan Minkiewicz, in *Chrystianizacja Litwy* [*The Christianization of Lithuania*], ed. by Jerzy Kłoczowski (Cracow: Społeczny Instytut Wydawniczy ZNAK, 1987), pp. 15–126
Jasudowicz, Tadeusz, *Śladami Ludwika Ehrlicha: Do Pawła Włodkowica po naukę o prawach człowieka* [*After Ludwik Ehrlich: Approaching Paulus Vladimiri for the Concept of Human Rights*] (Torun: Comer, 1995)
Kowalski, Marek D., 'Zapomniany kalendarz-nekrolog kapituły krakowskiej z XV wieku' ['The Forgotten Calendar-Necrology of the Chapter of Cracow of the 15th Century'], *Nasza Przeszłość*, 87 (1997), 123–45
Kuczyński, Stefan M., *Bitwa pod Grunwaldem* [*The Battle of Grunwald*] (Katowice: Śląsk, 1985)
Kwiatkowski, Stefan, *Zakon niemiecki w Prusach a umysłowość średniowieczna: Scholastyczne rozumienie praw natury a etyczna i religijna świadomość Krzyżaków około 1420 roku* [*The Teutonic Order in Prussia and Medieval Mentality: A Scholastic Comprehension of the Law of Nature and the Ethical and Religious Awareness of the Teutonic Knights to about 1420*] (Torun: Wydawnictwo Uniwersytetu Mikołaja Kopernika, 1998)
Muldoon, James, *Popes, Lawyers and Infidels: The Church and the Non-Christian World 1250–1550* (Philadelphia: University of Pennsylvania Press, 1979)
Nikodem, Jarosław, *Polska i Litwa wobec husyckich Czech w latach 1420–1433: Studium o polityce dynastycznej Władysława Jagiełły i Witolda Kiejstutowicza* [*Poland, Lithuania and Hussite Bohemia in the Years 1420–1433: A Study of the Dynastic Policy of Wladyslaw Jagiello and Witold Kiejstutowicz*] (Poznan: Instytut Historii UAM, 2004)
Ochmański, Jerzy, *Biskupstwo wileńskie w średniowieczu: Ustrój i uposażenie* [*The Bishopric of Vilna in the Middle Ages: Its Organization and Assets*] (Poznan: Wydawnictwo Uniwersytetu im. A. Mickiewicza, 1972)
Ożóg, Krzysztof, *The Role of Poland in the Intellectual Development of Europe in the Middle Ages* (Cracow: Wydawnictwo Naukowe Societas Vistulana, 2009)
Rebeta, Jerzy, 'Czy notatka "Revocatur" należy do polskiej szkoły prawa stosunków międzynarodowych z połowy XV wieku?' ['Does the Note "Revocatur" belong to the Polish School of the Law of International Relations from the Mid-15th Century?'], *Kwartalnik Nauki i Techniki*, 20 (1975), 533–39

Reid, Charles J., 'Paulus Valdimiri, the "Tractatus Opinio Hostiensis" and the Rights of Infidels', in *Sacri canones servandi sunt: Ius canonicum et status ecclesiae saeculis XIII–XV*, ed. by Pavel Krafl (Prague: Historycký ústav AV ČR, 2008), pp. 418–23

Rodriguez Bachiller, Anchel, 'Paulus Wladimiri, precursor de Francisco de Vitoria', in *L'Homme et son univers au Moyen Âge: Actes du septième congrès international de philosophie médiévale (30 août – 4 septembre 1982)*, ed. by Christian Wenin (Louvain-le-Neuve: Éditions de l'Institut Supérieur de philosophie, 1986), pp. 863–68

Sousa Costa, Antonius Domingues de, 'Canonistarum doctrina de Judaeis et Saracenis tempore concilii Constantiensis', *Antonianum*, 40 (1965), 3–70

Swieżawski, Stefan, *Eklezjologia późnośredniowieczna na rozdrożu* [*Late Medieval Ecclesiology at the Crossroads*], Studia do dziejów Wydziału Teologicznego Uniwersytetu Jagiellońskiego, 1 (Cracow: Polskie Towarzystwo Teologiczne, 1990)

Śliwa, Tadeusz, 'Kościół prawosławny w państwie litewskim w XIII–XIV wieku' ['The Orthodox Church in the Lithuanian State in the 13th–14th Centuries'], in *Chrzest Litwy: Geneza, przebieg, konsekwencje* [*The Baptism of Lithuania: Origin, Process, Consequences*], ed. by Marek T. Zahajkiewicz (Lublin: Katolicki Uniwersytet Lubelski, 1990), pp. 15–32

Świeboda, Wojciech, *Innowiercy w opiniach prawnych uczonych polskich w XV wieku: Poganie, żydzi, muzułmanie* [*Infidels in Juridical Opinions of Polish Intellectuals in the 15th Century: Pagans, Jews, Muslims*] (Cracow: Towarzystwo Naukowe Societas Vistulana, 2013)

Winowski, Leszek, *Innowiercy w poglądach uczonych zachodniego chrześcijaństwa XIII–XIV wieku* [*Infidels in the Eyes of the Western Christian Intellectuals of the 13th–14th Century*] (Wroclaw: Zakład Narodowy im. Ossolońskich, 1985)

Woś, Jan Władyslaw, 'Appunti per la biografia di Paulus Wladimiri canonista Polacco del secolo XV', *Studi Senensi*, 83 (1971), 57–124

———, 'Sul concetto della "guerra giusta" e l'intervento degli "infideles" alla bataglia di Grunwald (1410)', *Annali della Scuola Normale Superiore di Pisa: Classe di lettere e filosofia*, Serie III, 2.2 (1972), 597–627

Wyrozumski, Jerzy, 'L'idée de tolérance à l'Université de Cracovie dans la première moitié du XVe siècle', in *Societé et Église: Textes et discussions dans les Universités d'Europe Centrale pendant le Moyen Âge tardif*, ed. by Sophie Włodek, Rencontres de Philosophie Médiévale, 4 (Turnhout: Brepols, 1995), pp. 133–43

———, 'Próba chrystianizacji Litwy w czasach Giedymina' ['Attempts at Christanizing Lithuania in the Times of Gedymin'], *Analecta Cracoviensia*, 19 (1987), 69–90

Zahajkiewicz, Marek T., 'Chrzest Litwy' ['The Baptism of Lithuania'], in *Chrzest Litwy: Geneza, przebieg, konsekwencje* [*The Baptism of Lithuania: Origin, Process, Consequences*], ed. by Marek T. Zahajkiewicz (Lublin: Katolicki Uniwersytet Lubelski, 1990), pp. 33–56

Zacour, Norman, *Jews and Saracens in the Consilia of Oldradus de Ponte* (Toronto: Pontifical Institute of Medieval Studies, 1990)

WALDEMAR KOWALSKI

Peasants and 'Sectarians'

On the Ineffectiveness of Evangelical Persuasion in Sixteenth-Century Poland

Religious Instruction and Social Reality

Within the Kingdom of Poland, the religious Reformation progressed more slowly in Lesser Poland than in the neighbouring provinces of Silesia or Pomerania. After the initial period of crypto-Reformation in 1550, Mikołaj Oleśnicki, a wealthy nobleman and the owner of the town of Pińczów, ordered the expulsion of Paulines from the local parish church, which was then given to local followers of Protestantism.[1] This incident initiated numerous similar, although not so spectacular, events in private townships and villages in that province. The eviction of Catholic priests, however, was not always followed by immediate arrangements for an Evangelical place of worship. Moreover, the break with the Roman creed was not always ideologically motivated. Sometimes, having expelled the parson, the noble owner appropriated the liturgical utensils and other valuable church furnishings, and the parish benefice became part of the manorial estate. In the late Middle Ages and in the early modern epoch, it was the widespread opinion of the Polish nobility[2] that the right of patronage over

1 This has been sketched by Benedict, *Christ's Churches*, pp. 257–71; Małłek, *Opera selecta*, pp. 179–90; Bem, *Calvinism*, pp. 25–26. See also Nowakowska, 'High Clergy and Printers', pp. 46–47. Most of Silesia was part of the Bohemian Crown.

2 In the sixteenth century, the noble estate of the Kingdom of Poland (*szlachta*) comprised the following strata, which were equal under law but differentiated by wealth and access to public offices. A small number of the *illustres et magnifici* were at the top of the social hierarchy, with the *generosi* below and the *nobiles* at the bottom, and the latter were numerically dominant. While the first and the second group comprised wealthy owners of landed estates, the *nobiles* possessed one village, part of a village or had no land nor subject peasants. In this chapter, I use the term 'nobility' as the equivalent of the *szlachta* in its entirety.

Waldemar Kowalski • (waldemar.kowalski@ujk.edu.pl) is Professor of Early Modern History at Jan Kochanowski University in Kielce, Poland.

Religious Transformations in New Communities of Interpretation in Europe (1350–1570): Bridging the Historiographical Divides, ed. by Élise Boillet and Ian Johnson, New Communities of Interpretation, 3 (Turnhout: Brepols, 2022), pp. 209–237.

DOI 10.1484/M.NCI-EB.5.131221

a parish church gave unlimited prerogatives, which included not only appointing the parson, but also ultimate ownership of the benefice. Despite the fact that under canon law the bishop was always to be responsible for appointments within his diocese, with the Church the sole owner of its benefices, the sentences of ecclesiastical courts were extremely difficult to carry out. This was especially the case after 1556–57 when the Diet finally rescinded the *brachium sæculare*, that is, the ability of the royal captains (*capitaneus*, *starosta*) to enforce canon law.[3]

As a rule, however, after the Catholic priests had been evicted and church property appropriated, an Evangelical minister was introduced without much delay. Unlike a Catholic priest, who, when in conflict with his patron, could expect protection from his bishop, an Evangelical minister was completely dependent on the noble owner of the demesne and its parish church. The changes discussed here turned violent at times, especially when patronage rights were shared by a number of landowners who were not able to reach a compromise regarding whether they should break off with the Roman creed or remain faithful to it. Pro-Catholic collators engaged their subjects in these conflicts and organized them to defend the Catholic parson against the opponents of Rome. Initiatives taken by townsfolk or peasants are poorly documented.[4]

The diocese of Cracow was founded in 1000 and its borders were delineated at the beginning of the twelfth century. After the rebirth of the kingdom in the fourteenth century, the diocese comprised Lesser Poland (without Red Ruthenia), and its area encompassed 53,000 sq. km. This was roughly equivalent to the three palatinates of the province of Lesser Poland: Cracow, Sandomierz, and Lublin. In the mid-sixteenth century, the diocese was inhabited by approximately one million Catholics.[5] At that time and in the following decades, about 250 Protestant places of worship were organized there. Some of them were poorly documented ephemera. The number of relatively long-lasting Reformation centres, those that were active for at least ten years, is estimated at 110 in the Palatinate of Cracow, ninety-seven in the Palatinate of Sandomierz, and thirty-two in the Palatinate of Lublin. During the first general Catholic visitation in Lesser Poland in the 1590s, the diocese of Cracow comprised 924 parishes, 827 of which were active. Those labelled in the visitation protocols as 'profaned' were used by

3 Wiśniowski, 'Parish Clergy', pp. 119–38; Wójcik, 'Ecclesiastical Local Legislation', pp. 247–60; Wójcik, *Ze studiów* [*Studies on Synods*], pp. 33–98; Bruździński, *Działalność prymasa Stanisława Karnkowskiego* [*The Primate Stanisław Karnkowski's Activity*], pp. 122–23; Urban, *Et hæc facienda, et illa non omittenda*, pp. 25–39.

4 For a more detailed presentation of this process, see Kowalski, 'Change in Continuity', pp. 692–97.

5 Kłoczowski, *A History of Polish Christianity*, pp. 14–19, 45–64; Plisiecki, 'The Parochial Network', pp. 223–34.

Evangelical congregations, usually Reformed, less frequently Lutheran or Polish Brethren.[6]

Not without difficulty, the provincial followers of Protestantism built the structure of the movement in continual synodal debate from 1554 onwards. Intellectual and doctrinal inspiration was borrowed from various authorities, beginning with Erasmus, Melanchthon, and Luther. The religious programme of that initial period can be adequately summarized as a generally Protestant anti-Roman approach, a sort of 'middle-of-the-road' theology originating from the cardinal Reformation keynotes: by faith alone, by Scripture alone, through Christ alone, by grace alone, and glory to God alone. Although Calvin's *Catechism* was already recommended in the Church of Lesser Poland in the 1550s, a wider appreciation of his theology is noticeable only in the 1560s.[7]

It is a well-known fact that, in Lesser Poland, the Reformation was organized and supported almost exclusively by the nobility.[8] However, the reason why the majority of burghers and peasants remained reluctant to engage in the movement remains open to debate. This article discusses some poorly investigated aspects of the failure of the Reformed Church. They are, first and foremost, the programme of religious education that was offered to rural folk and their landlords' support for instruction in matters of faith. To date, these issues have only been investigated on a wider scale by Wacław Urban. His presentation of the spread of Reformation ideas and of opposition to them was heavily influenced by the oppressive Marxist culture in which the book was researched and published.[9] Nevertheless, the source information presented by him and his main conclusions are still worth considering. The relevant publications by Janusz Tazbir are more general and are based on a selective source collection; moreover, they were also written from a Marxist perspective.[10]

The wider cultural context of Evangelical persuasion in terms of the extended intellectual horizons of an individual and the group they belong to, especially the importance of spiritual heritage, has not been sufficiently

---

6 Kracik, 'Przeciw Reformacji' ['Against the Reformation'], pp. 169, 184; *Województwo sandomierskie* [*The Palatinate of Sandomierz*], ed. by Pałucki, pp. 65–66; *Województwo krakowskie* [*The Palatinate of Cracow*], ed. by Rutkowski, pp. 55–58; Chachaj, *Bliżej schizmatyków* [*Closer to Schismatics*], pp. 232–40.

7 Ptaszyński, 'The *Polish-Lithuanian Commonwealth*', pp. 48–50, 57–58; Benedict, *Christ's Churches*, pp. 257–71; Kowalska-Kossobudzka, 'Wpływ Jana Łaskiego' ['Jan Łaski's Influence'], pp. 15–26; Maciuszko, 'Poglądy religijne Mikołaja Reja' ['Mikołaj Rey's Religious Convictions']', pp. 287–308.

8 Ptaszyński, 'The *Polish-Lithuanian Commonwealth*', pp. 40, 52–57; Knoll, 'Religious Toleration in Sixteenth-Century Poland', pp. 30–52; Wijaczka, 'The Reformation in Sixteenth-Century Poland', pp. 9–26.

9 Urban, *Chłopi wobec Reformacji* [*Peasants and the Reformation*].

10 Tazbir, *Reformacja a problem chłopski* [*The Reformation and the Peasant Issue*]; Tazbir, 'Ze studiów nad stosunkiem polskich protestantów do chłopów' ['On the Relation of Polish Protestants toward Peasants'], pp. 32–61.

explored. At the turn of medieval times and the modern epoch, the postulated religious formation of the laity in the Cracow diocese was reduced to the observance of basic rules of morality and the fulfilment of duties such as participation in the Sunday Mass, Easter confession and the Eucharist, and last, but not least, material support for the parish rector. Christian awareness was founded on knowledge of the Apostles' Creed, the Lord's Prayer, and the Ten Commandments. In other words, the pastoral recommendations formulated in *De instructione confessorum* (*On the Instruction of Confessors*) in 1444 were reissued almost unchanged until the turn of the seventeenth century. The implementation of this pastoral programme was a long and arduous process, which brought only limited success.[11] The rudimentary education of the clergy was practical in its subject matter, with a focus on the proper reading of the liturgy. Only university graduates could gain thorough theological knowledge, but they were few and far between. It is estimated that fewer than 30 per cent of parsons were recruited from among the nobility. This clerical minority shared the social and economic standing of their collators, which explains why a larger percentage of those noble-born priests were able to benefit from university training than priest who hailed from the lower reaches of Polish society.[12]

From the late Middle Ages through to the mid-seventeenth century, the implementation of even such basic goals of the cure-of-souls was far from satisfactory. Although it is highly problematic to estimate Sunday church attendance realistically,[13] it seems that only a small percentage of parishioners did not attend regularly. Those who were discouraged from regular Mass participation because of the distance between the church and their home took part in paraliturgical services held at field chapels or crosses. Such 'field and forest liturgy', with which anonymous friars distracted rural folk from their parish church for over a year, was documented in a visitation protocol of the diocese of Cracow at the turn of the seventeenth century.[14] It is also impossible to estimate credibly the wider-scale effectiveness of religious education that was provided at parish elementary schools.

---

11 See, first of all Bruździński, *Działalność prymasa Stanisława Karnkowskiego* [*The Primate Stanisław Karnkowski's Activity*], pp. 137–38, 148; Bylina, 'La catéchèse du peuple en Europe du Centre-Est', pp. 40–53; Bylina, *Chrystianizacja wsi polskiej* [*The Christianization of the Polish Countryside*], pp. 46–95; Litak, *Parafie w Rzeczypospolitej* [*The Parish in the Polish-Lithuanian Commonwealth*], pp. 369–71. Such accessible forms of instructing the laity in spiritual matters were recommended all over Europe at the beginning of early modern times; cf. Duffy, *The Stripping of the Altars*, pp. 53–68; Małłek, *Opera selecta*, pp. 300–02.

12 Kowalski, 'Jan Długosz a tzw. szlachecki antyklerykalizm' ['Jan Długosz and the so-called Noblemen's Anticlericalism'], pp. 191–93.

13 Bylina, *Chrystianizacja wsi polskiej* [*The Christianization of the Polish Countryside*], pp. 15–45; Chachaj, *Bliżej schizmatyków* [*Closer to Schismatics*], pp. 194–95; Skierska, *Obowiązek mszalny* [*Church Attendance*], pp. 131–33.

14 Kowalski, 'Change in Continuity', p. 708.

The Lost Hope of Evangelization for Those Who Ignore the True Word of God

It is within such circumstances that the newly founded Reformed Church appealed to its prospective flock. The polemics between two neighbours near Cracow, Hieronim Rzeszowski, an Evangelical nobleman and the landlord of the township of Kossów and the village of Kwilina,[15] and Rev. Józef Konarzewski, the Catholic rector in the nearby village of Dzierzgów,[16] constitutes exceptional evidence of landlords' efforts to secure salvation for their subjects. The pamphlet that reveals their exchange of opinions was only cursorily referenced by Wacław Urban,[17] and it deserves further attention because Evangelical proselytism in sixteenth-century Poland is sparsely documented and hence poorly studied. That neighbourly dispute was conducted via correspondence, of which only two letters have been made available in print and published in a brochure titled *Catholici et sectarii concertatio* (*A Polemic Between a Catholic and a Sectarian*). The nobleman's note of 14 October 1568 opens the pamphlet, and is followed by the response from his clerical polemicist dated 4 December. The priest's initial letter, which had encouraged its addressee to a lengthy presentation of his evangelizing endeavours, is known only from the relevant quotes in the nobleman's response.

In his first letter, Rev. Konarzewski informs his neighbour that his subjects from Kossów have begged him with tears in their eyes to visit and teach them how to proceed on the way to salvation. The priest asked them about the Evangelical minister who had been located in the manor house, and whether that servant of God's word had taught them the way to salvation.[18] Rzeszowski strongly expresses his conviction that if the peasants who had visited the priest had had their wits about them, they must have confirmed that the way to achieve salvation had been explained. However, it is also possible that the imploring peasants were undeserving of the holy, eternal, and true Word, and refused God's mercy. That said, Rzeszowski graciously explains that he trusts in Konarzewski's experience and intuition, and consoles himself that in such a case the pious and reverend man would have observed the peasants' true state.[19]

---

15 In 1581, property tax was paid by a Rzeszowska, first name unknown, probably the widow of the said Hieronim; *Polska XVI w.* [*The Poland of the Sixteenth Century*], ed. by Pawiński, p. 69.

16 Died in 1591; Iwańska-Cieślik, 'Aspekty badań nad księgozbiorami' ['Some Aspects of the Research on the Book Collections'], p. 198.

17 Urban, *Et hæc facienda, et illa non omittenda*, p. 33; Urban, *Chłopi wobec Reformacji* [*Peasants and the Reformation*], pp. 136–38.

18 This was Wojciech of Ujście, who was sent to Kossów by the synod in 1557; *Akta synodów różnowierczych* [*The Minutes of the Protestant Synods*], ed. by Sipayłło, pp. 239, 263, 265, 304, 310.

19 *Catholici et sectarii concertatio*, fols Aii^{v}–Aiii^{r}.

Because the subjects did not want to, or were not able to, reveal the scope of the religious education provided by the Evangelical minister in the local church at Kossów, the nobleman explains it himself as follows. Man can only receive salvation through Christ, who was given to man by God solely as a result of His mercy and love. This is the foundation of faith and the source of its principles: justification, spiritual and carnal rebirth, the absolution of sins, resurrection, baptism, the sacrament of the Lord's supper, the Christian life, and good deeds.[20] These principles were explained, one can assume, with the help of manuals by Johannes Brenz, the famous Lutheran theologian. His large catechism, written in the early 1530s, was translated into Polish and printed in Königsberg in 1556. Brenz's catechetical works were very popular in Poland-Lithuania, not only among Lutherans but also among adherents of other Evangelical denominations.[21]

Hieronim Rzeszowski strongly emphasizes that Christ is the basis of faith; without a sound knowledge of Scripture the absolution of sins and justification are not possible. 'Tego tedy nie znać, ktory dawa wszyćko, szalona to wiara, a prawie bydlęca' (Not to know this one, who gives everything, is an insane faith and almost bestial folly).[22] Any polemics over the principles of faith cannot be productive unless one knows the Lord, God's Son. It can be assumed that the principles of religious education outlined here are representative of the general programme of Evangelical instruction that was realized all over Poland-Lithuania.[23] Rzeszowski presents the canon which is concurrent with the principles of faith publicized with the *Heidelberg Catechism* (1563). The Polish translation of this confessional document was published in Cracow in 1564 and was accepted by Evangelicals in Poland-Lithuania.[24]

The landlord laments that ungrateful peasants were unwilling to accept the simple and sincere Word, which had been sent to them through the Lord's love and mercy. Rzeszowski concludes that the reason may just be that man generally prefers the darkness to the light. Those who refuse to listen to the truth are left to believe in a lie. Such people have been seduced by Satan.

---

20 *Catholici et sectarii concertatio*, fols Aiii^{v}–u. fol.

21 Bock, 'Die Anfänge des polnischen Buchdrucks in Königsberg', p. 137; Korzo, 'W sprawie jednego z XVI-wiecznych katechizmów kalwińskich' ['On a Sixteenth-Century Calvinist Catechism'], pp. 184–87. For Brenz's catechetical exposition of Lutheran theology, see Corzine, 'Assuring the Faithful', pp. 98–116. In 1564, a Polish translation of John Calvin's *The Geneva Catechism* (1542, 1545) was published in Cracow, but this edition enjoyed a limited popularity; Korzo, 'Jeszcze raz w sprawie nieznanego tłumaczenia' ['Further Comments on the Unknown Translation'], pp. 191–201.

22 *Catholici et sectarii concertatio*, u. fol.

23 This assumption is made as a result of cursory remarks concerning education at the Lesser Poland Evangelical churches at the turn of the 1580s; see *Akta synodów różnowierczych* [*The Minutes of the Protestant Synods*], ed. by Sipayłło, pp. 50–68.

24 Leszczyński, 'Nauka ewangelicko-reformowana' ['Reformed Evangelical Teaching'], p. 62. More on this source, see Bierma, Gunnoe, Maag, and Fields, *An Introduction to the Heidelberg Catechism*.

Although God has shown them the way to salvation, they look for a wider path, but only find a road to hell. The nobleman does not recommend the latter choice to anyone, and he concludes that a subject is not a child. He knows what he is doing.[25]

The nobleman presents himself as one who always tries to live, together with his family and subjects, for God's glory, following his vocation. His pronouncing God's glory should bring him nothing more than salvation. He hopes to fulfil the Lord's plan for his life, specifically in gaining for the kingdom the expected number of elected. Those who refuse to listen to God's word, the nobleman proclaims, will not escape vengeance. Although this is not explicitly declared, the implication is that they should fear God's judgement and not the worldly wrath of their lord. Grace and salvation are rendered by the Word of God because 'faith comes from hearing' (Romans 10. 17), and the Gospel is the power leading to salvation. The canons of faith pronounced by Rzeszowski are deeply rooted in the teachings of mostly South-German and Swiss theologians like Ulrich Zwingli, Heinrich Bullinger, and John Calvin.[26]

This outline of theological principles is supplemented with polemics. Rzeszowski complains that his contemporaries rely more on themselves than on God. Many of them are satisfied with just observing tradition, that is 'dawność wiary' (the oldness of faith), in which they follow what was suitable for their fathers. They rely on the Doctors of the Church and preachers, and can see no reason to read the Bible for themselves.[27] In this way, the nobleman has joined the many Protestant pamphleteers who questioned the points the Catholics commonly referred to in arguing for the truthfulness of the Roman creed. His argumentation is typical of Evangelical polemicists. 'The oldness of faith', which was often referred to in the sermonizing of the day, comprised the tradition of the Catholic Church, the diocesan rite, and the paraliturgy, which had acculturated a body of pagan practices. In the widely shared opinion of the pastoral clergy, that heritage determined the vitality of the faith, as is testified, among others, by Benedykt Herbest, the author of a popular Catholic catechism in Poland at that time.[28] The effectiveness of the

---

25 *Catholici et sectarii concertatio*, fols B^{r}–Bii^{v}. The theme of the two ways one must wisely choose from to earn salvation (Matthew 7.13–14) recurred in late medieval sermonizing in Poland; see Wojciechowska, 'Stanisława ze Skarbimierza rozważania' ['Stanisław of Skarbimierz's Reflections'], pp. 195–205.

26 *Catholici et sectarii concertatio*, fol. Bii^{v}. See, among others, Picirilli, *Grace, Faith, Free Will*, pp. 139–48; Zachman, *John Calvin as Teacher, Pastor, and Theologian*, pp. 40–43; Opitz, 'Huldrich Zwingli', pp. 119–21.

27 *Catholici et sectarii concertatio*, fols Biii^{r}–Biii^{v}.

28 Herbest, *Nauka* [*The Teaching*], fols 112^{v}–19^{v}. Cf. Hanusiewicz-Lavallee, 'Dawne i nowe' ['The Old and the New'], pp. 103–44. On the religiousness of Polish commoners at the beginning of the modern era, see Bylina, 'The Church and Folk Culture', pp. 27–42; Bylina, 'La religion civique et la religion populaire', pp. 323–35; Wojciechowska, *Od godów do św. Łucji* [*From Twelvetide to St Lucy's Day*].

paraliturgy and of the sacramentals was successfully advertised by the Jesuits who converted Livonian peasants.[29]

As one can see, Rzeszowski accentuates the profits coming from an individualized reading of the Bible, which cannot be replaced with a preacher's interpretation. Rzeszowski suggests that unassisted Bible studies allow the laity to assess the veracity of the teaching from the pulpit. This conviction seems to derive from the assumption that the scriptural fluency of laypeople is equal to that of the clergy, and that individual studies cannot result in a misunderstanding of the biblical narrative. The nobleman must be transferring to society as a whole his own experience of the benefits of reading the Gospel. It is highly unlikely that the peasants in Lesser Poland would have been able to study the Bible individually, as only about 2 per cent of them were literate at that time.[30] It is more probable that peasants gathered to listen to Scripture, as was the practice in other lands,[31] although Rzeszowski suggests that even this custom was not widespread among his contemporaries. His criticism of their indifference suggests a limited readership of the first Polish translation of the Bible, which had been commissioned by the Polish Reformed Church and was published in 1563.[32]

Encouraging Bible study among the laity is one of the foundational postulates of the sixteenth-century reformers, as the 'true' faith is based solely on Scripture. Rzeszowski proves with scriptural passages that Christ taught only according to the commandments of His Father, as did Moses. Paul the Apostle also spread the teachings of Jesus without additions. These are common Evangelical arguments raised against Catholics. The nobleman adds that God ordained the prophets, Apostles, and Doctors of His Church; the latter referring to saints known for their depth of understanding and the orthodoxy of their teachings. Satan also did this for his own servants, but he cannot threaten God and the wind will blow away his promptings like chaff (Psalm 1. 4).[33]

Rzeszowski explains that if he had known which of his subjects had requested Catholic indoctrination, he would have exhorted them with the Gospel, as he always does together with the minister he employs. He sadly remarks that for several years he has been begging, admonishing, and threatening his

---

29 Tazbir, 'Propaganda kontrreformacji' ['The Counter-Reformation Propaganda'], pp. 729–30.

30 Urban, *Et hæc facienda, et illa non omittenda*, p. 451.

31 Cf. Pettegree, *Reformation and the Culture of Persuasion*, pp. 8, 118, 176.

32 On this edition, see Frick, *Polish Sacred Philology*, pp. 67–80, here especially 72–73. In 1573, the future translator of a Polish Catholic edition of the Bible, Jakub Wujek SI still remained convinced that no private reading had such a positive impact on the faithful as an explanation from a wise priest. He admitted, however reluctantly, that a sanctioned vernacular interpretation of Scripture must be edited to prevent Catholics from erroneous publications; see Hanusiewicz-Lavallee, 'Dawne i nowe' ['The Old and the New'], pp. 130–31. On Polish Evangelicals' complaints about 'the weakness of faith' of their coreligionists, see Augustyniak, *Państwo świeckie czy księże?* [*A Lay or a Clerical Polity?*], pp. 47–48.

33 *Catholici et sectarii concertatio*, fol. Biii^{v}.

subjects with the Lord's wrath, and finally with His disgrace. 'Chowam sługi Boże ku obwoływaniu głosu Bożego, ale iż nie chcą bieżeć do tej łagodnej a wdzięcznej trąby Bożej, biada będzie im onego przyszłego nieodmiennego sądu Boga' (I have been keeping ministers of the Lord to reverberate His voice, but they do not want to come to that gentle and resonant trumpet call of God. Woe betide them at that irrevocable Lord's judgement).[34] He asks Rev. Konarzewski to tell him who the peasants were because he would like to know why they are treating the Lord's grace with contempt. He does not intend to excuse himself, and if he can find out what mistake he has made, he will correct it, although he feels justified before God. As always, he is ready to show the way of salvation not only to his kin and servants, but to everyone. The nobleman's narrative demonstrates the frustration and disappointment of a devout man who, as a Christian, feels obliged to teach the Gospel in its uncontaminated, true version.

The priest replies that he did not want to give a straightforward answer to the peasants without communicating with their landlord, and the latter readily agrees with this. At the same time, Rev. Konarzewski declares his eagerness to serve both Rzeszowski and his subjects. Rzeszowski expresses his understanding of the offer and does not want to criticize the cleric for his willingness to serve. However, he is explicit about the consequences, which would be equivalent to committing idolatry. He is grateful to God that He liberated him 'z brzydliwej a obłędliwej sekty papieskiej i antychrystusowej' (of that abominable and insane popish and antichrist sect).[35] Once again he commends his neighbour for not engaging in the education of his subjects without his knowledge. He emphasizes how much he would like his kin and subjects to praise the Lord truly. However, if they do not want to, they are free to worship Baal and other idols, but not openly and not with his consent. This declaration is supplemented with biblical arguments commonly referred to on such occasions.

Rev. Konarzewski explains that he defends the teachings one can find in all Christian kingdoms. Rzeszowski agrees, but explains why the Catholic doctrine is so widespread. Satan occupies the throne in Rome with his assistant, the pope, 'z synem zatracenia' (with the son of perdition). All his kingdoms are worthless against the Kingdom of the Lord. When Jesus was tempted by Satan, He demonstrated how we should respond to such temptations. Rzeszowski declares that his obedience is to his monarch alone, as the sovereign instituted by God. He strongly believes that the eternal Kingdom is the greatest treasure with everlasting life and joy awaiting him there. This has been promised to all those chosen before the creation of the world (Ephesians 1. 4).[36] The priest calls his neighbour a friend and

---

34 *Catholici et sectarii concertatio*, fol. Cii^{r}.

35 *Catholici et sectarii concertatio*, fol. Ciii^{r}–u. fol.

36 *Catholici et sectarii concertatio*, fol. D^{v}.

the latter gratefully acknowledges it. He is afraid, however, that this kind of amity offends God.[37]

In his response to the letter, the clergyman demonstrates the cure-of-soul duties of a parish priest, who is obliged to serve all those in need. He explains that the 'true' faith must be accessible to everyone. Thus, no one can be blamed for sharing the Gospel, if done according to the rules codified at Trent. In accordance with the synodal legislation, parsons take under their protection Catholics in neighbouring 'profaned' parishes. Rev. Konarzewski readily admits that idolatry is in evidence. Although he does not declare it explicitly, he seems to have discerned such behaviour among the nobleman's subjects. He does not openly criticize the efforts of Rzeszowski or his Evangelical minister, but he does not express approval of them either. In his response, the priest concentrates on a typical, but not aggressive, well-balanced defence of the hierarchical Roman Church. He reminds his interlocutor that if people declare that they love God, they should love each other. Every teaching that refers to the Gospel must result in love because the cardinal duty of every Christian is to reflect their Master. Rev. Konarzewski asks if one who calls another Christian 'a son of perdition' really loves God.[38]

Not only does the pamphlet make it possible to scrutinize closely attempts to evangelize the rural population of sixteenth-century Lesser Poland, it also presents a very rare example of polemics in that both participants exhibit the true and genuine faith and their language is almost void of aggression. One can expect that this resulted from that fact that both interlocutors belonged to the nobility, namely, to the *generosi*. This is evident when Rzeszowski calls his clerical neighbour 'uczciwym szlacheckim człekiem' (an honest nobleman).[39] Rzeszowski is aware that his efforts to secure heaven for his subjects are the only right way to smooth the path to salvation, while the priest declares his readiness to perform his pastoral duties. They both remember the warning of Paul the Apostle: 'Woe to me if I do not preach the Gospel' (I Corinthians 9. 16).

We know nothing about the circumstances in which the correspondence analysed here was delivered to Stanisław Scharffenberger, one of the less active Cracow typographers. Although his workshop produced religious books in addition to academic manuals and cheap popular literature, *Catholici et sectarii concertatio* is one of only three prints in which he engaged himself in anti-Reformation polemics.[40] The title and the arrangement of the publication leave no doubt that the initiative came from the cleric. He must have availed himself of the possibility of pronouncing the ineffectiveness of Evangelical

37 *Catholici et sectarii concertatio*, fol. Dii^{r}.

38 *Catholici et sectarii concertatio*, fols E^{r}–Giii^{v}; cf. Kowalski, 'Change in Continuity', pp. 696–97.

39 *Catholici et sectarii concertatio*, fol. Aii^{v}.

40 See Dyl, 'Książki teologiczne polskich drukarń' ['Theological Books published by Polish Typographers'], p. 113.

persuasion without the consent of his neighbour. However, on the whole, he presents Rzeszowski in a positive light.

The reasons why the peasants stayed indifferent to Evangelical instruction for so long remain veiled in obscurity. The most probable causes given by scholars trying to explain peasants' uninterest are an attachment to the old, showy liturgy, which was less demanding when it came to participation in Church life.

Principles of the 'vivacious old faith'

Unfortunately, there are no sources penned by Polish peasants themselves that provide first-hand knowledge about their religious engagement. Moreover, other sixteenth-century narratives that shed light on this issue are few and far between.[41] The book entitled *Rozmowa nowa niektorego pielgrzyma z gospodarzem o niektorych cerymoniach kościelnych* (*The New Discourse betwixt the Pilgrim and the Innkeeper about Some Church Ceremonies*),[42] which was published in Cracow in 1549, gives a unique opportunity to understand at least partially why the lower strata of society could not accept Evangelical teachings. At the turn of the twentieth century, the polemic was known only by its unique extant printed copy when it was reprinted by Zygmunt Celichowski.[43]

Very little is known about the author; the only information comes from the introduction to his book. He presents himself as Stanisław of Szczodrkowice,

41 For a thorough evaluation of the sources that shed light on the religious life of peasants in early modern Poland, see Wiślicz, *Earning Heavenly Salvation*, pp. 17–20.

42 I place this pamphlet in the context of Church reform and discipline in sixteenth-century Poland in my 'Model chrześcijańskiego postępowania' ['A Model of Christian Behaviour'], pp. 77–113. Natalia Nowakowska ('High Clergy and Printers', p. 52 n. 53) briefly mentions this print as 'the first Polish-language anti-Reformation polemic'. She gives, however, the wrong date of its publication (1546) and misspells the name of its author. In fact, the source was preceded by an earlier anti-Protestant print in Polish, which was issued in 1545; cf. Dyl, 'Pierwsze krakowskie drukowane dzieła teologiczne' ['The First Cracow Printed Theological Works'], p. 90.

43 Celichowski assumes that the edition employed here was preceded by another one in the same year with a slightly different title; *Stanisława ze Szczodrkowic Rozmowa pielgrzyma z gospodarzem* [*Stanisław of Szczodrkowice's Discourse betwixt a Pilgrim and an Innkeeper*], pp. 1, 4–5. The Universal Short Title Catalogue shows the discussed book with an abbreviated title, with Cracow as the place of publication and Hieronim Wietor as the typographer on the first page http://ustc.ac.uk/index.php/record/241481. The title page of the copy used in this article has Cracow as the place of its publication, but it was handwritten in the sixteenth century and there is no mention of the typography. Celichowski, *Stanisława ze Szczodrkowic Rozmowa pielgrzyma z gospodarzem* [*Stanisław of Szczodrkowice's Discourse betwixt a Pilgrim and an Innkeeper*], p. 5 and Estreichr, *Bibliografia polska* [*Polish Bibliography*], p. 224 identify this copy as coming from a workshop owned by the Scharffenbergs.

a village in the vicinity of Cracow. He shared an armorial crest with Andrzej Tęczyński, palatine of Lublin, to whom he dedicates his work. Stanisław mentions his low social status as 'ubogiego a barzo już zeszłego domu' (of a poor and almost extinct house). Tęczyński is said to have taken him 'jakoby pastucha od bydła' (as a herdsman from cattle). The nobleman took care of him, sponsored his education in Krasnystaw, a provincial town in the palatinate of Red Ruthenia, and then employed him at his court.[44] On this basis, Celichowski connects him with the family of Morawicki, who owned part of Szczodrkowice in the sixteenth century. The author's erudition in the Bible and his good knowledge of the Church Fathers' works, along with his vivid description of the cure-of-souls and of the everyday life of the lower clergy, allow us to suppose that he had been ordained.[45] His lifestyle and mentality place him among the upper echelons of peasants or those of the poor *nobiles*. They and the middle strata of urban people are the intended readership of his book, which was written to mobilize them in defence of their 'old' faith. The book is dedicated 'wszystkim dobrym krześcijanom […], dla prostych ludzi, zwłaszcza nad Pismem Świętym, albo w ustawicznym Pisma czytaniu się nie obierającym […] przeciwko luteranom albo odszczepieńcom' (to all good Christians […], for the common folk, especially for those who do not choose systematically to scrutinize the Holy Scriptures, against Lutherans or apostates).[46] The book distinguishes itself from the relatively small number of printed sixteenth-century anti-Protestant Polish polemics by skilfully interweaving theological and social issues, with the latter dominating.[47] Pro-Catholic and anti-Lutheran arguments are arranged in the then-popular form of a dialogue between a Pilgrim, who visits holy places to earn indulgences, and an Innkeeper, at whose place the Pilgrim intends to stay for the night. The Pilgrim relies on the common sense of the reader, who should trust tradition because it is entirely based upon Scripture and appreciated especially by the older generation.[48] The verse dialogue is unwieldy and coarse at times, but this language seems to have met the expectations of the readership.

The main part of the polemic focuses on burials, salvation, and the Last Things. The author notices that Lutherans compose their own chants, but they do not sing them at funerals. They simply 'wloką zmarłego do grobu, jak świnię

44 *Rozmowa nowa* [*The New Discourse*], u. fol.–Aii^{r}.

45 Celichowski, *Stanisława ze Szczodrkowic Rozmowa pielgrzyma z gospodarzem* [*Stanisław of Szczodrkowice's Discourse betwixt a Pilgrim and an Innkeeper*], pp. 3–4) is of a different opinion, however. He thinks that Morawicki was a lay courtier of the aforementioned palatine.

46 *Rozmowa nowa* [*The New Discourse*], fol. Aii^{r}.

47 Cf. Dyl, 'Pierwsze krakowskie drukowane dzieła teologiczne' ['The First Cracow Printed Theological Works'], pp. 67–95. For a broad context, see Nowakowska, 'High Clergy and Printers', pp. 53–58.

48 *Rozmowa nowa* [*The New Discourse*], p. Aiii^{v}.

zdechłą z barłog' (drag the dead to the grave, like a dead hog from its lair).[49] It is very difficult to verify this observation unambiguously; however, it seems that hymns were sung during Lutheran burials in the Kingdom of Poland in the sixteenth century.[50] Morawicki comments on the Catholic symbolism of lit candles and explains their role at exequies conducted by parish fraternities. The custom of a farewell procession for the dead with lit candles was deeply rooted in Polish culture at this time.[51] According to Morawicki, Lutherans scorn the black funeral attire in which brotherhood members following the coffin were clad. They are also said generally to dislike processional crosses.[52] Lutherans are wrong, Morawicki explains, because the Cross provides protection against Satan. This belief was widespread all over late medieval Central Europe, but those who criticized it saw making the sign of the cross as one of the superstitious practices that distracted the faithful from Scripture.[53] Morawicki's appreciation of the custom recalls the solemn atmosphere of the famous hymn *Vexilla Regis* (*The Banners of the King*) by Venantius Fortunatus.[54] He also declares his disapproval of the theatricality of noble funerals. This opinion, exceptional in the first half of the sixteenth century, demonstrates that the arrangement of pompous burials by the nobility was already a widespread practice, and it also represents a very early critical comment on such celebrations. Morawicki explains that a 'knightly' funeral is justified only if the buried nobleman really had proved his valour on the battlefield. Nevertheless, there was a much greater chance that the object of praise, resting on his *bier*, had earned his disputable fame only by robbing his subjects.[55]

The author explains why Evangelicals refute the effectiveness of prayers for the dead and all related Catholic rituals. They are viewed to be ineffectual as Christ is man's only mediator at the Last Judgement.[56] The Evangelicals order followers to support the poor with alms and the Pilgrim is of the same opinion: 'co macie, to poprzedajcie, Jałmużnę nędznym dawajcie' (Sell all

---

49 *Rozmowa nowa* [*The New Discourse*], p. B^{r}.

50 Cf. Nowicka-Jeżowa, *Pieśń czasu śmierci* [*The Chant at the Time of Death*], pp. 44–63; Kizik, *Śmierć w mieście hanzeatyckim XVI-XVIII wieku* [*Death in the Hanseatic City of the Sixteenth-Eighteenth Centuries*], pp. 162–68; Koslofsky, *The Reformation of the Dead*, pp. 59–60, 94–111.

51 Zaremska, '*Żywi wobec zmarłych*' ['The Living for the Dead'], p. 733; Bruździński, 'Forms of Piety', pp. 109, 126; Wojciechowska, 'The Remembrance of the Deceased', p. 43; Wiślicz, *Earning Heavenly Salvation*, pp. 139–40.

52 *Rozmowa nowa* [*The New Discourse*], u. fol.; cf. Zaremska, '*Żywi wobec zmarłych*' ['The Living for the Dead'], pp. 745–46.

53 Bracha, *Des Teufels Lug und Trug*, pp. 47–80.

54 The hymn was sung or recited as part of paraliturgy in Poland, which was documented at the turn of the seventeenth century; Kowalski, *Do zmartwywstania swego za pewnym wodzem Kristusem* [*'To One's Resurrection, Following Christ, the Steadfast Master …'*], pp. 88–89; Cf. Szövérffy, 'Venantius Fortunatus and the Earliest Hymns to the Holy Cross', pp. 107–22; Thompson, 'Agency and Appetite for Religious Song', pp. 604–12.

55 *Rozmowa nowa* [*The New Discourse*], fol. Iiii^{v}; cf. Chrościcki, *Pompa funebris*, pp. 48–80.

56 *Rozmowa nowa* [*The New Discourse*], fol. B^{r}.

that is yours, give alms to the poor).[57] This is a time-sanctioned custom, which Augustine mentions in *De libero arbitrio* (*On Free Choice of the Will*). Distribution of alms earns God's grace and salvation. The Pilgrim also argues for the necessity of prayers for the dead. He has no doubt that it provides succour to the soul, but concentrates only on the mediation of Christ. He adds that there are Christians who have earned salvation with their faultless life and do not need any help from the living. There are also people who cannot benefit from any prayers. Referring to Augustine, the author teaches that everyone will be paid in heaven according to their deeds in this world. The relinquishment of enjoyment in this world helps prepare one for eternal life.[58]

Morawicki highly recommends the benefits of the veneration of Mary and the saints. He assures his readers that, contrary to assertions made by Evangelicals, angels and saints, whom he only mentions collectively, know people's needs. The Apostles especially deserve veneration because they never demanded it, and they ascribed all supernatural interventions to God. He adds that kneeling at a saint's grave is not idolatry. Christians praise the Lord by praying to the saints. Christ is a brother to man. He served people during His earthly life and still does so in heaven. A prayer connects man with God:

> Dusza, co Boga miłuje
> częstokroć w niebo wstępuje [...]
> tam po ulicach wędruje
> stolec boski oględuje
> apostoły nawiedzając i proroki pozdrawiając
> tudzież świętych męczenników
> patryjarchów, spowiedników
>
> > (A soul that loves the Lord
> > often visits the afterworld. [...]
> > There it walks heavenly streets,
> > admires the throne on which God sits.
> > The apostles and confessors,
> > holy martyrs, prophets, blessers,
> > all are praised by the soul
> > during its heavenly stroll).[59]

The Pilgrim describes to his interlocutor the eschatological visions that had circulated all over Europe and had been passed down from generation to generation. The way to the Heavenly Kingdom is paved with the misery one experiences during life on earth and then in Purgatory, the latter being either

57 *Rozmowa nowa* [*The New Discourse*], fol. E^{r}.

58 *Rozmowa nowa* [*The New Discourse*], u. fol.–K^{r}.

59 *Rozmowa nowa* [*The New Discourse*], fols Dii^{v}–Diii^{v} and u. fol. The translation of passages from this text here and subsequently endeavours to take account of verse structure, rhyme, and poetic style and is therefore not strictly literal.

scorned or awaited with anxiety. Poor peasants, who are deprived of their property by landlords, and those who are affected by natural calamities, experience Purgatory on earth. There are some who struggle against the odds and suffer everyday hardships to exchange finally their savings for prayers that may reduce their stay in Purgatory, but the Pilgrim doubts if they are right. Others simply do not believe in that place of post-mortem purgation, and they are wrong. Although there are no first-hand accounts, people should believe in it as part of the Tradition of the Church. The Pilgrim is sure that the stay in Purgatory is meted out by God. The most severe sentence is declared to those who abuse their subjects; he states that no intermediary prayer can help such people. It is an idealized vision of the Church which has realized the Evangelical message that 'the last will be first, and the first will be last' (Matthew 20. 16). Morawicki also refers to the late medieval heritage when he illustrates the distress caused by purgatorial penance with a detailed picture of souls writhing in the flames of Hell that reach Purgatory. There is no accent here on the distinction between Hell and Purgatory, which was popular in late medieval Church didactics.[60] His presentation of Paradise is not innovative either. Following late medieval preachers, the Pilgrim briefly describes the Heavenly Kingdom as a city full of various goods, but surrounded by fire and water. There is only one narrow path leading there, and only a third of all the souls in Purgatory will follow it. The rest have been destined for Hell, a place of fire, pain, and misery.[61]

This very conventional narrative, describing the places to which souls migrate after the Particular Judgement,[62] is the starting point to his polemic on the significance of sins and good deeds. Whoredom, idolatry, adultery, sodomy, theft, greed, slander, drunkenness, and robbery lead one straight to Hell.[63] The author communicates this truth with simple but pungent language, which was used, one may assume, on a daily basis by people of various social strata and professions, including preachers. Like the authors of late medieval cure-of-souls manuals,[64] Morawicki is sure that Jesus himself guides all those who perform good deeds to Heaven. This conviction must have impressed the imaginations of peasants, who expected their release from manorial dependence and aspired to citizenship; all those for whom the promise 'the city air makes you free' was out of reach received the compensation of the *urbs cœlestis*. The

---

60 Cf. *Rozmowa nowa* [*The New Discourse*], fols Hiii^{v}–u. fol. Cf. Bylina, 'Le problème du purgatoire', pp. 473–80; Bylina, *Człowiek i zaświaty* [*Man and the Other World*], pp. 120–28; Bylina, *Religiousness*, pp. 129–33, 135–38, 149.

61 *Rozmowa nowa* [*The New Discourse*], fols Iii^{r}–Iii^{v}. For a detailed discussion of the two popular visions of Heaven (the garden and the city) in late medieval Poland, see Bylina, *Religiousness*, pp. 138–42.

62 Bylina, 'Wyobrażenia raju w Polsce średniowiecznej' ['Imagining Paradise in Medieval Poland'], pp. 137–53; Bylina, *Religousness*, p. 138.

63 *Rozmowa nowa* [*The New Discourse*], fol. Hiii^{v}.

64 Cf. Włodarski, *Obraz i słowo* [*The Picture and the Word*], pp. 3–12, 59–68; Wojciechowska, 'Stanisława ze Skarbimierza rozważania' ['Stanisław of Skarbimierz's Reflections'], pp. 197–98.

Pilgrim then teaches that faith redeems, but only a faith stimulated by good deeds. Thus, he repudiates the *sola fide* attitude propagated by Luther and his followers. This dialogue echoes the inter-faith debate that took place at the Imperial Diet in Regensburg in 1541.[65]

Morawicki explains that Lutherans deny the existence of Purgatory because Catholic priests had made money from the faithful with votive masses. He reproaches Protestants for their criticism of the alleged greed of Catholic priests and says that such a generalization is unjust. One is obliged to support the poor clergy 'obiadem i monetą' (with dinner and coin), and those who assist 'inne mnogie' (other numerous), namely opulent clerics, 'z nieświętą sprawą dają' (add themselves to an unholy matter).[66] The polemic with Lutherans allows the Pilgrim to diagnose the condition of his Church. He begins this diagnosis with a straightforward statement about the deficit of good governance. Moreover, while Lutheran priests can take wives, Catholic ones are reduced to sinful concubinage when they take on 'a cook'. This situation is lavishly documented in the first visitation protocols of the Cracow diocese at the turn of the seventeenth century.[67] Morawicki suggests that concubinage is, in fact, inevitable because of their solitary life. He does not go as far as to appeal for the annulment of the celibacy law. He suggests returning to the former tradition, in which parsons shared the table with their clerical personnel, so the latter did not have to care for their daily nourishment and did not have to keep 'cooks'. In this ideal order of clerical discipline, which is undoubtedly unrealistic, parsons would control the morality of subordinate clergy and alert the bishop ordinary in case of debauchery without delay. 'A takiego nie chowano, gdzie go być z małpą widziano' (One was pushed out by his nape, when he was seen with an ape),[68] which means that laxity was punished with deprivation of benefice. Morawicki sadly concludes that in his time clerics live as they pleased.[69] He blames the nobility for the harmful personnel policies in the Church, but he also criticizes the higher clergy for accumulating benefices and renting them out. The nobility prefer to keep the property of the Church and gratify the hired clerics with small incomes rather than risk a lack of parish administration:

Więc dziesięcinę przepije
A ksiądz się w kąt ze mszą kryje
Śpiewa *Requiem* pod strzechą

---

65 *Rozmowa nowa* [*The New Discourse*], fols H^r–Giii^r; cf. Heinz, *Justification and Merit*; Sproul, *Faith Alone*; Mattes, 'Luther on Justification as Forensic and Effective', pp. 264–73.

66 *Rozmowa nowa* [*The New Discourse*], fols Eii^r–Eii^v.

67 Kowalski, 'Change in Continuity', p. 710; cf. Parish, *Clerical Celibacy*, pp. 143–207.

68 In early modern Polish 'ape' was a synonym of 'whore'. Cf. Zygner, 'Vision der Kirchenreform', pp. 209–35.

69 *Rozmowa nowa* [*The New Discourse*], fol. Kii^v; Morawicki's complaints reflected problems that reoccurred at synods of the Polish Church at the turn of the modern epoch; see Fijałek, *Życie i obyczaje kleru*, pp. 66–79; Zygner, 'Późnośredniowieczne synody narzędziem reformy Kościoła' ['Late Medieval Synods as a Tool of Church Reform'], p. 440.

Tylko żacy z głupim klechą
Bo deszcz kapie do kościoła
Nie masz rządu prawie zgoła
A tam ksiądz pleban dworuje
Dwornikowi tam najmuje.

(So the noble wastes on drink church tithes,
and the priest with the Mass hides.
Only pupils with the tonsured goof,
sing *Requiem* under the leaking roof.
That's the parson who's not sad
letting land to the manor's head).[70]

Some scholars believe that this dialogue was penned in response to publications by Jan Seklucjan, who, starting from 1544, spread Lutheranism in the Polish language under the auspices of Duke Albert of Prussia.[71] This may be true. Both authors accept the recurring postulate that the Church should return to Evangelical modesty.[72] Morawicki's comments aptly reflect the reasons behind the enduring conflicts between the clergy and the privileged social strata, as well as dissension within the Church.

Conclusion

Historians who have previously focused on the formative period of the Reformed Church in Lesser Poland, primarily Wacław Urban, leave no doubt that only an insignificant number of peasants and of the township population attended the Reformed Evangelical Church. Their limited engagement is said to have often been short-term and superficial. The principalities of Zator and Oświęcim, the borderlands of Silesia and Lesser Poland, which were incorporated to the Polish Crown in 1563–1564, were exceptions to that rule and their rural population readily turned to the Reformed faith or to Lutheranism in significant numbers. The usual explanation of that phenomenon is the influence of neighbouring Silesian communities that had readily adopted Protestantism. Moreover, for the ethnically mixed Czech, Polish and German population of these principalities there were not the same language barriers to adapting the new ideas as there were in the central and northern territories of Lesser Poland.[73]

---

70 *Rozmowa nowa* [*The New Discourse*], fol. Kiii^{v}–u. fol. *Requiem* is the Latin name of Mass for the Dead.

71 Dyl, 'Pierwsze krakowskie drukowane dzieła teologiczne' ['The First Cracow Printed Theological Works'], p. 91. For an analysis of Albert's influence on the early stage of Reformation in Poland, see Nowakowska, *King Sigismund of Poland and Martin Luther*.

72 Cf. Kowalski, '"Verily, This Is the Sheepfold of that Good Shepherd"', pp. 24–26.

73 Urban, *Et hæc facienda, et illa non omittenda*, pp. 211–31; Bem, *Calvinism*, pp. 202–05.

From 1557 onwards, the problem of attracting peasants to the 'true' faith was often raised at Evangelical synods. In 1559, the lay and clerical elders of the Evangelical Church expressed support for enforcing their faith upon Catholic peasants and burghers in private domains. This statute allowed for forced baptism and the education of children according to the principles of the Evangelical Church. Two years later, the synod stressed the need regularly to instruct members of the Evangelical Church and converts in matters of faith. While acknowledging the importance of the sacraments, the synod condemned any attempts to enforce them. Catholics and Evangelicals both accused each other of religious coercion. Although Evangelicals officially renounced exerting such pressure, some landlords would forbid 'idolatry', that is the participation of their subjects in the Mass. At the beginning of the 1560s, the lay leaders of the Church were reminded that they should guide their peasants toward the Gospel with their own teachings and example. Wacław Urban noticed that Evangelical propaganda addressed to commoners increased no earlier than the mid-1560s as a response to the Antitrinitarian offensive with its escalating radicalism; nevertheless, it was still not interpreted as enforcement of the faith.[74] Then nobility declared freedom of religious expression in the Warsaw Confederation Act (1573). This was primarily to protect their right to choose their own faith and express it without restrictions.[75] The provision that a landlord should punish those subjects who skip religious practices, yet must not force them to practise his religion, was included in the bill penned by Evangelicals *c.* 1588–1589. In the same draft, they guaranteed commoners unlimited freedom of religion, no matter whose domain they inhabited.[76] A survey of mid-sixteenth-century declarations from various places in Lesser Poland shows that the official disapproval of religious coercion was often ignored by Evangelical landlords. This dissonance may have resulted from the dilemma that proved troublesome even for Augustine: how far the necessity of showing your neighbour the way to salvation justifies limiting their free will.[77]

The limited success of the Lesser Poland Reformed Church in gaining converts is often pointed to as one of the main reasons for its withering and consequent total marginalization in the second half of the seventeenth century.[78] It is worth remembering, however, that in the formative period of the Reformation in Poland,

74 Urban, *Chłopi wobec Reformacji* [*Peasants and the Reformation*], pp. 42–45; Tazbir, 'Ze studiów' ['On the Relation'], pp. 51–56; Tazbir, *Reformacja a problem chłopski* [*The Reformation and the Peasant Issue*], pp. 78–82. Cf. Bem, *Calvinism*, pp. 196–203.

75 Tazbir, 'The Fate of Polish Protestantism', pp. 203–04; Benedict, *Christ's Churches*, p. 264; Ptaszyński, 'The Polish-Lithuanian Commonwealth', pp. 55–57.

76 Augustyniak, *Państwo świeckie czy księże?* [*A Lay or a Clerical Polity?*], pp. 45–46; cf. Wijaczka, 'The Reformation', pp. 19–20.

77 More on this, see Brown, 'St Augustine's Attitude to Religious Coercion', pp. 107–16.

78 Benedict, *Christ's Churches*, pp. 365–67; Wijaczka, 'The Reformation', pp. 19–21; Ptaszyński, 'The Polish-Lithuanian Commonwealth', p. 65; Kriegseisen, *Between State and Church*, pp. 400–01, 455–56; Bem, *Calvinism*, pp. 175–95.

at least some of its leaders stood by the opinion, expressed in 1556, that 'melius [...] est habere parvum numerum ovium Christi, quam ingentem cohortem luporum et porcorum' (It is better to have a small number of Christ's sheep than a multitude of wolves and swine).[79] This may explain why some noble adherents to the Reformation movement employed an Evangelical minister to serve in their manor chapel but still tolerated a Catholic priest who provided cure-of-souls to their subjects. They seem to have been convinced that it was the lesser of two evils for their peasants to hear popish indoctrination than be left to total ignorance in spiritual matters. This may have been the case with the well-to-do nobleman, poet, and theologian, Mikołaj Rey (1505–1569). Although his pro-Reformation attitude is evident in his works written as early as the 1540s, he did not dismiss Catholic clergymen from his demesne earlier than *c.* 1563, probably seeing the threat of Antitrinitarianism, of which he was a vigorous opponent, or, possibly, an early stage of a Catholic revival.[80]

The hypothesis that only a minority of Evangelical landowners seriously engaged in the evangelization and conversion of their peasants is well grounded.[81] They were those who took the words of Jesus seriously: '[...] go and make disciples of all nations' (Matthew 28. 19), and who, like Rzeszowski, saw their own way to salvation tied to assuring a straight path to Heaven for all those around them, including their subjects. Driven by their Zwinglian eagerness, they did not see that their evangelizing efforts did not have much chance of success. The reasons for this were revealed by Morawicki. His verse teaching does not have much in common with polemics circulated in sixteenth-century Poland. Morawicki raises only one of the fundamental theological problems of the day: justification by faith alone, which he touches on when discussing the importance of good deeds. He also discusses the intercession of saints. He ignores, however, such vital issues that divided Christians as the sacraments, including the Eucharist, and the primacy of the pope. During the last decades of the sixteenth century, there were parishes in Lesser Poland in which only a few parishioners participated in the obligatory Easter communion.[82] Morawicki is exceptionally restrained in his anti-Lutheran attacks. He often condemns Luther's followers, but there is only one invective personally directed against the great reformer: 'chytry wąż, który wypuścił jad ze swej paszczęki' (the sly snake that threw poison from its jaws).[83] For Morawicki's prospective readers, Luther was at most a vague synonym of evil, just as the pope could only be a distant and abstract personification of holiness. Instead, the author strongly

---

79 *Akta synodów różnowierczych*, [*The Minutes of the Protestant Synods*], ed. by Sipayłło, p. 61. This problem has been outlined recently by Bem, *Calvinism*, pp. 196–206.

80 Kowalski, 'Change in Continuity', p. 694; Urban, *Et hæc facienda, et illa non omittenda*, pp. 545–49; Maciuszko, 'Poglądy religijne Mikołaja Reja' ['Mikołaj Rey's Religious Convictions'], 287–308, 400–03.

81 See Wijaczka, 'The Reformation', p. 20.

82 Kowalski, 'Znaczenie archiwów parafialnych' ['The Importance of Parish Archives'], p. 23.

83 *Rozmowa nowa*, p. Cii^{v}; Reference to Romans 3. 1, 4, 13.

suggests that there is the chance of avoiding the torments of Hell and entering the Heavenly Kingdom if the faithful avoid evil and sin, praise the saints, remember the dead in their prayers, and defend the liturgy, especially funeral practices. This simple programme of religious teaching came down to the observation of traditionally accepted customs. The concern for a funeral as rich as possible and post-mortem remembrance was always a vital part of religious life in the Polish countryside.[84] Evangelical landlords intended to deprive their peasants of that heritage. The peasants resisted this, one can assume, individually and as a community, just as they would oppose growing manorial encumbrances. For some commoners, participation in liturgical or paraliturgical services compensated for more devout and regular engagement in church life. The office of churchwarden, a lay representative of the community whose duty it was to assist the parson in the administration of church property, was well documented in Polish dioceses as early as the fifteenth century. At the end of the sixteenth century, the visitors sent by the Bishop of Cracow to inspect parishes all over the large diocese often had problems with finding peasants ready to take on this office.[85] Undoubtedly, an unknown percentage of the faithful stayed indifferent to the needs of their parish community and ignored matters of faith, an attitude which was recorded in other regions of Central Europe as well.[86] One cannot ignore the fact that Rzeszowski's Evangelical minister at Kossów, Wojciech of Ujście, seems to have expected from his parishioners religious knowledge and morals far above the spiritual code that had been formulated locally by the Catholic priest before him. On the other hand, there is no doubt that, just like in the neighbouring German-speaking countries, the Sunday instruction, also in the form of the sermon, had long been the key medium for teaching the rudiments of the faith. Unfortunately, its effectiveness cannot be convincingly evaluated.[87]

By publishing his correspondence with his Evangelical neighbour together with his comments, Rev. Konarzewski showed the chapter clergy and bishops

---

84 As part of pan-European preoccupation with the last things, in which donations, that is, individual acts of piety, especially at the point of death, constituted a widespread feature of medieval popular devotion; cf. for example, Duffy, *The Stripping of the Altars*, pp. 301–78. On the realities of the Polish situation, see Wojciechowska, 'The Remembrance of the Deceased', pp. 41–42; Wiślicz, 'Chłopskie pogrzeby' ['Peasant Funerals'], pp. 351–69; Wiślicz, 'Ile kosztował pogrzeb chłopa' ['What was the Cost of a Peasant Funeral'], pp. 276–80.

85 Wiśniowski, *Parafie w Polsce średniowiecznej* [*The Parish in Medieval Poland*], pp. 175–90; Kowalski, 'Change in Continuity', p. 699; Wiślicz, *Earning Heavenly Salvation*, pp. 32, 87, 114 concludes optimistically that seldom were churchwardens absent, but this results from the scrutiny of records documenting early modern Lesser Poland through to the eighteenth century. The *Gemeinde* was the arbiter in the matters of faith in the German-speaking lands; see Blickle, 'Communal Reformation and Peasant Piety', p. 219. This activity of village communities in sixteenth-century Poland is poorly confirmed with extant sources. On the office of churchwarden in England, see French, *The People of the Parish*, pp. 68–99.

86 For example, Dixon, *The Reformation and Rural Society*, pp. 176–80.

87 Cf. Frymire, *The Primacy of the Postils*, pp. 15–25.

that they need not fear that commoners, a substantial part of Polish society, would leave Catholicism for a Protestant creed. This motivation explains why the letters were published in Polish, to retain the expression and authenticity of speech, while the comments were formulated in Latin, for the convenience of the papal nuncio.

Works Cited

Primary Sources

Akta synodów różnowierczych w Polsce [*The Minutes of the Protestant Synods in Poland*], I: *(1550–1559)*, ed. by Maria Sipayłło (Warsaw: Państwowe Wydawnictwo Naukowe: 1966)

Catholici et sectarii concertatio (Cracoviæ: Stanislaus Scharffenber, 1569), Biblioteka Kórnicka, Cim. O. 184

Herbest, Benedykt, *Nauka prawego chrześcijanina* [*The Teaching of a Righteous Christian*] (Cracow: Mateusz Siebeneicher, 1566); Biblioteka Jagiellońska, Cim. 339

Rozmowa nowa niektorego pielgrzyma z gospodarzem o niektorych cerymoniach kościelnych, jako o pogrzebie, o krzyżu, o Salwe, o czyscu, o swiecach, o kapach, y o inssych pompach. Przeciw Luteryanom y inssym przeciwnikom wiary krzescijańskiey. Wsselkiemu człowiekowi ku wiedzeniu potrzebna y pożyteczna. Teraz nowo uczyniona y wydana 1549 [*The New Discourse betwixt the Pilgrim and the Innkeeper about Some Church Ceremonies: That is about the Funeral, the Cross, the Salve, Purgatory, Candles, Copes, and of Other Grandiosities. Against Lutherans and Other Enemies of the Christian Faith. Necessary and Useful for the Knowledge of Every Man. Now Made Anew, and Published 1549*], Biblioteka Kórnicka, Cim. O. 92

Stanisława ze Szczodrkowic Rozmowa pielgrzyma z gospodarzem o niektórych ceremoniach kościelnych (1549) [*Stanisław of Szczodrkowice's Discourse betwixt a Pilgrim and an Innkeeper about Some Church Ceremonies*], ed. by Zygmunt Celichowski, Biblioteka Pisarzów Polskich, 37 (Cracow: Akademia Umiejętności, 1900)

Secondary Studies

Augustyniak, Urszula, *Państwo świeckie czy księże? Spór o rolę duchowieństwa katolickiego w Rzeczypospolitej w czasach Zygmunta III Wazy. Wybór tekstów* [*A Lay or a Clerical Polity? The Confrontation over the Role of Catholic Clergy in the Polish-Lithuanian Commonwealth in the Times of Sigismund III Vasa: A Selection of Surces*] (Warsaw: Semper, 2013)

Bem, Kazimierz, *Calvinism in the Polish-Lithuanian Commonwealth, 1548–1648: The Churches and the Faithful*, St Andrews Studies in Reformation History (Leiden: Brill, 2020)

Benedict, Philip, *Christ's Churches Purely Reformed: A Social History of Calvinism* (New Haven: Yale University Press, 2002)

Bierma, Lyle D. with Charles D. Gunnoe Jr., Karin Maag, and Paul W. Fields, *An Introduction to the Heidelberg Catechism: Sources, History, and Theology: With a translation of the smaller and larger catechisms of Zacharias Ursinus*, Texts and Studies in Reformation and Post-Reformation Thought (Grand Rapids: Baker Academic, 2005)

Blickle, Peter, 'Communal Reformation and Peasant Piety: The Peasant Reformation and Its Late Medieval Origins', *Central European History*, 20 (1987), 216–28

Bock, Vanessa, 'Die Anfänge des polnischen Buchdrucks in Königsberg. Mit einem Verzeichnis der polnischen Drucke von Hans Weinreich und Alexander Augezdecki', in *Königsberger Buch- und Bibliotheksgeschichte*, ed. by Axel E. Walter (Cologne: Böhlau, 2004), pp. 127–55

Bracha, Krzysztof, *Des Teufels Lug und Trug: Nikolaus Magni von Jauer: Ein Reformtheologe des 15. Jahrhunderts gegen Aberglaube und Götzendienst*, trans. by Peter Chmiel, Quellen und Forschungen zur Europäischen Ethnologie, 25 (Dettelbach: J. H. Röll, 2013)

Brown, P. R. L., 'St Augustine's Attitude to Religious Coercion', *The Journal of Roman Studies*, 54.1 and 2 (1964), 107–16

Bruździński, Andrzej, *Działalność prymasa Stanisława Karnkowskiego w zakresie wprowadzania uchwał Soboru Trydenckiego w Polsce 1581–1603* [*The Primate Stanisław Karnkowski's Activity for the Implementation of the Tridentine Statutes in Poland, 1581–1603*], Rozprawy Doktorskie. Papieska Akademia Teologiczna w Krakowie. Wydział Teologiczny [Doctoral Dissertations. The Pontifical Theological Academy. The Department of Theology] (Cracow: Wydawnictwo Naukowe Papieskiej Akademii Teologicznej, 1996)

———, 'Forms of Piety Among Members of Religious Confraternities in Krakow in the Early Modern Period', *Folia Historica Cracoviensia*, 21 (2015), 103–46

Bylina, Stanisław, 'Le problème du Purgatoire en Europe Centrale et Orientale au bas Moyen Âge', in *The Use and Abuse of Eschatology in the Middle Ages*, ed. by Werner Verdeke, Daniel Verhelst, and Andries Welkenhuysen (Leuven: Leuven University Press, 1988), pp. 473–80

———, *Człowiek i zaświaty. Wizje kar pośmiertnych w Polsce średniowiecznej* [*Man and the Other World: Imaginations of After-Death Punishments in Mediaeval Poland*] (Warsaw: Polska Akademia Nauk. Instytut Historii, 1992)

———, 'The Church and Folk Culture in Late Medieval Poland', *Acta Poloniæ Historica*, 68 (1993), 27–42

———, 'La religion civique et la religion populaire en Pologne au bas Moyen Âge', in *La religion civique à l'époque médiévale et moderne (chrétienté et islam): Actes du colloque de Nanterre (21–23 juin 1993)*, ed. by André Vauchez, Collection de l'École française de Rome, 213 (Rome: École française de Rome, 1995), pp. 323–35

———, 'Wyobrażenia raju w Polsce średniowiecznej' ['Imagining Paradise in Medieval Poland'], in *Wyobraźnia średniowieczna* [*Medieval Imagination*], ed. by Teresa Michałowska (Warsaw: IBL, 1996), pp. 137–53

———, 'La catéchèse du peuple en Europe du Centre-Est au XIVe et XVe siècles', in *Christianity in East Central Europe: The Late Middle Ages*, ed. by Jerzy Kłoczowski, Paweł Kras, and Wojciech Polak, Proceedings of the Commission Internationale d'Histoire Ecclesiastique Comparée, 2 (Lublin: Instytut Europy Środkowo-Wschodniej, 1999), pp. 40–53

———, *Chrystianizacja wsi polskiej u schyłku średniowiecza* [*The Christianization of the Polish Countryside in the Later Middle Ages*] (Warsaw: Instytut Historii PAN, 2002)

———, *Religiousness in the Late Middle Ages: Christianity and Traditional Culture in Central and Eastern Europe in the Fourteenth and Fifteenth Centuries*, trans. by Alex Shannon, Polish Studies. Transdisciplinary Perspectives, 25 (Berlin: Peter Lang, 2019)

Chachaj, Jacek, *Bliżej schizmatyków niż Krakowa… Archidiakonat lubelski w XV i XVI wieku* [*Closer to Schismatics than to Cracow* […] *The Archdeaconry of Lublin in the Fifteenth and the Sixteenth Centuries*] (Lublin: Werset, 2012)

Chrościcki, Juliusz A., *Pompa funebris: Z dziejów kultury staropolskiej* [*Pompa funebris: On the History of Early Modern Polish Culture*], Idee i sztuka: studia z dziejów sztuki i doktryn artystycznych [Ideas and Art: Studies in Art History and Artistic Doctrines] (Warsaw: Państwowe Wydawnictwo Naukowe, 1974)

Corzine, Jacob, 'Assuring the Faithful: On Faith and Doubt in Lutheran Preaching', in *Feasting in a Famine of the Word: Lutheran Preaching in the Twenty-First Century*, ed. by Mark W. Birkholz, Jacob Corzine, and Jonathan Mumme (Eugene: Pickwick, 2016), pp. 98–116

Dixon, C. Scott, *The Reformation and Rural Society: The Parishes of Brandenburg-Ansbach-Kulmbach, 1528–1603* (Cambridge: Cambridge University Press, 1996)

Duffy, Eamon, *The Stripping of the Altars: Traditional Religion in England, 1400–1580* (New Haven: Yale University Press, 2005)

Dyl, Janusz, 'Książki teologiczne polskich drukarń XV i XVI wieku' ['Theological Books Published by Polish Typographers in the Fifteenth and Sixteenth Centuries'], *Archiwa, Biblioteki i Muzea Kościelne*, 69 (1998), 101–70

———, 'Pierwsze krakowskie drukowane dzieła teologiczne obcych i rodzimych polemistów antyprotestanckich' ['The First Cracow Printed Theological Works of Foreign and Native Anti-Protestant Polemicists'], *Roczniki Teologiczne*, 48 (2001), 67–95

Estreichr, Karol, *Bibliografia polska* [*Polish Bibliography*], pt. 3, XIX (30) (Cracow: Akademia Umiejętności, 1934)

Fijałek, Jan, *Życie i obyczaje kleru w Polsce średniowiecznej: na tle ustawodawstwa synodalnego* [*The Life and Morals of Clergy in Medieval Poland in the Context of Synodal Legislation*] (Cracow: Universitas, 1997)

French, Katherine L., *The People of the Parish: Community Life in a Late Medieval English Diocese*, The Middle Ages Series (Philadelphia: University of Pennsylvania Press, 2001)

Frick, David A., *Polish Sacred Philology in the Reformation and the Counter-Reformation: Chapters in the History of the Controversies (1551–1632)*, University of California Publications in Modern Philology, 123 (Berkeley: University of California Press, 1989)

Frymire, John M., *The Primacy of the Postils: Catholics, Protestants, and the Dissemination of Ideas in Early Modern Germany*, Studies in Medieval and Reformation Traditions, 147 (Leiden: Brill, 2010)

Hanusiewicz-Lavallee, Mirosława, 'Dawne i nowe. Tożsamość wyznaniowa katolików świeckich w potrydenckiej Rzeczypospolitej' ['The Old and the New. Confessional Identity of Lay Catholics in the Post-Tridentine Polish-Lithuanian Commonwealth'], in *Formowanie kultury katolickiej w dobie potrydenckiej: Powszechność i narodowość katolicyzmu polskiego* [*Forming a Catholic Culture in the Post-Tridentine Epoch: The Universality and Ethnicity of Polish Catholicism*], ed. by Justyna Dąbkowska-Kujko, Kultura Pierwszej Rzeczypospolitej w dialogu z Europą. Hermeneutyka wartości [The Culture of the Polish-Lithuanian Commonwealth in Dialogue with Europe: Hermeneutics of Values], ed. Alina Nowicka-Jeżowa, 6 (Warsaw: Wydawnictwo Uniwersytetu Warszawskiego, 2016), pp. 103–44

Heinz, Johann, *Justification and Merit: Luther Vs. Catholicism* (Merrien Springs: Andrews University Press, 1984)

Iwańska-Cieślik, Bernadeta 'Aspekty badań nad księgozbiorami członków kapituły katedralnej we Włocławku' ['Some Aspects of the Research on the Book Collections of Members of the Cathedral Chapter in Włocławek'], *Studia Włocławskie*, 13 (2011), 189–203

Kizik, Edmund, *Śmierć w mieście hanzeatyckim XVI–XVIII wieku: Studium z nowożytnej kultury funeralnej* [*Death in the Hanseatic City of the Sixteenth-Eighteenth Centuries: Studies in Early Modern Funeral Culture*] (Gdańsk: Wydawnictwo Uniwersytetu Gdańskiego, 1998)

Kłoczowski, Jerzy, *A History of Polish Christianity* (Cambridge: Cambridge University Press, 2000)

Knoll, Paul W., 'Religious Toleration in Sixteenth-Century Poland: Political Realities and Social Constraints', in *Diversity and Dissent: Negotiating Religious Difference in Central Europe, 1500–1800*, ed. by Howard Louthan, Gary B. Cohen, and Franz A. J. Szabo, Austrian and Habsburg Studies, 11 (New York: Berghahn, 2011), pp. 30–52

Korzo, Margarita, 'W sprawie jednego z XVI-wiecznych katechizmów kalwińskich w Rzeczpospolitej' ['On a Sixteenth-Century Calvinist Catechism in the Polish-Lithuanian Commonwealth'], *Odrodzenie i Reformacja w Polsce*, 52 (2007), 177–98

———, 'Jeszcze raz w sprawie nieznanego tłumaczenia Jana Kalwina w Polsce' ['Further Comments on the Unknown Translation of John Calvin in Poland'], *Odrodzenie i Reformacja w Polsce*, 56 (2012), 191–201

Koslofsky, Craig M., *The Reformation of the Dead: Death and Ritual in Early Modern Germany, 1450–1700* (Houndmills: Macmillan, 2000)

Kowalska-Kossobudzka, Halina, 'Wpływ Jana Łaskiego na kształtowanie się reformacyjnego Kościoła w Małopolsce' ['Jan Łaski's Influence on the Formation of the Reformed Church in Lesser Poland'], in *Jan Łaski 1499–1560: W pięćsetlecie urodzin* [*John a Lasco, 1499–1560: On the Quincentenary of His Birth*], ed. by Wojciech Kriegseisen and Piotr Salwa (Warsaw: Semper, 2001), pp. 15–26

Kowalski, Waldemar, 'Znaczenie archiwów parafialnych w badaniach nad dziejami przedrozbiorowymi' ['The Importance of Parish Archives for Early Modern Studies'] *Archiwa, Biblioteki i Muzea Kościelne*, 75 (2001), 19–63

———, 'Change in Continuity: Post-Tridentine Rural and Township Parish Life in the Cracow Diocese', *The Sixteenth Century Journal*, 35 (2004), 689–715

———, *'Do zmartwywstania swego za pewnym wodzem Kristusem…'. Staropolskie inskrypcje północno-zachodniej Małopolski* [*'To One's Resurrection, Following Christ, the Steadfast Master …'. The Medieval and Early Modern Inscriptions of North-western Lesser Poland*], (Kielce: Wydawnictwo Akademii Świętokrzyskiej, 2004)

———, '"Verily, This Is the Sheepfold of that Good Shepherd": The Idea of the "True" Church in Sixteenth-Century Polish Catechisms', *Odrodzenie i Reformacja w Polsce*, SI (2016) 5–47

———, 'Jan Długosz a tzw. szlachecki antyklerykalizm w siedemnastowiecznej Rzeczypospolitej' ['Jan Długosz and the So-Called Noblemen's Anticlericalism in Seventeenth-Century Poland-Lithuania'], in *Jan Długosz w kręgu badań historyków i literaturoznawców* [*Jan Długosz in Historical and Literary Research*], ed. by Tomisław Giergiel (Sandomierz: Urząd Miejski & Muzeum Okręgowe, 2017), pp. 187–207

———, 'Model chrześcijańskiego postępowania w świetle dwóch druków polemicznych z połowy XVI wieku' ['A Model of Christian Behaviour in the Light of Two Polemical Pamphlets from the Mid-Sixteenth Century'], in *Reformacja: między ideą a realizacją. Aspekty europejskie, polskie, śląskie. Reformation: zwischen Idee und ihrer Umsetzung. Die europäische, polnische und schlesische Aspekte* [*The Reformation: Between Idea and Realisation. European, Polish, Silesian Aspects*] ed. by Lucyna Harc and Gabriela Wąs (Cracow: Księgarnia Akademicka, 2019), pp. 77–113

Kracik, Jan, 'Przeciw Reformacji' ['Against the Reformation'], in *Kościół krakowski w tysiącleciu* [*The Cracow Church in the First Millennium*] (Cracow: Znak, 2000), pp. 169–303

Kriegseisen, Wojciech, *Between State and Church. Confessional relations from Reformation to Enlightenment. Poland-Lithuania – Germany – Netherlands*, trans. by Bartosz Wójcik, Polish Studies. Transdisciplinary Perspectives, 16 (Frankfurt am Main: Peter Lang, 2016)

Leszczyński, Rafał Marcin, 'Nauka ewangelicko-reformowana w polskojęzycznych katechizmach z XVI wieku' ['Reformed Evangelical Teaching in the Polish-language Catechisms of the Sixteenth Century'], in *Ewangelicyzm reformowany w Pierwszej Rzeczypospolitej: Dialog z Europą i wybory aksjologiczne w świetle literatury i piśmiennictwa XVI–XVII wieku* [*Reformed Evangelism in the Polish-Lithuanian Commonwealth: A Dialogue with Europe and Axiological Choices in Light of Literature and Writings of the Sixteenth and Seventeenth Centuries*], ed. by Dariusz Chemperek, Kultura Pierwszej Rzeczypospolitej w dialogu z Europą: Hermeneutyka wartości [The Culture of the Polish-Lithuanian Commonwealth in Dialogue with Europe: Hermeneutics of Values], 9 (Warsaw: Wydawnictwa Uniwersytetu Warszawskiego, 2015), pp. 57–87

Litak, Stanisław, *Parafie w Rzeczypospolitej w XVI–XVIII wieku. Struktura, funkcje społeczno-religijne i edukacyjne* [*The Parish in the Polish-Lithuanian Commonwealth in the Sixteenth-Eighteenth Centuries: Structure, Socio-religious and Educational Roles*], Dzieje chrześcijaństwa Polski i Rzeczypospolitej Obojga Narodów [A History of Christianity in Poland and in the Commonwealth of the Two Nations], 2 (Lublin: Wydawnictwo KUL, 2004)

Maciuszko, Janusz T., 'Poglądy religijne Mikołaja Reja' [Mikołaj Rey's Religious Convictions], in *Mikołaj Rej z Nagłowic: W pięćsetną rocznicę urodzin* [Mikołaj Rey of Nagłowice: in Commemoration of His 500th Birthday], ed. by Waldemar Kowalski (Kielce: Kieleckie Towarzystwo Naukowe, 2005), pp. 287–308

Małłek, Janusz, *Opera selecta*, II: *Poland and Prussia in the Baltic Area from the Sixteenth to the Eighteenth Century*, trans. by Hazel Pearson, Studies Presented to the International Commission for the History of Representative and Parliamentary Institutions, 91 (Toruń: Wydawnictwo Naukowe Uniwersytetu Mikołaja Kopernika, 2013)

Mattes, Mark C., "Luther on Justification as Forensic and Effective," in *Oxford Handbook of Martin Luther's Theology*, ed. by Robert Kolb, Irene Dingel, and Lubomir Batka (Oxford: Oxford University Press, 2014), pp. 264–73

Nowakowska, Natalia, 'High Clergy and Printers: Anti-Reformation Polemic in the Kingdom of Poland, 1520–36', *Historical Research*, 87 (2014), 43–64

———, *King Sigismund of Poland and Martin Luther: The Reformation before Confessionalization* (Oxford: Oxford University Press, 2018)

Nowicka-Jeżowa, Alina, *Pieśń czasu śmierci. Studium z historii duchowości XVI–XVIII wieku* [*The Chant at the Time of Death: A Study in the History of Spirituality of the Sixteenth-Eighteenth Centuries*] (Lublin: Towarzystwo Naukowe Katolickiego Uniwersytetu Lubelskiego, 1992)

Opitz, Peter, 'Huldrich Zwingli', in *The Cambridge Companion to Reformed Theology*, ed. by Paul T. Nimmo and David A. S. Fergusson (Cambridge; Cambridge University Press, 2016), pp. 117–31

Parish, Helen, *Clerical Celibacy in the West: c. 1100–1700* (Farnham: Ashgate, 2010)

Pettegree, Andrew, *Reformation and the Culture of Persuasion* (Cambridge: Cambridge University Press, 2007)

Picirilli, Robert E., *Grace, Faith, Free Will: Contrasting Views of Salvation: Calvinism and Arminianism* (Nashville: Randall House, 2002)

Plisiecki, Piotr, 'The Parochial Network and the Tithes System in the Medieval Diocese of Cracow', in *Pfarreien im Mittelalter: Deutschland, Polen, Tschechien und Ungarn im Vergleich*, ed. by Nathalie Kruppa and Leszek Zygner, Studien zur Germania Sacra, 32 (Göttingen: Vandenhoeck & Ruprecht, 2008), pp. 223–34

Polska XVI w. pod względem geograficzno-statystycznym [*The Poland of the Sixteenth Century in Respect of Geographical and Statistical Data*], III: *Małopolska* [*Lesser Poland*], ed. by Adolf Pawiński, Źródła dziejowe [Historical Sources], 14 (Warsaw: Księgarnia Gebethnera i Wolffa, 1886)

Ptaszyński, Maciej, 'The Polish-Lithuanian Commonwealth', in *A Companion to the Reformation in Central Europe*, ed. by Howard Louthan and Graeme Murdock, Brill's Companions to the Christian Tradition, 61 (Leiden: Brill, 2015)

Skierska, Izabela, *Obowiązek mszalny w średniowiecznej Polsce* [*Church Attendance in Medieval Poland*] (Warsaw: Wydawnictwo Instytutu Historii PAN, 2003)

Sproul, Robert Charles, *Faith Alone: The Evangelical Doctrine of Justification* (Wheaton: Crossway, 1995)

Szövérffy, Joseph, 'Venantius Fortunatus and the Earliest Hymns to the Holy Cross', *Classical Folia*, 20 (1966), 107–22

Tazbir, Janusz, *Reformacja a problem chłopski w Polsce XVI wieku: oddziaływanie walki klasowej na wsi polskiej na kształtowanie się ideologii religijnej szlachty w okresie reformacji* [*The Reformation and the Peasant Issue in Sixteenth-century Poland: The Influence of Class Conflict in the Polish Countryside on the Formation of Noblemen's Religious Ideology*], Studia staropolskie [Old Poland Studies], 2 (Wrocław: Zakład Narodowy im. Ossolińskich, 1953)

———, 'Ze studiów nad stosunkiem polskich protestantów do chłopów w XVI wieku [On the Relation of Polish Protestants Toward Peasants in the Sixteenth Century]', *Reformacja w Polsce*, 12 (1956), 32–61

———, 'Propaganda kontrreformacji wśród chłopów inflanckich (1582–1621)' ['The Counter-Reformation Propaganda Amongst Livonian Peasants'], *Kwartalnik Historyczny*, 65 (1958), 720–41

———, 'The Fate of Polish Protestantism in the Seventeenth Century', in *A Republic of Nobles: Studies in Polish History to 1864*, ed. by J. K. Fedorowicz, Maria Bogucka, and Henryk Samsonowicz (Cambridge: Cambridge University Press, 1982), pp. 198–217

Thompson, John J., 'Agency and Appetite for Religious Song: *Vexilla Regis* and its First Thousand Years', *English Studies*, 93 (2012), 604–12

Universal Short Title Catalogue, http://ustc.ac.uk/index.php

Urban, Wacław, *Chłopi wobec Reformacji w Małopolsce w drugiej połowie XVI w.* [*Peasants and the Reformation in Lesser Poland in the Second Half of the Sixteenth Century*], Prace Komisji Nauk Historycznych PAN Oddział w Krakowie [Works of the Commission for Historical Disciplines of the Polish Academy of Sciences. Cracow Department], 3 (Cracow: Państwowe Wydawnictwo Naukowe, 1959)

———, *Et hæc facienda, et illa non omittenda: profesor Wacław Urban w swych dziełach wybranych* [*Et hæc facienda, et illa non omittenda: Selected Works of Professor Wacław Urban*], ed. by Anna Kądziela, Waldemar Kowalski, Jadwiga Muszyńska, and Zdzisław Pietrzyk, Opera necessaria (Warsaw: Wydawnictwo DiG, 2012)

Wijaczka, Jacek, 'The Reformation in Sixteenth-Century Poland: A Success Story or a Failure?', *Reformation & Renaissance Review*, 17 (2015), 9–26

Wiślicz, Tomasz, 'Chłopskie pogrzeby w Polsce od drugiej połowy XVI do końca XVIII wieku' ['Peasant Funerals in Poland from the Second Half of the Sixteenth to the End of the Eighteenth Century'], *Kwartalnik Historii Kultury Materialnej*, 45 (1997), 351–69

———, 'Ile kosztował pogrzeb chłopa w Polsce XVII–XVIII wieku (i kto za to płacił?) [What Was the Cost of a Peasant Funeral in Poland of the 17th–18th Centuries (and Who Paid for It?)]', in *Wesela, chrzciny i pogrzeby. Kultura życia i śmierci* [*Weddings, Christenings and Funerals: The Cultures of Life and Death*], ed. by Henryk Suchojad (Warsaw: Semper, 2001), pp. 273–86

———, *Earning Heavenly Salvation: Peasant Religion in Lesser Poland: Mid-Sixteenth to Eighteenth Centuries*, trans. by Tristan Korecki, Studies in History, Memory and Politics, 34 (Berlin: Peter Lang, 2020)

Wiśniowski, Eugeniusz, 'Parish Clergy in Medieval Poland', in *The Christian Community of Medieval Poland: Anthologies*, ed. by Jerzy Kłoczowski (Wrocław: Zakład Narodowy im. Ossolińskich, 1981), pp. 119–38

———, *Parafie w średniowiecznej Polsce: struktura i funkcje społeczne* [*The Parish in Medieval Poland: Structures and Social Roles*], Dzieje chrześcijaństwa Polski i Rzeczypospolitej Obojga Narodów, 1: Średniowiecze [The History of Christianity in Poland and in the Commonwealth of the Two Nations, 1: The Middle Ages] (Lublin: Wydawnictwo Katolickiego Uniwersytetu Lubelskiego, 2004)

Włodarski, Maciej, *Obraz i słowo. O powiązaniach w sztuce i literaturze XV–XVI wieku na przykładzie 'ars moriendi'* [*The Picture and the Word: On the Correspondence of Art and Literature in the 15th–16th Centuries as Exemplified by the Ars Moriendi*] (Cracow: Universitas, 1991)

Wojciechowska, Beata, *Od godów do św. Łucji: Obrzędy doroczne w Polsce późnego średniowiecza* [*From Twelvetide to St Lucy's Day: Annual Folk Celebrations in Late-Medieval Poland*] (Kielce: Wydawnictwo Wyższej Szkoły Pedagogicznej im. Jana Kochanowskiego, 2000)

———, 'The Remembrance of the Deceased in the Traditional Polish Culture of the Middle Ages', *Collegium: Studies across Disciplines in the Humanities and Social Sciences*, 18 (2015), 32–48

———, 'Stanisława ze Skarbimierza rozważania "o dwóch drogach, którymi podąża się do nieba"' ['Stanisław of Skarbimierz's Reflections on the Two Ways Leading to Heaven'], in *Ambona: Teksty o kulturze średniowiecza ofiarowane Stanisławowi Bylinie* [*The Pulpit: Texts on Medieval Culture Dedicated to Stanisław Bylina*], ed. by Krzysztof Bracha and Wojciech Brojer (Warsaw: IH PAN, 2016), pp. 195–205

Województwo krakowskie w drugiej połowie XVI wieku [*The Palatinate of Cracow in the Second Half of the Sixteenth Century*], II: *Komentarz, indeksy* [*Commentaries, Indices*], ed. by Henryk Rutkowski, Atlas historyczny Polski, mapy szczegółowe XVI wieku [A Historical Atlas of Poland: Thematic Maps of the Sixteenth Century] (Warsaw: Neriton, 2008)

Województwo sandomierskie w drugiej połowie XVI wieku [*The Palatinate of Sandomierz in the Second Half of the Sixteenth Century*], II: *Komentarz, indeksy* [*Commentaries, Indices*], ed. by Władysław Pałucki, Atlas historyczny Polski, mapy szczegółowe XVI wieku [A Historical Atlas of Poland: Thematic Maps of the Sixteenth Century] (Warsaw: Wydawnictwo Naukowe PWN, 1993)

Wójcik, Walenty, 'Ecclesiastical Local Legislation in Poland before the Partitioning in the Light of the Legislation of the Universal Church', in *Poland's Millennium of Catholicism*, ed. by Marian Rechowicz, I (Lublin: The Scientific Society of the Catholic University in Lublin, 1969), pp. 247–60

———, *Ze studiów nad synodami polskimi* [*Studies on Synods of the Polish Church*] (Lublin: Towarzystwo Naukowe Katolickiego Uniwersytetu Lubelskiego, 1982)

Zachman, Randall C., *John Calvin as Teacher, Pastor, and Theologian: The Shape of his Writings and Thought* (Grand Rapids: Baker Academic, 2006)

Zaremska, Hanna, '*Żywi wobec zmarłych*: Brackie i cechowe pogrzeby w Krakowie w XIV-pierwszej połowie XVI w.' ['The Living for the Dead: Brotherhood and Guild Funerals in Cracow from the Fourteenth to the Mid-Sixteenth Century'], *Kwartalnik Historyczny*, 81 (1974), 733–49

Zygner, Leszek, 'Późnośredniowieczne synody narzędziem reformy Kościoła' ['Late Medieval Synods as a Tool of Church Reform'], in *Ecclesia semper reformanda. Kryzysy i reformy średniowiecznego Kościoła* [*Ecclesia semper reformanda. Crisis and Reform in Medieval Church*], ed. by Tomasz Gałuszka, Tomasz Graff, and Grzegorz Ryś (Cracow: Towarzystwo Naukowe Societas Vistulana, 2013), pp. 423–41

———, 'Vision der Kirchenreform im Spiegel der polnischen Synodalstatuten um 1400', *Bulletin der Polnischen Historischen Mission*, 11 (2016), 209–35

DANIELA RYWIKOVÁ

Religious Transformation on the Early Modern Periphery – Law and Gospel

Image, Place, and Communication in the Multi-Confessional Community of Sixteenth-Century Moravian Ostrava

The Place and the Times: A Town on the Periphery and Religious Transformation in Sixteenth-Century Moravia[1]

Present-day Ostrava, the third largest town in the Czech Republic and a crucial industrial conurbation, was in the Middle Ages a small town on the periphery of the Moravian dominion of the bishops of Olomouc.[2] The town's early modern history is closely connected with its parish church. The first written reference to the parish church of St Wenceslas dates to as early as 1297, when the parish priest and bishop's notary, whose name was Jindřich, appeared as a witness in a deed of the Bishop Dětřich of Olomouc.[3] It is nonetheless probable that the church was founded earlier, even before the foundation of the town, probably around the mid-thirteenth century.[4] In 1378–1379 the papal curia enabled the priest of Ostrava Master Adam Benešů of Nežetice to reserve some of the more prominent vacated parish prebends, since he claimed that the parish of Ostrava did not yield more than one third from

1 The study is supported by the research grant project The Construction of the Other in Medieval Europe (University of Ostrava, IRP 201820).

2 The town was founded by the Bishop of Olomouc, Bruno of Schauenburg (1245–1281), before 1267. This is apparent from the bishop's testament dated 29 November 1267. Bakala, 'Ostrava v období' ['Ostrava During the Period of the High Middle Ages'], p. 29.

3 Adamus, *Dějiny města Ostravy v přehledu až do r. 1860 [History of Moravian Ostrava up to 1860]*, p. 27. For the history of the Moravian parish of Ostrava, see also Wolný, *Kirchliche Topographie*, pp. 117–23.

4 Bakala, 'Ostrava v období' ['Ostrava During the Period of the High Middle Ages'], p. 45.

Daniela Rywiková • (daniela.rywikova@osu.cz) is Associate Professor of Art History at the University of Ostrava.

Religious Transformations in New Communities of Interpretation in Europe (1350–1570): Bridging the Historiographical Divides, ed. by Élise Boillet and Ian Johnson, New Communities of Interpretation, 3 (Turnhout: Brepols, 2022), pp. 239–266.

DOI 10.1484/M.NCI-EB.5.131222

the fifteen pounds of tithe annually. This makes it clear that the parish was small and poor, just like the entire town of Ostrava.[5]

Until the early fifteenth century, written records are limited to stating the existence of Ostrava Church. The Hussite wars did not have a large effect on Ostrava, except in 1428 when the town became a direct target of a military campaign and was occupied by the Hussites for a short period.[6] Around the mid-fifteenth century, both Moravian and Polish Ostrava was acquired by Hussite hejtman Jan Čapek of Sány, who brought with him a priest, Augustin, mentioned in 1444 as the priest of Polish Ostrava.[7] It is very likely that this is the same Augustin mentioned ten years later, this time as the priest of St Wenceslas's Church, in a deed to the Bishop of Olomouc, JanHáz, when he joined the municipality to ask for permission to found an altar 'jenž vystaven jest ke dveřím pobočným, ke cti Pánu Bohu všemohoucímu, Panně Marii a svaté Cecílii, kterou chceme míti za patronku' (placed by the side door to praise the Lord Almighty, the Virgin Mary, and St Cecilia, whom we wish to have as our patron saint).[8]

The foundation of the altar refers to the Catholic faith of the burghers of Ostrava and raises questions about the form of the Masses celebrated in the parish church as well as the confessional loyalties of the above-mentioned priest Augustin.[9] Most likely, St Wenceslas's Church held both Catholic and Utraquist services. This was not unique, as, in the region, similar dual masses were held in parish churches in Odry and Fulnek, which essentially

5 Bakala, 'Ostrava v období' ['Ostrava During the Period of the High Middle Ages'], p. 45.

6 For more details on the Hussites in Northern Moravia, see Jurok, *Moravský severovýchod* [*Northeast Moravia*], pp. 87–153; Rohlová, 'Středověká Ostrava' ['Medieval Ostrava'], pp. 48–50.

7 Pitronová, 'Rozvoj města' ['Development of the Town'], p. 55; Barcuch, 'Ostrava v letech 1437–1618' ['Ostrava between 1437 and 1618'], pp. 52–53.

8 'altare, quod aedificatum est circa ostium laterale ad laudem Dei omnipotentis et in honorem servulae Domini Nostri Jesu Christi, gloriosae Virginis Mariae, Sanctaeque Caeciliae Virginis et martyris, quam volumus esse patronam', *Codex diplomaticus*, ed. by Adamus, no. 18, p. 28. We can only speculate on the appearance of the altar. It could have been a larger polyptych and its commissioning by the burghers of Ostrava was undoubtedly perceived not only as a material expression of their Catholic faith but also as a representative, collective, and prestigiously pious act of the entire town community, since the priest celebrating Masses at the altar was also supposed to pray for 'omnius civibus, incolis nostrae supradictae civitatis Ostraviae.' (all inhabitants, the locals in the aforementioned city of Ostrava). Ostrava, Archiv města Ostravy, Fond Farní úřad Ostrava, Farní kronika Moravská Ostrava, [Ostrava, The City Archive of Ostrava, The Ostrava Parish Office Fund, The Parish Chronicle Moravian Ostrava], inv. no. 6a., p. 9.

9 According to a royal privilege from 1461, Ostrava was to hold an annual eight-day-long fair on the occasion of the Feast of St Cecilia (22 November). Pitronová, 'Rozvoj města' ['Development of the Town'], p. 55. That the burghers did not profess affiliation with Utraquism at this time tends to be accounted for mainly by the predominant German ethnicity of the burghers. This demographic composition changed in favour of Czech ethnicity only at the turn of the fifteenth and the sixteenth century, as is also evidenced by the fact that the oldest surviving deed in the Czech language in the Ostrava municipal

reflected religious practice in Bohemia and Moravia following the Compacts of Basel (1436).[10] Until the beginning of the sixteenth century, written sources pertaining to the church are limited to a handful of notes relating to Ostrava priests. In 1511, the town of Moravian Ostrava returned to the ownership of the bishops of Olomouc.[11]

Soon after this, and as early as 1520, Martin Luther's new teaching started to spread through the Czech lands. At this time, Bohemia was already more or less a Utraquist country (as late as the end of the sixteenth century, 85 per cent of the population of Bohemia were Utraquists and only 10 per cent were Catholics, whereas in Moravia 75 per cent were Utraquists).[12] The new Protestant teaching was mainly absorbed by the more radical fraction of Czech Utraquism and, understandably, by the German-speaking population. Their syncretism led to the emergence of so-called Neo-Utraquism.[13]

---

office is dated 1496. For the latest discussion on the subject, see Knop, 'Čeština ostravských' ['The Czech Language'], p. 325; Turek, 'Národnostní poměry v Ostravě' ['The Nationality Situation in Ostrava'], p. 96.

10 Šmahel, *Basilejská kompaktáta* [*Compacts of Basel*]; Krchňák, *Čechové na basilejském sněmu* [*Czechs at the Council of Basel*]; Bechyně, 'Kompaktáta' ['The Compacts'], pp. 37–40; Pitronová, 'Rozvoj města' ['Development of the Town'], p. 75. For the religious situation in sixteenth-century Moravia, see Hrubý, 'Luterství a kalvinismus na Moravě' ['Lutheranism and Calvinism in Moravia'], pp. 17–18; Hrejsa, 'Luterství, kalvinismus a podobojí na Moravě' ['Lutheranism, Calvinism and Utraquism in Moravia'], pp. 296–326, 474–85; Dvořák, *Dějiny Moravy* [*History of Moravia*]; Válka, *Husitství na Moravě* [*Hussites in Moravia*]; Válka, *Dějiny Moravy* [*History of Morava*]; Pojar, 'Reformace a protireformace' ['Reformation and Counter-Reformation'], pp. 44–75; Mezník, 'Tolerance na Moravě v 16. století' ['Tolerance in Sixteenth-Century Moravia'], pp. 76–85; *Morava v době renesance* [*Moravia in the Age of the Renaissance and Reformation*], ed. by Knoz; Jakubec, *Kulturní prostředí a mecenát* [*The Culture and Artistic Patronage*]; Vorel, *Velké dějiny zemí Koruny české* [*The Great History of the Czech Lands*], pp. 255–63.

11 The town was bought out by Bishop Stanislav Thurzo (1497–1540). He gained substantial financial support from his brother, the Kremnica count Juraj Thurzo, who lent him 3000 Hungarian Guldens to buy out the Hukvaldy estate. For this sum the bishop granted him tenure of Ostrava but held all incomes from the town. Starting in 1511, however, the bishop acted as the real owner of Moravian Ostrava. Pitronová, 'Rozvoj města' ['Development of the Town'], p. 58.

12 Pojar, 'Reformace a protireformace' ['Reformation and Counter-Reformation'], p. 56. Sadly, the newest history of Ostrava, published in 2006, *Ostrava*, ed. by Przybylová, only summarizes the previous research and deals but briefly with the religious situation in the sixteenth-century town: Barcuch, 'Ostrava v letech 1437–1618' ['Ostrava between 1437 and 1618'], pp. 60–61.

13 At the land Diet in 1543 representatives of radical Utraquism influenced by Luther's teaching, Jan Mystopol, Václav Mitmánek, and the nobleman Jan of Pernštejn attempted to enforce Lutheran ideas within the Czech Utraquist environment. They raised three essential doctrinal questions with the Diet: whether the Mass constitutes a sacrifice; whether it is appropriate to worship saints; and whether only faith without merciful works can redeem the Christian. The Diet's response can be called appropriate as the first thesis was passed whereas it could not reach agreement on the second thesis. The third and decisive thesis was not even discussed as: 'mlčením pominuli a žádný o něj nic neříkal' (it was passed over in silence and nobody commented on it). See Halama, *Otázka svatých v české reformaci* [*The*

The Czech lands observed a certain religious status quo established by the Basel Compacts, which had determined the political legalization of religious duality — Catholicism and Utraquism — in this territory. Although the Compacts guaranteed religious 'tolerance' and coexistence between the two factions, they simultaneously created a rather conservative environment, since they practically prevented assimilation of new reformed teachings (such as Luther's teaching on justification by faith alone — iustificatio sola fide), placing them de jure outside the law side by side with 'heretical' communities such as the Unity of Brethren, Antitrinitarians, and Anabaptists.

Compliance with the Compacts was strictly required for keeping the peace in the land, and any new theological Lutheran ideas met with the suspicion of the majority of Czechs (and, to a much lesser degree, Moravian Utraquists), leading to nationwide bans of the new faith. In 1575 the theological compromises resulted in the passage of the so-called Bohemian Confession or Vyznání víry svaté křesťanské všech tří stavův Království českého Tělo a Krev Krista Pána pod obojí přijímajících (Confession of the Holy Christian Faith of all three Estates of the Realm in the Kingdom of Bohemia receiving the Body and Blood of Christ the Lord under both species), which was supposed to lead to the legalization of Lutheranism and the Unity of Brethren in Bohemia.[14] Although the document was not enforced, as it was approved neither by the ruler nor the land diet, it paved the way for the so-called Emperor Rudolf II's Letter of Majesty issued in 1609, which granted religious freedom to people of all ranks in the Kingdom of Bohemia.[15]

Ostravia, as the town was called in the written sources, was situated on the border with Lutheran Cieszyn Silesia. The burghers of Ostrava were naturally in touch with Lutheranism, not least because of the lively trade connections with nearby Silesian towns. In Silesia, the Reformation had been spreading from the beginning of the sixteenth century, thanks mainly to close commercial and cultural connections with Nuremberg, a major Reformation hub. Wrocław was the largest Silesian town and the region's cultural centre; it was also one of the first towns to join the Protestant movement. The first Reformation prints were published there as early as 1519.[16] One of the first reformers preaching in the town was Johannes Hess, and Catholic services

---

Question of Saints in the Bohemian Reformation], p. 80; Pojar, 'Reformace a protireformace' ['Reformation and Counter-Reformation in Central Europe'], pp. 56–57; David, 'The Integrity of the Utraquist', pp. 329–51; David, *Finding the Middle*, pp. 220–31.

14 David, *Finding the Middle Way*, pp. 168–78; Bartlová, 'Renesance a reformace v českých dějinách umění' ['Renaissance and Reformation in Czech Art History'], p. 36; Říčan, *Čtyři vyznání* [*Four Confessions*].

15 On Rudolf II's Letter of Majesty, see Just, *9. 7. 1609*.

16 For more details on the subject of the Reformation and art in Silesia, see Harasimowicz, *Treści i funkcje* [*The Content and Ideological Functions*]; Baumgarten, *Konfession, Bild und Macht*; Harasimowicz, *Schwärmergeist und Freiheitsdenken*.

were banned here as early as 1525.[17] The Reformation process in Silesia was completed in 1545 when Cieszyn Silesia, the last of the Silesian Duchies, became fully Lutheran.

It is probable that, in addition to the Catholic burghers, the ethnically German burghers mainly professed the Lutheran faith, while some Ostrava nobles demanded communion sub utraque specie,[18] thus putting the priest of St Wenceslas's Church, Jan Jilovský, also called Gitorius, in a rather difficult situation. As late as 1522, Jilovský was praised by the Bishop of Olomouc, Bernard Zoubek of Zdětín, as 'muž hodný a oblíbený' (a good and well-liked man). However, the new bishop, Marek Khuen (1553–1565), summoned the priest to Kroměříž in 1559 to answer for offering the local nobility the Utraquist communion and for degrading the sacrament of confession.[19] Jilovský was clearly thought to be overstepping his authority here.

The episode is important testimony to the religious situation, not only in mid-sixteenth century-Moravian Ostrava but also in the whole of Moravia. While the situation could be described as chaotic, it was 'liberal' compared with the contemporary state of affairs in the rest of Europe, even though it was still following the rule cuius regio, eius religio. Even the religious Peace of Augsburg, promulgated in the German lands in 1555, only applied to landlords and knights.[20] The religious practices and denominations of most people, then, completely depended on the religious 'tolerance' of the landlord. In Moravia, it was typical for subjects and villeins in a single domain to profess multiple denominations. This was obviously the case in the episcopal town of Moravian Ostrava, except that it was impossible to assume religious tolerance from the landlord — the bishop of Olomouc. It is also important to note that in 1553 Bishop Khuen founded a deanery in St Wenceslas's Church in Moravian Ostrava. This, no doubt, should have strengthened Catholicism in the town, improving not only the parish's

---

17 Pojar, 'Reformace a protireformace' ['Reformation and Counter-Reformation'], p. 60. For the Reformation in Central Europe, see Scribner, *For the Sake of Simple Folk*; Kaufmann, *Court, Cloister and City*; *Public Communication*, ed. by Bartlová and Šroněk; Keul, *Early Modern Communities in East-Central Europe*; *Umění české reformace* [*Art of the Bohemian Reformation*], ed. by Horníčková and Šroněk; *From Hus to Luther*, ed. by Horníčková and Šroněk.

18 The owners of Polish Ostrava, Sedlničtí z Choltic, were not Catholics, probably like other local aristocrats in the region. It is known, for instance, that some aristocrats even supported the Unity of Brethren and allowed it to set up congregations on their estates, e.g. Jan Petřvaldský z Petřvaldu, who was one of the bishop's vassals. Turek, 'Čeští bratři v okolí Ostravy' ['Czech Brethren in the Surroundings of Ostrava'], pp. 319–24; Barcuch, 'Ostrava v letech 1437–1618' ['Ostrava between 1437 and 1618'], p. 60.

19 In the end, Gitorius was forced to write a statement and publicly expressed his remorse on the second fast, Sunday 10 March 1560. Adamus, *Dějiny města Ostravy v přehledu až do r. 1860* [*History of Moravian Ostrava up to 1860*], p. 27; Wolný, *Kirchliche Topographie*, pp. 120–21.

20 Augsburger Reichs- und Religionsfrieden. Wüst, 'Der Augsburger Religionsfrieden', pp. 147–63; Schorn-Schütte, *Die Reformation*, pp. 88–90.

reputation within Church administrative structures but also the prestige of the town more generally.

It is at this time, in 1555, as the surviving inscriptions in Ostrava parish church make clear, that St Wenceslas's Church was painted with murals. Their iconography, as I will demonstrate below, reflects the complicated religious situation not only in the town but also in the larger border region of Moravian Silesia. Despite the attempts of the diocese, the numbers of inhabitants in Ostrava professing Lutheranism and other non-Catholic affiliations were increasing from the mid-1560s. As early as 1535, sources document 'Picards', i.e. the Unity of Brethren, in Polish Ostrava. There is also evidence of their congregations in Paskov, Fulnek, and Petřvald, as well as in Trnávka, Zábřeh nad Odrou, and Místek, and thus also in the immediate proximity of Moravian Ostrava.[21]

In the spring of 1570 Jan Chololecký was appointed as the new priest in Ostrava. At first, he had differences with the local burghers, who demanded 'věci nové, nebývalé ve zpovědi' (new and unprecedented things in the confession), probably public confession.[22] Gradually, the priest adjusted to the local situation, whereas his altarist Peter complained to the bishop both about the priest's Protestantism and the municipal council's denial of his benefits and monetary salary.

In 1571 Bishop Vilém Prusinovský sent, as part of a general visitation of Ostrava, a scribe Jiřík Kamenohorský, to counsel the town and threaten the priest with punishment. But the priest Chololecký did not change his attitude and was jailed at the bishop's castle in Hukvaldy. In March 1571 the bishop ordered the municipal council and a newly appointed priest, Jan Rokyta, to collect all the books and written documents that Chololecký used for confessions and during his preaching and to send them to Kroměříž. The imprisoned Chololecký was vouched for by his brother and other burghers that he would neither flee nor preach against the Catholic faith — so the bishop released him after he promised to do penance and make do with whatever parish was allocated to him.[23]

The newly appointed priest in Ostrava, Jan Rokyta, Vicar of the Olomouc chapter, was also given the task of counselling the burghers of Ostrava on the difference between communion under one kind and sub utraque specie, and

---

21 According to a preserved deed of the nobleman Jan Petřvaldsky z Petřvaldu a Zábřehu, from 1561 he gifted a house along with property to the Unity of Brethren in Zábřeh. In Paskov, a Brethren congregation is documented for period 1525–1617. See Turek, 'Čeští bratři v okolí Ostravy' ['Czech Brethren in the Surroundings of Ostrava'], p. 320. For the Unity of Brethren generally, see Atwood, *The Theology of the Czech Brethren*.

22 Pitronová, 'Rozvoj města' ['Development of the Town'], p. 65.

23 Nevertheless, Chololecký did not fulfil his promise to the bishop and fled to Klimkovice owned by the nobleman Hynek Bruntálský z Vrbna. Eventually, he ended up in Hukvaldy prison again. For more details, see Adamus, *Dějiny města Ostravy v přehledu až do r. 1860* [*History of Moravian Ostrava up to 1860*], p. 29; Barcuch, 'Ostrava v letech 1437–1618' ['Ostrava between 1437 and 1618'], p. 60.

on Catholic theology per the conclusions of the Council of Trent. Between 1572 and 1578, however, Protestantism continued to spread successfully in Ostrava. In September 1582, the new bishop, Stanislav Pavlovský (1579–1598), arranged a general visitation of Ostrava so as to learn more about the situation in the town and to draw appropriate conclusions. The burghers of Ostrava complained to the canons sent, Václav Šturm and Petr Illicinus, that their priest Jan Ocellius possessed inadequate theological knowledge and could not even name the Seven Sacraments. They claimed that all of them were Catholics, and that there was no non-Catholic chapel in the town.[24]

The committee's activity was resolved in a dramatic way when it initiated the appointment of the Catholic Martin Omeis as the Burgermeister, but the town council refused to give its approval. As a result, the bishop sentenced the councillors to a month-long imprisonment in Hukvaldy Castle jail. On 10 December 1584 the bishop issued Ostrava with the so-called Reformation and Instruction for Burgomaster, Vogt and councillors of the town of Ostrava, who, in the spirit of Trent, are ordered thus:

> V témž městě Ostravě nyní i budoucně nikdo z obyvatelův, též podruhův a hoferův trpěn a přijímán nebyl, než toliko kteříž by nepodezřelí a dobře zachovalí lidé, jsouc religii svaté katolické římské byli [...]
>
> > (In the town of Ostrava for now and in the future, there shall be no residents, tenants and wage labourers tolerated or accepted, except those non-suspicious and well-behaved people who would keep the Catholic faith [...])[25]

In other words, all the town's inhabitants and officials were to be Catholics. The 'reformation' further stipulated that no non-Catholics were to reside in Ostrava and that guild members had to make annual confession and participate in Holy Communion. A much stricter supervision over town finances was also established, and a chaplain, whose duties were to supervise the school and to serve Holy Mass, was appointed to the parish church. The burghers had to contribute financially to his livelihood from the town's toll income. The bishop similarly called on other towns in northern Moravia in a bid to force them to receive the Holy Communion under one kind.

However, the uneasy task for the bishops of Olomouc was to find well-educated and reliable priests for their provincial parishes. This is well evidenced by the fact that the local northern Moravian parishes were almost exclusively

---

24 All Ostrava's inhabitants were summoned to the main square, where the bishop's visitors publicly asked who among them did not hold the Catholic faith. The general visits were one of the instruments of the Catholic Church reform that the bishops used in the post-Tridentine period. The first such visit was organized by Bishop Prusinovský as early as 1566. For more details, see Jakubec, *Kulturní prostředí a mecenát* [*The Culture and Artistic Patronage*], pp. 30–31.

25 *Codex diplomaticus*, ed. by Adamus, p. 30.

filled with priests from Lower Silesia and Poland. It was probably shortly after 1591 that the Ostrava Literary Brotherhood was set up by St Wenceslas's Church. Its task was to strengthen the Catholic faith and solidify the success of the re-Catholization process in the town.[26] In 1596, the Polish dean Jan Hřeblovský (1593–1600) is mentioned as priest of Ostrava; he complained that people in Ostrava were lukewarm in faith.[27] However, with the exception of this note and a mention of some bacchanalia[28] held in the parish, there is no reference to non-Catholic profession among the burghers of Moravian Ostrava at the beginning of 1590s. This presumably means that they had succumbed to the Counter-Reformation campaign of the bishops of Olomouc.

Image, Confession, and Communication: Law and Gospel or the Ostrava Allegory of Salvation?

As mentioned above, the donor inscriptions on the walls of St Wenceslas's parish church record that, in 1555, they were decorated with an originally extensive cycle of mural paintings.[29] Older fragments of saints' figures are

26 Maňas, 'Náboženská bratrstva na Moravě' ['The Religious Fraternities in Moravia'], p. 52.

27 In 1597 the priest further complained that he was physically attacked by scribe Ondřej Slezinger during a feast. Although the bishop admonished people in Ostrava and urged them to be more pious during church services, observe holy days, and keep the fast days, as well as demanding that the scribe Slezinger be disciplined, he also admonished the priest for wandering and attending feasts and cautioned him instead to stay at home and fulfil his duties. The owner of Polish Ostrava, Jiří Sedlnický z Choltic, also complained about the priest for, allegedly, publicly offending his wife. The investigation of the incident revealed that the priest's offending words were in response to Ms. Sedlnická's words that he belonged in the pillory and on the gallows. The story may seem banal; however, it demonstrates resistance on the part of Ostrava burghers and a tension in town society during the period of forceful recatholization executed by the Olomouc bishopric. See Adamus, *Dějiny města Ostravy v přehledu až do r. 1860* [*History of Moravian Ostrava up to 1860*], p. 33.

28 It is unclear what exactly happened in the parish. It probably concerned the overt drinking of a chaplain from Mohelnice whose name we are not familiar with. The chaplain was severely disciplined by the bishop. Adamus, *Dějiny města Ostravy v přehledu až do r. 1860* [*History of Moravian Ostrava up to 1860*], p. 33.

29 The paintings were uncovered in 1966 and began to weather soon after. This becomes evident from O. Pechová's letter (from the State Institute of Heritage and Nature Preservation in Prague) addressed to the National Heritage Institute in Ostrava dated 30. 6. 1977, no. 4310/77. The findings were published by Hlubinka in, 'Významné objevy' ['Important Discoveries'], pp. 365–78. The interior of the church was painted with a narrative Christological cycle of unknown extent that included a Passion cycle. Only two monumental scenes remained. These are located in the southern nave of the church and depict the Adoration of the Magi and their companions (scene on the south wall of the nave) and a fragment of Christ before Pilate. The poor and fragmentary appearance of the paintings does not allow for a thorough formal and iconographic analysis, and only very general and hypothetical observations can be made. The stylistic character of the paintings suggests artistic affinity to Germany (Saxony) and Silesia. For the Ostrava paintings and history of their uncovering and restoration, also revealing the careless attitude towards preservation in socialist times, see Rywiková, *Renesanční nástěnné* [*Renaissance Mural Paintings*],

preserved in the presbytery while an extensive Christological cycle is situated in the southern nave of the church, even though only the monumental scene depicting the Adoration of the Magi survives. Its composition obviously draws on graphic templates produced in contemporary German workshops, specifically the Hans Süss Kulmbach workshop — as is visible today.[30] Only one scene from the assumed decoration is preserved in the northern nave. The front wall of the northern nave under the vault is filled with ornamental decor under which, separated by a moulding, is situated a relatively well-preserved monumental allegorical image composed of several scenes.

The painting is dominated by a monumental figure of Moses holding the Tables of the Law, showing the verses from the Decalogue:

> [UNUM | C]R[E] | D[E] | DEUM | NEC | VANE | IURES | PER ° I || [PSUM SABBATA] | SAN | CTIF | [I]CES ° | HAB[E] | AS | [IN HONORE PARENTES][31]

Situated on Moses's right side is the Mouth of Leviathan with two visible figures inside — a human soul and a devil pulling it into Hell. On the left side a plate with a Latin inscription quoting I Corinthians 15. 55–57 is still visible; it can be reconstructed as follows:

> UBI TU(U)S MORS ACULEUS UBI | TU[A] INFE[R]N[E] [VICTO] RIA ° ACU | [LEUS AU]TE(M) ° MORTIS [PECCATUM] ° PO | [TENT]IA VERO [PECCAT]I LE[X SED] | DE[O G]R[AT]IA QUI DEDIT NO[BIS] | VICTORIAM P(ER) DOMINU(M) NOS[TRUM] | [I]ESUM XRISTU(M) [---].[32]

---

pp. 6–10; Dědková, *Významné nálezy* [*Important Discovery*]; Indra, 'Ostravští malíři' ['Ostrava Painters']), p. 387; Dědková, 'Kostel sv. Václava v Ostravě' ['St Wenceslas's Church in Ostrava'], p. 80; Dědková, 'Torzo souboru maleb' ['Torso of Mural Paintings'], cat. no. 337, p. 428.

30 This is clear from a comparison of the Ostrava composition with Kulmbach's Adoration from 1511, which shows an identical composition of the front plan, as well as of details of the figures (location of the lower limbs, hand gestures, etc.). Berlin, Gemäldegalerie, inv. no.: VD 2056. Koelitz, Hans Suess.

31 I thank Jan Dienstbier for deciphering this and the inscription cited below. Both are yet unpublished. I am quoting both according to his transcription: 'Unum crede deum, nec vana iures per ipsum; sabbata santifices, habeas in honore parentes' (Believe in one God, do not swear by him in vain. Keep the Sabbath holy, honour your parents.). These are the beginning of catechetic verses summarizing the Decalogue used in medieval pastoral education. They continue as follows: 'Non sis occisor, fur, mechus testis iniquus. Vicinique thorum resque caueto suas.' Altogether: 'Believe in one God, do not swear by him in vain. Keep the Sabbath holy, and honour your parents. Do not be a killer, thief, adulterer, or false witness. Beware of your neighbour's spouse and goods.' *Handbook for Curates*, trans. by Thayer, p. 305.

32 'Ubi est mors victoria tua? Ubi est mors stimulus tuus? Stimulus autem mortis peccatum est; virtus vero peccati lex. Deo autem gratias, qui dedit nobis victoria per Dominum nostrum Jesum Christum.' (O death, where is thy sting? O grave, where is thy victory? The sting of death is sin; and the strength of sin is the law. But thanks be to God, which giveth us the victory through our Lord Jesus Christ). The missing end of the text was probably a reference to the relevant biblical verses from Paul.

A dead human body is depicted above the plate, and visible only in contours is the Lamb of God with a banner symbolizing victory over death and commenting on Paul's verses.

The trunk of the Tree of Life is situated above Moses, apostrophized by plant decor above the painting. A relatively well-preserved scene of the lifting up of the brazen serpent in the desert, traditionally understood to be a typological prototype of the crucified Christ, is situated on his right side.[33]

Another figure carrying a vessel filled with manna is visible further left. This is part of the scene of the raining down of manna that continues on the side wall with a tent with a sitting male figure gathering manna. Like the previous scene, this was interpreted by biblical expositors as the Old Testament archetype of the Lord's Supper, which is also visually accentuated in the Ostrava composition, where the shape of the manna decidedly reminds the onlooker of the host.[34] A further fragment of another of Moses's miracles is visible on the opposite side of the lifting up of the serpent — the gushing of water from the rock that Moses struck with his rod.[35]

Christ the Judge, seated on the rainbow and globe with a sword and a lily at his mouth, is painted in the upper right corner next to the crown of the Tree of Life. Underneath him is situated a now barely legible scene of Moses striking the water from the rock. Incomplete inscriptions in the upper part of the image frame refer to the miracles of Moses depicted below: the lifting up of the brazen serpent and the gushing of the water from the rock, and, as they are incomplete, we might speculate that there was also one, now missing, referring to the raining down of manna. It is intriguing that, whereas the first inscription referring to the lifting up of the brazen serpent is a verbatim quotation of the biblical verse, the second is only a loose paraphrase of it:

> SICUT ° MOGIZES ° EX[A]LTA[VIT ° SERP]ENTEM ° IN ° DESERTO ° | ITA ° EXALTARI ° OPORT[ET ° FILIU]M ° HOMINIS °[36]

> EDVXIT ° IVDEIS ° M[OG]I[ZES PET]RA | ASICA ° AQUAM °[37]

---

33 John 3. 14–15, 'And as Moses lifted up the serpent in the wilderness, even so must the Son of man be lifted up'.

34 John 6. 49–51, 'Your fathers did eat manna in the wilderness, and are dead. This is the bread which cometh down from heaven, that a man may eat thereof, and not die. I am the living bread, which came down from heaven: if any man eat of this bread, he shall live for ever: and the bread that I will give is my flesh, which I will give for the life of the world'.

35 Exodus 17.6, 'en ego stabo coram te ibi super petram Horeb percutiesque petram et exibit ex ea aqua ut bibat populus fecit Moses ita coram senibus Israhel' (I will stand before thee there upon the rock in Horeb and thou shalt smite the rock, and there shall come water out of it, that people may drink. And Moses did so in the sight of the elders of Israel).

36 John 3.14, 'Sicut Moses exaltavit serpentem in deserto, ita exaltari oportet filium hominis' (And as Moses lifted up the serpent in the wilderness, even so must the Son of man be lifted up). Inscription cited by Hlubinka, 'Významné objevy' [Important Discoveries], p. 369.

37 The inscription is cited according to Hlubinka, 'Významné objevy' ['Important Discoveries'], p. 369.

side wall **front wall**

Composition Scheme of the Ostrava Allegory: 1. Moses 2. Christ the Judge (Last Judgement) 3. Virgin Mary with the infant Jesus 4. Tree of Life 5. The Brazen Serpent 6. Lamb of God 7. John the Baptist with a sinner 8. Hell – Mouth of Leviathan 9. Raining down of manna 10. Original Sin – Adam and Eve 11. The gushing of the water from the rock. Drawing by Nela Parmová.

The Virgin Mary, holding the infant Jesus in the image in the upper left corner, represents the compositional counterpart of the Last Judgement. Visible underneath are standing figures of Adam and Eve at the scene of the Original Sin. The first plan on the sidewall part of the composition shows two male figures — a fully-bearded John the Baptist in a brown cape accompanying a naked man with hands in a gesture of prayer and the fragment of 'blood line' stretching around the vessel with manna and extending possibly as far as the front wall (to the Tree of Life image?), and falling down on him.

For easier orientation around the complex composition of the painting, it is useful to summarize it following the partial scenes from left to right:

First Plan: John the Baptist with a believer — Lamb of God and a cadaver — Moses — Hell

Second Plan: Original Sin — The gathering of manna — The lifting of the brazen serpent — The gushing of the water from the rock

Third Plan: Virgin Mary with the infant Jesus — Tree of Life — Christ the Judge

Previous scholarship wrongly identified this Ostrava painting described above as a well-known Lutheran theme composed by Lucas Cranach the Elder — the allegory of the Law and the Gospel.[38] At first glance, the Ostrava composition really appears to be an example of the famous dogmatic image (Dogmenbild). However, there are iconographic differences that challenge the ideological and doctrinal concept of a Lutheran motif. The Ostrava image composition is based on different doctrinal principles, and, as I will demonstrate, it does not clearly express the cardinal Lutheran idea of the Law and the Gospel — iustificatio sola fide — the justification of the Christian by faith alone and the antithesis between the Old (sub lege) and the New Testament (sub gratia).

The essential visual difference between the Ostrava painting and the Law and Gospel is that the former lacks an antithetical division into two halves, sub lege and sub gratia, and, in particular, its more or less syncretic character combines individual scenes in the manner of a 'jigsaw puzzle' lacking a deliberate dogmatic theme or a message proclaiming confessional affiliation.

Although the Tree of Life forms, as is the case with Cranach's models, both the visual and the semantic axis, the depiction of the tree lacks the ideological meaning essential in the depictions of this motif: that is, the withering part of the crown of the tree on the Old Testament side symbolizing damnation, and the green part on the Gospel (New Testament) side expressing salvation and eternal life through Christ's sacrifice.[39] The crown of the tree in the Ostrava painting is green on both sides — even on the side depicting Hell as the symbol of damnation.

Another motif that raises questions about the meaning of the entire painting is the centrally positioned and visually dominating figure of Moses.

---

38 The composition was identified as the Law and Gospel by Libuše Dědková: Dědková, 'Kostel sv. Václava v Ostravě' ['St Wenceslas's Church in Ostrava'], p. 80; Dědková, 'Torzo souboru maleb' ['Torso of Mural Paintings'], p. 428; and questioned by Rywiková, *Renesanční nástěnné* [*Renaissance Mural Paintings*], pp. 66–72; Royt, 'The Allegory', p. 255; and Přidalová, 'The Wall Painting', pp. 175–82.

39 The following are selected essential scholarship and reference works from the extensive body of literature on the subject of the Law and Gospel in Bohemian art and Central European iconography: Lilienfein, *Lucas Cranach*; Thulin, *Cranach – Altäre*; Christensen, *Art and Reformation*, pp. 124–30; Hintzenstern, *Lucas Cranach*; Koepplin, 'Kommet her zu mir alle', pp. 75–96; *Martin Luther*, ed. by Löcher, pp. 398–99; Scribner, *For the Sake of Simple Folk*, pp. 216–17; Grossmann, 'A Religious Allegory', pp. 491–94; Schiller, *Iconography*, pp. 161–64; Steinborn, 'Malowane epitafia mieszczańskie' ['Burgher Painted Epitaphs'], pp. 7–138; Harasimowicz, 'Typy i programy śląskich ołtarzy' ['Types and Programmes of Silesian Altarpieces'], pp. 7–27; Harasimowicz, *Treści i funkcje* [*The Content and Ideological Functions*], pp. 40–46; Harasimowicz, *Mors janua vitae*, pp. 133–37; Michalski, *Protestanci a sztuka* [*Protestants and Art*], pp. 19–22; Hrubý and Royt, 'Nástěnná malba s námětem Zákon a milost' ['The Law and Gospel Mural Painting'], pp. 124–37; Schulze, *Lucas Cranach*, pp. 11–22; Royt, 'The Allegory'; Royt, 'Grafický list s luteránským námětem Zákona a milosti' ['The Engraving with the Lutheran Motif of the Allegory of Law and Mercy'], pp. 45–62; Noble, *Lucas Cranach*, pp. 27–66.

He stands alone and, in contrast to the Law and Gospel models, there is missing a figure of the sinner deciding between the Law, represented by Moses, and Christ's mercy. In the Cranach models Moses is often joined by the figure of John the Baptist, who guides the sinner and represents Moses's ideological 'rival' encouraging the Christian to accept Christ's sacrifice and mercy.[40] In the first plan of the painting's sidewall part we can certainly see, albeit not completely clearly, two male figures of the faithful and John the Baptist, as presented in one of two Cranach's versions of the Law and Gospel from 1529 — the Gotha version.[41] In Ostrava, however, the scene with John the Baptist and the believer is depicted on the sidewall and not directly next to Moses as in the Gotha painting or in the Prague composition of the same theme (1529), where the believer is seated under the Tree of Life and both Moses and John the Baptist are pointing at the crucified Christ and the Lamb of God. In both iconographic prototypes of the Law and Gospel, John the Baptist points at Christ, his right hand bent at the elbow. The Gotha prototype of the Law and Gospel served as the iconographic model for this motif in the Ostrava painting, where it is positioned as a visually distant counterpart of Moses. However, this is only visible if we look at the painting diagonally from the nave, in other words from the space occupied by the laypeople during the Mass and sermons. Whoever conceived the Ostrava allegory probably adjusted the composition to the fact that the scene needed to be for some reason divided over the corner into two adjacent church walls, obscuring the 'reading' of the scene if looking at it stationary and en face.

The Ostrava painting also incorporates scenes that do not appear in the 'conventional' depictions of the Law and Gospel. In the first plan, on Moses's right side, we would expect a scene of the resurrected Christ and the Lamb of God as the symbols of Christ's victory and a defeated Devil and death. However, the Ostrava painting instead depicts Hell in the form of Leviathan's mouth embracing the human soul. In Cranach's compositions of the Law and the Gospel, Hell, represented by flames, is always placed on the Old Testament side. The Ostrava allegory completely omits the resurrected Christ scene, leaving only the victorious Lamb of God. We would expect the Lamb to be placed underneath the Crucifixion: this, however, is also missing in the Ostrava composition and, moreover, it is visually and semantically substituted by the typological scene of the Lifting of the brazen serpent.

40 Martin Luther described John the Baptist as 'der Finger und der Zeiger des Messias' (the finger and the pointer of Messiah). Schulze, *Lucas Cranach*, p. 12.

41 According to the oldest painting with the image of Law and Gospel originating from the castle of Gotha. The second compositional model is the so-called Prague type. Gotha panel: Gotha, Stiftung Schloss Friedenstein, oil on wood, 71.9 × 59.6 cm, inv. no. FR221. Prague panel: Prague, National Gallery, linden wood, 72 × 88.5 cm, inv. no. O 10732. For a recent study on the subject, see Kotková, 'Lucas Cranach st. Zákon a milost, 1529' ['Lucas Cranach the Elder: Law and Gospel, 1529'], pp. 74–78.

The compositional location of the Last Judgement in the Ostrava allegory is rather unusual. The Last Judgement, depicted here as Christ the Judge sitting on a globe, is represented only in the Gotha type, where it is always placed on the left side, above the scene of the Original Sin. In Ostrava, it is placed in the upper right corner of the painting as a compositional counterpart to the standing Madonna with the infant Jesus.

Again, the compositional counterpart is only visible if we perceive the painting on both walls of the nave as a whole. Whoever conceived the Ostrava painting, however, switched both scenes (Last Judgement and Mary with Jesus), so that Christ the Judge was visually moved above the scene of Hell, thus creating part of the traditional narrative depiction of the Last Judgement placing Christ above Heaven and Hell. The Virgin Mary, depicted above the scene of the Original Sin, can be understood as the 'second Eve' who redeems people from sin through her son. Both semantic, vertical pairs (Virgin Mary — Original Sin versus Christ the Judge — Hell) simultaneously form a logical, eschatological framework of the image and human history: its beginnings in Paradise, Original Sin — the 'birth' of sin and death; and the Last Judgement — the end of history, sin, and Death that is, in an eschatological sense, with eternal damnation in Hell or eternal life by the grace of Christ.

The painting shows more pairs that are similarly symbolic: these, I would suggest, are key to understanding the allegory and its function. It is an antithetical image iconographically based on the Protestant Law of the Gospel, but it utilizes its soteriological motifs in a completely different way.

The scene of the lifting of the brazen serpent is such an example. It represents a popular, independent, and relatively frequent motif in Protestant art that appears both in the Law and Gospel and as a stand-alone scene.[42] According to Martin Luther, gazing at the brazen serpent represents faith itself — faith that vindicates and leads to salvation[43] and visually expresses the essential Lutheran thesis of iustificatio sola fide.

The lifting of the brazen serpent in the Ostrava allegory probably totally substitutes for the Crucifixion, as it is unusually placed between two Old Testament scenes anticipating the sacrament of Eucharist (the gathering of manna and the gushing of the water from the rock). We can consider them to be an original 'contribution' or innovation upon the original Law and Gospel by whoever conceived the Ostravian painting. Both scenes are not positioned next to each other, symbolically representing both kinds of the holy sacrament. Their sacramental and possibly Utraquist symbolism is presented contextually as an interpretative possibility, suggested only through

42 In Bohemian art it is exemplified by the panel painted by a Bohemian follower of Lucas Cranach the Elder, Master IW, from 1550. Ústí nad Labem, Národní památkový ústav (National Heritage Institute), inv. no. MO 2. Hamsíková, 'Mistr IW / dílna. Kovový had, kolem 1550' ['Master IW / Workshop. Brazen Serpent, around 1550'], p. 144.

43 Steinborn, 'Malowane epitafia mieszczańskie' ['Burgher Painted Epitaphs'], p. 24.

the manna and water gushing from the rock. In the same way, the brazen serpent symbolically refers to Christ crucified and his body as the source of all sacraments. By incorporating both scenes into the Ostrava composition, its originator surely intended to strengthen the sacramental symbolism of an allegory that would possibly be acceptable to Catholics, Protestants, and Utraquists alike.

Potentially more problematic for Protestants was the traditional motif of the double composition of the Man of Sorrows and the Sorrowful Mother placed directly under the allegory and therefore impossible to be viewed separately. This composition expresses the traditional soteriological idea of Christ completing his messianic task with the participation of his mother, expressed by the compassionate pain she shares with her son (compassio).[44] Engelbertus of Admont was among the first theologians in the first half of the fourteenth century to describe Mary as 'the partaker of the passion', since, as he argued, she was the only one who did not leave Christ in the moment of his greatest suffering and did not turn away from him like his disciples.[45] Martin Luther, contrary to most Bohemian Utraquists, rejected the aforementioned speculative aspects of Marian devotion, including their articulation in art.[46] For him, the essential principle was sola scriptura: iconography ought to reflect the biblical text and art ought to illustrate the Word, leading the believer to the meaning of Scripture and to faith (sola fide) in the absolute and exclusive sacrifice and mercy (sola gratia) of Christ, as expressed by the premise of solus Christus.

We need to acknowledge, however, that theological knowledge of the ordinary sixteenth-century Ostrava believer probably would not exceed a basic knowledge of the Creed, the Lord's Prayer, Ave Maria, and Ten Commandments, and therefore that he or she would not likely be able to differentiate between the theological subtleties reflected by the allegory. I believe that the strong (and the only obvious) Catholic motif accompanying

---

44 Carol, *De corredemptione*; Schiller, *Iconography*, pp. 225–26; Dobrzeniecki, 'Gotycki obraz z Olbierzowic' ['Gothic painting from Olbierzowice'], p. 41.

45 Engelberti Abbatis Admontensis Ord. S. Ben. Tractatus de Gratis et Virtutes Beatae Mariae Virginis, Caput XXXIII: 'Stabat igitur ut fixa in fide [...] existens individua socia passionis'. (Stands constant in faith [...] person indivisibly participating in the passion). Thesaurus Anecdotorum Novissimus, col. 556.

46 Martin Luther honoured the Virgin Mary; nevertheless, he denied any suggestion that she is a mediatrix or coredemptrix. However, he did not disapprove of the image of Virgin Mary (he was known to have a painting of her in his study), as long as it did not serve for worship. In other words, Mary is not understood as a helper or advocate. For Luther's theological views on the Virgin Mary, see Kreitzer, *Reforming Mary*, pp. 6–11. For the development of Martin Luther's ideas on images and his polemics with the German iconoclasts and followers of Thomas Munzer, see Michalski, *Protestanci a sztuka* [*Protestants and Art*], pp. 30–55; *Representing Religious Pluralization in Early Modern Europe*, ed. by Höfele, Laqué, and Ruge; Wenzel, 'Konfese a chrámová' [Confession and Church Architecture], pp. 31–103; Noble, *Lucas Cranach*, pp. 33–34.

the Ostrava allegory could also represent a 'confessionally appropriate' sign that would allow local Catholics to proclaim and explain the entire allegory as 'Catholic', when this might be needed, for example, during the canonical visitations by the owners and patrons of the Moravian Ostrava parish, the bishops of Olomouc. On the other hand, the Virgin Mary compassio motif did not prevent Protestant believers expressing their own faith and devotion. The painting caters for a 'catechetic minimum' and an ethical outlook common to all Christian confessional communities in mid-sixteenth-century Ostrava. This, together with the pastoral and homiletic potential of the image, substantially determined its composition and an iconography that succeeded in establishing a compromise of 'supra-confessional' communication between all Christians who attended the Masses and sermons in St Wenceslas's Church.

Conclusion: Confessional Identity and Artistic Innovation

I suggest that the author of the allegory, possibly the Ostrava priest Jan Gitorius or maybe even one of the educated canons of the Olomouc chapter, intended to create a painting that would communicate across confessional divides. In addition, the iconographic analysis of the painting demonstrates that its composition may well be a syncretic assemblage, with a logical and ideologically meaningful framework. This framework, however, is not a specific confessionally deterministic dogmatic motif or narrative, but rather a 'jigsaw puzzle' of individual motifs distilled both from the Law and Gospel and earlier medieval typological allegories of Crucifixion, sin, and salvation.[47] It incorporates commonplaces of all Christian confessions, following, as it does, the Ten Commandments, a belief not only in the sacrifice of Christ for the purposes of salvation but also in the power of the Sacraments, to which may be added fear of the Last Judgement, Hell, and eternal damnation. All this is

47 Listed below are selected works from the extensive literature dealing with religious confessionality as an art historical category (including the so called 'confessional style') and simultaneously part of a larger sociocultural context of the European Reformation: *In puncto religionis*, ed. by Horníčková and Šroněk; Horníčková, 'Konfesionalita díla' ['Confessionality of Artwork'], pp. 9–20; Bartlová, 'Renesance a reformace v českých dějinách umění' ['Renaissance and Reformation in Czech Art History'], pp. 23–48; Harasimowicz, 'Sztuka jako medium nowożytnych konfesjonalizacji' ['Art as the Medium of Early Modern Confessionalization'], pp. 51–76; Jakubec and Malý, 'Konfesijnost' ['Denominationality'], pp. 79–112; Deventer, 'Confessionalisation', pp. 403–25; Wetter, *Formierungen des konfessionellen*; Wegmann and Wimböck, *Konfessionen im Kirchenraum*; Wenzel, 'Konfese a chrámová architektura' ['Confession and Church Architecture'], pp. 31–103; Malý, Smrt a spása [Death and Salvation]; Backus, *Historical Method*; *Proměny konfesijní kultury* [*Transformations of Confessional Culture*], ed. by Ferencová, Chmelařová, Kohoutová, and Prchal Pavlíčková, pp. 9–20; Jakubec, *Kde jest, ó smrti, osten tvůj?* [*Where, O Death, is Your Sting?*], esp. pp. 235–52, dedicated to an epitaph as 'confessional object'.

articulated through confessionally neutral accompanying texts paraphrasing biblical verses in the manner of contemporary pastoral manuals.

In fact, the only motif exclusively tied to Cranach's dogmatic image of the Law and Gospel is the figure of the faithful accompanied by John the Baptist and (in the Prague prototype case) Moses. As Martina Kratochvílová has shown, similar reception of the individual motifs based on the new Protestant iconography can be seen in the Czech lands in sixteenth-century Utraquist hymn books: these depict an interesting 'distillation' and subsequent semantic transformation of these motifs from the complex composition of the Law and Gospel with reference to the liturgical classification of the borrowed motif.[48] Perhaps the general motif of the Law and Gospel could have worked in a similar way. Such an idea may be supported by the presence of this motif in the wall painting (*c.* 1590) of the cloister of the Dominican monastery in České Budějovice, an exclusively Catholic space.[49]

The Ostrava allegory is not a chaotic representation of the Law and Gospel, but rather an innovative assemblage of its motifs that could have been used universally in pastoral education and homiletics. However, it was more than a form of preaching illustration; it was, rather, a visual, rhetorical, and hermeneutic framework opening up layers of the biblical text and its exegesis. Important new interpretative perspectives could be freed by placing the individual biblical events into new contexts that enabled a sort of 'supra-confessional' approach to both the individual scenes as well as to the imagery as a whole. The principles of the recontextualisability of the individual allegorical scenes provide a key to the function of the imagery in Ostrava Church amongst local Christian communities. The painting also illustrates the pastoral strategy used by the priest of Ostrava or even by the episcopate itself — although we may question how far it really made an impact on the peripheral regions of its dominion. This is well illustrated by the Bishop of Olomouc Marek Khuen's words addressed to the Holy Roman Emperor Ferdinand I, complaining about the poor state of Catholicism and Catholic priests in mid-sixteenth-century Moravia:

> Jest na větším díle takových zmatených a ženatých kněží v tom markrabství Moravském [...] někteří luteriáni, cvingliáni, jiní o mšech sv. nic nedrží žádných ceremonií a svátostí v kostelích nezachovávají než každý káže, puosobí, jak se jemu aneb pánu jeho dobře líbí a takoví všickni se zastírají spuosobem sub utraque [...] Protož nebude-li se vlastní osobů vaší Císařské

48 Kratochvílová, 'Recepce a transformace protestantské ikonografie' ['Reception and Transformation of Protestant Iconography'], p. 456.

49 The painting represents an epitaph. This situation testifies either to a 'liberal' attitude of the Catholics to this Protestant motif or more likely the fact that it did not need to be perceived necessarily as theologically controversial or confessionally identifying. On the painting, however, without reference to its confessional identity, see Royt, 'The Allegory', p. 255.

> Milosti v tomto markrabství takového bludu v kněžství přetržení, skrze osobu mů to se přetrhnúti nemuože.[50]
>
> > (There is a larger proportion of confused and married priests in the Margraviate of Moravia [...] some of them are Lutherans, Zwinglians and others; they do not observe any ceremonies during the Holy Mass, and the Sacraments they do not serve, yet everyone preaches and acts as it suits him and his lord; all of them hide themselves behind the sub utraque [...] Therefore if Your Majesty will not be able to break off such a fallacy of priesthood in this Margraviate, through my person this cannot be stopped.)

The financial difficulties of Moravian monasteries and the Olomouc diocese, the generally poor state of Church organization, weak discipline, and the frequently inadequate theological knowledge of the Catholic clergy, together with the growing ambitions of the Moravian nobility for confessional 'independence', limited the bishop's power to intervene in political and religious affairs and to launch the process of the Catholic Counter-Reformation, as customarily documented in Central Europe during the latter half of the sixteenth century.[51] All this led, beside other issues, to a growing confusion about theological doctrines among the ordinary believers as well as among the lower clergy. In addition, the Moravian Estates of the realm actively strove for general religious freedom for all confessions and believers.[52]

Paradoxically, the situation described above could have contributed to a more positive atmosphere around questions regarding Christian orthodoxy and even to a degree of permissiveness and 'tolerance' towards other confessions. In the case of the fine arts, it left room for a 'grey zone', in which images of a supra-confessional and non-conflictual character might operate and even thrive.[53] They did not often, in the sacred environment, demonstrate the confessional identity of their commissioners, audience, or priest; moreover, they could only have been perceived and understood in terms of their dependence on each occasion of use within a particular and shifting context and environment. In Moravian religious practice, the bishops of Olomouc had officially to tolerate Utraquism as per the Basel Compacts; they focused instead on suppressing non-official confessions or those regarded as heretics (such as the Unity of Brethren, for example), and in particular on the activities of Lutheran preachers who often acted under the guise of tolerated Utraquism.

The unfavourable situation of the Moravian Catholic Church began to improve only due to more intense interventions by the bishops of Olomouc

---

50 Jakubec, *Kulturní prostředí a mecenát* [*The Culture and Artistic Patronage*], p. 45.

51 The bishops of Olomouc were among the most active promoters of the process of confessionalization in Moravia and exerted pressure mainly in the royal towns but also on their estates. Malý, '"Confessional Identity"', pp. 324–25.

52 Mezník, 'Tolerance na Moravě v 16. století' ['Tolerance in Sixteenth-Century Moravia'], p. 79.

53 Horníčková, 'Konfesionalita díla' ['Confessionality of Artwork'], p. 13.

after the mid-sixteenth century, and also due to the summoning of the Jesuit order to Moravia in 1566 and the foundation of the Jesuit College in Olomouc. Emperor Ferdinand I succeeded in getting Pope Pius IV to recognize access to the chalice for all lay inhabitants of the Habsburg lands in 1564, including Catholics. This strategy was intended to lead not only to lay conformity but also to control by the authorities of the Czech and Moravian Utraquist clergy, whose members were to be newly consecrated by the archbishop of Prague.[54]

A letter sent in 1571 by the Bishop of Olomouc, Vilém Prusinovský, to the Ostrava priest Jan Rokyta, provides important evidence that directly concerns the Moravian Ostrava parish and illustrates the religious situation described above, specifically the diocese's attempt to control the Utraquist structure in Moravia during the second half of the sixteenth century:

> Sobě nestejskej, lid ten vyučujíc, aby pro velikou vážnost té velebné svátosti k tomu hodně a slušně vnitř i zevnitř připravovali, muži brady, aby tady skrz omočení fúsů irreventia sacrosanti sacramenti se nezačala, holiti, nýbrž s zkroušeným srdcem k tomu přistupujíc tak se na to, jakž před tváří Boží atd. náleží, chovali [...] aby jinak nesmejšleli než podle vyměření koncilu tridentského, kdo pod obojí způsobů tu velebnou svátost přijímá více jako ten, kdo pod jednou béře, nepřijímá, aby v tom jedni druhých nepotupovali, myslíc na to, aby pro takové nebezpečenství, poněvadž obé jedno a tak mnoho jedno jako druhé jest, raději pod jednou přijímali.[55]
>
> (Do not be sorrowful while instructing people on the great importance of the Blessed Sacrament [...] Men should not shave out of great

54 This happened through the papal brief of 16 April 1564. Other than denomination, the only condition was to confess that Christ is present in both parts of the Eucharist and that the Catholic Church did not stray when establishing communion under one kind for laypeople and priests. The brief was ceremoniously read in St Vitus's Cathedral on 23 July 1564 and was also delivered to the bishop of Olomouc, including practical instructions on performing the sub utraque rite. For more on the Council's proceedings and negotiations on allowing the lay chalice, see Kavka and Skýbalová, *Husitský epilog na koncilu tridentském* [*The Hussite Epilogue at the Council of Trent*], pp. 154–57.

55 Quoted by Adamus, *Dějiny města Ostravy v přehledu až do r. 1860* [*History of Moravian Ostrava up to 1860*], pp. 28–29. The implications of the papal concession of the lay chalice for Moravia are well summarized by Ondřej Jakubec: 'Ve snaze o konsolidaci náboženských poměrů na Moravě se, jako pražský arcibiskup Antonín Brus v Čechách, přikláněl k možnosti vyřešit situaci zavedením papežské koncese, povolující přijímat sub utraque, která měla podle jejich nadějí sjednotit utrakvisty s katolíky. Toto úsilí bylo také projevem snahy biskupů podřídit si moravské podobojí. Podobně jako i v Čechách se vyhlášení koncese setkalo s odmítnutím již většinou protestantské populace' (Attempting to consolidate religious affairs in Moravia, the archbishop of Prague, Antonín Brus, leaned in Bohemia toward the possibility of solving the situation by establishing a papal concession allowing communion sub utraque. This was also an expression of the bishop's attempt to subdue Moravian communion under both kinds. As in Bohemia, the proclamation of the concession was met with rejection from the already mainly Protestant-affiliated population). Jakubec, *Kulturní prostředí a mecenát* [*The Culture and Artistic Patronage*], p. 44.

reverence for the Blessed Sacrament, fearing to wet their beard, but receive it with a crestfallen/contrite heart before of the Face of God [...] they should not question the Council of Trent's orders. Those who receive the Blessed Sacrament sub utraque specie should not chide those who receive sub una specie, as both ways are as one and equal. They should also consider that, rather than risk a danger [of conflict – D.R.], it is better to receive the Blessed Sacrament under one kind.)

Such a religious situation reveals the significance of the Ostrava composition. At the same time, it exemplifies the difficulty for modern scholars of interpreting religious images in the context of the dynamic religious and social transformations that Central Europe and other regions experienced during the sixteenth century.[56] Is it possible that the Ostrava painting reflects and promotes the diocese's earlier attempts to 'conquer' the Utraquist structures in the town as suggested above? Was it a visual tool or at least a manifestation of the Catholic attempt to gain control peacefully over the public space of Ostrava Church? Is the painting evidence of an artistic 'grey zone' reflecting a measure of liberal, supra-confessional approach, and religious tolerance? These are difficult questions to answer, but it is evident that the painting's final, theologically non-conflicting iconography illustrates relatively precisely Bishop Prusinovský's later reconciliatory words fearing and preventing possible religious conflict and in practice making equal Holy Communion both sub utraque and sub una.

The Ostrava allegory was able to communicate with the individual believer as well as with a whole Christian community within the terms of generally valid values, Christian ethics, and a shared identity and culture.[57] Whoever designed the painting strove, like the bishop, for reconciliation and the preservation of cohesion among the various Christian denominations living side by side in a small town. The Ostrava painting illustrates a sort of umbrella-like Christian 'supra-identity',[58] with a common basis in the interpretation of Holy Scripture, Christian morality defined by the Ten Commandments, and pastoral care as practised across three Christian denominations by a single Catholic priest.

In a sense, it is actually pointless to inquire after the confessional affinity or affiliation of the Ostrava allegory, since its interpretation and the correct understanding of its historical functions necessarily derive from multiple

---

56 Kateřina Horníčková summarizes this well: 'Svébytnost náboženského obrazu 15.–16. století vyrůstá z trojího základu: 1. Z imaginace vycházející ze společného křesťanského obsahu, 2. z vyjadřovací specifičnosti obrazového jazyka, 3. z kulturně-historické výpovědi ve vztahu k lokální situaci.' (The distinctiveness of the fifteenth- and sixteenth-century religious image stems from a threefold basis: 1. Imagination deriving from a common Christian content, 2. Expressive specifics of the visual language, and 3. Cultural-historical testimony relating to the local situation). Horníčková, 'Konfesionalita díla' ['Confessionality of Artwork'], p. 13.

57 Horníčková, 'Konfesionalita díla' ['Confessionality of Artwork'], p. 18.

58 Horníčková, 'Konfesionalita díla' ['Confessionality of Artwork'], p. 18.

contexts, including the time and place of origin, the audience, and the expansive contours of the period's cultural and religious interconnections. It illustrates a new strategy of commissioners and artists towards the traditional as well as towards new themes created by Protestant theologians. It helps us to understand better (though not completely) the migration of Protestant visual subjects and the possible reasons for their original, innovative transformations as well as for their re-use in specific religious contexts. This opened up new possibilities of 'reading' and using such images in religious practice across the Christian denominations through their iconographic demontage, compositional assemblage, and re-contextualization.[59] To put it simply: the iconographic transformation of the imagery (in our case the Law and Gospel) reflects a semantic, utilitarian and generally contextual transformation that is above and beyond the period's confessional controversies at the same time as reflecting and responding to them.

The Ostrava allegory is a precious illustration of such a case. It is a unique witness of multi-confessional coexistence and religious 'tolerance out of necessity' in sixteenth-century Moravia that was highly praised by contemporaries. The Moravian Margraviate hauptmann, Václav z Ludanic, described this best when he concluded his speech against Emperor Ferdinand I's attempt to curb religious freedom in Moravia at the 1550 Brno Diet: 'Moravia will sooner perish in fire and ashes than suffer from the forcing of faith'.[60]

Works Cited

Manuscripts and Archival Sources

Ostrava, Archiv města Ostravy, Fond Farní úřad Ostrava, Farní kronika Moravská Ostrava [Ostrava, The City Archive of Ostrava, The Ostrava Parish Office Fund, The Parish Chronicle Moravian Ostrava], inv. no. 6a

Primary Sources

Codex diplomaticus civitatis Ostraviae: Sbírka listin k dějinám Moravské Ostravy, ed. by Alois Adamus (Moravská Ostrava: Lidová knihtiskárna, 1929)

Engelberti Abbatis Admontensis Ord. S. Ben. Tractatus de Gratis et Virtutes Beatae Mariae Virginis, Caput XXXIII. Thesaurus Anecdotorum Novissimus. Veterum Monumentorum, praecipue Ecclesiasticorum, ex Germanicis potissimum Bibliothecis adornata Collectio recentissima. Tomus I, ed. by Bernhard Pez (Augsburg and Graz: n. pub, 1721)

---

59 Horníčková, 'Konfesionalita díla' ['Confessionality of Artwork'], p. 14.

60 'Dříve Morava v ohni a popeli zahyne, než aby trpěla nějakého u víře nucení'. Dvořák, *Dějiny Moravy* [*History of Moravia*], p. 422.

Handbook for Curates: A Late Medieval Manual on Pastoral Ministry. By Guido of Monte, trans. and ed. by Anne T. Thayer (Washington, DC: The Catholic University of America Press, 2011)

The Holy Bible, containing the Old and New Testaments (London: Cambridge University Press, 1921)

Vulgata. Biblia Sacra iuxta vulgatam versionem, Bible Gateway, 1969 <https://www.biblegateway.com/versions/Biblia-Sacra-Vulgata-VULGATE> [accessed 8 April 2017]

Secondary Studies

Adamus, Alois, *Dějiny města Ostravy v přehledu až do r. 1860* [*History of Moravian Ostrava up to 1860*] (Ostrava: Lidová knihtiskárna, 1927)

Atwood, Craig D., *The Theology of the Czech Brethren from Hus to Comenius* (University Park: Pennsylvania State University Press, 2004)

Backus, Irena, *Historical Method and Confessional Identity in the Era of the Reformation (1378–1615)* (Leiden: Brill, 2003)

Bakala, Jaroslav, 'Ostrava v období vrcholného středověku (do roku 1437)' ['Ostrava During the Period of the High Middle Ages (before 1437)'], in *Dějiny Ostravy*, ed. by Karel Jiřík (Ostrava: Sfinga, 1993), pp. 25–49

Barcuch, Antonín, 'Ostrava v letech 1437–1618' ['Ostrava between 1437 and 1618'], in *Ostrava: Historie, kultura, lidé, ed. by Blažena Przybylová* (Prague: Nakladatelství Lidové noviny, 2013), pp. 51–80

Bartlová, Milena, 'Renesance a reformace v českých dějinách umění: otázky periodizace a výkladu' ['Renaissance and Reformation in Czech Art History: Questions of Periodization and Interpretation'], in *In puncto religionis: Konfesní dimenze předbělohorské kultury Čech a Moravy*, ed. by Kateřina Horníčková and Michal Šroněk (Prague: Artefactum, 2013), pp. 23–48

Baumgarten, Jens, *Konfession, Bild und Macht: Visualisierung als katholisches Herrschafts- und Disziplinierungskonzept in Rom und im habsburgischen Schlesien (1560–1740)* (Hamburg: Dölling und Galitz, 2004)

Bechyně, Jan, 'Kompaktáta' ['The Compacts'], *Historický obzor*, 7 (1996), 37–40

Carol, Junipero B., *De corredemptione Beatae Virginis Mariae: Disquisitio Positiva* (Civitas Vaticana: Typ. Polygl. Vat., 1950)

Christensen, Carl C., *Art and Reformation in Germany* (Athens: Ohio University Press, 1979)

David, Zdeněk V., *Finding the Middle Way: The Utraquists' Liberal Challenge to Rome and Luther* (Washington DC: Woodrow Wilson Center Press and The Johns Hopkins University Press, 2003)

———, 'The Integrity of the Utraquist Church and the Problem of Neo-Utraquism', in *The Bohemian Reformation and Religious Practice. Vol. 5. Part 2, Papers from the Fifth International Symposium on The Bohemian Reformation and Religious Practice held at Vila Lanna, Prague 19–22 June 2002* (Prague: Akademie věd ČR, 2005), pp. 329–51

Dědková, Libuše, *Významné nálezy maleb v památkových objektech Severomoravského kraje: Příspěvek k 25letému trvání památkové péče v Severomoravském kraji* [*Important Discovery of Mural Paintings in Preserved Buildings in the Northern Moravian Region: The Contribution to 25 Years of Monument Care in Northern Moravia*] (Ostrava: Krajské středisko státní památkové péče a ochrany přírody v Ostravě, 1984)

———, 'Kostel sv. Václava v Ostravě – několik nových informací' ['St Wenceslas's Church's in Ostrava – Two New Items of Information'], in *Památkový ústav v Ostravě: Výroční zpráva 1997*, ed. by Jiří Gwuzd (Ostrava: Památkový ústav v Ostravě, 1998), pp. 80–81

———, 'Torzo souboru maleb' ['Torso of Mural Paintings'], in *Od gotiky k renesanci: Výtvarná kultura Moravy a Slezska 1400–1550. III. Olomoucko*, ed. by Ivo Hlobil (Olomouc: Muzeum umění Olomouc, 1999), cat. no. 337, pp. 428–29

Deventer, Jörg, 'Confessionalisation – a Useful Theoretical Concept for the Study of Religion, Politics, and Society in Early Modern East-Central Europe?', *European Review of History: Revue Européenne D'histoire*, 11 (2003), 403–25

Dobrzeniecki, Tadeusz, 'Gotycki obraz z Olbierzowic: Zagadnienia ikonografii i stylu' ['Gothic Painting of Olbierzowice: Iconography and Style'], *Biuletyn historii sztuki*, 31 (1969), 41–59

Dvořák, Rudolf, *Dějiny Moravy od nejstarších dob až do r. 1848, díl III. Země a lid* [*History of Moravia from the Earliest Period until 1848. Part III: The Country and People*] (Brno: Moravské akciové tiskárny, 1901)

From Hus to Luther: Visual Culture in the Bohemian Reformation (1380–1620), ed. by Kateřina Horníčková and Michal Šroněk (Turnhout: Brepols, 2017)

Grossmann, Fritz A., 'A Religious Allegory by Hans Holbein the Younger', *Burlington Magazine*, 103 (1961), 491–94

Halama, Ota, *Otázka svatých v české reformaci: Její proměny od doby Karla IV. do doby České konfese* [*The Question of Saints in Bohemian Reformation: Its Transformation from the Period of Charles IV to the Bohemian Confession*] (Prague: Nakladatelství L. Marek, 2001)

Hamsíková, 'Mistr IW / dílna: Kovový had, kolem 1550' ['Master IW / Workshop: Brazen Serpent, around 1550'], in *Lucas Cranach a české země: Pod znamením okřídleného hada*, ed. by Kaliopi Chamonicola (Prague: KANT – Karel Kerlický, 2005), pp. 144–45

Harasimowicz, Jan, 'Typy i programy śląskich ołtarzy wieku reformacji' ['Types and Programmes of Silesian Altarpieces from the Age of the Reformation'], *Roczniki sztuki śląskiej*, 12 (1979), 7–27

———, *Treści i funkcje ideowe sztuki śląskiej Reformacji 1520–1650* [*The Content and Ideological Functions of the Art of the Silesian Reformation 1520–1650*] (Wrocław: Wydawnictwo Uniwersytetu Wrocławskiego, 1986)

———, *Mors janua vitae: Śląskie epitafia, nagrobki wieku reformacji* [*Mors janua vitae: Silesian Epitaphs and Tombstones in the Age of the Reformation*] (Wrocław: Wydawnictwo Uniwersytetu Wrocławskiego, 1992)

———, 'Sztuka jako medium nowożytnych konfesjonalizacji' ['Art as the Medium of Early Modern Confessionalization'], in *Sztuka i dialog wyznan w XVI i XVII wieku*, ed. by Jan Harasimowicz (Warsaw: Stowarzyszenie Historyków Sztuki, 2000), pp. 51–76

———, *Schwärmergeist und Freiheitsdenken: Beiträge zur Kunst- und Kulturgeschichte Schlesiens in der frühen Neuzeit* (Cologne: Böhlau, 2010)

Hintzenstern, Herbert, *Lucas Cranach d. Ä.: Altarbilder aus der Reformationszeit* (Berlin: Evangelische Verlagsanstalt, 1975)

Hlubinka, Milan, 'Významné objevy při stavebně historickém průzkumu kostela sv. Václava v Ostravě' ['Important Discoveries During Surveying for Construction in St Wenceslas's Church in Ostrava'], *Ostrava: Sborník příspěvků k dějinám a výstavbě města*, 8 (1975), 365–78

Horníčková, Kateřina, 'Konfesionalita díla' ['Confessionality of Artwork'], in *In puncto religionis: Konfesní dimenze předbělohorské kultury Čech a Moravy*, ed. by Kateřina Horníčková and Michal Šroněk (Prague: Artefactum, 2013), pp. 9–20

Hrejsa, Ferdinand, 'Luterství, kalvinismus a podobojí na Moravě před Bílou horou' [Lutheranism, Calvinism and Utraquism in Moravia before the Battle of Bílá Hora], *Český časopis historický*, 44 (1938), 296–326, 474–85

Hrubý, Vladimír, and Jan Royt, 'Nástěnná malba s námětem Zákon a milost na zámku v Pardubicích' ['The Law and Gospel Mural Painting in the Pardubice Chateau'], *Umění*, 40 (1992), 124–37

Hrubý, František, 'Luterství a kalvinismus na Moravě před Bílou horou' ['Lutheranism and Calvinism in Moravia before the Battle of Bílá Hora'], *Český časopis historický*, 41 (1935), 1–40

In puncto religionis: Konfesní dimenze předbělohorské kultury Čech a Moravy [*In puncto religionis: The Confessional Dimensions of Culture in Bohemia and Moravia*], ed. by Kateřina Horníčková and Michal Šroněk (Prague: Artefactum, 2013)

Indra, Bohumír, 'Ostravští malíři od 16. do poloviny 19. století' ['Ostrava Painters from the Sixteenth to the mid-Nineteenth Century'], *Ostrava: Sborník příspěvků k dějinám a výstavbě města*, 10 (1979), 387–400

Jakubec, Ondřej, *Kulturní prostředí a mecenát olomouckých biskupů potridentské doby: Umělecké objednávky biskupů v letech 1533–1598, jejich význam a funkce* [*The Culture and Artistic Patronage of the Bishops of Olomouc in the Period after the Council of Trent: Bishops' Artistic Commissions, 1553–1598 and Their Meaning and Function*] (Olomouc: Univerzita Palackého v Olomouci, 2003)

———, *Kde jest, ó smrti, osten tvůj? Renesanční epitafy v kultuře umírání a vzpomínání raného novověku* [*Where, O Death, is Your Sting? Renaissance Epitaphs in the Early Modern Culture of Dying and Commemorating*] (Prague: Nakladatelství Lidové noviny, 2015)

Jakubec, Ondřej, and Tomáš Malý, 'Konfesijnost – (nad)konfesijnost – (bez) konfesijnost: Diskuse o renesančním epitafu a umění jako zdroji konfesijní identifikace' ['Denominationality – (Supra)-Denominationality – (Non)-Denominationality: On the Renaissance Epitaph and Art as a Source of Denominational Identification'], *Dějiny – teorie – kritika*, 1 (2010), 79–112

Jurok, Jiří, *Moravský severovýchod v epoše husitské revoluce: Poodří a Pobečví v husitském období v letech 1378–1471* [*Northeastern Moravia during the Hussite Revolution: The Odra and Bečva Regions during the Hussite Period between 1378 and 1471*] (Nový Jičín: J. Jurok, 1998)

———, *9. 7. 1609. Rudolfův majestát. Světla a stíny náboženské svobody* [*9. 7. 1609: The Letter of Majesty of Rudolf II: Lights and Shadows of Religious Freedom*] (Prague: Havran, 2009)

Kaufmann, Thomas DaCosta, *Court, Cloister and City: The Art and Culture of Central Europe 1450–1800* (Chicago: University of Chicago Press, 1995)

Kavka, František, and Anna Skýbová, *Husitský epilog na koncilu tridentském a původní koncepce habsburské rekatolizace Čech: Počátky obnoveného pražského arcibiskupství 1561–1580* [*The Hussite Epilogue at the Council of Trent and the Original Conception of the Habsburg Recatholicization of Bohemia: Origins of the Renewed Archbishopric of Prague 1561–1800*] (Prague: Univerzita Karlova, 1969)

Keul, István, *Early Modern Religious Communities in East-Central Europe: Ethnic Diversity, Denominational Plurality, and Corporative Politics in the Principality of Transylvania (1526–1691)* (Leiden: Brill, 2009)

Knop, Alois, 'Čeština ostravských písemných památek do roku 1620' ['The Czech Language in Ostrava Written Sources before 1620'], *Ostrava: Příspěvky k dějinám a výstavbě Ostravy a Ostravska*, 16 (1991), 325–37

Koelitz, Karl, *Hans Suess von Kulmbach und seine Werke: Ein Beitrag zur Geschichte der Schule Dürers* (Leipzig: Seemann, 1891)

Koepplin, Dieter, 'Kommet her zu mir alle: Das tröstliche Bild des Gekreuzigten nach dem Verständnis Luthers', in *Martin Luther und die Reformation in Deutschland: Vorträge zur Ausstellung im Germanischen Nationalmuseum Nürnberg*, ed. by Kurt Löcher (Schweinfurt: Weppert GmbH, 1983), pp. 153–90

Kotková, Olga, 'Lucas Cranach st. Zákon a milost, 1529' ['Lucas Cranach: Law and Gospel, 1529'], in *Lucas Cranach a české země: Pod znamením okřídleného hada*, ed. by Kaliopi Chamonicola (Prague: KANT – Karel Kerlický, 2005), cat. no. 11, 12, pp. 74–78

Kratochvílová, Martina, 'Recepce a transformace protestantské ikonografie: Lounský graduál Jana Táborského' ['Reception and Transformation of Protestant Iconography: The Louny Hymn Book of Jan Táborský'], *Umění*, 53 (2005), 445–64

Kreitzer, Beth, *Reforming Mary: Changing Images of the Virgin Mary in Lutheran Sermons of the Sixteenth Century* (Oxford: Oxford University Press, 2004)

Krchňák, Alois, *Čechové na basilejském sněmu* [*Czechs at the Council of Basel*] (Svitavy: Trinitas and Křesťanská akademie, 1997)

Lilienfein, Heinrich, *Lucas Cranach und seine Zeit* (Bielefeld: Velhagen und Klasing, 1942)

Malý, Tomáš, '"Confessional Identity" in Moravian Royal Towns in the 16th and 17th Centuries?', in *Public Communication in European Reformation: Artistic and Other Media in Central Europe 1380–1620*, ed. by Milena Bartlová and Michal Šroněk (Prague: Artefactum, 2007), pp. 323–34

———, *Smrt a spása mezi Tridentinem a sekularizací: Brněnští měšťané a proměny laické zbožnosti v 17. a 18. století* [*Death and Salvation between Trent and Secularization: The Citizens of Brno and the Transformations of Lay Piety in the 17th and 18th Centuries*] (Brno: Matice moravská, 2010)

Maňas, Vladimír, 'Náboženská bratrstva na Moravě do josefínských reforem' ['The Religious Fraternities in Moravia before the Reforms of Joseph II'], in *Bratrstva: Světská a církevní sdružení a jejich role v kulturních a společenských strukturách od středověku do moderní doby*, ed. by Tomáš Jiránek and Jiří Kubeš (Pardubice: Univerzita Pardubice, 2005), pp. 37–77

Martin Luther und die Reformation in Deutschland: Vorträge zur Ausstellung im Germanischen Nationalmuseum Nürnberg, ed. by Kurt Löcher (Schweinfurt: Weppert GmbH, 1983)

Mezník, Jaroslav, 'Tolerance na Moravě v 16. století' ['Tolerance in Moravia in the Sixteenth Century'], in *Problém tolerance v dějinách a perspektivě*, ed. by Milan Machovec (Prague: Academia, 1995), pp. 76–85

Michalski, Sergiusz, *Protestanci a sztuka: Spór o obrazy w Europie nowożytnej* [*Protestants and Art: A Controversy on Images in Early Modern Europe*] (Warsaw: PWN, 1989)

Morava v době renesance a reformace [*Moravia in the Age of the Renaissance and Reformation*], ed. by Tomáš Knoz (Brno: Moravské zemské muzeum, 2001)

Noble, Bonnie, *Lucas Cranach the Elder: Art and Devotion of the German Reformation* (Lanham: University Press of America, 2009)

Pitronová, Blanka, 'Rozvoj města v letech 1437–1620' ['Development of the Town between 1437 and 1620'], in *Dějiny Ostravy*, ed. by Karel Jiřík (Ostrava: Sfinga, 1993), pp. 55–68

Pojar, Miloš, 'Reformace a protireformace ve střední Evropě' ['Reformation and Counter-Reformation in Central Europe'], in *Problém tolerance v dějinách a perspektivě*, ed. by Milan Machovec (Prague: Academia, 1995), pp. 44–75

Přidalová, Jana, 'The Wall Painting "The Law and Gospel"? in St Wenceslas Church in Moravian Ostrava, its Iconography and the Influence of Utraquism', in *Public Communication in European Reformation: Artistic and Other Media in Central Europe 1380–1620*, ed. by Milena Bartlová and Michal Šroněk (Prague: Artefactum, 2007), pp. 175–82

Proměny konfesijní kultury: Metody – témata – otázky [*Transformations of Confessional Culture: Methods – Topics – Questions*], ed. by Hana Ferencová, Veronika Chmelařová, Jitka Kohoutová, and Radmila Prchal Pavlíčková (Olomouc: Univerzita Palackého, 2015)

Public Communication in European Reformation: Artistic and Other Media in Central Europe 1380–1620, ed. by Milena Bartlová and Michal Šroněk (Prague: Artefactum, 2007)

Representing Religious Pluralization in Early Modern Europe, ed. by Andreas Höfele, Stephan Laqué, and Enno Ruge (Berlin: Lit, 2008)

Rohlová, Eva, 'Středověká Ostrava, 1267–1437' ['Medieval Ostrava, 1267–1437'], in *Ostrava: Historie, kultura, lidé*, ed. by Blažena Przybylová (Prague: Nakladatelství Lidové noviny, 2013), pp. 32–50

Royt, Jan, 'The Allegory of Salvation and Sin', in *The Bohemian Reformation and Religious Practice: Vol. 6, Papers from the Sixth International Symposium on the Bohemian Reformation and Religious Practice Held at Vila Lanna, Prague 23–25 June 2004*, ed. by Zdeněk V. David and David Holeton (Prague: Akademie věd ČR, 2007), pp. 247–64

———, 'Grafický list s luteránským námětem Zákona a milosti ve vydáních Melantrichovy bible' ['The Engraving with the Lutheran Motif of the Allegory of Law and Mercy in Editions of the Melantrich Bible'], *HOP*, 5 (2013), 45–62

Rywiková, Daniela, *Renesanční nástěnné malby v kostele sv. Václava v Moravské Ostravě: Ikonografická studie* [*Renaissance Mural Paintings in St Wenceslas's Church in Moravská Ostrava: An Iconographic Study*] (Ostrava: Ostravská univerzita, 2005)

Říčan, Rudolf, *Čtyři vyznání: Vyznání, Augsburské, Bratrské, Helvetské a České se čtyřmi vyznáními stare církve a se Ctyřmi články pražskými* [*Four Confessions: Augsburg, Brethren, Helvetic and Czech with four Credos of the Old Church and with Four Articles of Prague*] (Prague: Komenského evangelická bohoslovecká fakulta, 1951)

Schiller, Gertrude, *Iconography of Christian Art. Vol. II: The Passion of Christ* (New York: Graphic Society Ltd, 1972)

Schorn-Schütte, Luise, *Die Reformation: Vorgeschichte, Verlauf, Wirkung* (Munich: Beck, 2006)

Schulze, Ingrid, *Lucas Cranach d. J. und die protestantische Bildkunst in Sachsen und Thüringen: Frömmigkeit, Theologie, Fürstenreformation* (Bucha bei Jena: quartus-Verlag, 2004)

Scribner, Robert W., *For the Sake of Simple Folk: Popular Propaganda for the German Reformation* (Cambridge: Cambridge University Press, 1981)

Šmahel, František, *Basilejská kompaktáta, Příběh deseti listin* [*Compacts of Basel: The Story of Ten Charters*] (Prague: Nakladatelství Lidové noviny, 2012)

Steinborn, Bożena, 'Malowane epitafia mieszczańskie na Śląsku w latach 1520–1620' ['Burgher Painted Epitaphs in Silesia in the Years 1520–1620'], *Roczniki sztuki śląskiej*, 4 (1967), 7–138

Thulin, Oskar, *Cranach – Altäre der Reformation* (Berlin: Evangelische Verlagsanstalt, 1955)

Turek, Adolf, 'Národnostní poměry v Ostravě a okolí do poloviny 17. století' ['The Nationality Situation in Ostrava and its Surroundings before the Mid-Seventeenth Century'], *Ostrava: Sborník příspěvků k dějinám a výstavbě města*, 3 (1966), 88–111

———, 'Čeští bratři v okolí Ostravy do počátku 17. století' ['Czech Brethren in the Surroundings of Ostrava before the Beginning of the Seventeenth Century'], *Ostrava: Příspěvky k dějinám a výstavbě Ostravy a Ostravska*, 16 (1991), 319–24

Umění české reformace (1380–1620) [*Art of the Bohemian Reformation 1380–1620*], ed. by Kateřina Horníčková and Michal Šroněk (Prague: Academia, 2010)

Válka, Josef, *Dějiny Moravy, díl II. Morava reformace, renesance a baroka* [*History of Moravia: Part II, Reformation, Renaissance, and Baroque*] (Brno: Muzejní a vlastivědná společnost, 1996)

———, *Husitství na Moravě: Náboženství a snášenlivost – Jan Amos Komenský* [*Hussites in Moravia: Religion and Tolerance – Jan Amos Comenius*] (Brno: Matica moravská, 2005)

Vorel, Petr, *Velké dějiny zemí Koruny české, VII. 1526–1618* [*The Great History of the Czech Lands: VII, 1526–1618*] (Prague: Paseka, 2005)

Wegmann, Susanne, and Gabriele Wimböck, *Konfessionen im Kirchenraum. Dimensionen des Sakralraums in der Frühen Neuzeit* (Korb: Dydimos, 2007)

Wenzel, Kai, 'Konfese a chrámová architektura: Dva luteránské kostely v Praze v předvečer třicetileté války. 1. díl' ['Confession and Church Architecture: Two Prague Lutheran Churches before the Thirty Years' War. Part 1'], *Pražský sborník historický*, 36 (2008), 31–103

Wetter, Evelin, *Formierungen des konfessionellen Raumen in Ostmitteleuropa* (Stuttgart: Franz Steiner Verlag, 2008)

Wolný, Gregor, *Kirchliche Topographie von Mahren, meist nach Urkunden und Handschriften, I. Abteilung, Ölmutzer Erzdiöcese. IV. Band* (Brünn: Selbstverlag, 1863)

Wüst, Wolfgang, 'Der Augsburger Religionsfrieden: Seine Rezeption in den Territorien des Reiches', *Herbergen der Christenheit: Jahrbuch für deutsche Kirchengeschichte, Der Augsburger Religionsfrieden*, 11 (2006), 147–63

Index of Persons and Places

New Communities of Interpretation

Contexts, Strategies, and Processes of Religious Transformation in Late Medieval and Early Modern Europe

All volumes in this series are evaluated by an Editorial Board, strictly on academic grounds, based on reports prepared by referees who have been commissioned by virtue of their specialism in the appropriate field. The Board ensures that the screening is done independently and without conflicts of interest. The definitive texts supplied by authors are also subject to review by the Board before being approved for publication. Further, the volumes are copyedited to conform to the publisher's stylebook and to the best international academic standards in the field.

Titles in Series

Religious Connectivity in Urban Communities (1400-1550): Reading, Worshipping, and Connecting through the Continuum of Sacred and Secular, ed. by Suzan Folkerts (2021)

Religious Practices and Everyday Life in the Long Fifteenth Century (1350–1570): Interpreting Changes and Changes of Interpretation, ed. by Ian Johnson and Ana Maria S. A. Rodrigues (2022)